LEGISLATIVE POLITICS U.S.A.

WITHDRAWN

LEGISLATIVE POLITICS U.S.A.
Third Edition

Edited by

Cornell University **Theodore J. Lowi**

The Ohio State University **Randall B. Ripley**

Little, Brown and Company  Boston

Library of Congress Catalog Card No. 73-9206

First Printing

Published simultaneously in Canada
by Little, Brown & Company (Canada) Limited

Printed in the United States of America

PREFACE

When *Legislative Politics U.S.A.* was first published ten years ago, it was a ripple in a tidal wave of legislative research. Nevertheless the academic commitment to the study of legislative politics was completely overshadowed at that time by the political fact of presidential power. Mainly because of the power and poetry of John F. Kennedy, the prevailing attitude toward presidential power was reaching a state of virtual enthralment. Although some serious congressional researchers remained quietly pro-Congress, most political leaders, journalists, an overwhelming majority of political scientists, and even many congressional researchers were caught up in the executive fever.

Not even the assassination of President Kennedy put out the fires. In fact, the assassination probably gave presidential power a momentary boost. All the Kennedy program, and more, was passed by the first Johnson Congress during one of the most active periods in the history of national government.

The unprecedentedly high presidential batting average depended upon an unprecedentedly docile Congress. Congress rarely put its creative touch upon the most fundamental pieces of legislation in the 1960's. The second edition of *Legislative Politics U.S.A.* was published, for example, at the time of the Gulf of Tonkin resolution, which even congressional leaders admit was a new high (or low) in congressional cooperation with the executive. Distinguished congressional research continued to take place, despite the ever-weakening basis for optimism about the place of Congress in the system. After all, even an unimportant Congress was a good laboratory for studying political behavior. Nevertheless, presidential power was the fashion.

But in 1965 or later, the presidency began to show some stress. Some important failures in executive effort began to shake the rosy view that presidential power could set the world to rights. Thanks to broad congressional delegation, the extension of federal power at home and abroad had meant an unprecedented extension of presidential power. But exercising this power did not bring commensurate returns. Time-tested techniques were producing unexpected woes. Popular remedies were being rejected by many who had been enthusiastic about their adoption. Established theories of social control were being regularly disproved, first in the ghettos, then in the cities at large, and ultimately in favorite suburbs and independent towns. By 1968 it appeared almost as if problems expanded directly with the efforts to solve them. Violent reaction to federal, therefore presidential, power reached its extreme in 1968–69. But the reduction of violence since then has merely revealed a much more widespread and long-term disenthralment with executive power.

Citizen response to this disenthralment has expressed itself in many ways, but most noticeably in a clamor for representation. "Participatory democracy" began as a radical appeal for virtual disestablishment. But it was not long before the radical position was raped by the center, with such notions as "maximum feasible participation," reapportionment, ethnic proportionality (quotas), and, by 1972, a quest for proportional allocation of almost all social values inside the national political parties. The "McGovern Rules" of the reconstituted Democratic Party are, more than anything else, an attack on the extent and the composition of presidential power in America.

The demand for increased representation was made first on the presidency and its agencies because the executive was the most clearly identified source of failure, and America's defense against illegitimate power has always been expressed in efforts to expand "access." Moreover, although the principle of representation applied to lower administrative levels may have gained some support for the regime in the short run, it was mainly providing frustration at the center. If representation at local levels was to be sincere, local agencies had to be given a great deal of discretion; otherwise, a decision would have to be imposed from above after all the participatory time had been spent. This discretion involved a direct and deliberate drainage of power from the chief executive down and down, by successive subdelegations, until real discretion and real resources were in the hands of local interests. But responsibility, compounded by tremendously strong expectations of efficacy, continued to be held at the center, primarily upon the chief executive. The buck stopped there even if the president did not want it to. The final blow to overwhelming presidential prestige was experienced in Chicago in 1968, when an incumbent president of the United States was not welcome at a convention of his own party. In turning their backs on the president, the delegates of the Democratic Party were in effect turning their backs on the presidency. No such changes alone can bring the presidential system down into a shambles, but could, and did, begin a long and arduous process of reevaluation and rebalancing of that system. Inevitably, concern about representation slowly turned back toward Congress.

The turning point was the curdling dissatisfaction with the Vietnam war. The final souring of the prevailing relationship between the president and Congress was expressed in remorse over the Gulf of Tonkin resolution. Because this resolution had been the most extreme case of Congress's abdication to the president, it became the most important issue about which to express remorse, self-pity, and ultimately a determination to recover some of Congress's lost prestige and power.

It is significant that dissatisfaction with the war took the form of constitutional arguments over the Separation of Powers. Yet it is no paradox. Both issues were inextricably involved. War may be war in some countries, but war cannot be mere war in a real democracy where constitutional forms are expected to prevail at all times. When under stress, democracies are notorious for abandoning constitutional forms; and all sides seem to agree that much form was set aside during the Vietnam war. Nevertheless, the faith remains strong that a vigorous legislative politics will restore and maintain constitutional uses of power.

The Age of Aquarius has not arrived for legislative politics U.S.A. Such an age will probably never arrive for legislatures *or* for human beings. But some signs indicate a changing balance of relationships among the branches in the 1970's. If this is true, it will be of great importance, at least to students of politics. Legislatures are the enemies of secrecy. Legislative competition provides its own publicity and opens many routes of access to the secret councils of the executive branch, for study if not for influence. As observers we of course celebrate such a development, because it gives us more and better things to study. But we think all citizens in a democracy should celebrate this development and should do whatever they can to commend and encourage it.

Changes over the past decade have of course dictated changes in the selection of readings in this volume. In some instances we have prepared our own selections because times have changed faster than research can keep up with. To ensure the proper selection of materials, I have taken on as coeditor a man known throughout the profession for his work on Congress and for his love affair with Congress. What may not be as generally appreciated is Ripley's complete command of the literature, both published and prepublished. Though we share responsibility for errors and other weaknesses, Ripley deserves far more than half the credit for any virtues of balance and comprehensiveness the new edition possesses.

Changes in the decade have not changed the basic theme of the book: Congress *is* shaped by the contradictory demands of representation and decision making, by the competition between participation and policy. Consequently, though its illustrations may be dated and though the argument may be stilted by the enthusiasm and sentimentality of youth, the introductory essay remains substantially as written over ten years ago. This new preface captures the only important cleavage with the recent past, which is a change of mood rather than analysis: Congress is coming back closer to the center of a system that is no longer quite so optimistic about its ability to survive. And this is fitting. When you are not certain you can win, it is time to start worrying about how you play the game.

Cumulatively, the changes in spirit and in the selection of readings may indicate that, twenty-five years after George Galloway's observation, Congress may no longer be "at the crossroads." But which route has been taken? We may not have the answer to that question until everybody has decided which route Congress ought to have taken. We dedicate this book to that choice.

Theodore J. Lowi

ACKNOWLEDGMENTS

The senior editor would like first to single out Professor Duncan MacRae for a special expression of gratitude. The MacRae-Lowi course at the University of Chicago was a more important source of instruction than Congress itself. But MacRae is only one of several colleagues who, though not represented by selections in this volume, are in spirit present in any work on Congress. Richard Fenno, Ralph Huitt, Charles Jones, Donald Matthews, Robert Peabody, and David Truman have nothing in this volume only because no part of their excellent work fits one pedagogical need within the space constraints that necessarily face any editor. However, they and their work have meant so much to the study of Congress that no student should consider himself fully educated without being aware of their research. We are pleased to call them friends and eager to reveal how much their work has influenced us as well as everyone else who spends part of his or her professional life studying Congress. We are sure that every living author represented in this volume would agree.

We are also indebted to Grace A. Franklin for a wide variety of skillful labors that put the book together in good order.

CONTENTS

LEGISLATIVE POLITICS U.S.A.

INTRODUCTION
REPRESENTATION VERSUS DECISION

In all forms of collective life there is at least one simple division of labor — leaders and followers. Most people accept the fact until it is called to their attention.

Popular government has first to recognize the inevitability of leadership and power, not to deny it: to establish some fair and regular pattern for selecting leaders and, further to secure minimum control over leaders once they are granted authority over others. "Representation" is such an attempt. Theories of representation are made for *legitimizing* leadership. Obeisance to the proper rituals converts "leaders" into "representatives"; popular election converts "power" into "authority." Where doctrines of representation are accepted, the probability that followers will do the bidding of representatives rather than of leaders is much higher.

Constitutionally, the representation formula works a limitation on governmental power, along with other constitutional formulas such as separation of powers and federalism. Our form of representation requires not only the periodic election of officeholders; it also requires that the law-making body be drawn from every geographical area of the country.[1] Thus we attempt to limit our legislators by making them electorally dependent *and* by placing in the assembly a very hetero-

---

[1] The "geographical constituency" is not the only method of representation, and it is not universally accepted as the best. See below.

1

geneous collection of leaders, giving our system several hundred checks and balances.

The concept also has an ideological dimension that is not always sufficiently appreciated. Acceptance of the doctrine of representative government directs the representative to act "in a representative way." His role requires that he seek the perceived and even the unperceived needs of his constituency. Since the Supreme Court handed down *Baker v. Carr* much has been made of the problem of apportionment, for *Baker v. Carr* and succeeding decisions require much greater effort to achieve a closer approximation of equality in the numbers of people each legislator represents. But even under conditions of near perfection in the mechanics of representation a truly representative government could still be unattainable. Mechanical accountability to an electorate is a necessary but, in itself, insufficient condition for representative government. Without a widely shared acceptance of representation as a "good thing" regardless of the price, the whole structure becomes a sham.

A successful system of representation, therefore, requires a special kind of leader. This man is generally outgoing and casual in personality, good in small gatherings but generally poor and bumbling in large ones.[2] Besides his belief in the goodness of the role of representative, his ideology tends to be vague and basically methodological. He is a man of many interests but rarely does he seriously rationalize those interests to fit more grandiose concepts. If he does, he is never quite too serious to refuse to submit interests or grandiose concepts to mediation. To him any interest can win or lose as long as existing institutions and procedures are preserved. In the United States this type of leader is the creature of the process of nomination and election that has developed around him over two centuries. Leadership selection in the United States is more open, uncontrolled, and unpredictable than anywhere else in the world. There are many problems with such a system, the most important being that national party responsibility is next to impossible to achieve. But it does ensure the selection of the type required by our mixed and decentralized legislatures. No matter what formal basis of representation is used, and no matter how consistently the criteria of unit size are enforced, the resulting units of representation will always be composed of too many diverse elements to allow for clean lines of authority and accountability. Uncertainty about the size of his own local following and the

[2] Former Speaker Joseph Martin, whose public image was one of colossal clumsiness, was more typical of the true representative than was his Massachusetts colleague, John F. Kennedy.

amount of support for those who would unseat him renders the representative vulnerable to a far wider range of interests than those he himself might choose if he were totally a free agent. Uncertainty in the chamber itself about where the opposition to his interests might come from simply reinforces his sense of the essential ambiguity of political life. As he and others like him begin to believe in this system and the amoral manner in which it deals with interests, then they begin to make the system work. Whatever the Supreme Court says after *Baker v. Carr,* their original position on apportionment, which was reversed by *Baker v. Carr,* will always be the inescapable truth: that representative government is a *political question.*[3] Many districts are going to change as a result of the reapportionment cases, but the essential problem of Congress and of representative government will remain.

That problem is the inconsistency between *representation* and *government* or, synonymously, participation and decision. The inconsistency of the two basic norms is the determining characteristic of the institution. The interplay between the two types of forces, of representation *versus* decision, is the integrating theme of this volume. Achieving a balance between these two forces is the basic problem of all authoritative institutions — American and non-American, democratic and nondemocratic — for even an autocrat cannot depart too far or too long from the prevailing values of his subjects. The autocrat, feeling the pressures for representation, typically creates the myth of *virtual* representation — that he *is* the people or the vanguard of the people. But of course the significance lies in where the balance is struck. With the autocrat the reality is the overwhelming stress put on efficiency and decision. The problem of successful limited government is to balance the two forces without getting a maximum of either.

A healthy fear and hatred of autocracy and irresponsibility in the United States, as well as all Western democracies, led to a strong preference for government by representation, government that would be both limited and popularly based. But government can all too easily be made *too* representative; we can react too strongly to fear of irresponsible, unlimited government. In the immortal words of James Thurber, "You might just as well fall flat on your face as lean

[3] *Colegrove v. Green,* 328 U.S. 549 (1946). Professor of Political Science Colegrove sought to prevent the conducting of the 1946 Illinois election until the state obeyed the laws of Illinois and the requirements of the Constitution and eliminated the inequities among congressional districts. The Supreme Court simply refused to review on grounds that it lacked jurisdiction over "political questions." All *Baker v. Carr* did was to reverse Colegrove and to redefine apportionment as within judicial scope.

over too far backwards." A *perfectly representative* government would be virtually incapable of making a decision. The reformer's schemes of proportional or occupational representation, recall, or referendum are schemes that could, if employed meticulously, make the legislature an almost perfect replica of the society; but how would the members of such a legislature face the problem of agreement? If a majority vote is required, and a *two-thirds* majority must be ready for many controversial matters (to close debate and bring the question to a vote, as in our Senate), we can easily see that perfect representation would result in complete stalemate. It cannot be emphasized too strongly or too often that you can surround government with innumerable restraints, but not to the extent of taking away its capacity to act. The answer to autocracy is not a completely popular government. Every degree of representativeness is likely to be paid for in inefficiency.

Because the problem of achieving a proper balance between these two forces is best seen in Congress, Congress (with one look at American state legislatures and one look at the Soviet legislature) becomes our laboratory for studying representative government. Beyond its intrinsic importance for study as an instrument of government, Congress serves as an excellent laboratory for the study of politics and the political process. The political process begins when many people perceive that they have some sense of distress or injustice in common. Through many successive stages of organization, which may take years, these common interests become legislative problems. Congress and legislation are, therefore, located at a very late and very mature stage of social life. However, Congress can only be understood in terms of all that went into making up its agenda and all the forces that militate for and against Congress' action on any specific item on its agenda. Factors such as the committee and subcommittee system, the opposition or minority party, most of the parliamentary rules (dull and dry in themselves but politically potent — no rule is neutral!), seniority, floor debate, interest groups, and regional blocs are almost constantly working for delay, for the fullest possible deliberation of one interest or another. Against those the (usually weaker) forces of the president and his immediate following in the executive branch, the president's party in Congress, the speaker and other congressional officers, "gag rules" in the House, are supposedly at work molding the variety of interests into policy. (Of course expediting decisions is not a synonym for progress. A decision can amount to "turning the clock back.") To complicate matters further, the contribution of any one of these factors or participants to the legislative process depends upon the issue in question. For example, a committee chairman who strongly favors a piece of legislation becomes a strong force for result rather than for deliberation. The fight in 1961 to enlarge the Rules Committee was a struggle to convert that powerful committee from an instrument of delay into a lever of expedition. And the congressman least involved in an issue usually supports its quick settlement in order to get on with business he deems most important. Thus, the process of representative government can be characterized abstractly in simple terms, but in practice it is very complex. Each factor must be assessed carefully. The intelligent, sophisticated student of Congress is one who does not take any participant at face value but tries instead to assess each participant's *functional* value within the total context of which the participant is only one small part.

It is difficult to determine just where the balance between representation and government has been struck in the United States, and surely it must shift from one period to the next. But it is certain that Congress has always shared in the real powers of government and therefore in the responsibility for making decisions. And Congress is the sort of representative institution it is, precisely because it is a real governing body. The responsibilitiy and need for making decisions converts an otherwise somber debating society into a *power arena*. Congressional life becomes something quite separate and distinct from, albeit influenced by, constituencies. The constant attempt to put issues on the agenda for serious consideration and to reach agreement on them requires organization, skill, and compromise. In a collective decision-making body like Congress, agreement *equals* power. Every participant in the "legislative struggle" is seeking at least enough agreement or power either to enact a law or to prevent one from being enacted. Only a body without important decisions to make can afford the highest degree of representation, and only in such a body can the members afford to be perfectly straightforward and perfectly equal. Our representative institutions can afford neither. But the consequences of this, sometimes ludicrous, more often mystifying, are all too easily denounced. A representative system not only depends upon partisanship, compromise, manipulation; it could hardly work without them. This is why it will always be true that in a real governing legislature "the socialist deputy," as the saying goes, "is more deputy than socialist." Professor Dexter later on in the volume provides reasons why the representative *can* as well as *must* behave as a legislator as well as a delegate.

The precise location of the balance between representation and government, as well as the very role of the legislative assembly in it is further complicated by modern problems and new requirements The twentieth century is an "executive-centered" era. We achieve productivity and abundance through specialization, but specialization leads to *interdependence*. Few men are now autonomous; all the rest are part of a very common destiny because each depends on others as well as himself for sustenance. The farmer lives by market patterns set by anonymous others. Laborer and manager alike have become part of a product over which they have no personal control, to which they contribute in only a minuscule way, in which they can take only the remotest pride. Informal ties such as family, community, and traditional values are weakening. An increasing number of class and intergroup relations must therefore be regularized by deliberate and formal procedures — *administered* social relations. Not all these administered relationships are governmental — for example, trade associations and other interest groups, labor unions, civic groups, and "red feather" ("family service" and the like) agencies — but an increasing number *are* governmental.

And this means that legislators have less and less time and less and less slack in the system within which to play at their deadly serious game of bargaining with unpredictable compromise as the result. With government's more frequent direct involvement in crises, representation can lead to stalemate only at the risk of becoming illegitimate. Twentieth-century America is not a happy time or place for government by representative assembly. The technical complexities of modern life that require "administered" social relations also require expert administration and continuity in administration. Statutes become less and less self-executing. The legislature must delegate to the administrative agency a larger and larger role in legislation, which is done by leaving the administrator an increasingly large scope for making his own decisions and writing his own rules for the conduct of citizens. In delegating discretion, Congress is also delegating conflict, and the management and settlement of conflict comprise the essence of Congress.

The growing burden of public management coupled with America's sudden exposure to the uncontrollable outside world have made us an executive-centered government. Congress' response to this undeniable fact comprises the real history of representative government in America in the twentieth century.

Out of all this, the president has emerged as the most important legislator, the most imporant force for decision in our scheme of representative government. In the past, only "strong" presidents have taken the initiative and set the agenda of Congress (in a "program"). Nowadays, this initiative is the norm; it is virtually thrust upon every president. So often is this the case that the relations between the two branches have in large part been *reversed,* with the president proposing (in budget, State of the Union, and special messages) draft legislation and the like, and Congress exercising the powers of amendment and veto.

But the president, with his advantageous position and vast resources, does not *legislate.* His powers, like congressional statutes, are not self-executing. The president has become the most important but not the only pariicpant in the legislative process. Modern problems may have shifted the centers of power, but laws must still be made in Congress. Thus the struggle is not materially different from the struggle of earlier days. In the age-old way, *a majority must be created for every issue,* and every participant plays some role in the creation or the obstruction of that majority. The difference from earlier times lies in the need to bring each struggle sooner to a close. We may, then, be witnessing a decline of representation without a decline in representative government.

Thus, there is no longer any controversy over the fact that relations between president and Congress have been profoundly altered in the past generation or two. But this is not to say that the power of Congress has declined. As an instrument of national government Congress is more powerful than ever. Congress' power over domestic economic effairs was set anew in 1937 with a single Supreme Court decision (*NLRB v. Jones and Laughlin Steel Corporation*) that has needed little enhancement since that time. By 1964 interstate commerce powers were found adequate for getting at local discriminatory practices that had heretofore existed behind a wall of protective Federalism.

In the field of foreign affairs, always considered executive business par excellence, congressional power has also vastly increased. The charge that the executive has "usurped" the power of Congress by use of executive agreements rather than treaties [4] has been much too strongly emphasized. Because we are a world leader, most of our international affairs involve money, or troops which involve money. And money involves Congress — not only the Senate but now the House of Representatives — in foreign policy as never before. The degree of congressional participation in foreign policy decisions

---

[4] Executive agreements have all the force and effect of treaties but do not require approval by two-thirds vote of the Senate. The question of usurpation is dealt with at length in the Cooper-Church debate in Selection 1.

depends, of course, on the nature of the decision. A quickly developing crisis might require an executive action with congressional approval only after the fact. But more often than not, some congressional leaders become involved in even the most urgent cases, as shown in "The Day We Didn't Go to War." On the longer range, more elaborately considered policies, Congress is intimately involved. Marshall Plan, NATO, and the other bulwarks of our international involvements were as much congressional as executive. The problem of enactment is about the same here as in the domestic field; presidential initiative is simply more frequent and presidential power is more telling. However, when enough congressional leaders feel strongly enough on an issue, Congress can grab the initiative as it did in some part during the late stages of the Vietnam war.

Thus, it is not toward decline of the governing power of Congress that we must look for the meaning of the influence of twentieth-century developments on the assembly. Rather, as the relation of Congress to the executive suggests, it is the very nature of the problem itself ·that has changed: The power of Congress, still immense, manifests itself in new ways. Legislation remains the most important power of Congress, and without it Congress would possess no power at all. But even the problem of legislation has changed as part of the new forms of congressional power. In brief, the major problem and major focus of Congress is no longer simply that of prescribing the behavior of citizens but more often that of *affecting the behavior of administrators.* This is the constitutional implication of "executive-centered" government.

This aspect of the problem facing Congress is often dignified in the political rhetoric as the achievement of a "responsible bureaucracy," and indeed this would be the ideal outcome. But the workaday problem is one of power, electoral power versus the power of organization and specialization. Until the twentieth century no power in the West (where violence was not involved) matched electoral power. Wealth, status, monarchy fell before it. Now, however, it faces a sturdier foe in the esoteric authority of *expertise.* Almost every statute passes through the hands and the discretion of the full-time, expert administrator. As never before Congress faces the truth — that its laws are not self-executing. With the president, although too often at cross-purposes with the president, Congress *must reduce the discretion of the administrator,* if it is to enjoy its status as creator of law and not merely the enunciator of a pious, platitudinous public will.

The process of influencing administrative behavior begins with the statute, substantive, and appropriations enactments; nothing, including presidential orders, influences administrative decision like a statute, *if said statute is a clear expression.* But that is only a beginning even when the statute is unambiguous, which is almost never. In an executive-centered world it is not only the administrator but also Congress whose job is continuous. More than ever before, congressional government is government by committee and subcommittee. Most of the important legislative decisions are still made in committees as in the days of Woodrow Wilson's "Imperious Authority of the Standing Committees." Now these committees are almost exclusive agents of continuing congressional supervision ("oversight") and clarification of law. Hence, the new forms of congressional power.

Inquiry is not a new device. It is as old as Congress itself, having developed along with the committee system. What may be new is the growing importance of hearings and investigations, which stems from the increasing need of Congress to grant discretion and therefore to delegate its intrinsic powers of legislation. What Congress gives away in chunks it tries to take back in bits.

Hearings are used for various purposes. The manifest purpose in all cases is that of collecting information from administrators, non-governmental experts, and interest-group leaders for the drafting and revising of proposed legislation. As such, hearings are intimately connected with the process of representation, a crudely systematic means of taking the largest possible number of views into account. But hearings are also used effectively as a strategy for building support or opposition in the legislative struggle. The chairman of a committee or subcommitteee has the power to pick his witnesses, the order of their appearance, the time to be devoted to the issue, and most key questions. This includes the power to avoid witnesses if publicity is expected to bring adverse reactions.

Most significantly, hearings are a lever for influencing the administrator. The standing committees are organized mainly along departmental lines (e.g., Committees on Foreign Relations, Agriculture, Labor and Education), and the vital subcommittees of the House and Senate Appropriations Committees are organized in the same manner. The occasion of a hearing can be a time of trepidation for the bureaucrats; no hearings are taken lightly. Many committee chairmen are old-timers who consider the bureaucrats either birds of passage (which is *true* of the top political appointees!) or their own servants. These old men get to know departmental business as well as any bureaucrat, and when one threatens to examine appropriations "with a fine-tooth comb" you can be sure that it is not an idle promise. These hearings can be effective even if no new laws are passed, and often it is understood that no important new legislation is even contemplated. Every administrator called as a witness can expect to defend last year's activities and to receive some instructions on expected practice for next year. The hearings in general build up a record of "legislative intent," before *and* after the fact, that has great bearing on administrative conduct even if it does not, as is often hoped, influence the judiciary very much when their turn comes to interpret a statute.

The second tool of "oversight" is the investigation. Roughly the same as the hearings in outward appearance, the investigation covers a problem area (which can be co-extensive with one department or can include more or less than a department) rather than a specific piece of proposed legislation. For this reason, the investigation can be a more potent device, but it is also more slipshod in that it usually covers so much territory. Investigation has become a discredited technique in the estimation of many because of abuses of witnesses. But there is an important distinction to be made between investigation of the executive branch and investigation (in the manner of a grand jury) of the past and present conduct of private citizens. It is only in the latter case that constitutional problems of procedural due process arise.

Through hearings and investigations Congress carries the process of representation over into the bureaucracy. And it may well be that the most abiding role of Congress in the years to come will be its *service as a place where the needs of the bureaucracy are continually being balanced against the prevailing special interests in the community*. We call this our insurance against an irresponsible administrative government, but it is not quite so simple. We pay the price in decentralized and inefficient administration. Congress reaches down into the departments creating split loyalties between the president and the committees. Thus Congress builds into the executive its own problem of representation versus decision, creating many barriers to effective presidential coordination. The continuing relations between Congress and the executive tend to create a kind of triangular trading pattern involving a standing committee or appropriations subcommittee (or both), an executive agency, and one or more agency clientele groups. The situation in "How the Farmers Get What They Want" suggests possible consequences. In many agriculture agencies it is very difficult to find just where "public" ends and "private" begins. It is representation carried to its outer limits in a pattern not unlike European corporatism. Here is a problem of balance that must be solved in every generation and for every area of policy. Continuous congressional committee participation short-circuits presidential responsibility and can lead to patterns of economic privilege. But, on the other hand, how centralized and independent and efficient a bureaucracy can we afford? [5]

These problems can only be raised; they cannot be solved. Every area of governmental activity challenges Congress in its own peculiar way. The balance between administrative autonomy and political control must be adjusted accordingly. In older, well-established activities Congress might, for instance, slacken its reins. In new and unplotted areas, where every adminstrative decision may be a "hard case" or a precedent, closer congressional-administrative relations might follow.

In sum, the representative assembly performs several functions vital to the democratic political order. Making laws is its manifest or constitutional function and is the most important if only because without it no other functions would follow. But legislation is not the only function of the assembly; if legislation *were* the only function, the assembly could hardly justify its existence. A totally bureaucratic organization, for instance, would be a much more efficient instrument and would probably be more rational and fair, however these ambiguous terms might be defined. It is the subsidiary, extraconstitutional or "latent" functions of the assembly that make it an indispensable feature of government.

The most important subsidiary or latent function of the representative assembly is — through its powers of policy, appropriation, inquiry, and supervision — that of balancing administrative needs against organized community desires. This extension of the representative principle into the bureaucracy may, so I have argued, prove to be its most abiding function as its legislative power atrophies into general, even if significant, policy expressions.

Also, several equally significant functions are not so directly involved in statutes or administrative control as such but are part of the legislative struggle itself. Exact assessment of these functions is impossible but their importance cannot be doubted. These will be briefly summarized: [6]

1. *Communications.* The exposed deliberations of the assembly enlarge the area of conflict and widen public awareness of problems

---

[5] Ironically, the sins associated with "bureaucracy" in its pejorative sense, such as inefficiency, waste, overlapping, and duplication, result from not enough bureaucratization! The perfect bureaucracy would have none of these.

[6] See Harold Lasswell and Abraham Kaplan, *Power and Society.* (Yale University Press, New Haven, 1950, pp. 161–169.)

and proposed solutions. Woodrow Wilson offers suggestions for improving this function.

2. *Legitimacy*. The ritual of formulating public policy among 535 participants and hundreds of influential outsiders tends to reaffirm faith in democratic procedures. Modern civilizations never entirely eliminate the more primitive instincts, including the need for ritual. By acting out the social struggle before the world, Congress is the grandest of all stages for the political passion play. Furthermore, to commit the powerful to this *method* of settling conflicts tends also to commit them to the *outcomes,* even in adversity. And, to be Machiavellian, with so many participants it is possible for dissatisfied groups to blame individual members *without losing faith in the institution itself*. Majority rule, said Toqueville, "made obedience very easy; it enabled the subject to complain of the law without ceasing to love and honor the lawgiver."

3. *Power*. "Representation stabilizes the power structure by providing a mean between the extremes of concentration and dispersion of power.[7] The one is intolerable, the other is impractical. There may be more powerful men in the country than ordinary congressmen, but they must eventually go to Congress to build greater support if their demands are to be made legitimate claims. Again to be Machiavellian, the size of the assembly makes it easier for the individual congressman to hide his pursuit of the public interest when such pursuit conflicts with constituency interests.

Here then are some fragments and intimations of the context of representative government. It is the responsible student's task to study and evaluate the workings of the system for himself. We can only provide a balanced selection of materials and a few guides to method and theory.

In Part I we set up the problems of legislative politics with a single selection, a long excerpt from the Cooper-Church debate. To a discerning reader this single debate is a veritable textbook in powers, strategies, motives, and interests. We hope that the student will read through the debate and then return frequently to it, perhaps following each new level of sophistication.

Parts II, III, and IV are designed to put the student in the presence of the ongoing legislative process, piece by piece and act by act. Distortion is of course involved as soon as one factor is drawn out from the tightly connected flow of events in the real world. However, the order of presentation maintains the sequence in which the actual

[7] Lasswell and Kaplan, p. 166.

legislative process flows, and that provides an approximation of reality even if not reality itself. An introductory essay for each part directs the reader toward the larger picture.

In Part V we put back together what we took apart in order to analyze. Each selection here is a detailed case study of some fundamental event or process. These, we hope, put all the influences and actions back into context.

The final part will remind students of their own obligation to take personally the problems and prospects of legislative politics. We hope each student comes to feel, as we do, that every political institution is a human contrivance that is capable of improvement by normal human action. Because analysis should always precede reasonable action, our modest reform proposals come naturally at the end. But the desire for reform should nevertheless accompany every effort to analyze. Hence, be critical at every turn. Do not be too impressed, or if impressed, do not admire too much. Legislative politics is dead the minute we decide the world cannot be better.

I

REPRESENTATIVE GOVERNMENT
IN THE AGE OF THE EXECUTIVE
VIETNAM AND AN EIGHTEENTH-CENTURY
IDEAL OF GOOD GOVERNMENT

War is a terrible time for everyone, but especially for representatives and representative assemblies. Assemblies can declare war and they can support it with money and manpower; they can contribute to the moral fervor necessary when democracies go to war. But apparently assemblies are far less capable of restraining war, guiding it, stopping it, and setting the terms of victory or defeat.

Economists often say that monetary policy is like a string: you can pull with it but you cannot push very well. In the same spirit, Congress seems to be like a battering ram. You can push with it, but you cannot pull. Its functions can also be compared to a shillelagh or a rusty knife. You can frighten with it, you can bash and flail, but it is hard to do precise surgery with it. These metaphors may always be applicable. War simply exposes them for all to see and none to deny.

But are Congress' limitations inevitable and intrinsic or are they produced merely by bad habits? Would relations with the executive be significantly different if enough congressmen decided to make it so? How would our system be affected if a few congressmen seriously decided to try? Such efforts could make the conduct of government far more inefficient than it already is. Consequently, many are very happy with Congress' incapacities and with Congress' willingness to delegate its powers to the executive. But such efforts could also make government more legitimate and citizens better educated by maintaining full public awareness of the problems of constitutionality, law, and propriety; the publicity alone can help maintain a sense of proportion.

Vietnam has been a great ordeal for the United States. Our treasury and our will have been tested to the limit. But in the end it may have been our constitutional system that was tested most severely. Totally aside from its direct impact on the conduct of the Vietnam war, the debate triggered by the Cambodian incursion raised the most fundamental questions about the proper functions of executive and legislature under the American constitutional scheme. In many respects, the debate made Congress look ridiculous. To the hawks it was ridiculous to pretend ever to tell the president what to do in his capacity as commander-in-chief. To the doves Congress looked ridiculous for having been taken in by the executive for years and for not trying hard enough early enough to hold the president in check. But there is good constitutional reasoning on both sides, and constitutional government probably gained a great deal from the encounter.

Students of Congress have most to gain from the debate on the wisdom and constitutionality of our Vietnam involvement. It provides a unique opportunity to study parliamentary practice and the possibilities of government by assembly. Even the prerogatives of government-by-committee are defended — by Senator Fulbright of all people, a man known mostly for his interest in purely substantive issues. This only emphasizes how tightly bound the members of Congress tend to be in procedural matters. Control of the floor, making amendments and amendments to amendments, respect and pseudo-respect among colleagues, bringing debate to an end, tabling and reconsideration, conferences with the other chamber, presidential power, facing the prospect of presidential veto, plus many other basic features of true representative government arise again and again in the debates that spread across many legislative days. These procedural matters arise in a context where their importance to the very notion of representative government cannot be doubted. Often these procedural matters make all the difference, and that may be why when the chips are down the executive takes over. But that would be too bad if it were permanently true. Democracy without procedure is likely to be nothing more than a rhetorical mask for the real distribution of power. Formal debate exposes, educates, and restrains power. Rich or poor, any country that espouses the representative form may be faced with the dilemma of not being able to live with the formalisms, yet not being able to live without them.

Nevertheless, was the Senate's decision to stage a debate on congressional power and national goals appropriate in the midst of an expensive and embarrassing war? Does something about Congress make debate, if it is to come at all, come at the wrong time? Was there anything peculiar or limited about the fact that so many major spokesmen in this debate were senators from small and isolated states and senators who had never served abroad in any official capacity? Or could the involvement of laymen be actually good? And is there anything about the way the debate was conducted that would leave one to celebrate or to mourn the structure, procedures, and processes of legislative politics U.S.A.?

These questions are worth attacking. But a sensible attack will require a careful study of the Cooper-Church debate and an even more careful study of the research on Congress that attempts to understand the conduct, motives, and institutions that make such a debate, for better or worse, possible.

1

Amending the Foreign Military Sales Act

MR. MANSFIELD. Mr. President, I ask unanimous consent that the Senate turn to the consideration of Calender No. 868, H.R. 15628, I do this so that the bill will become the pending business.

THE PRESIDING OFFICER (Mr. Cranston). The bill will be stated by title.

THE LEGISLATIVE CLERK. A bill (H.R. 15628) to amend the Foreign Military Sales Act.

From U.S. Senate, *Congressional Record* (May 13–June 30, 1970), pp. S7098–S10285.

The work that Eugene P. Dvorin did in editing *The Senate's War Powers* (Chicago: Markham, 1971) has been very helpful to the editors in preparing this selection.

THE PRESIDING OFFICER. Is there objection to the present consideration of the bill?

There being no objection, the Senate proceeded to consider the bill, which had been reported from the Committee on Foreign Relations with amendments.

MR. FULBRIGHT. . . . Mr. President, it is with both a sense of great reluctance and a feeling of guarded accomplishment that I present this bill to extend the foreign military sales program to the Senate.

My reluctance derives from the fact that I take no pride in asking my colleagues to approve the portion of this bill which contributes to the spread of conventional military hardware. On the other hand, there is a feeling of accomplishment because of the committee's adoption of a number of significant amendments, including the prohibition on further involvement in Cambodia and a number of restrictions on the military aid and sales programs.

The basic purpose of this bill is to authorize continuation of the military credit sales program for fiscal years 1970 and 1971.

It would authorize credit sales of $300 million in military arms and equipment for each of those years and would authorize the appropriation of $250 million each year to finance the sales. The sales financed under this program are made primarily to less developed countries.

But the credit sales program must be viewed in the context of the total picture of U.S. arms exports. The Department of Defense estimates that in the current fiscal year the United States will sell abroad a total of about $1.9 billion in arms and military equipment. Of that, $300 million will be financed under authority of the Foreign Military Sales Act. In addition to the sales volume, the United States will supply $392 million in arms through the military grant aid program and will have an additional $166 million in surplus arms and equipment — valued at one-fourth of acquisition cost — to give away. Thus, the United States will sell or give away nearly $2.5 billion in military materials this fiscal year.

I point out also that there are some $9 billion worth of surplus arms and military equipment now available for the Department of Defense to give away — even to Cambodia — without any congressional limits. And the total is mounting rapidly as U.S. forces are withdrawn from Vietnam. In addition to the excess arms, the funds available under the regular grant aid and sales program, the President may, under section 506 of the Foreign Assistance Act, give other nations up to $300 million of arms and equipment out of the Department of Defense's stock if he considers it vital to our national security. The sources of U.S. arms are many and the volume is vast. The credit sales program authorized by this bill is only the tip of the iceberg. . . .

Nothing was more indicative of the Pentagon's blatant disregard for the intent of Congress than its giving away of some $140 million in surplus military equipment to Taiwan following Congress' refusal to appropriate $54.5 million in additional military aid above the amount authorized. As a result of this attempt to increase appropriations over the authorization level, and the Pentagon's attempt to make an end run around the Congress by using the surplus program, two amendments have been added to this bill to prevent such developments in the future.

The first, dealing with the excess property issue, restricts the Department of Defense's authority by imposing a $35 million ceiling on the amount of surplus military arms or equipment that may be given away in any fiscal year. A portion of the original cost of any surplus material given away above that amount would be deducted from the funds available for granting military aid.

The second, relating to appropriations, simply states that any appropriation above the amount authorized cannot be used and that any appropriation for which there is not an authorization cannot be expended. This amendment writes into law the principle, supported by the Senate in two votes last year, that the appropriation of funds which are not authorized is bad practice and, if carried to extremes, could seriously undermine the authority of all legislative committees. . . .

[In addition, the] Cooper-Church-Aiken-Mansfield amendment, to prevent any further U.S. involvement in Cambodia, is a small, but important step in the recovery process.

Last year, by a vote of 70 to 16, the Senate adopted the national commitments resolution expressing the sense of the Senate that "a national commitment by the United States results only from affirmative action taken by the executive and legislative branches of the U.S. Government by means of a treaty, statute, or concurrent resolution of both Houses of Congress specifically providing for such commitment." By its action of April 1970 in initiating hostilities within the territory of Cambodia without the consent or even the prior knowledge of Congress or any of its committees, the executive branch has shown disregard not only for the national commitments resolution but for the constitutional principles in which that resolution is rooted. In the wake of recent events, there is reason to reassert, with renewed conviction, a statement made in the Foreign Relations Committee's report of April 16, 1969, on the national commitments resolution:

> Our country has come far toward the concentration in its national executive of unchecked power over foreign relations, particularly over the disposition and use of the Armed Forces. So far has this process advanced that, in the committee's view, it is no longer accurate to characterize our Government, in matters of foreign relations, as one of separated powers checked and balanced against each other.

The notion that the authority to commit the United States to war is an Executive prerogative, or even a divided or uncertain one, is one which has grown up only in recent decades. It is the result primarily of a series of emergencies or alleged emergencies which have enhanced Executive power, fostered attitudes of urgency and anxiety, and given rise to a general disregard for constitutional procedure.

In fact, there was neither uncertainty nor ambiguity on the part of the framers of the Constitution as to their determination to vest the war power exclusively in the Congress. As Thomas Jefferson wrote in a letter to Madison in 1789: "We have already given in example one effectual check to the Dog of war by transferring the power of letting him loose from the Executive to the Legislative body, from those who are to spend to those who are to pay."

As to the powers of the President as Commander in Chief, Alexander Hamilton, an advocate of strong executive power, wrote in Federalist No. 69:

> The President is to be commander in chief of the army and navy of the United States. In this respect his authority would be nominally the same with that of the King of Great Britain, but in substance much inferior to it. It would amount to nothing more than the supreme command and direction of the military and naval forces, as first General and admiral of the Confederacy, while that of the British king extends to the declaring of war and to the raising and regulating of fleets and armies — all which, by the Constitution under consideration, would appertain to the legislature.

The present administration's view of the President's power as Commander in Chief is almost the polar opposite of Hamilton's. In its comments of March 10, 1969, on the then pending national commitments resolution, the Department of State made the following assertion:

> As Commander in Chief, the President has the sole authority to command our Armed Forces, whether they are within or outside the United States. And, although reasonable men may differ as to the

circumstances in which he should do so, the President has the constitutional power to send U.S. military forces abroad without specific congressional approval.

Like a number of its predecessors, the present administration is basing its claim to war powers on either a greatly inflated concept of the President's authority as Commander in Chief, or in some vague doctrine of inherent powers of the Presidency, or both. Another possibility is that the matter simply has not been given much thought.

Whatever the explanation may be, the fact remains that the Executive is conducting a constitutionally unauthorized, Presidential war in Indochina. The commitment without the consent or knowledge of Congress of thousands of American soldiers to fight in Cambodia — a country which has formally renounced the offer of protection extended to it as a protocol state under the SEATO Treaty, and to which, therefore, we are under no binding obligation whatever — evidences a conviction by the Executive that it is at liberty to ignore the national commitments resolution and to take over both the war and treaty powers of Congress when congressional authority in these areas becomes inconvenient.

It is noteworthy that, in his address to the Nation of April 30 explaining his decision to send American troops to Cambodia, the President did not think it necessary to explain what he believed to be the legal ground on which he was acting, other than to refer to his powers as Commander in Chief of the Armed Forces. Equally noteworthy was the President's repeated assertion in his press conference of May 8 that he — and he alone — as Commander in Chief was responsible for the conduct of the war and the safety of our troops. This sweeping assertion of the President's authority as Commander in Chief amounts to the repudiation of those provisions of article I, section 8 of the Constitution, which empower Congress not only to "declare war" but to "raise and support armies," "provide and maintain a Navy," and "make rules for the Government and regulation of the land and naval forces." It is true, of course, that the present administration's attitude in this area hardly differs from that of its predecessors — except that preceding administrations took no special pride, as the present administration does, in adherence to a "strict construction" of the Constitution.

The Senate's adoption of the Church-Cooper-Aiken-Mansfield amendment will be a significant step toward restoring the health of our constitutional system of checks and balances. Both its purpose and language are simple and straightforward. Its purpose is simply to prevent involvement by the United States in a wider war in Asia by insuring that our forces are withdrawn from Cambodia and that the United States does not end up fighting a war in behalf of Cambodia. I will not go into the several points of the amendment since the sponsors of it will discuss its details in their presentations. . . .

MR. CHURCH. Mr. President . . . The United States is still stuck fast in the longest war of its history in the former French properties known as Indochina. Three Presidents, representing both political parties, have been unwilling to put an end to the American involvement in this Asian war.

Throughout this protracted period, the Congress of the United States has permitted each President to exercise blank-check powers. In so doing, we have shrunk from the use of our own authority under section 8 of article I of the Constitution, which vests in Congress the purse strings, together with the power to declare war, to raise and support armies, to provide and maintain a navy, and to make rules for the government and regulation of the land and naval forces. Our failure to make effective use . . . of any of these powers, while the war was passed from one President to another, is one for which historians may judge us harshly.

Within the past 2 weeks, another front has been opened in this interminable war — again as the result of a Presidential decision taken without so much as a bow to Congress. The dispatch of American troops into Cambodia, though presently limited in scope, could easily become the first step toward committing the United States to the defense of still another government in Southeast Asia. Sobering as this specter should be, in light of our experience in Vietnam, it nonetheless presents Congress with a historic opportunity to draw the limits on American intervention in Indochina. This is the purpose of the amendment that Senator Cooper and I, joined by Senators Mansfield and Aiken, urge the Senate to approve. If enacted into law, it would draw the purse strings tight against a deepening American involvement in Cambodia.

There is a precedent for what we are asking the Senate to do. It lies in the action taken last December when, you will recall, the Senate adopted overwhelmingly a modification I proposed to an amendment offered by Senators Cooper and Mansfield to the military appropriations bill for fiscal year 1970. It provided that "none of the funds appropriated by this act shall be used to finance the introduction of American ground combat troops into Laos or Thailand." There is reason to believe that this amendment, which became law, had a restraining effect on our newest venture, because the President is said to have rejected recommendations that the current operation include Laos as well as Cambodia. To have done otherwise, might well have placed the President in the untenable position of breaking the law.

We now seek to do for Cambodia what our earlier amendment did for Laos. But since American forces have already entered Cambodia, the amendment we propose would set limits on their intervention, prevent them from remaining in Cambodia, and preclude any military entanglement on our part with the government of that country.

Unquestionably, Congress has the power to accomplish these objectives. But this power, so little used in recent years, amounts to so much idle talk, unless a majority proves willing to invoke it. Our amendment is drafted in such manner as to invite, and offered in the hope that it will attract, majority support.

Some have argued that it is useless for the Senate to legislate limits, when the House of Representatives has already backed away from them. I do not agree. Nor do I believe the Senate should be put off on such a pretext. . . .

The amendment itself is a realistic one. It is no exercise in futility; it does not attempt to undo what has been done. Instead, it is addressed to the immediate need of preventing the United States from bogging down in Cambodia, and from committing itself to the defense of another Asian government on a new front.

It does this by: First, denying funds for the retention of American forces in Cambodia; second, prohibiting funds for the instruction of Cambodian military forces or for hiring mercenaries to fight for Cambodia; and, third, forbidding the use of any appropriation for conducting combat activity in the air above Cambodia in support of Cambodian forces.

In sum, the amendment is directed against those very activities which led to our entrapment in Vietnam. Its adoption would erect a legal barrier against further penetration of American forces into the jungles of Southeast Asia and help expedite the withdrawal of our troops from Vietnam. . . .

Mr. President, when the amendment was originally offered, Senators Mansfield and Aiken joined Senator Cooper of Kentucky and myself in recommending it to the Committee on Foreign Relations. The committee adopted the amendment by a vote of 9 to 5 and affixed it to the Foreign Military Sales Act now pending before the Senate.

Since the committee took that action, many other Senators have asked to be listed as cosponsors of the amendment. . . .

Mr. President, as of now, the total number of Senators sponsoring the amendment is 30. . . .

Mr. President, I also ask that a text of the amendment in its revised form, as reported from the Committee on Foreign Relations, be printed at this point in the *Record.*

There being no objection, the text was ordered to be printed in the Record *as follows:*

Church-Cooper Amendment

Sec. 7. The Foreign Military Sales Act is amended by adding at the end thereof the following new section:

"Sec. 47. Prohibition of assistance to Cambodia. — In order to avoid the involvement of the United States in a wider war in Indochina and to expedite the withdrawal of American forces from Vietnam, it is hereby provided that, unless specifically authorized by law hereafter enacted, no funds authorized or appropriated pursuant to this Act or any other law may be expended for the purpose of —

"(1) retaining United States forces in Cambodia;

"(2) paying the compensation or allowances of, or otherwise supporting, directly or indirectly, any United States personnel in Cambodia who furnish military instruction to Cambodian forces or engage in any combat activity in support of Cambodian forces;

"(3) entering into or carrying out any contract or agreement to provide military instruction in Cambodia, or to provide persons to engage in any combat activity in support of Cambodian forces; or

"(4) conducting any combat activity in the air above Cambodia in support of Cambodian forces."

. . . Mr. Stennis. Yes, Mr. President, it is true I am a strict constructionist of the Constitution. But the time has long since passed for making a strict construction here, when we have been sending these men into battle for months and years, and still are, right this minute — right this minute — not as a part of an act of aggression, but as a part of an action, now, of receding and trying to pull out.

It is under those conditions, and for those reasons — and because blood is being spilled, and lives lost, and will continue to be as a result of the use of just such ammunition as we are destroying here — that I say, let us not stay our hand now, and thus send the enemy word that, "You will never be subjected to this again."

I hope we can pull out. I wish we could pull out tomorrow, out of Cambodia, and stay out forever. But I know as long as we are there, engaged in these battles, we ought not to be sending word to the enemy, "We are going to leave you alone hereafter as far as this area is concerned."

That is what we will be doing if we pass a law saying that our Commander in Chief is prohibited from doing anything like this again, regardless of the circumstances, unless he can get another law passed.

There are a lot of things about this war that are not pleasing to me. We have made plenty of mistakes. But I pray we will not make this mistake. Not this one, sending such glad tidings to our adversaries, not only those in Hanoi, but those who are allied with them — Peking, Moscow, and others — that we are not going to tie a part of our other hand behind us, and we are not going to proceed unless another law can be passed.

Mr. President, I believe that when all these facts are exposed, and this has sunken into the commonsense of the American people, their verdict will be, "No; do not do it."

This is not a time to be stepping in here and stopping a procedure of battle that has every evidence of being highly profitable. There is no reason to promise now that we will never do it again unless we can get a law passed.

Mr. GRIFFIN. Mr. President, I wish to commend the distinguished Senator from Mississippi. Once again he has demonstrated that he is not only very learned and knowledgeable, but he is also a statesman as he rises at this point in the history of our country to say some things that ought to be said now on the floor of the Senate.

I am as concerned as any Senator about the prerogatives and the powers of the Congress, and particularly of the Senate.

But I do not understand the argument of some who support the amendment and variations thereof being talked about today. The Constitution says Congress shall have the power to declare war. Any Senator is perfectly within his rights if he wishes to introduce a resolution to declare war, or to argue the point that war ought to be declared or ought not to be declared, because the Constitution does say that Congress has the power to declare war.

It should be noted, however, that a declaration of war is a very broad policy declaration on the part of the Congress. On the other hand, the Constitution gives the President, as Commander in Chief of the Armed Forces, the responsibility for military decisions, strategy, tactics, and so forth. In Congress we cannot, and should not, attempt to make battlefield decisions, or to draw precise lines or to make decisions regarding the time or scope of a battle, nor should we try to direct the Commander in Chief specifically with regard to how battles should be conducted, or exactly where they should be conducted. Such decisions are beyond the Constitutional powers of Congress and it would not be in the interests of the United States for the Congress to attempt to make such decisions. I am very much concerned that the amendment before us gets into that territory and that area of decision-making — areas which are appropriately and properly left to the Commander in Chief. . . .

As we consider these amendments' resolutions, particularly the so-called Church-Cooper amendment, it is important to keep in mind that one person is absolutely essential to the hope of negotiating a peaceful settlement of this war, and one person is absolutely essential to the success of an orderly withdrawal of our troops. Of course, that person is the President of the United States.

The credibility of the President of the United States is very important. That the President of the United States should be believed; that others realize that he means what he says and says what he means, is of utmost importance — not only in the United States, but more important, as far as the enemy is concerned. Because if the Senate should infer by the adoption of this amendment that we doubt, or do not believe the President, then how can we expect the enemy to believe what the President of the United States is saying? . . .

THE PRESIDING OFFICER. The clerk will report the final committee amendment.

THE LEGISLATIVE CLERK. On page 4, line 21, insert the language down to and including line 21 on page 9. . . .

The Cooper-Church amendment was inserted in the text of the bill.

MR. DOLE. Mr. President, will the Senator from Idaho yield?

MR. CHURCH. I am happy to yield for questions.

MR. DOLE. Mr. President, on Tuesday of this week, the junior Senator from Kansas submitted an amendment which I may offer as substitute language for the so-called Church-Cooper amendment. At that time I said, and repeat today, that I applaud the sincere efforts, of the Senator from Idaho, the Senator from Kentucky, and other sponsors of the Church-Cooper amendment; but I also share the concerns of others in this Chamber regarding the right of any President to protect American troops.

I am wondering whether the Senator from Idaho has had an opportunity to study the proposed amendment that I submitted on Tuesday. It reads:

> In line with the expressed intention of the President of the United States, no funds authorized or appropriated pursuant to this Act or

any other law shall be used to finance the introduction of American ground combat troops into Laos, Thailand, or Cambodia without the prior consent of the Congress, except to the extent that the introduction of such troops is required, as determined by the President and reported promptly to the Congress, to protect the lives of American troops remaining within South Vietnam.

This was commonly known in the other body as the Findley amendment. It was adopted by the other body and later dropped from the Military Sales Act.

It occurs to me this language does, in essence, what the authors of the Church-Cooper amendment intend to do or propose to do. At the same time, it does give the President that right, the right which he might have in any event, to protect American troops remaining in South Vietnam.

I take this opportunity to exchange my views with those of the Senator from Idaho, if he has any comment to make.

MR. CHURCH. I would say, first of all, to the Senator that the substitute he proposes would, in my judgment, render the Cooper-Church effort meaningless. If this language is adopted, the Senate will merely be making an idle gesture. With all deference to the Senator, the exception he recommends provides a loophole big enough to drive the Pentagon through.

If we are to make a serious effort, within the constitutional powers of Congress, to establish the outer perimeters on American penetration into Cambodia, it will be necessary, then, to adopt the language that the committee approved, or something very close to it.

The proposed substitute offered by the disitnguished Senator from Kansas is unacceptable. It would gut the amendment, rendering it meaningless. . . .

MR. DOLE. Mr. President, let me say and make it very clear that I share some of the reservations of the distinguished Senator from Idaho, and so stated at the outset publicly, that I hope our efforts in Cambodia were to protect American troops, and to keep the Vietnamization program on schedule, not an effort to shore up the Lon Nol government. Thus, I share the concern of the Senator from Idaho, the Senator from Kentucky, and others who have joined as cosponsors; but the point is that, notwithstanding the language in the Senator's amendment, or consistent with the language in the Senator's amendment, does the Senator from Idaho agree or disagree that the President, as Commander in Chief, notwithstanding the passage of the amendment and the enactment of the amendment as part of the Military Sales Act, would still have the power, under the Constitution, to go back into Cambodia or any country to protect American troops?

MR. CHURCH. Whatever authority the President has under the Constitution, Congress cannot take from him. That is, however, only one side of the coin. The other side has to do with the authority of Congress, as vested in it by the Constitution. The Cooper-Church amendment is designed to assert that authority in such a way as to keep the present Cambodian operation within the limits declared by the President as his objective. It is idle for us to write language regarding the President's own constitutional authority. That is why we have avoided any reference to the President or to his responsibilities as Commander in Chief. We have confined our amendment to that authority which belongs to Congress — determining how and where public money can be spent.

Further, the Senator mentioned, in connection with his proposed amendment, that the Senate had earlier passed an amendment, which became law, limiting the expenditure of funds in regard to the introduction of American ground combat troops into either Laos or Thailand.

That amendment passed this body on December 15, 1969. It reads as follows:

> In line with the expressed intention of the President of the United States, none of the funds appropriated by this act shall be used to finance the introduction of American ground combat troops into Laos or Thailand.

We did not then go on to say —

> . . . except to the extent that the introduction of such troops is required, as determined by the President and reported promptly to the Congress, to protect the lives of American troops remaining within South Vietnam.

It was not thought necessary, then, to say that. It is not necessary now. Whatever power the President has under the Constitution we cannot take from him. But we can establish limits on the expenditure of public money, so that, if he wants to exceed those limits, he must then come back to Congress, present his case, and ask us to lift the limitations. . . .

MR. SYMINGTON. Would the Senator have included Cambodia in his resolution last December if he had had the remotest conception that we would be attacking Cambodia at this time?

MR. CHURCH. If anyone had suggested that Cambodia was on the list, there is no question in my mind that Cambodia would have been added to Laos and Thailand. I am sorry it was not. Perhaps if we had added it then, we would not be faced with this serious crisis now. . . .

MR. DOLE. I take issue with the word "attack" used by the distinguished Senator from Missouri. I also remind him that another great Missourian, former President Truman, went into Korea without the consent of Congress. . . .

MR. GORE. I have listened with a great deal of interest to this colloquy, which deals with a fundamental constitutional question. I would like briefly and impromptu to express some views.

The genius of our system is that we have coordinate, coequal branches of government, with checks and balances one upon the others and the others upon the one. The warmaking powers are vested in the legislative and the executive. A war cannot be waged except with the support of both.

By the rationale advanced, by my distinguished and able friend the junior Senator from Kansas, the President would have the authority to launch an attack upon China tomorrow, or tonight, or at this moment, without the approval of Congress. China is a sanctuary, indeed the greatest sanctuary of the war, to the enemy in Southeast Asia. It supplies rice, ammunition, the supplies, equipment, and materiel of all sorts. So by that reasoning, by that rationale, without the approval of the elected representatives of the people, the Congress, indeed, even without any consultation with them, the President could say, it is in the interest of saving American lives, the lives of those who are now in Vietnam, to bomb, to attack, to eradicate the sanctuary in Red China.

Would not that be just as logical, just as constitutional, as what we have just heard?

MR. CHURCH. I must concede that it would. The senator's argument underscores the fact that the authors of our Constitution never envisioned that a President, on his own decision, would send American troops to a war in a distant, foreign country.

The whole purpose of placing the war power in the hands of Congress was to make certain that such a fateful decision would be formulated by the representatives of all the people, including the President, and not by the Chief Executive alone. Why, the framers of the Constitution would turn in their graves if they knew how the shared responsibility, which they provided in that document, has eroded away. . . .

MR. PELL. Along the line of the previous questions and points, when the patriotism of those of us who support this amendment, who believe our present policies wrong, is questioned by the two largest veterans' organizations, I think it is of interest to note that 82 percent of the sponsors of the amendment under discussion are veterans, as opposed to 71 percent in this body as a whole. I think it is an interesting statistic.

Now I would like to ask the Senator, who, as a lawyer, is more educated in the law than I am, and is also versed in international law, what is the difference between the sanctuaries in Thailand from which our bombers move and the sanctuaries in Cambodia from which the North Vietnamese move.

MR. CHURCH. The difference is that the Thai sanctuaries are ours and the Cambodian sanctuaries are theirs. . . .

Mr. President, I know that the Senator from Kansas wishes the floor, and I will not detain him much longer!

I do think it is interesting, however, in view of the questions he posed earlier, to remember that in 1846 President Polk sent American forces into disputed territory in Texas which precipitated the clash that began the Mexican War.

Abraham Lincoln was then a Congressman from Illinois, and he took strong exception to the Presidential decision that led to our involvement in the Mexican War. He wrote some memorable words concerning the Constitution and the intended limits on Presidential discretion in the matter of war. I should like to read those words to the Senate. Abraham Lincoln wrote:

> Allow the President to invade a neighboring nation whenever he shall deem it necessary to repel an invasion, and you allow him to do so whenever he may choose to say he deems it necessary for such purpose — and you allow him to make war at pleasure. Study to see if you can fix any limit to his power in this respect, after you have given him so much as you propose.
>
> The provision of the Constitution giving the war-making power to Congress, was dictated, as I understand it, by the following reasons. Kings have always been involving and impoverishing their people in wars, pretending generally, if not always, that the good of the people was the object. This, our convention undertook to be the most oppressive of all kingly oppressions; and they resolved to frame the Constitution that no one man should hold the power of bringing this oppression upon us. . . .

MR. STENNIS. Mr. President. . . . We are now attempting to legislate with respect to a battle which is actually being fought now — today — near the Cambodian-South Vietnamese border. By the assurances which have been given us by our highest officials, from the President on down, we know that the present action is limited in scope, limited in purpose, limited in geography, limited in size, and limited in time. I submit to all Senators that, under the circumstances, there is no precedent in all history for Congress to outline, limit, or define the perimeter of a battlefield here in the halls of the Congress. I believe this is the first time it has ever been undertaken. That is exactly what we will be trying to do, in this Chamber, to form the perimeter of a battlefield, where the battle is already in progress and men are dying today — I repeat, today.

If we are going to do that, we should draw every one of those men out immediately, not only from Cambodia but also from Vietnam. We cannot have it both ways at once. That is clear to me.

I believe that as this sinks into the minds of the American people, concerned as they are and vexed as they are about this war, their thoughts will be, "Do not stay the hands of our Commander in Chief. If we are going to stay there at all, do not put bonds on him; instead come out altogether."

I know of no one in this body who wants to increase the hazards to our young men in Vietnam and Cambodia. Of course not. It is a matter of judgment. I am glad that we have a President who had the courage to act on the facts as he saw them.

If we adopt this amendment, it would be unthinkable and an affront to reason and to the President.

Mr. President, I am not thinking in terms of President Nixon. I am thinking in terms of a constitutional American Commander in Chief, a constitutional Chief Executive who has been chosen by the people and who is known throughout the world as our Commander in Chief, who know that he is the only American who can carry out that role. We cannot put in a substitute for Mr. Nixon just because we do not like his judgment. . . .

I want to make it clear that I think Congress has the power — I am not arguing that Congress does not have the power — to withhold an appropriation. . . .

I find it difficult to believe that we really want to convert the Senate of the United States into a war room and to try to direct battle, prescribe tactics, control strategy, draw boundaries, and otherwise to usurp the responsibilities and the prerogatives of the President and our military leaders. This is not a proper function of the Congress; and it should not be. And I do not believe that it ever will be. . . .

Mr. President . . . going back to the constitutional question involved, I do not know of any sound, legal basis or any real and valid precedent for that which is being proposed here. Under article 2 of the Constitution the President is made Commander in Chief of the Armed Forces. As early as *Fleming v. Page,* 50 U.S. 602, 614 (1850), the U.S. Supreme Court held that the responsibility of the President under article 2 is "to direct the movement of the naval and military forces placed by law at his command and to employ them in the manner he may deem most effectual." . . .

As far as I can ascertain, the nearest thing to a precedent along these lines was the adoption of the amendment to the defense appropriation bill last year — which now appears as section 643 — providing that —

> In line with the expressed intention of the President of the United States, none of the funds appropriated by this Act shall be used to finance the introduction of American ground troops into Laos or Thailand.

Aside from the fact that this is far less restrictive than the proposed amendment, at that time the American troops were not on the mission which the statute was designed to prevent and were not engaged in the prohibited combat. Incidentally, I opposed that amendment and voted against it. But there was no one being sent into battle, no battle was going on, men were not called upon to die in those battles, and that is the big distinction, as a practical matter, from the conditions today.

While the Cooper-Church amendment and its general thrust is somewhat similar to the President's expressed intention concerning our limited role in Cambodia and the completion of our operations by July 1, there are certain elements of it which raise serious questions and which could affect adversely the President's policy on Vietnamization and the steady withdrawal of American combat forces from Vietnam. Therefore, I think that it would be wise to look at the provisions of the amendment.

Before I leave that point, I wish to say with respect to the subject of declarations of war: I remember standing within a few feet of where I am now standing when word came that President Truman had sent our Armed Forces into Korea. I realized very clearly then that act, within itself, even though I supported the concept of the United Nations, was a terrific precedent and that it might plague us. But I also noted that, for many years after I came here, the idea of the issuance of a declaration of war by Congress was laughed at and scoffed at as being old-fashioned and out of the times; why, it was ridiculous. Some of you remember that. I can give names and I can almost give dates, if you want me to.

Most of the thought behind all of these alliances that we signed up for, whereby we tried to underwrite everything all over the world, was based partly on the idea that declarations of war were old-fashioned and out of date. There is very much concern about it now. I am glad there is. I hope we can bridge that gap as a general proposition, but now it is too late with respect to South Vietnam. We stood here and sent all of those men over there to fight and now we talk about a declaration of war, and some say, "We ought to declare war." We are now on the way out. It is too late in this war. We are on the way out; we are withdrawing. We are trying to cover our withdrawal and make it safe for ourselves and our allies. . . .

MR. COOPER. The Senator stated — and many have stated their comments on this amendment, that we are inhibiting the constitutional powers of the President to protect the lives of American soldiers. Of course, this argument has great appeal. It has appeal to me. The President of the United States, as Commander in Chief, does have large wartime powers. But I do not believe this power can be employed to enter a new war in another country —for Cambodia — particularly when there is no obligation, no treaty obligation, no obligation under the SEATO Treaty, which Cambodia denounced. Certainly, we have no obligation to engage in the self-defense of Cambodia. And it would be extreme to enter a larger, expanded war in Cambodia upon the basis of the protection of our forces.

The President has great powers as Commander in Chief in wartime to protect our Armed Forces. With respect to this power, this amendment would not limit, except in one respect, and I want to be frank about the exception. It would say to the President, "We respect your power to defend our forces and to protect their lives, but you cannot use that power to enter into another war in another country without the consent of Congress."

Without trying to delineate his powers, we are saying to him, "Mr. President, with great respect for you, if this amendment becomes law, you cannot use the authorized and appropriated funds of the United States to become involved in a larger and wider war in Cambodia." It shows our respect for him. It also shows our respect for our obligations and duties as Senators. I have supported the President's program of Vietnamization. It represents a change from the policies of the past and represents what I consider to be an irreversible policy to bring our forces home. . . .

The only certain constitutional power that Congress has over a war is through its power of the purse strings. That is all.

It can pass resolutions. We can through sense of the Senate resolutions and sense of the House resolutions express our positions to the Executive. But if he thinks we are incorrect, he does not have to follow our suggestions. The purse is our power.

Mr. President, the Constitution did not give the Congress the power lightly. The Constitutional Convention made a distinction between the King of England and the President of the United States. The King of England had the power both to declare war and to raise armed forces for war.

The Constitution gave to Congress the power to raise and support an army and navy.

The logic of the argument the Senator makes is that we can never use this constitutional power, because he says the soldiers will not be paid and their wives, their widows and children, will not receive allowances.

That decision would be a matter for the President.

If the Congress passes this amendment, it will then be a matter for the President to decide whether it shall be followed. If by some mischance, there was a period of time when this was not observed or any other factor intervened to affect the rights of our servicemen, that matter could be corrected. We respect our servicemen. I know that Congress and the President of the United States would see that such a situation would not remain.

We are trying to deal with the large question of avoiding another war. That far overshadows these objections.

Mr. Williams of Delaware. Mr. President, I respect the position of the Senator from Kentucky. And I do not advance this in a critical manner, but that is the mathematical effect of his amendment. . . .

I think this point should be clear.

I agree that the power of the purse is in the hands of Congress, and perhaps directing that power in certain directions would have influence on the Government.

Rather than using the power of the purse to withhold pay from the boys in Vietnam and Cambodia who are there through no fault of their own, let us put our own salaries on the line and put them on the line as a demonstration of our good faith. We should not put their pay on the line.

I think it would be most unfortunate for the families of the servicemen to feel that they are being cut off from all benefits under any circumstances regardless of how short this period may be.

I question the effect of such action on the morale of our troops. If we could do this today for troops in Cambodia we could do it tomorrow in Vietnam. Does anyone dare suggest we stop the pay of all military personnel in Southeast Asia? . . .

MR. FULBRIGHT. Mr. President, . . . I think this is the most irrelevant argument that one could make. I cannot imagine why anyone would make such an argument. I have never heard the Senator from Delaware, in the 20 years I have been in the Senate, make an argument with no more substance than that. . . .

MR. McGEE. . . . I can recall well how, in the first critical test of our role as leaders of the world in the 1950's, those of us in the liberal community were groping for some middle ground in exercising our responsibility between the "massive retaliation" that John Foster Dulles was talking about on the one hand, which meant nuclear weapons, and "Fortress America" on the other.

It was then that we felt crowded into a position of at least weighing the dimensions of a limited, undeclared war. Our belief was that in the nuclear age we did not dare take the risk of a declared war unless it was total war, "The" war, whatever that means. Hopefully, that will never occur.

To fend off the holocaust of nuclear warfare on the one hand and the ridiculousness of such a policy as "Fortress America" on the other, we thought it was better to learn from World War II, from the experiences with Japan, which began to nibble at Manchuria and then to dominate Asia, which involved us in war as a result of Pearl Harbor; from the experiences with Hitler, who nibbled away at the Versailles Treaty until he occupied the Rhineland in violation of that treaty, and involved us all in world war at such terrible cost. So it is understandable that our generation sought some alternative. That alternative was a limited war without a declaration.

That is what I think poses the problem now with us today.

Under the Constitution of the United States, our Founding Fathers never envisaged such an exigency as that, and understandably so. They envisaged a declaration of war in what would be today an old-fashioned war. There are a great many gray areas in question as to the role of the Senate which derive from the circumstance of an undeclared war.

I must confess, as a student of the problem, that I am not sure to this day whether we, as a free society, can wage an undeclared war.

We are spending a great deal of time on this subject here today. We are caught up in where we are, for better or for worse. I think it would behoove us all to devote more of our energies, and all the foresight that we can mobilize to figure out how we best should conduct the role of the Senate in this nuclear age in its relationships with the President of the United States. . . .

I have no doubt that in terms of this war, that, had it been successfully concluded in a year or 18 months, members of this body would have been bragging about how the Senate of the United States approved the Gulf of Tonkin resolution and participated in that decision, and they would be seeking the credit for that resolution; but because of the mystery of the Orient, because of the vagaries of the new kinds of conflict that guerrilla warfare has raised in the East, and because of all the other pressures and the timetables in the world crowding in on us, it did not go as Republicans and Democrats would have preferred. It turned out to be much more complicated and much larger than partisan politics, even larger than Presidents of the United States, or the American people as a whole.

For that reason, I would express my desperate wish that we not take a step here that will, in fact, jeopardize the leadership role of the President of the United States as Commander in Chief in the midst of a conflict, when we should be readdressing ourselves to his proper role in cooperation with the Senate in all future such decisionmaking processes in the kind of world in which we live. . . .

The amendment, in effect, states that U.S. war power resides in the Congress, that the power of the purse may legitimately be extended in such a way as to shape the course of a war in which we are already deeply involved.

I oppose this position. I believe the framers of the Constitution meant it when they said that the President shall be the Commander in Chief of the Army and Navy of the United States. I believe they meant it when they said that the Congress shall declare war, not make war. The language is clear. . . .

Never in our history has it been a function of the Senate to advise and consent on operational military decisions made by the Commander in Chief.

Never in our history have we conducted a war by committee.

And on many different occasions prior to World War II, U.S. Presidents have ordered undeclared acts of war.

The Congress is the greatest deliberative body in the world, but as a military leadership group, notoriously unable to arrive at rapid decisions, it could become a multiheaded monster if it attempted to second-guess the conduct of a war. . . .

MR. CHURCH. . . . Warmaking was supposed to be a shared responsibility. The framers of the Constitution did not conceive the Presidency to be an autocracy. They never intended that one man, as President, should have all the power to decide where, when, and under what circumstances the United States would fight. They never intended that he alone should pass upon the vital questions of war and peace which would involve the life or death of this Republic. No, indeed. The framers of the Constitution and Presidents for nearly two centuries, in adherence to the provisions of the Constitution, have recognized that Congress has its role to play, as well as the President, when it comes to the matter of war. . . .

MR. PELL. I wonder if the Senator is as struck as I am with the fact that under our system of government it is rather hard, sometimes, for the people of our country to make their will known, if the President is in opposition.

Under a parliamentary democracy, we have the vote of confidence, and upon a failure in it, the representatives go back to the people. Even in the Soviet Union, certainly the opposite of a democracy, a committee form of government exists where, if there is a consensus within the committee that the head of government is going too far in an incorrect direction, he is quietly nudged aside, as we have seen happen to Mr. Khrushchev and his predecessors. But with our system, there is very great difficulty in the majority will expressing itself except at 4-year intervals.

We also have the question of what is the majority will. How do you weigh the intensity of feeling?

We have at this time, it seems to me, a very dangerous situation developing within the country, developing with great intensity of feeling — one might call it decibels, if such a term could be used relating to emotion — decibels of emotion of high intensity and high anguish on the part of many young people who believe they are not being heard, that there is no dialog or communication, and who want to see some action taken.

At the same time, I think there is a majority opinion in the Nation that somewhat apathetically believes these decisions are best left to the President alone — the old idea of "father knows best."

This is a situation that can lead to real confrontation and real violence, unless some means are found of permitting the high decibel emotions of our younger people also to vent. . . .

MR. CHURCH. I agree with the Senator . . . that public confidence in our political institutions is at stake here. During previous years, the direction of protest, demonstration, and antiwar effort was pointed at the White House. When 250,000 young Americans came to the Capitol last November, hardly any of them came up to Capitol Hill. They all turned their backs on the Capitol and went down and faced the White House. They recognized that we had permitted enormous powers to be concentrated in the President's hands, and unless they could convince the President, they had no chance. Congress was irrelevant.

That was the pattern of the protest until the distinguished Senator from Kentucky (Mr. Cooper) and I went to the press galleries a couple of weeks ago and suggested that the time had come for Congress to begin to use some of its power, so long overlooked, for the purpose of establishing the outer limits to American participation in this widening war. Ever since, for the first time, attention has been directed at Congress. Indeed, Congress has been rediscovered. The issue is whether we can summon up the resolution to use the powers which were meant to be not only lodged in Congress, but also exercised by Congress. . . .

MR. BYRD of West Virginia. Let me say, if the distinguished Senator will yield, that I have not made up my mind as to whether I shall vote for or against the amendment. But, if I decide to vote for the amendment, it will never be because of threats of demonstrations, or violence in the streets, or on the campuses. If it is to be adopted on that basis, then I will not vote for it.

MR. CHURCH. May I say, with respect to the Senator's statement. that I believe he misunderstands the point I made.

MR. BYRD of West Virginia. I may have. I hope that I have. . . .

MR. CHURCH. It was certainly not because Congress is bending to any such threats, but because the place to settle this question is in the Halls of Congress, not in the streets. . . .

MR. ERVIN. Mr. President I rise to voice my opposition to the so-called Church-Cooper amendment. . . .

Section 8 of article I of the Constitution declares that Congress shall have the power to declare war. Section 10 of article I of the Constitution contains a provision that no State shall, without the consent of Congress, engage in war unless actually invaded or "in such imminent danger as will not admit of delay." Section 4 of article IV of the Constitution provides that the United States shall guarantee to every State in this Union a republican form of government and shall protect each of them against invasions.

Mr. President, the provisions of the Constitution which I have just read make these things clear. First, Congress and Congress alone has the power to declare a national or foreign war; and second, that the United States or even a State may engage in war without waiting for the consent of Congress when the United States or the State so acting is invaded or threatened with imminent invasion. . . .

Mr. President, let us see what words the framers used in setting out the congressional power to declare war. They said, "Congress shall have the power to declare war."

Now there is no obscure meaning in the word "war." There is no obscure meaning in the word "declare."

Anyone can pick up a dictionary and find that the word "war" means — "A state of open, armed conflict carried on between nations, states, or parties."

He will also find that the word "declare" means — "To state officially or formally, to state with emphasis or authority."

It also means — "To affirm."

Now, Mr. President, I maintain that the Gulf of Tonkin resolution, which is technically known as the Southeast Asia resolution, constitutes a declaration of war in a constitutional sense.

It asserts in its preamble —

> Whereas naval units of the Communist regime in Viet Nam, in violation of the principles of the Charter of the United Nations and of international law, have deliberately and repeatedly attacked United States naval vessels lawfully present in international waters, and have thereby created a serious threat to international peace. . . .

That is one of the assertions in the preamble, a preamble passed by both Senate and House with only two dissenting votes.

The next assertion is that —

> Whereas these attacks are part of a deliberate and systematic campaign of aggression that the Communist regime in North Viet Nam has been waging against its neighbors and the nations joined with them in collective defense of their freedom. . . .

Thus, here in the preamble of the Southeast Asia resolution, the Congress of the United States declares two significant facts. First, that the naval vessels of the United States have been deliberately and repeatedly attacked by North Vietnamese naval forces; and, second, that the attacks are a part of a deliberate and systematic campaign of aggression that North Vietnam is waging against South Vietnam.

Then, after the account of those recitations and those facts, it states:

> *Resolved by the Senate and House of Representatives of the United States of America in Congress assembled.* That the Congress approves and supports the determination of the President, as Commander-in-Chief, to take all necessary measures to repel any armed attack against the forces of the United States and to prevent further aggression.

Mr. President, there is no other way that has ever been devised by the mind of man to repel an armed attack except by force. Thus, Congress expressly stated in the first paragraph, following the preamble to the Southeast Asia resolution, that the President was empowered to take all the necessary measures to repel any armed attack against the forces of the United States and to prevent further aggression. Now, "aggression" as mentioned in the resolution means the aggression of North Vietnam upon its neighbors and the nations joined with them in collective defense of their freedom.

Section 2 of the resolution states in effect that —

> Consonant with the Constitution of the United States and the Charter of the United Nations and in accordance with its obligations under the Southeast Asia Collective Defense Treaty, the United States is, therefore, prepared, as the President determines, to take all necessary steps, including the use of armed force, to assist any member or protocol state of the Southeast Asia Collective Defense Treaty requesting assistance in defense of its freedom.

Mr. President, that is strikingly in harmony with the declaration that the United States made when it went to war with Spain in 1898.

On April 20, 1898, after the sinking of the battleship *Maine* in the harbor of Havana, the Congress of the United States passed . . . [a] resolution, which every one who has studied the subject admits to being a declaration of war. It is strikingly similar to the Southeast Asia resolution and even contains the same assertion made in the closing paragraph of the Southeast Asia resolution, that the United States has no territorial ambitions. . . .[1]

I am certain that when Congress passed the Gulf of Tonkin joint resolution, it was aware of what authority it was granting to the President of the United States. This is made exceedingly clear by a statement which one of the opponents of the resolution made on the floor of the Senate.

Former Senator Wayne Morse made this statement:

> We are, in effect, giving the President of the United States warmaking powers in the absence of a declaration of war. I believe that to be an historic mistake.

Former Senator Morse stated that by passing the Gulf of Tonkin joint resolution Congress was giving to the President warmaking powers. I agree with that statement of former Senator Morse to that extent. But I disagree with the statement that Congress was doing it

---

[1] Senator Ervin then introduced the Cuba resolution in full. — Eds.

without a declaration of war, because I contend that the Gulf of Tonkin resolution is clearly a declaration of war.

Let us now examine another facet of this situation. When the resolution was under consideration in the Senate, the Senator from Kentucky (Mr. Cooper) put this question to the distinguished Senator from Arkansas (Mr. Fulbright), the floor manager of the Gulf of Tonkin joint resolution:

> MR. COOPER. Does the Senator consider that in enacting this resolution we are satisfying that requirement of Article IV of the Southeast Asia Collective Defense Treaty? In other words, are we now giving the President advance authority to take whatever action he may deem necessary respecting South Vietnam and its defense, or with respect to the defense of any other country included in the treaty?
>
> MR. FULBRIGHT. I think that is correct.
>
> MR. COOPER. Then looking ahead, if the President decided it was necessary to use such force as could lead into war we will give that authority by this resolution?
>
> MR. FULBRIGHT. That is the way I would interpret it.

Mr. Fulbright added:

> If a situation later developed in which we thought approval should be withdrawn it could be withdrawn by concurrent resolution.

... I think that the Church-Cooper amendment is unconstitutional, in that it attempts to have Congress usurp and exercise some of the powers to direct the military forces in the theater of operations which belong, under the Constitution, to the President of the United States. ...

MR. BENNETT. . . . [While] I am opposed to the various amendments now pending before the Senate designed to limit the President's authority in Vietnam and Cambodia, [this] does not mean that I believe the President should have unlimited authority to expand the war. It means that I think such amendments as those before us are unnecessary and illtimed particularly under the circumstances. It is interesting to note that the sponsors of the pending amendments have fastened upon the power of the Congress to appropriate money as a means of stopping the President. It is my feeling that this attempt to use the power of the purse usurps the responsibility clearly vested in the President to issue orders for the protection of our Armed Forces. The President has determined that the limited actions he has ordered within Cambodia are necessary for the protection of our forces in South Vietnam. The proposed amendments would try to substitute the judgment of the Congress on that question for the judgment of the President. Knowing a little about both the Congress and the President, having been a Member of Congress for 18 years, and knowing my own weakness in this respect, I am choosing the Commander in Chief in this instance. . . .

MR. CRANSTON. Mr. President . . .

The Cooper-Church amendment is essentially a conservative document based on a strict constructionist view of the Constitution of the United States.

I view the amendment as a second step in an effort to restore Congress to its proper role in controlling the funding of military operations and giving the people a greater voice in the issues of war and peace through their elected representatives. . . .

I want to make it clear that the Cooper-Church amendment is a document of restraint — not isolation.

In no way are its supporters advocating a return to "fortress America." . . .

The issue of the war in Vietnam has become so vital and significant to America in the last 10 days that references to the intent of the Founding Fathers in granting Congress the power to fund and declare war have become more than patriotic sloganeering.

At stake is the separation of powers upon which our experiment in democratic government is based. . . .

MR. TOWER. . . . How many times has the legislative power of Congress been usurped by this agency, that agency, this department, that department, or the courts of the United States, and yet we have done nothing?

The fact of the matter is that our power over the conduct of foreign policy is essentially a negative power. We have the right to ratify treaties. We have the right to confirm appointments. We have the right to raise the stop sign. But seldom in our history have we gone over to the positive business of saying, "You may not do something in the future that we think you might do."

The supporters of this amendment have contended that this is in pursuance to what the President has said he will do: this is pursuant to presidential policy. Why not nail it down to this specific respect? If it is pursuant to presidential policy, then I submit that it is redundant for us to seal it into law here, in a really unprecendented action, at a time when we run the risk of convincing the world that we all disagree with our President, that we are not going to allow him to implement his policy and, from this point forward, "Ye shall know, be ye friend or foe, what the United States of America is going to do. We tie our hands." . . .

MR. TYDINGS. Mr. President . . . the facts are that the plain meaning of our Constitution, the recorded intentions of our Founding Fathers who framed this great document, the opinions of the Justices of the Supreme Court, and the statements and actions of the leaders of our country throughout its history squarely support the authority of Congress to enact the Church-Cooper amendment.

Congress' fundamental authority to keep Federal funds from being used for military matters in Cambodia after July 1, 1970, is founded in two important clauses in the Constitution. First, in clause 1 of article 1, section 8 of the Constitution it is provided that Congress shall have the power "to lay and collect taxes, duties, in posts and excises, to . . . provide for the common defense." Second, in clause 11 it is provided that Congress shall have the power "to declare war, grant letters of marque and reprisal, and make rules concerning captures on land and water."

Our forefathers were indeed wise in giving to Congress both the power to initiate and generally control war and the power of the purse to ensure that its wishes with regard to war were not abused. They remembered the long history of kings and rulers who plunged their countries into disastrous wars without the approval of their parliaments and people. They sought to insure that no U.S. President would ever involve this country in a war without the stated consent of the peoples' elected representatives in the Congress. . . .

In brief, it is clear that the war-declaring clause of the Constitution independently empowers Congress to specify the outer boundaries of our Nation's involvement in the war in Southeast Asia.

Some might conclude that the President's decision to send American troops into Cambodia without congressional authorization represents an infringement of Congress' warmaking authority and an abuse of his own authority as Commander in Chief. I am somewhat puzzled by the way this matter has been answered. For while it has been argued on the Senate floor that the Gulf of Tonkin resolution supplies adequate authority for the President's action in Cambodia, the administration has told us that it is not relying on the Tonkin Gulf resolution as support for its Vietnam policy.

However, it is not my purpose to question the President's Commander in Chief authority. Rather, the point I wish to make is that the argument of the distinguished Senator from North Carolina (Mr. Ervin), that Congress does not have the constitutional right to limit the perimeters of U.S. military activity is completely without support in the constitutional history of the Nation; indeed, it is contrary not only to the language of the Constitution but also to the words of the Founding Fathers and the great opinions of the Supreme Court that were addressed to this vital matter.

It is clear that Congress has been granted by the Constitution, at the very least, an equally important role to play with regard to the issue of war and peace. We must no longer ignore that responsibility. . . .

MR. WILLIAMS of Delaware. . . . Much is said about the President's usurping the powers of Congress. As one who has served here for 23½ years I am just as jealous as any Member of Congress of the powers of the Senate. But let us face it: The criticism of the President's usurping the powers of Congress is not the President's fault. It is because we in Congress have delegated to the President many of these powers which we should have kept right here in the Congress and discharged ourselves. This matter of easy delegation of powers I shall discuss further in a moment. Congress has delegated these powers, oftentimes, and then acted as a Monday morning quarterback after the decision was made. If the President's decision through these powers works out well we take the credit. If it is bad we can then say it is all his fault.

I think Congress should stop this delegation of these broad powers to the President and then trying to second guess him after it is over with as to whether he should or should not have acted. . . .

MR. MANSFIELD. Let me say that I am in accord with what the distinguished Senator has said. It is not the fault of the President that the executive branch has been able to retain these powers over the past 4 decades; it is because we gave those powers. We did not try to pull them back. If there is any blame, I would attach it to no President, but I would attach it to Congress as a whole, because we have been derelict in our duty and derelict in facing up to our responsibilities in that regard.

MR. WILLIAMS of Delaware. The Senator from Montana has said it better than I could.

I mentioned particularly that the Secretary was primarily before the committee on that Monday, before the President made the decision regarding Cambodia, to discuss with us and to get our opinion on the question of large-scale shipment of arms for the Cambodian Government which had been requested. There is no secret about this. It was in the press, so we can mention it. Yet under the powers which Congress in earlier years delegated to the President he did not have to come to Congress. He did not have to come to the Committee on Foreign Relations and get our opinion on this question of arms for Cambodia because in the passage of these bills in past months and years we delegated to the President this power to grant these arms to any nation in the world if he thought it was in the best interests of the U.S. Government.

MR. MANSFIELD. That is inherent in the bill under discussion. I do not think that the Foreign Relations Committee was aware of just how all embracing, how far embracing the authority in this bill is until the bill was before us a week or two ago.

As the Senator has said, the President, on his own initiative can empty the arsenal of the United States and give it to any country or any set of countries he wants to. Is that correct?

MR. WILLIAMS of Delaware. That is correct both under prior laws and so far as this bill is concerned. The bill before the Senate carries appropriations of $250 million in cash sales of military equipment and $350 million in credit sales, which is approximately $600 million. Under this pending bill the President will have the authority to use that $600 million to furnish military equipment, either sales or guarantee credits, to any nation in the world where he thinks it is in the best interests of the United States Government. The only requirement in the existing law or the bill before the Senate is that the President reports to Congress at the end of the fiscal year and tells us what he has done with it. This pending bill is only one of three such laws. . . .

I do not think Congress will get control of this until we stop this delegation of authority. The irony of the present situation right here is that Congress under the Cooper-Church amendment would be questioning the word of the President. I cannot get away from the fact that approval of the amendment as proposed to be modified would write into law that the troops must be out by July 1, which is an indication that we are accepting the President at his word but are not quite sure he means it and that therefore Congress is going to write into law a penalty if he does not keep his word. Immediately thereafter, the next vote would be to delegate to the President broad powers to sell $600 million in military equipment anywhere in the world — Thailand, Taiwan, Israel, or even Red China if he desired. Yes, any nation in the world? Does this make sense?

We have had the situation, as Senators know, in Pakistan and India where we were furnishing arms to both sides. When one got ahead of the other we would give arms to the other country. The result is that in any border dispute whoever got killed on either side had the satisfaction of being killed with an American bullet. . . .

The point I am making is this: If we want to regain the power of Congress why do we not just say we are going to stop delegating this authority to the President? In the future let there be line items in the appropriation bills for each country by name. Then Congress can accept or reject the request. . . .

In the bill before us Congress would delegate to the President authority to sell or guarantee payment of $600 million in military equipment to any country anywhere in the world — to Red China if he wants — there is no prohibition except that the President cannot make the equipment available to Cambodia. . . .

MR. FULBRIGHT. First, I would certainly join the Senator in support of limiting the arms aid and sales program further. But I thought that we obtained about as many improvements as was feasible during the committee's work on the bill. I supported those changes and I believe the Senator did also. I would be perfectly willing to go further in limiting giveaway of excess arms, for example. There was a good deal of discussion in the committee on that problem. I thoroughly agree with the Senator that Congress has been improvident in giving extraordinary discretion to Presidents past as well as present. This practice of giving them vast authority did not start with President Nixon. . . .

The only reason we did not go further than we did is that we did not think we had the votes to support more drastic changes.

I agree with much that the Senator has said. About 3 years ago the Senate put in strict controls on the number of countries that could receive aid without further congressional approval. But we could not hold that provision in conference. . . .

I do not think the Senator can deny that the Military Establishment, through its powerful and distinguished leaders in both Houses of Congress, have for all practical purposes dominated Congress on these matters. Whenever efforts have been made to do some of the things the Senator has suggested, we have failed for lack of votes. . . .

The Senator is well aware of the extent of the influence of the Military Establishment on the other body. It is very powerful.

MR. WILLIAMS of Delaware. Mr. President, I point out that the Military Establishment is not responsible for my vote in the Senate. The Senator is correct that Congress has tried on occasion to limit sales with respect to certain countries. Greece was one counry, and we have tried to limit sales to other countries.

The point I make is, why approve a bill which provides $600 million and delegates the President this broad authority only by negative action then to say that the authority is good anywhere in the world, "except in Cambodia and maybe Greece"?

Why single out two or three countries? That is always embarrassing for diplomatic reasons. Why not take our action affirmatively? Why delegate this $2 billion and this $600 million of authority and then start limiting this authority by two or three countries? Why not act affirmatively? Let the administration come down and ask for the authority, mentioning each country by name and amounts, and then let Congress vote on the specific request.

MR. FULBRIGHT. Mr. President, I agree with the Senator.

MR. WILLIAMS of Delaware. If the Senator will join with me we will defeat the bill where it is and at least stop the delegation of the power to use this $600 million.

MR. FULBRIGHT. Mr. President, I would like to stop it. But the Senator is confusing two very different things. One is the sale of military weapons. The second is the question of this President's right to go into Cambodia without coming to Congress.

We have not delegated, and the Congress would not allow us to delegate, wide open authority for the President to go to war with any country in the world. Going to war is supposed to be done only in accordance with constitutional procedures.

We have never been faced with a situation quite like the present one.

It is not the arms sales program in which we are particularly interested. The Cooper-Church amendment does not involve the arms sale program. We are concerned in this amendment with the Congress' powers in the field of foreign affairs. I do not think it contributes to public understanding to confuse those two issues.

I say again that I agree with the Senator on the matter of arms sales. I think that it has been a bad program and is not in the national interest. . . .

MR. HOLLAND. Mr. President, I certainly enjoyed this exchange between two very able Senators whom I respect very much. I do not think I ever heard so much wisdom coupled with so much unrealistic idealism in my life, and that goes back a number of years.

The fact is that everyone in the Senate knows the President has to have consent with reference to furnishing arms where they are badly needed. There is not a citizen in the United States who does not know how he has been pressed to furnish very much needed planes to Israel. Most of the people in the United States feel the

President is using proper restraint. I do not suppose you will find one person in ten who does not admit that there has to be somebody in power to act and act when the facts require it.

The same thing is true with reference to this whole question of supplying arms. We live in a world that moves fast.

A while ago I reported to the Senate that the ticker tape indicated that within an hour four different things had happened at an airport in Phonm Phen, halfway around the world. They were very interesting things, too, because they differed so greatly in importance. We live in a fast world, and somebody has to be empowered to act. We love the republican form of government and we like to live under what we call a democracy. But we know its greatest weakness is the inability to act fast unless we delegate some power for fast action in those areas that require it.

With all due respect to my distinguished friend from Delaware and my distinguished friend from Arkansas, I know that they know that Congress does not act fast. They know the Senate frequently exercises its prerogatives for long hearings, for exhaustive reports, and then long debates before it ever acts. At the other end of the Capitol, something of the same situation exists when one considers the long time taken by the Rules Committee to act. So we have to delegate authority.

In this important question of trying to supply arms where they are needed to keep weakness from being overthrown by force and innocence to be overthrown by violence, we have to give the power to somebody, and the President, chosen by all the people in the Nation, is the one who should receive such power. It is utter idealism to suggest he should not have that power. . . .

Following a long discussion of U.S. prestige and Senate reaction to President Nixon's speech on the Cambodia incursion, debate resumes on June 4.

MR. HANSEN. Mr. President . . . it could very well be that the vote on the Byrd amendment will be the decisive vote on the whole proposition that has been before this body for some days. I say that, first of all, because it is my conviction that the language itself cuts right down to the basic issue that must be faced by the people of America. I read from the amendment:

> Except that the foregoing provisions of this clause shall not preclude the President from taking such action as may be necessary to protect the lives of United States forces in South Vietnam or to facilitate the withdrawal of United States forces from South Vietnam. . . .

MR. GRIFFIN. Mr. President . . . last night, the Senator from Pennsylvania (Mr. Scott) received a letter from the President regarding the pending Byrd amendment to the Cooper-Church amendment.

I ask unanimous consent that the letter from the President to the Republican leader be printed at this point in the *Record*.

There being no objection, the letter was ordered to be printed in the Record, *as follows:*

The White House,
Washington, June 4, 1970.

Hon. Hugh Scott,
U. S. Senate,
Washington, D.C.

Dear Hugh: You have requested my views on an amendment offered by Senator Robert Byrd of West Virginia to the Cooper-Church amendment to the Foreign Military Sales bill now being considered by the Senate.

As you know, I am opposed to the language of the Cooper-Church provision in its present form. Nevertheless, I fully appreciate the concerns of many Senators anxious that the Cambodian expedition not involve our nation in another Vietnam-type conflict. As I reported to the American people last night, this has been the most successful operation of this long and difficult war and will be completed by June 30. The results will be fewer casualties and continued withdrawals from Vietnam — objectives that Senators share with me.

The Byrd amendment reaffirms the Constitutional duty of the Commander in Chief to take actions necessary to protect the lives of United States forces and is consistent with the responsibilities of my office. Therefore, it goes a long way toward eliminating my more serious objections to the Cooper-Church amendment.

You will recall that last year in Guam I outlined the Nixon doctrine establishing a policy for Asian nations to defend themselves, with American material assistance and technical help. If a stable lasting peace is to emerge in that beleaguered region, it is important that we promote regional cooperation. Therefore, I should hope that the Senate would also adopt an amendment supporting the Nixon doctrine of American material and technical assistance toward self-help.

I appreciate your continued deep interest in this subject and the untiring effort you and your colleagues have made in an effort to achieve meaningful legislation in the best interest of the American people.

Sincerely,
Richard Nixon.

MR. DOLE. Mr. President, I wish to commend the President of the United States on the letter forwarded to our distinguished minority leader, the senior Senator from Pennsylvania (Mr. Scott), in which the President indicates his willingness to compromise and to work out some accommodation with the Senate with reference to the pending business, the so-called Cooper-Church amendment.

The President indicates in clear and concise terms his support for the Byrd amendment. He states that the Byrd amendment does reaffirm his constitutional power and the constitutional power of any Commander in Chief to take necessary action to protect the lives of American forces consistent with his responsibilities and obligations.

I believe that the President by indicating his intentions is saying to the Senate that now is the time for compromise, not the time for confrontation. . . .

By crossing the Cambodian border to attack sanctuaries used by the enemy, the United States has in no sense gone to "war" with Cambodia. United States forces are fighting with or in support of Cambodian troops, and not against them. The Cambodian incursion has not resulted in a previously uncommitted nation joining the ranks of our enemies, but instead has enabled us to more effectively deter enemy aggression heretofore conducted from the Cambodian sanctuaries.

Only if the constitutional designation of the President as commander in chief conferred no substantive authority whatever could it be said that prior congressional authorization for such a tactical decision was required. Since even those authorities least inclined to a broad construction of presidential power concede that the commander in chief provision does confer substantive authority over the manner in which hostilities are concluded, the President's decision to invade and destroy the border sanctuaries in Cambodia was authorized under even a narrow reading of his power as commander in chief. . . .

So I say again today, as I have said time after time after time concerning the constitutional right and the constitutional power and constitutional obligation a President has, what harm can it do to adopt the language of the Byrd amendment and make it part of the Cooper-Church amendment. . . .

MR. MANSFIELD. Mr. President. . . . Six years ago the U.S. Military presence was confined largely to Saigon and a few coastal Vietnamese cities. The U.S. involvement was still indirect and peripheral. Now 6 years after the Tonkin Gulf resolution, U.S. servicemen are scattered through Vietnam, Laos, Thailand, Cambodia. The involvement is direct and, notwithstanding the so-called Vietnamization program, it is central to the entire structure of the war in Indochina.

I do not recall this history without a painful awareness of the Senate's part in its writing. Yet, it must be recalled. It must be recalled because the Senate is, again, face to face with another Tonkin Gulf resolution. I refer to the Byrd-Griffin modification which is now pending to the Cooper-Church amendment.

Once again, the Senate is asked, in effect, to accept what the executive branch has done, what it is doing, and what it may do with regard to Cambodia. That is the price the Senate is quoted if we would retain even a promise of preventing the further spread of the war under the Cooper-Church amendment. We are asked by the Byrd-Griffin modification to give legal endorsement to whatever course may be set by the executive branch in Cambodia. We are asked to subscribe not only to what is done in Cambodia in the name of the Commander in Chief under this President but, if the war persists, under his successor, whomever he may be and, perhaps, his successor's successor. . . .

The Byrd-Griffin modification is a direct descendant of the Tonkin Gulf resolution. The clay carries the same imprint. The door to further involvement in Cambodia is not closed by Byrd-Griffin. Byrd-Griffin opens the door wider. It sanctions an in-and-out entanglement in Cambodia. It sanctions a direct or indirect entrapment in Cambodia. It sanctions an ad infinitum involvement in Cambodia even as the Tonkin Gulf resolution did the same for the open-ended involvement in Vietnam.

Byrd-Griffin lifts the Congressional counterweights which Cooper-Church seeks to place against the pressures for expanding involvement in Indochina. It shackles the Senate's responsibility to join its separate constitutional authority with that of the President in a common effort to confine the war and withdraw U.S. forces.

If Byrd-Griffin is adopted on Thursday next, let there be no Monday morning regrets. Let there be no shocked indignation later. Whatever our intent, we will have cleared the way for another Vietnam in Cambodia and, perhaps, for still others elsewhere. The time to face the implications of Byrd-Griffin is now. It is not next year or the year after. . . .

I am aware that the President has expressed some sort of unofficial endorsement of the pending modification. The White House has written a letter. That is the President's right and his comments — solicited or unsolicited — deserve the most careful consideration of the Senate. Let us be clear, however, on one point. The President's constitutional responsibility in this matter does not begin at this time. His constitutional responsibility is not activated unless and until this legislation has passed, not only the Senate but also the House. Then and only then does the measure become subject to the President's approval or rejection. Then and only then does it become the Constitutional business of the President. . . .

The Byrd-Griffin modification, in my judgment, is the critical vote of this issue. Reject it and the Senate will say that the way out of Vietnam is not by way of Cambodia. Adopt Byrd-Griffin to Cooper-Church and the Senate will still say that the way out of Vietnam is not by way of Cambodia, but only if the executive branch also says the same thing.

The Constitutional message of Cooper-Church without this proposed addition is clear. The Senate acts in concert with the President's expressed determination but under its own legal responsibility in an effort to curb the further expansion of the war in Indochina. The Byrd-Griffin modification clouds that message.

In my judgment, the Senate should keep the Cooper-Church amendment free of distortion. The credibility of the Senate demands it. The urgencies of the Nation require it. . . .

MR. BYRD. . . . Mr. President, I ask unanimous consent to modify my amendment No. 667 as follows:

> On page 5, line 7, before the semicolon insert a comma and the following: except that the foregoing provisions of this clause shall not preclude the President in the exercise of his constitutional authority, powers and duties as Commander in Chief, from taking only such temporary action as is clearly necessary to protect the lives of United States forces in South Vietnam or to facilitate the withdrawal of United States forces from South Vietnam, in which circumstances the President is requested to first consult with Congressional leaders; . . .

There are those who say that my amendment will gut the Cooper-Church amendment. It was said last night by one Senator, although facetiously, that he would prefer to have the first amendment because it would more clearly gut the Cooper-Church amendment.

But what are we looking for here? Are we looking for an issue, or are we looking for the enactment into law of meaningful language that will help avoid another Vietnam but which, at the same time, will make clear that the President can act, decisively and promptly, for the protection of American troops in South Vietnam?

The amendment makes clear that he cannot use it as a guise to get us into a new war, into a permanent war, into a new commitment.

I use the word "guise" only because it has been used in discussions heretofore.

So here is an effort to meet the objections to close the gap and to come up with language — . . . which might stand a slim chance of acceptance in the other body, once it is passed by the Senate. . . .

THE VICE PRESIDENT. All time on the amendment has now .expired.

The question is on agreeing to the amendment No. 667 of the Senator from West Virginia (Mr. Byrd) as modified. . . .

The assistant legislative clerk called the roll. . . .
The yeas and nays resulted — yeas 47, nays 52. . . .

MR. BYRD of West Virginia. Mr. President, again I want to express my thanks to the sponsors, the cosponsors, and the supporters of the Cooper-Church amendment. I thank especially those who participated in the debate last evening, the able Senator from Idaho (Mr. Church), the able Senator from Kentucky (Mr. Cooper), the able Senator from Arkansas (Mr. Fulbright), and other Senators who participated in that debate, who took the side of the opposition to my amendment. I express my appreciation to them for the way they conducted their remarks and for the fine presentation they made with respect to their objections to my amendment. They conducted what I consider to be a very high level of debate on their part. . . .

MR. MANSFIELD. Mr. President, the [Mansfield-Dole] amendment that is now at the desk and is the pending business needs no explanation. The language is clear, to the point, concise, brief, and answers, I believe, a doubt which has been in the minds of some Senators. I think that without question that doubt will be removed.

The modification reads as follows.

> Nothing contained in this section shall be deemed to impugn the constitutional power of the President as Commander in Chief. . . .

MR. DOLE. The amendment offered by the Senator from Montana, the Senator from Kentucky (Mr. Cooper), the Senator from Vermont (Mr. Aiken), and the Senator from Idaho (Mr. Church) does, in large measure, answer some of the criticisms that have been raised with reference to the Church-Cooper amendment. I would hope that in a very few minutes we might discuss how the proposed amendment would relate to each of the four sections of the Church-Cooper amendment and what effect and bearing it would have. I should think that it would not take long to discuss the amendment and that there would be no reason why, so far as I know, we could not proceed to vote on it.

I would also ask the Senator from Montana whether he would have any objection to changing the word "impugn" to words "in any way modify." It would be a very minor change.

MR. MANSFIELD. I would prefer to leave the language just as it is, not because of any pride of authorship, but because the amendment is a combination of the thinking of several Senators. I think the same objectives can be achieved. I would prefer to stand on the amendment as it is. . . .

THE PRESIDING OFFICER. . . . The question is on agreeing to the amendment of the Senator from Montana (Mr. Mansfield) and other Senators. The yeas and nays have been ordered, and the clerk will call the roll.

The assistant legislative clerk called the roll. . . .
The result was announced — yeas 91, nays 0. . . .

MR. COOPER.[2] Mr. President, after Byrd amendment No. 1 was defeated on June 11, several supporters of the Byrd amendment and of the Cooper-Church amendment expressed a desire to see included in the Cooper-Church amendment language recognizing the constitutional authority of the President as Commander in Chief to protect the Armed Forces. Several Members, among them Senator Spong of Virginia, Senator Percy of Illinois, Senator Dole of Kansas, made valuable contributions through amendments and discussion on the floor toward specifying recognized powers of the President to protect the Armed Forces of the United States. . . .

Senator Byrd has continued his work to develop an amendment which would recognize the authority of the President to protect the U.S. Armed Forces and he has done so in a very systematic and scholarly fashion. . . .

The amendment now pending is an amendment to the Mansfield amendment which was adopted on June 11 by the unanimous vote of those present.

I shall read the language of the Mansfield amendment:

> Nothing contained in the Section shall be deemed to impugn the Constitutional power of the President as Commander in Chief.

If the Byrd amendment is approved, his language will read as follows:

[2] Debate is resuming here on June 22. — Eds.

Including the exercise of that Constitutional power which may be necessary to protect the lives of United States forces wherever deployed. . . .

MR. CHURCH. . . . Mr. President, I see no objection to the amendment, in its new form, offered by the Senator from West Virginia. It is consistent with the action the Senate took more than a week ago when it adopted the Mansfield amendment by a unanimous vote of 91–0. I will, therefore, cast my vote in favor of the new Byrd amendment.

MR. MANSFIELD. Mr. President, I wish to join my distinguished colleague, the senior Senator from Idaho, in what he has just said.

To me, what the Byrd-Griffin amendment does is in no way comparable to the Gulf of Tonkin resolution. If I had even the slightest suspicion that that would be the result of this amendment to the Cooper-Church amendment, I would vote against it unhesitatingly.

THE PRESIDING OFFICER (MR. HOLLINGS). . . . The question is on agreeing to the amendment, No. 708, of the Senator from West Virginia (Mr. Byrd).

On this question the yeas and nays have been ordered, and the clerk will call the roll.

The bill clerk called the roll. . . .
The result was announced — yeas 79, nays 5. . . .[3]
Debate turns now to repeal of the Gulf of Tonkin Resolution.

MR. DOLE. Mr. President. . . . recent Senate debate has repeatedly emphasized the responsibility of Congress to assume its obligation in the formulation and conduct of foreign policy. While care should be taken to avoid actions which would appear to limit or transgress upon the President's prerogatives in this field, Congress, the Senate in particular, has a significant role to play in establishing policy objectives and guidelines. By repealing the Tonkin Gulf resolution we can exercise our powers and fulfill our responsibilties in a positive and meaningful way. Having provided the peg upon which the Vietnam escalation was hung, we can make a start at exerting congressional influence and wisdom by removing that peg and clearing the way for other worthwhile achievements in defining foreign policy and national priorities. . . .[4]

---

[3] The five holdouts were Senators Fulbright, Goodell, Javits, Hughes, and McGovern, with Senator Ribicoff paired against. — Eds.
[4] The main elements of the Gulf of Tonkin Resolution were quoted by Senator Ervin above, p. 39–40. — Eds.

Mr. President, it occurs to me this is a very important amendment. The original Gulf of Tonkin joint resolution was enacted by Congress after brief debate. There was some reason for urgency at the time. Action on it was expedited through the House and through the Senate. It was approved on August 10, 1964. In effect, we have debated Southeast Asia, if not specifically the Gulf of Tonkin resolution and its repeal, for over 30 days on this floor, compared with 2 days when it was enacted in 1964, almost 6 years ago. By virtue of the Gulf of Tonkin resolution, which I voted for as a Member of the other body, and which every Member of the Senate who was there at that time voted for as Members of this body, the war has been escalated.

As I said at the outset, the present occupant of the White House, President Nixon, has indicated no need for the Gulf of Tonkin resolution. I would guess that the majority of the Members of the Senate and the House of Representatives would indicate no need for the Gulf of Tonkin resolution. I would say, in conclusion, that the earlier we can repeal the Gulf of Tonkin resolution the better. . . .

Mr. Ervin. Mr. President, it is a most surprising development that the President would seek to defeat the Cooper-Church amendment which merely undertakes to put limits upon his power to wage war in Cambodia and Laos, and then have his spokesman propose to the Senate an amendment which would not only take away his power to act in Cambodia and Laos, but also take away his power to act in South Vietnam. That is exactly what this amendment does.

It is true that when Congress passed the Gulf of Tonkin resolution it inserted a section in which it said, among other things, that Congress could repeal the Gulf of Tonkin resolution by a concurrent resolution. Congress reserved the right to repeal by concurrent resolution. But here the proposal, instead of repealing it by concurrent resolution, would repeal it by an amendment to an act of Congress having no connection with the subject.

The Senate is getting itself in a rather perplexing state. . . .

Mr. Dole. . . . We have been debating the general issue of Southeast Asia and the effect of the Gulf of Tonkin resolution. The President has made it clear that he does not rely on the Tonkin Gulf resolution. The Senator from Arkansas and other Senators have made it clear that they do not rely on the Tonkin Gulf resolution now. It seems an appropriate time to act now.

I apologize if I have trespassed on the rights of any Member or any committee. That was not the purpose of my amendment. We were debating a measure relating to the Tonkin Gulf resolution, not trying to deal lightly with it. I may say the Tonkin Gulf resolution passed, after a brief debate, by a vote of 88 to 2. Because of passage, the war escalated until there were approximately 550,000 troops there. Perhaps it was dealt lightly with at the time the resolution was passed. I do not pass judgment on that. But now that we have expressed ourselves many times, why is it inappropriate to act now? This is an appropriate time to pass on the proposition. If it fails, we still have the concurrent resolution. This procedure will give the President an opportunity, by appending his signature to it, to affirm that he favors repeal of the Gulf of Tonkin resolution. . . .

MR. FULBRIGHT. Mr. President, I cannot say any more than I have as to why the Senator's amendment is inappropriate. It departs from the usual procedure. . . . I can only conclude that the Senator has not listened very carefully and has not observed what the proper procedures are. After he has been here a while, I think he will come to appreciate the procedures of the Senate. One of the important parts of the procedures of the Senate is following the committee procedure. In fact, following the proper procedure is very relevant to our democratic form of government. One does not override the established procedures of a body like this and still reach any kind of result.

I do not blame the Senator, in view of his brief attendance here, for not having learned all of the proper procedures. . . .

I do not know what more I can say to the Senator from Kansas — his amendment does not accord with the proper procedure. . . .

No; there is no rule that one has to clear anything with me, but all of the standing committees have a function to play in this body. If the Senator will read the rules of the Senate, he will see each committee has certain jurisdictions. The Senator can make any motion he wants to. Of course he can. That does not mean we have to accept it. I am not saying the Senator cannot make a motion. I am going to move to table the motion, because the procedure proposed by the Senator is highly improper. . . .

The result was announced — yeas 15, nays 67. . . . So Mr. Fulbright's motion to table Mr. Dole's amendment was rejected.

MR. JAVITS. Mr. President, the Gulf of Tonkin resolution, it seems to me, is one of the keys to the argument now preoccupying the Senate with respect to the power of the President in this war and future wars. Unless it is cleared from the books we will not, and cannot, face the issue before the Senate and the country — the division of the warmaking powers between Congress and the President. If the President has the power to initiate undeclared war can Congress "undeclare" such wars, as part of its constitutional power to declare war? Can Congress stop a President other than by denying funds?

Perhaps the President could find funds in the Federal cupboard and use them to support troops. There is always the great argument that you would be depriving the men in combat who are in jeopardy of the means to do their job. It would be an unfortunate course but it may be the one we have to take if Congress does not resurrect the now atrophying policy war powers, so deliberately and explicitly reserved to it in the Constitution.

By clearing the decks of the Gulf of Tonkin resolution, we will have taken a step in dealing with a problem which American youth has so passionately and insistently demanded an answer on. That is: Who has the warmaking power? Can a President place us in a war — as we have been involved in a war since 1965 by a President — without public and congressional approval?

Unless this resolution is cleared from the books, President Nixon could subsequently make use of it, even though he says he is not now relying on it. It is there, and it gives him a lawful cloak of sorts for what he is doing, or might later seek to do. . . .

In the current debate we are writing a legislative record which history may deem as second in importance only to the deliberations of the Constitutional Convention itself. . . .

The Constitution divides and balances power. It deliberately tries to keep the power to get the Nation into war in the hands of Congress, as close to the people as possible, and away from the arbitrary exercise of Executive power.

We will only be able to face up fully to the truly historic challenge we now face when we have terminated the Tonkin Gulf resolution. This resolution, in addition to its legal implications, is a symbol of ill-considered congressional acquiescence in, and rubberstamping of, unlimited Presidential authority in warmaking. It wounds the wisdom of the Constitution. We are all agreed that it should be terminated. . . .

The Presiding Officer. The clerk will call the roll. . . .

The assistant legislative clerk proceeded to call the roll. . . .
The result was announced — yeas 81, nays 10. . . .[5]

[5] The amendment to repeal the Tonkin Resolution was thus agreed to, and would take effect at the end of the 1970 Congressional session. — Eds.

Mr. Griffin. Mr. President, the debate in which the Senate is engaged is an historic one. It concerns the manner in which the United States will meet its responsibilities as leader of the free world. It concerns such questions as whether and how the United States will use its influence to preserve peace and stability in Asia and the Pacific.

It concerns the very heart of the Nixon doctrine.

Mr. President, I shall, upon conclusion of my remarks, offer an amendment to subsection (3) which would modify the Church-Cooper language to make it read as follows:

> No funds authorized or appropriated pursuant to this Act or any other law may be expended after July 1, 1970 for the purpose of —
> (3) entering into or carrying out any contract or agreement to provide military instruction in Cambodia by United States personnel or to provide United States personnel to engage in any combat activity in support of Cambodian forces;

The operative change in the amendment to subsection (3) is to insert the words "by United States personnel" in two places.

The purpose of the amendment is to make clear that the United States would not be enjoined by the Church-Cooper language from assisting non-Communist nations in Asia which stand prepared to cooperate in lending support to a neighboring country in dire need, in this case, particularly Cambodia.

The amendment we offer would not authorize anything, but it would modify the broad language of subparagraph 3 of the Church-Cooper amendment, which goes far beyond the "mercenary" issue; it would actually nullify the Nixon doctrine so far as Cambodia is concerned. . . .

In the President's statement at Guam in mid-1969, and in his report to the Congress on U.S. foreign policy for the 1970's, Mr. Nixon observed that we look to Asian nations to increasingly assume the primary responsibility for their own defense. He said:

> This approach requires our commitment to helping our partners develop their own strength. In doing so, we must strike a careful balance. If we do too little to help them . . . they may lose the necessary will to conduct their own self-defense or become disheartened about prospects of development. Yet if we do too much, and American forces do what local forces can and should be doing, we promote dependence rather than independence. . . .

I realize the sponsors of the Cooper-Church language want us to disconnect ourselves in such a way from Asian efforts at collective self-defense that we will not become directly involved in Cambodia.

But as the amendment now stands, it would mandate abdication of our responsibility, and it would discourage our friends from shouldering theirs.

On the other hand, our amendment recognizes American supportive responsibility, and would enable us to carry it out in a way that makes clear to other countries that the direct burden for their defense rests with them and not in the United States. . . .

There are some who will say that the United States intends to hire mercenaries to act as proxy warriors. They point to the fact that during the previous administration arrangements were made under which the United States agreed to meet the operating expenses of certain units in Vietnam. They argue that the previous administration, in order to fly more flags in Vietnam, paid for units which otherwise would not have been sent.

Nothing of that kind is contemplated by this administration with respect to Cambodia. What our amendment seeks to do is to keep the door open so that if other nations in Southeast Asia wish to assist Cambodia they can do so without being penalized by the loss of U.S. economic and military assistance, in accordance with the Nixon doctrine. . . .

It is essential to keep in mind that other countries in the area, such as Thailand, have a direct national interest in aiding Cambodia. If Cambodia should fall to Communist aggression, who will say that neighboring countries such as Thailand woulld not be in grave danger?

If one man's mercenary is another man's patriot, then clearly much depends upon which side of the coin we examine. . . .

MR. CHURCH. . . . There are reasons why we feel so strongly [about an amendment which allows Asians to help Asians]. The previous administration did not consult with Congress in regard to agreements the United States made with Asian countries whereby their troops were hired at a profitable price to fight in South Vietnam.

In some instances, it has taken Congress years to find out about those agreements. It was the insistent investigatory effort of the Symington Subcommittee which enabled us to discover what was taking place in countries such as Laos; which enabled us to ascertain that large sums of money were paid to the Philippine Government for 2,500 troops sent to Vietnam, yet never fought there, and have now returned home. Many millions of dollars were involved, much of which was siphoned off in ways that have never been explained.

Throughout this unfortunate period, Congress remained ignorant of these secret agreements made with the Philippine, Korean, Lao, and Thai Governments. Only years later, left to our own investigatory devices, did we find out what had been done in secret dealings.

That may be the way some Members of the Senate view the conduct of constitutional government. That may be the demeaning role some Members want the Congress to play. If it is, then we no longer are the legislative body fashioned by the Constitution of the United States.

When Congress is not even informed of such dubious arrangements, let alone asked to consent, the President is being allowed to usurp congressional power. We should confess our error, and correct our practices before congressional power wastes away. . . .

Mr. Cooper. Mr. President, our amendment does not prohibit the use of other nationals in Cambodia. It says, "If you want to use them, pay for them."

There is no prohibition in the amendment against the use of other nationals without the advance approval of the United States. . . .

The Presiding Officer. . . . The question is on agreeing to the amendment offered by the Senator from Michigan (Mr. Griffin). On this question the yeas and nays have been ordered, and the clerk will call the role. . . .

The result was announced — yeas 47, nays 46. . . .

Mr. Mansfield. Mr. President, I move to reconsider the vote by which the amendment was agreed to. . . .

Mr. Dole. Mr. President, will the Chair advise me whether we are voting on a motion to table or a motion to reconsider?

The Presiding Officer. The Senate is voting on whether to table the motion to reconsider the vote by which the amendment was agreed to. On this question the yeas and nays have been ordered, and the clerk will call the role.

The legislative clerk proceeded to call the role. . . . The result was announced — yeas 46, nays 47. . . . So the motion to table the motion to reconsider the vote by which the Griffin amendment was agreed to was rejected.

Mr. Dole. Mr. President, a parliamentary inquiry.

The Presiding Officer. The question is on the reconsideration of the vote.

Mr. Mansfield. Mr. President, I ask for the yeas and nays.

*The yeas and nays were ordered. . . . The result was announced —
yeas 49, nays 46. . . . So the motion to reconsider was agreed to.
Mr. Byrd of West Virginia addressed the Chair.*

THE VICE PRESIDENT. The Senator from West Virginia is recognized. The Senate will be in order. . . .
The clerk will call the roll.

*The assistant legislative clerk proceeded to call the role. . . .
The yeas and nays resulted — 45 yeas, 50 nays. . . .*

THE VICE PRESIDENT. On this vote the yeas are 45 and the nays are 50. The amendment is rejected. A motion to reconsider is not in order. . . .

MR. MANSFIELD.[6] Mr. President, it is said that the House of Representatives will not approve Cooper-Church should it pass the Senate. It is said that if Cooper-Church clears the Congress, in all probability, it will be vetoed by the President.

Whether these predicates are true in whole or part or not true at all remains to be seen. I hope they are not true. True or not, however, they do not and cannot detract one iota from this vote today.

The Senate cannot answer for the President. The Senate cannot answer for the House. The Senate can speak only for the Senate. In the vote on Cooper-Church, today, Senators will most assuredly do so, as individuals and collectively. What is said will be most significant, in my judgment, to the future of this Nation. . . .

Cooper-Church is a response to a pattern of Executive actions in Southeast Asia which has been evolving for years and which has now raised constitutional questions regarding the responsibilities of the Senate in the gravest questions which confront the Nation — the questions for war and peace. It is a pattern whereby the Congress was first invited to join with the executive branch, as in the Tonkin Gulf resolution, in delineating a policy, presumably for peace in Vietnam. Therefore, the Congress discovered it had joined in a strategy which led to war. The Congress was carried along into the ever-deepening military involvement in Vietnam. . . .

MR. MCGEE. Mr. President, I want to say at this late hour that I still think we are missing the point, that the many weeks we have spent on this amendment should be addressed to the real problem before the Senate: How do we update the role of the Senate in the

[6] Following a brief debate on adoption of a perfecting amendment offered by Senator Jackson. — Eds.

latter half of the 20th century to exercise its responsibility in foreign policy in a nuclear age?

In a day when some people think we can only afford a limited war if we have to test strategic areas, where else can we find the answer to that but by a searching inquiry now? . . .

MR. THURMOND. Mr. President, I rise in opposition to the Cooper-Church amendment. . . . My opposition today to passage of the Military Sales Act in its present form rests on the crippling amendments affixed to the bill by the Senate Foreign Relations Committee. While I support military sales and credits to our allies abroad, the bill is replete with unwise amendments. These amendments, including the Cooper-Church amendment, repudiate the Nixon doctrine of providing sufficient military arms to our allies in Southeast Asia and encouraging them to provide for their own defense. . . .

MR. MANSFIELD. Mr. President, I ask for the yeas and nays on the bill.

The yeas and nays were ordered.

THE PRESIDING OFFICER. The bill is open to further amendment. If there be no further amendment to be proposed, the question is on the engrossment of the amendments, and the third reading of the bill.

The amendments were ordered to be engrossed and the bill to be read a third time. The bill was read the third time.

THE PRESIDING OFFICER (MR. ALLOTT.) The hour of 4 o'clock has arrived. The bill (H.R. 15628) having been read the third time, the question is, Shall it pass?

On this question the yeas and nays have been ordered, and the clerk will call the roll. . . .

The bill clerk called the roll. . . . The result was announced — yeas 75, nays 20, as follows:

Yeas — 75

Aiken	Brooke	Curtis
Allott	Burdick	Dole
Anderson	Byrd, Va.	Eagleton
Baker	Byrd, W. Va.	Fong
Bayh	Cannon	Fulbright
Bellmon	Case	Goodell
Bennett	Church	Gore
Bible	Cooper	Gravel
Boggs	Cranston	Griffin

Harris	McGee	Proxmire
Hart	McGovern	Randolph
Hartke	McIntyre	Ribicoff
Hatfield	Metcalf	Saxbe
Hollings	Miller	Schweiker
Hruska	Mondale	Scott
Hughes	Montoya	Smith, Maine
Jackson	Moss	Smith, Ill.
Javits	Murphy	Sparkman
Jordan, N.C.	Muskie	Spong
Kennedy	Packwood	Stevens
Long	Pastore	Symington
Magnuson	Pearson	Tydings
Mansfield	Pell	Williams, N.J.
Mathias	Percy	Yarborough
McCarthy	Prouty	Young, Ohio

Nays — 20

Allen	Fannin	Stennis
Cook	Goldwater	Talmadge
Cotton	Gurney	Thurmond
Dominick	Hansen	Tower
Eastland	Holland	Williams, Del.
Ellender	Jordan, Idaho	Young, N. Dak.
Ervin	McClellan	

Not Voting — 5

Dodd	Mundt	Russell
Inouye	Nelson	

So the bill (H.R. 15628) was passed. . . . The title was amended, so as to read: "An act to amend the Foreign Military Sales Act, and for other purposes."

Mr. Fulbright. Mr. President, I move that the Senate insist upon its amendments and request a conference with the House, and that the Chair be authorized to appoint the conferees on the part of the Senate.

The motion was agreed to; and the Presiding Officer (Mr. Allott) appointed Mr. Fulbright, Mr. Sparkman, Mr. Mansfield, Mr. Church, Mr. Aiken, Mr. Case, and Mr. Cooper conferees on the part of the Senate.

Mr. Fulbright. Mr. President, I ask unanimous consent that the bill be printed and passed, so that Senators may be informed of the many changes.

THE PRESIDING OFFICER. Without objection, it is so ordered. . . .

MR. MANSFIELD. Mr. President, having spent over 7 weeks on this one piece of legislation, it is impossible to single out any particular Senator for commendation; the Senate as a whole has participated in a truly historic event. The issue of the separate responsibilities of the Congress and the executive branch have never been more fully explored; the final action on this bill marks a significant breakthrough in the reassertion of the responsiblities of the Senate in the essential decisions affecting the foreign policy of this country as well as the issue of war and peace. . . .

[The following legislative chronology will assist the reader in understanding what happened to the Cooper-Church amendment and the Foreign Military Sales Act (HR 15628) following Senate debate and passage — Eds.:

> March 24, 1970–May 11, 1970 Senate Foreign Relations Committee held hearings on HR 15628 and related bills.
> May 12, 1970 HR 15628 is reported from committee with Cooper-Church provisions included.
> June 30, 1970 Following seven weeks of debate on the Senate floor, the Cooper-Church amendment to the Foreign Military Sales Act was adopted on a 58–37 roll call vote; the final version of the bill was adopted on a 75–20 roll call vote and was sent to conference committee.
> July 9, 1970 The House voted not to give its conferees any formal instructions in dealing with HR 15628. (The House version of the bill, which had passed on March 24, 1970, contained no restrictions on U.S. military activity in Cambodia.)
> Dec. 21, 1970 The conference report was filed following a six-month deadlock over the Cooper-Church amendment. The controversial amendment was dropped from the Foreign Military Sales bill, but a revised version of it was attached to another bill (a supplemental foreign aid authorization, HR 19911) that cleared Congress Dec. 22, 1970. That bill authorized $255 million in military and economic assistance to Cambodia.
> Dec. 31, 1970 The House and Senate agreed to the conference report in HR 15628 by voice votes.
> Jan. 12, 1971 The President signed HR 15628 into law (PL 91–672).]

II

WHAT IS A REPRESENTATIVE?

Representatives are a pretty standard lot, apparently, the world over. They emerge from their local environments and they carry a strong local stamp with them wherever they go. Most are of moderate temperament, not really standing out too far from their neighbors, whom they properly address on the streets and in their speeches as their fellows, or their comrades, depending on the country — or the translator.

Standing out too far can be a problem. Lasswell once suggested that the truly power-oriented personalities are usually relegated to secondary roles in politics. Agitators and compulsives, zealots and charismatic types, who almost by definition reject the slow committee-dominated deliberation in parliaments, are rarely elected to assemblies, and when they are they usually come from districts with weak political organizations or are elected during periods of social disorder when all political organizations are in a weakened condition. Mosca bitterly attacked the myth of representation by observing, quite appropriately, that "the people" don't choose their representatives from a wide variety of possibilities but rather that certain well-positioned persons settle on one of their own company, who, in turn, "gets himself elected." That may capture very well the typical manner of nomination and election where electoral committees of some sort coopt a familiar and safe person as their candidate. However, the man they pick to get himself elected tends nevertheless to be a very normal and rather ordinary, patient, long-suffering, nice guy. Richard Nixon was unusual in the partisan feeling he always seems to have engendered. And his exceptionally fast rise to the vice presidential nomination suggests some extraordinary personal characteristics as well as unusual good luck. But even so, his original nomination was probably typical in the rather mundane and workaday motivation that gave rise to it.

The very sameness or normality of character among representatives is precisely what makes so interesting the tremendous variation in their behavior and its consequences once they take up their membership. Three different and widely diverse contexts — the Supreme Soviet, the United States Congress, and four state legislatures — provide a strong sense of the situation: a very normal distribution of souls presenting wide discrepancies of action, a kaleidoscope of uniform materials producing multitudes of patterns.

But is the legislature, as a consequence, protean and not susceptible to further analysis? Does the legislature produce no patterns by which it allows itself to be understood, predicted, and reformed? First, let us establish the norm of legislative character. Then we can go on in following sections to the question of whether the tremendous complexities and varieties of legislative conduct can be explained.

2

The Role of the Representative: Some Empirical Observations on the Theory of Edmund Burke

Heinz Eulau, John C. Wahlke,
William Buchanan, and Leroy C. Ferguson

. . . The history of political theory is studded with definitions of representation,[1] usually embedded in ideological assumptions and postulates which cannot serve the uses of empirical research without conceptual clarification.[2] . . .

A convenient and useful starting point in theoretical clarification is Edmund Burke's theory of representation. For, in following his classic argument, later theorists have literally accepted Burke's formulation and ignored its contextual basis and polemical bias. Burke ingeniously combined two notions which, for analytical purposes, should be kept distinct. In effect, he combined a conception of the *focus* of representation with a conception of the *style* of representation. Parliament, Burke said in a famous passage,[3]

> is not a *congress* of ambassadors from different and hostile interests; which interests each must maintain, as an agent and advocate, against other agents and advocates; but parliament is a *deliberative* assembly of *one* nation, with *one* interest, that of the whole; where, not local purposes, not local prejudices ought to guide but the general good, resulting from the general reason of the whole.

From Heinz Eulau, John C. Wahlke, William Buchanan, and Leroy C. Ferguson, "The Role of the Representative: Some Empirical Observations on the Theory of Edmund Burke," *American Political Science Review,* 53 (September 1959), pp. 742–56.

[1] For a convenient and comprehensive summary of definitions, see John A. Fairlie, "The Nature of Political Representation," *American Political Science Review,* Vol. 34 (April–June, 1940), pp. 236–48; 456–66.

[2] An effort at conceptual clarification is made by Alfred De Grazia, *Public and Republic — Political Representation in America* (New York, 1951).

[3] In his "Speech to the Electors of Bristol" (1774), *Works,* Vol. II, p. 12.

The sentence indicates that Burke postulated two possible foci of representation: local, necessarily hostile interests, on the one hand; and a national interest on the other hand. He rejected the former as an improper and advocated the latter as the proper focus of the representative's role. But in doing so, he also linked these foci of representation with particular representational styles. If the legislature is concerned with only one interest, that of the whole, and not with compromise among diverse interests, it follows that the representative cannot and must not be bound by instructions, from whatever source, but must be guided by what Burke called "his unbiased opinion, his mature judgment, his enlightened conscience." Moreover Burke buttressed his argument by emphasizing the deliberate function of the legislature — presumably in contrast to its representational function. Yet if one rejects his notion of the legislature as only a deliberative body whose representational focus is the whole rather than its constituent parts, the logic of Burke's formulation is no longer necessary or relevant. . . .

Premises underlying decisions made by legislatures . . . may be of two kinds: (1) they may be premises relevant to the focus of representation; and (2) they may be relevant to the style of representation. With regard to the first kind, for instance, a representative may be guided by premises such as that legislation should benefit either his district or the state, that it should be "liberal" or "conservative," that it should or should not favor special interests, that it should or should not be in performance of his party's campaign pledges, and so on. With regard to the second kind of premises, the representative's choices may be circumscribed by his stylistic role orientation, whether he sees himself following his own conscience or instructions. In this dimension the premises involved in his decisional behavior refer not to the focus but to the style of his role as representative.

The issue of styles of representation — free agency versus mandate — has been confounded by the fact that the enabling source of a representative's power is the electorate of a geographical district. Representation of geographical areas introduces a certain amount of ambiguity into the relationship between representative and represented which is likely to be absent under schemes of proportional or vocational representation.[4] Part of this ambiguity is the widely held expec-

[4] For a perspicacious discussion of ambiguities in representation, see Harold F. Gosnell, *Democracy — The Threshold of Freedom* (New York, 1948), pp. 124–42.

tation, contested by Burke but shared by many citizens and politicians alike, that the representative is a spokesman of the presumed "interests" of the area from which he has been elected. Of course, implicit in this expectation is the assumption that a geographical unit has interests which are distinct and different from those of other units, and which should be represented in public decision-making. This assumption has been challenged on a variety of grounds: that the geographical area as such, as an electoral unit, is artificial; that it cannot and does not generate interests shared by its residents; that it has no unique interests; and so on. Schemes of proportional or vocational representation have been advanced to make possible the representation of allegedly more "natural" interest groupings, such as minority groups, skill groups or economic groups.[5]

The assumption that geographical districts have particular characteristics — such as population attributes and industrial, agricultural or commercial properties — and, hence, unique interests which are, or ought to be, factors influencing the direction of public decisions continues to be shared not only by voters, politicians and others involved in policy-making, but also by scientific students of the political process. It underlies many studies which seek to relate legislative roll-call votes to the socio-economic characteristics of electoral districts,[6] as well as those studies which analyze the socio-economic composition of legislatures.[7]

It is a further assumption of these studies that legislators, having lived in their districts for all or substantial parts of their lives, share the values, beliefs, habits and concerns of the people who elected them and whom they presumably represent. Indeed, a literal interpretation of "represent" is to make something present that is not actually present. But this interpretation is most tenuous under modern conditions. Electoral districts tend to be so heterogeneous in population attributes, so pluralistic in the character of their group life, so diverse in the kinds of values and beliefs held, that whatever measures of

[5] Most theories of functional or proportional representation are motivated or supported by tacit and untested assumptions about the relationship of legislators' behavior to the process by which they are selected. This is merely a special case of the general democratic assumption that political responsibility is the mechanism *par excellence* for bringing legislators' actions in line with the expectations of the represented.

[6] See, for instance, Julius Turner, *Party and Constituency: Pressures on Congress* (Baltimore, 1951); or Duncan MacRae, Jr., *Dimensions of Congressional Voting* (Berkeley, 1958).

[7] See, for instance, Donald R. Matthews, *The Social Background of Political Decision-Makers* (Garden City, 1954); or Charles S. Hyneman, "Who Makes Our Laws?" *Political Science Quarterly,* Vol. 55 (December, 1940), pp. 556–81.

central tendency are used to classify a district are more likely to conceal than to reveal its real character. The notion that elections are held as a method to discover persons whose attributes and attitudes mirror those most widely shared by people in their district appears to be of dubious validity.

This does not mean, of course, that the geographical district is dysfunctional from the point of view of maintaining the political system. The very circumstance of heterogeneity in the district tends to free the representative from being readily bound by a mandate, to make for discretion and political responsibility, and to enable him to integrate conflicting demands. The function of representation in modern political systems is not to make the legislature a mathematically exact copy of the electorate.

But the difficulty of finding an identity between representative and represented does not also mean that a representative's point of reference in making decisions cannot be his district. It may or may not be, and whether it is or not is a matter of empirical inquiry. We merely doubt that what orients a representative towards his district rather than some other focus of attention is the similarity between his district's characteristics and his own. We cannot assume, therefore, that even if a representative incorporates in himself the characteristics of his district — which, for argument's sake, may be admitted when he comes from a relatively homogeneous area — he will be more oriented towards the district than a representative who, from the point of view of district characteristics, is a deviant. In fact, the latter may be more concerned with his district and seek to discover its "interests," if they are discoverable, than the former. And if a district interest, so-called, can be specifically singled out, it is more likely to be the interest of a politically salient group in the district than of the district as an undifferentiated entity.

In so far as the district rather than some other unit, such as the entire commonwealth, is at the representative's focus of attention, it is more likely to be a function of political than of demographic or socioeconomic variables. The problem is one of discovering under what conditions the representative can afford to disregard the district and still hope to maintain the confidence of his constituents. We might speculate, for instance, that in so far as he cherishes the position of power he holds, he is unlikely to ignore his district. We should expect, therefore, that representatives from districts where competition between the parties is keen are more district-oriented than representatives from one-party districts. Yet, we also know that competitive districts are more likely to be found in the heterogeneous metropolitan areas where district "interests" are difficult to ascertain.[8] In other words, what tends to orient the representative towards his district is likely to be the mechanism of political responsibility effectuated by political competition. District-oriented representatives from metropolitan areas where party competition is strong are, therefore, likely to rely on their own judgment, for a mandate must yield here to discretion to satisfy the demands of political responsibility. Discretion, of course, does not mean that the representative is wholly free to act as he pleases. On the contrary, it means that he will have due regard for all the considerations relevant in the making of legislative decisions. And among these considerations, certainly, the "interests" of his electorate or segments of the electorate, as well as his own estimate of the limits which these interests set to his actions, are important. As Burke admitted,

> it ought to be the happiness and glory of a representative to live in the strictest union, the closest correspondence, and the most unreserved communication with his constituents. Their wishes ought to have great weight with him; their opinion high respect, their business unremitted attention. . . .

Though analytically the foci and the style of the representative's role are distinct, they can be expected to be related empirically in a system of mutually interpenetrating orientations. In other words, just as we need not assume that a commitment to district invariably involves the representative's following instructions from his district (the role orientation of Delegate), or that a commonweal-oriented representative is invariably a free agent (the role orientation of Trustee), so also we need not assume that the foci of a representative's role are invariably unrelated to his representational style. In fact, it is the functionally related network of roles which makes for a representational *system*. We can assume, for instance, that a representative who is highly sensitive to the conflict of pressure groups, but not committed to any one, is more likely to be a Trustee in his representational role than the representative who feels close to a particular group and, consequently, is more likely to be a Delegate. Similarly, we might expect that a representative not strongly attached to a party, but not independent of it, is likely to shift between his own judgment and instructions (the role orientation of Politico).

[8] See Heinz Eulau, "The Ecological Basis of Party Systems: The Case of Ohio," *Midwest Journal of Political Science,* Vol. 1 (August, 1957), pp. 125–35.

An opportunity to test the validity of the theoretical distinction here made, between the focus and style of representation, as well as of the representative's role, was afforded in connection with a comparative research project undertaken by the authors during the 1957 sessions of the state legislatures in California, New Jersey, Ohio, and Tennessee.[9] State legislators in these four states were asked the following question, among others: "How would you describe the job of being a legislator — what are the most important things you should do here?" Of the 474 respondents, 295 gave answers relevant to the stylistic dimension of the representative's role, and 197 of these gave additional answers referring to the areal focus of their role.[10]

Responses concerning the stylistic dimension yielded three major representational role types: Trustee, Delegate, and Politico.[11] These types may be described as follows:

1. *Trustee:* This role finds expression in two major conceptions which may occur separately or jointly. First, a moralistic interpretation: the representative is a free agent, he follows what he considers right or just — his convictions or principles, the dictates of his conscience. Second, a rational conception: he follows his own judgments based on an assessment of the facts in each case, his understanding of the problems involved, his thoughtful appraisal of the sides at issue.

The orientation of Trustee derives not only from a purely normative definition, but is often grounded in conditions which make it functionally necessary. The represented may not have the information to

[9] The samples for the four legislatures are 91 per cent in Tennessee, 94 per cent in California and Ohio, and 100 per cent in New Jersey. The four states composing the total sample represent different regions of the country, different ratios of metropolitan and non-metropolitan population, and different degrees of party competition. The interviews, using fixed schedules, uniform in all four states and including both open-ended, focussed-type questions as well as closed, or fixed-answer type questions, averaged about two hours. [Complete results of this study were later reported in a book by the same authors, *The Legislative System* (New York: Wiley, 1962) — Eds.]

[10] The reduction in the number of respondents from the total samples is, of course, due to the open-endedness of the question. Hence not all respondents could be used in the construction of the role types as they emerged from representatives' own definitions, and in the analysis.

[11] In constructing stylistic and areal-focal role orientation types, the responses to the question were coded in terms of (a) characterization of job; (b) objectives of job and (c) criteria of decision. Each total answer was broken up into individual statements and coded in terms of manifest content rather than latent meanings, though meaning was taken into consideration in locating manifest statements. Role orientation types were constructed by combining relevant manifest statements which seemed to make for a major orientational dimension. In general, data concerning criteria of decision yielded the stylistic orientation, and data concerning the objectives of the job yielded the areal orientation.

give intelligent instructions; the representative is unable to discover what his clienteles want; preferences remain unexpressed; there is no need for instructions because of a presumed harmony of interests between representative and represented — all of these circumstances may be cited as sources of the role orientation of Trustee.

2. *Delegate:* Just as the Trustee is by no means an empirically pure type, the orientation of Delegate allows for a number of conceptions. All Delegates are, of course, agreed that they should *not* use their independent judgment or convictions as criteria of decision-making. But this does not mean that they feel equally committed to follow instructions, from whatever clientele. Some merely speak of consulting their constituents, though implying that such consultation will have a mandatory effect on their behavior. Others frankly acknowledge their direct dependence on instructions and accept them as a necessary or desirable premise for their decisions. Some may even follow instructions counter to their own judgment or principles. In other words, the possibility of conflict in role orientations is clearly envisaged and resolved in favor of subordinating one's independence to what is considered a superior authority.

3. *Politico:* The classical dichotomization of the concept of representation in terms of free agency and mandate was unlikely to exhaust the possibilities of representational styles. Depending on circumstances, a representative may hold the Trustee orientation at one time, and the Delegate orientation at another time. Or he might seek to reconcile both in terms of a third. One can think of representation as a continuum, with the Trustee and Delegate orientations as poles, and a midpoint where the orientations tend to overlap and, within a range, give rise to a third role. Within this middle range the roles may be taken simultaneously, possibly making for conflict, or they may be taken serially, one after another as conditions call for.

Because the data do not permit sharp discrimination between the two possibilities, we shall speak of representatives who express both orientations, either simultaneously or serially, as Politicos. In general, then, the Politico as a representational role type differs from both the Trustee and the Delegate in that he is more sensitive to conflicting alternatives in role assumption, more flexible in the way he resolves the conflict of alternatives, and less dogmatic in his representational style as it is relevant to his decision-making behavior.

The spell of the Burkean formulation on the interpretation of representation tended to create reactions which, it seems, are almost as arbitrary as Burke's formula itself. In particular, the functional notion, itself quite realistic under modern conditions, that the legislature is an agency for the coordination and integration of diverse social, economic and political interests makes apparent the simple-mindedness of Burke's theory, now as then. Carl J. Friedrich, for instance, has pointed out that "the pious formula that representatives are not bound by mandate, that they are subject only to their conscience and are supposed to serve the common weal, which is repeated in so many European constitutions, while significant as a norm, may lead to differentiating as well as to integrating results." [12] Yet, in concentrating on the multiplicity of potential representational foci, Friedrich went too far in his rejection of Burke. For, once the distinction is made between the style of the representative's role and its focus, Burke's "pious formula" is still relevant. Both the focus and the style are likely to be influenced by the character of politics at a given time and by the demands of contemporary political circumstances on the representative as a decision-maker. Functional analysis cannot limit itself to the foci of representation alone, but must also pay attention to those political requirements which may be relevant to the representative's style.

Our hypothesis may be stated as follows: the exigencies of modern government, even on the relatively low level of state government, are exceedingly complex. Taxation and finance, education and public welfare, legal reform, licensing and regulatory problems, transportation, and so on, are topics more often than not, beyond the comprehension of the average citizen. Unable to understand their problems and helpless to cope with them, people are likely to entrust the affairs of government to the elected representatives who, presumably, are better informed than their constituents. People may pay lip service to the notion that a representative should *not* use his independent judgment,[13] but in fact they are unable, or do not care, to give him instructions as may once have been possible when the tasks of government were comparatively simpler. It is likely, therefore, that the representative has

---

[12] *Constitutional Government and Democracy* (Boston, rev. ed., 1950), p. 297.

[13] In the years before the second World War, public opinion polls several times sampled expectations in this regard. Relevant poll questions were: (1) Do you believe that a Congressman should vote on any question as the majority of his constituents desire or vote according to his own judgment? (2) Should members of Congress vote according to their own best judgment or according to the way the people in their district feel? (3) In cases when a Congressman's opinion is different from that of the majority of the people in his district, do you think he should usually vote according to his own best judgment, or according to the way the majority of his district feels? In three of four polls, 61, 63 and 66 per cent, respectively, of the respondents said the Congressman should vote the way people feel. In the fourth poll, only 37 per cent gave this answer. See Hadley Cantril, ed., *Public Opinion, 1935–1946* (Princeton, 1951), p. 133.

become less and less a Delegate and more and more a Trustee as the business of government has become more and more intricate and technical. Rather than being a "pious formula," the role orientation of Trustee may be a functional necessity, and one should expect it to be held by state legislators more frequently than that of Politico, and the latter more frequently than that of Delegate.

A test of this general proposition is possible by way of comparative analysis of the distribution of representational role styles in the four states. As Table 1 indicates the role orientation of Trustee is held by a greater number of legislators than that of either Politico or Delegate. In all four states it appears more frequently, and significantly more frequently, than the other two. Moreover, the Politico appears somewhat more frequently in all states than the Delegate.

Table 1

Distribution of Representational Role Orientations in Four States

Representational Role Orientation	Calif. (N = 49)	N.J. (N = 54)	Ohio (N = 114)	Tenn. (N = 78)	Total (N = 295)
Trustee	55%	61%	56%	81%	63%
Politico	25	22	29	13	23
Delegate	20	17	15	6	14
Total	100%	100%	100%	100%	100%

The Trustee orientation appears significantly more frequently in Tennessee than in the other three states, a fact that seems to contradict the proposition that the orientation of Trustee varies with the complexity of governmental affairs. As Tennessee is less urbanized and industrialized than the other states, one should expect Tennessee legislators to be less often Trustees and more often Delegates than legislators in California, New Jersey, or Ohio. But it may also be that "complexity" is a function of perceptions, regardless of the real situaiton. If so, then to Tennesseans the relatively less complex character of socio-economic life may appear more complex than it actually is, compared with the other states. The more frequent appearance of the Trustee orientation there may only be symptomatic of an even greater feeling of helplessness and inefficacy on the part of people *vis-à-vis* governmental problems, as it is perceived by state representatives.

Such perceptions may be a reflection of the lower educational level in Tennessee; but to demonstrate this is beyond the limits of this analysis.[14]

If, as suggested earlier, a representative's areal-focal orientation does not automatically derive from ascertainable district interests or from personal characteristics he may share with his constituents, the question arises where such orientations do come from, and how they intrude on the representative's conception of his role. For the purposes of this study, it was possible to delineate three areal-focal orientations which may be described as follows:

1. *District-orientation:* District-oriented representatives had essentially two alternatives: either they could simply mention their districts or counties as being relevant in their conception of their jobs, or they could explicitly place their districts as being above the state as an important factor in their legislative behavior. Among the former, the most frequent responses suggested that it is the representative's job to take care of his district's needs and pass legislation which will benefit his district or county. Others emphasized the policy problems involved in legislation and the necessity to protect what they considered district interests from the policy point of view. Or the emphasis was on the services which these representatives think they are expected to render for their district. Another group of district-oriented representatives specifically pointed to the importance of placing the interests of their district above those of the state, though they usually admitted that state concerns should also be given consideration.

2. *State-orientation:* As in the case of the district-oriented respondents, state-oriented representatives may either mention the state alone as the salient focus, or they may also mention the district, but clearly tend to place state above district. Some emphasized the need of state policy or state programs as an overriding consideration. A second group pointed to both state and district as relevant foci, but tended to give the benefit of doubt to the state. Finally, some state-oriented representatives explicitly emphasized the desirability of overcoming parochial considerations in favor of the state.

3. *District-and-state-orientation:* A third major group of respon-

[14] As the Trustee orientation includes responses stressing traditional moral values, it might be assumed that these virtues — such as following one's conscience or what one feels to be "right" — are more valued in rural Tennessee than in the three more urbanized states. But inspection of the frequency with which this attitude appears in Tennessee as against the other states does not reveal significantly different distributions of relevant responses: California — 18%; New Jersey — 8%; Ohio — 28%; and Tennessee — 23%.

dents who spontaneously concerned themselves with the areal focus of their role mentioned both district and state, but, apparently, did not envisage a possibility of conflict and thought that they could attend to both foci without undue difficulty. Yet, the generality of the responses given in this connection may be deceptive, and coding them under this rubric may have been somewhat arbitrary in a number of cases. Though the actual language used tended in the direction of the state as the focus of role orientation, the tone often appeared to be more indicative of a latent district orientation. One should expect these hyphenated representatives to resemble district- more than state-oriented representatives.

Areal role orientations may be assumed to be a function of the dynamics of the democratic political system with its emphasis on the responsibility of the representatives to the represented. Political responsibility — a set of relationships in which the elected are sensitive to the power of the electors over them, and in which the elected are aware of the sanctions which make responsibility a reality — is predicated on the existence of a competitive political system where constituents have a genuine choice, i.e., where the representatives are periodically confronted with the real possibility of removal from office. The sanction of removal inherent in a competitive party system serves to focus representatives' attention on their district rather than the state as the crucial point of reference. Representatives from competitive areas are more likely to be district-oriented than representatives from one-party areas, while representatives from one-party areas are more likely to be state-oriented than those from competitive areas.

An initial, though crude, test of this hypothesis is possible by examining the distribution of areal role orientations in the four states. Tennessee representatives might be expected to be less district-oriented than representatives in the other states, in view of the predominant one-party character of Tennessee politics. As Table 2 indicates, the data support this hypothesis. Though the percentage differences are small and statistically not significant, except in the California-Tennessee contrast, only 21 per cent of the Tennessee representatives are district-oriented as against 35 per cent in California, 27 per cent in New Jersey, and 28 per cent in Ohio. But the most noticeable aspect of Table 2 is the fact that Tennessee representatives in significantly greater proportion failed to express themselves spontaneously in this connection. Why this is so can, at this point, be only a matter of speculation. Tennessee representatives may take whatever areal foci they have so much for granted that they feel no need to mention them,

Table 2

Role Orientations in Four States
Distribution of Areal

Areal Role Orientation	Calif. (N = 113)	N.J. (N = 79)	Ohio (N = 162)	Tenn. (N = 120)	Total (N = 474)
District	35%	27%	28%	21%	27%
District-and-state	14	28	25	8	19
State	20	14	16	9	15
No mention	31	31	31	62	39
Total	100%	100%	100%	100%	100%

or they may simply be less articulate than representatives elsewhere. Finally, while there is a somewhat sharper differentiation between district and state role orientations in California than in New Jersey and Ohio (where the combined category figures more prominently), relatively few representatives in all states mentioned the state alone as the focus of their areal orientation.

A more severe test of the hypothesis is possible by relating areal role orientations to the political character of representatives' home districts. Because party competition as an independent variable has no room for operation in predominantly one-party Tennessee,[15] Table 3 presents the combined data for California, New Jersey and Ohio alone.[16] As Table 3 shows, 53 per cent of the representatives from competitive districts were district-oriented, while only 33 per cent of those from one-party districts were so classified. On the other hand, one-party district representatives held in significantly greater proportion a state orientation than those from competitive districts.[17] The data support the hypothesis that areal orientation varies with the political character of the district in which representatives are elected.[18]

[15] Of the 46 Tennessee respondents who mentioned an areal orientation, only four came from competitive and five from semi-competitive districts.

[16] Competition in district was severally defined in the four states on the basis of past election returns. Space limitations prevent us from specifying the criteria here. They may be obtained from the authors.

[17] $\chi^2 = 9.238$ for the entire array where d.f. = 4 p $\geq$ .05. If the middle categories are omitted and only competitive and one-party districts are compared with respect to state and district orientation alone $\chi^2 = 7.12$; d.f. = 1; p < .01.

[18] However this finding may be spurious. It might be less a function of the political character of the district than of its ecological character. Competitive districts are, more often than not, located in metropolitan areas, while one-party

Table 3

**Political Character of Electoral Districts
and Areal Role Orientations in Three States** [a]

Areal Role Orientation	Political Character of District		
	Competitive (N = 72)	Semi-competitive (N = 77)	One-party (N = 96)
District	53%	48%	33%
District-and-state	28	34	33
State	19	18	34
Total	100%	100%	100%

[a] California, New Jersey, and Ohio. "Non-respondents" on the areal dimension have been omitted.

The analytical distinction between the foci and the style of representation is helpful in dissecting the representative's role. Actual behavior is not a function of discrete role orientations, however, but of a system of such orientations. It is the network of interpenetrating roles which gives pattern and coherence to the representational process. It is essential, therefore, to relate areal and stylistic role orientations to each other in terms of significant hypotheses about conditions of their co-variation in the representational system.

It has been suggested earlier that, analytically, stylistic role orientations are neutral. What correlation may be found empirically, therefore, should depend on some crucial attribute in the independent variable — in this connection the areal role orientation. It may be suggested that this crucial attribute is the condition of effective politi-

---

districts are more frequent in non-metropolitan areas. It seemed advisable, therefore, to control the districts' political character by their ecological character. For this purpose, the districts were divided on the basis of the 1950 Census specifications. The hypothesis concerning the relationship between political character of district and areal orientation was clearly maintained in both metropolitan and non-metropolitan districts. However, while the pattern proved similar in both ecological categories, a greater proportion of district-and-state-oriented representatives appeared in the non-metropolitan than in the metropolitan areas, suggesting a pull towards greater dichotomization of areal orientations in the metropolitan environment. In view of the intimate connection in industrialized states between metropolitan and state-wide problems, this result is not surprising. It seems that the state is more salient as a focus of attention for representatives from metropolitan districts (no matter what their political character) than from non-metropolitan districts.

cal responsibility. In so far as they differ, district-oriented representatives are ultimately responsible to their constituents, while state-oriented representatives are not responsible to an equivalent state-wide constituency. The state-oriented representative cannot point to a state-wide clientele from which he could possibly receive a mandate.[19] Hence the hypothesis may be advanced that state-oriented representatives are more likely to be Trustees than district-oriented representatives, whereas the latter are more likely to be Delegates than the former. As Table 4 demonstrates, this is in fact the case. While 84 per cent of the state-oriented representatives are Trustees, only 37 per cent of the district-oriented and 55 per cent of the district-and-state-oriented representatives are so. And while 36 per cent of the district-oriented representatives are Delegates, only 8 per cent of the district-and-state-oriented and none of the state-oriented hold a mandatory view of their representational role.

Table 4

Areal-Focal and Representational Role Orientations in Four States [a]

Representational Role Orientation	District-Oriented (N = 89)	State-District-Oriented (N = 64)	State-Oriented (N = 44)
Trustee	37%	55%	84%
Delegate	36	8	—
Politico	27	37	16
Total	100%	100%	100%

[a] χ^2 for the entire array = 37.759; d.f. = 4; p < .001.

Moreover, Table 4 supports some corollary hypotheses. In the first place, because a representative is district-oriented, he need not be a Delegate any more frequently than a Trustee. This simply means that though a representative may clearly have his district at his focus of attention, he may nevertheless act on behalf of the district, in his own conception, as a free agent. Such a representative will say that he knows and understands what the district needs and wants, and he

[19] He might, of course, receive instructions from a state-wide clientele such as a pressure group or political party, but these constitute other dimensions of his attention foci.

rejects the notion that anybody in the district can tell him what to do. As Table 4 shows, among the district-oriented representatives, almost equal proportions, 37 per cent and 36 per cent respectively, are Trustees and Delegates. On the other hand, state-oriented representatives are more likely to be Trustees than anything else. This hypothesis is based on the assumption that the state-oriented representatives do not and cannot recognize a state-wide areal clientele which could give them instructions. As Table 4 indicates, none of the state-oriented representatives is a Delegate, and only 16 per cent are Politicos.

Finally, if the representative's areal focus is both his district and the state, one should expect that he will take the role of Politico more frequently than either the district- or the state-oriented representative. For, because he stresses both foci, he is likely to be subject to cross-pressures: as a district-oriented representative he will take the role of Delegate at least as frequently as that of Trustee; as a state-oriented representative he will take the role of Trustee more frequently than any other. We should expect, therefore, that this representative will not only be a Politico more frequently than the other two areal-orientational types, but also that he will take the Trustee role more frequently than the Delegate role. Both hypotheses find support in the data reported in Table 4. While the differences are small, 37 per cent of the district-and-state-oriented representatives are Politicos, while only 16 per cent and 27 per cent of the other two groups admit to this representational style. Moreover, a majority are also Trustees, while only 8 per cent are Delegates — evidence of the differential effect of areal role orientations on the particular stylistic roles which seem most appropriate.

This analysis supports the notion that the areal-focal and stylistic dimensions of representation give rise to role orientations which, though analytically distinct, constitute a role system, and that this system gives the process of representation both its structure and its function.

3

The First Richard Nixon

Earl Mazo

Nixon registered as a voter in 1938. He was twenty-five and had missed four voting years. But his job as assistant city attorney of Whittier was a political plum, so to speak, and therefore he had become, in effect, a politican. But it was the late fall of 1945 before he went into politics in earnest.

Whittier and its environs, then the 12th Congressional District of California, was staunch Republican territory. Yet in 1936 it elected a Democrat for Congress, and kept re-electing him. Jerry Voorhis, the Congressman, was mild mannered, conscientious, likeable, and extremely popular. He was respected by fellow Congressmen and the press corps in Washington. He worked hard at his job, answered his mail promptly, dealt with personal problems of his constituents on an eagerly nonpartisan basis, and when Congress was not in session he seldom passed by opportunities to be guest teacher of Sunday-school classes or to address church and civic groups. Furthermore, the Congressman faithfully remembered births, anniversaries, and other happy occasions in his district. And, of course, that kept his name in the minds of many voters. In short, Jerry Voorhis was a smart politician.

As was customary for candidates in the crazy quilt of California politics, Voorhis always sought both the Democratic and the Republican nomination. He never ran as an out-and-out, partisan Democrat. In fact, the word "Democrat" rarely appeared in his advertisements and other paraphernalia (just as the word "Republican" almost never showed up on the material of his opponents). Several Republican organization leaders were among Congressman Voorhis' loyal supporters. This galled other rock-ribbed Republicans because, well known to the party faithful, Voorhis was no ordinary Democrat. He was raised in well-to-do circumstances, and that made him all the

From pp. 41–50 in *Richard Nixon: A Political and Personal Portrait* by Earl Mazo. Copyright © 1959 by Earl Mazo. By permission of Harper and Row, Publishers, Inc.

more sensitive to the woes of the poor. After graduating Phi Beta Kappa from Yale, he took a factory job at 39 cents an hour, worked as a freight handler in a railroad yard, where he saw two fellow workers killed for lack of adequate safety equipment, toured Europe, where he witnessed hunger everywhere, and then, after failing to get a job in a southern textile milll, and working awhile on a Ford assembly line, he married and with financial help from his father, opened a school and home for orphaned boys. In the mid-twenties Voorhis was a LaFollette Progressive. Then he became an active Socialist. And in the early depression years he embraced the "End Poverty in California" program of Upton Sinclair and ran for assemblyman on the ticket which Sinclair headed for governor. By 1936 Voorhis had become a bona fide Democrat and ran for Congress as a follower of Franklin D. Roosevelt. Although he grew increasingly conservative in Congress and became an energetic foe of Communism, his record as a whole was bitter medicine for most stalwart Republicans. Worst of all to them was his espousal of co-operatives and a Voorhis plan for altering the monetary system. They called the latter a "funny-money scheme."

When all else failed, the Republican hierarchy in California turned to the 1940 census for salvation. Since the legislature was Republican, the plan was to gerrymander Voorhis and several other Democratic congressmen out of office simply by redefining their districts. Two communities which Voorhis normally carried by a ratio of 5–1 were sliced from his district. Even so, Voorhis was re-elected in 1942 by a 13,000 vote majority and again in 1944, for a fifth term, by the same impressive margin. Other Democrats also survived the gerrymander. Therefore, in 1945, Republican professionals agreed to let complaining amateurs try their hand. These, most of them successful business, industrial, and professional figures, traced the trouble to low-grade candidates, known in the trade as "turkeys." It was decided to form a Fact-Finding Committee of leading citizens in each troublesome district. This committee would interview potential candidates, weed out the perennials and the misfits, and support with all available resources "sound-thinking, articulate, and respected" individuals, preferably newcomers. Murray M. Chotiner, a resourceful Beverly Hills lawyer-politician whose enterprises included a public relations firm, was designated by the party organization to help the amateurs. Chotiner had masterminded several exceptionally successful campaigns for Republicans, including Governor Earl Warren, and later was to become Richard Nixon's political manager.

Meanwhile the citizen fact-finders in the 12th District bestirred themselves well ahead of schedule. In the late spring of 1945 — a full year and a half before the target election — a group met in Arcadia. Stanley Barnes, an attorney who has since been appointed to the United States Circuit Court of Appeals, as chairman and Frank E. Jorgensen, a vice-president of the Metropolitan Life Insurance Company, were the spark plugs. Later, to assure unity, leaders of various regular Republican party organizations were added to the committee in time to hear the first aspirants for nomination. As might be expected, none of the eight applicants were satisfactory. In fact, Jorgensen and his group already knew the man they wanted. He was Walter Dexter, a former president of Whittier College who had become California's superintendent of education. To run for Congress Dexter would have had to resign his state position and, as Jorgensen recalls, "he couldn't afford to risk the financial loss that would result if he was not elected." Dexter therefore suggested one of his former students, Richard M. Nixon, whom he described as one of the most promising young men he had ever known. Jorgensen and two associates, Boyd Gibbons and Rockwood Nelson, drove over to the Nixon grocery store to make inquiries. Frank and Hannah Nixon were more than willing to talk about their oldest living son. They noted that a good friend in town Herman L. Perry, manager of the local Bank of America branch, also had mentioned that their son would be an ideal candidate.

Perry telephoned Nixon in Baltimore, where he was renegotiating Navy contracts while awaiting release from the service. Nixon flew to California, and on December 4, 1945, he formally accepted the fact-finding committee's endorsement in a letter to Roy O. Day, district Republican chairman. It was evident from his letter that the 32-year old Nixon was eager to be out of uniform and running for office. "I am going to see Joe Martin and John Phillips and try to get what dope I can on Mr. Voorhis' record," he wrote, in part. "His 'conservative' reputation must be blasted. But my main efforts are being directed toward building up a positive, progressive group of speeches which tell what *we* want to do, not what the Democrats have failed to do." The neophyte politician advised Day to "bring in the liberal fringe Republicans. We need *every* Republican and a few Democrats to win. I'm really hopped up over this deal, and I believe we can win."

In January Nixon was released from active duty, and he came west with a satchelful of ideas and a set of electioneering pictures from which he learned a fundamental political truth. It was that the great majority of veterans had been enlisted men for whom a politician campaigning in the uniform of an officer held little attraction. The photographs were thrown out, and the simple words "Dick Nixon" or just "Nixon" replaced "Lieutenant Commander Richard M. Nixon" on proposed literature. Nixon began his active campaign immediately. Shortly thereafter the Nixons' first daughter, Patricia, was born, and within three weeks Mrs. Nixon left the child with her mother-in-law and joined her husband.

Murray Chotiner was the principal professional member of Nixon's campaign organization. Chotiner was Senator Knowland's southern California campaign manager, in itself a full-time job. Roy Day retained him as publicity director for Nixon, on the side, at a fee of $500.

Voorhis and Nixon took advantage of California's peculiar cross-filing system to become candidates for the nominations of both parties. But, while Nixon worked at it energetically, Voorhis sent word that he was very busy looking after the people's welfare in Washington and therefore could not spare the time to campaign in the spring primaries. As usual, that was fine strategy. Voorhis won the Democratic nomination, got a substantial vote in the Republican primary, and gained the psychological advantage of beating Nixon by 7,000 votes in the over-all count. Normally this would have meant sure victory in the November general election. But Nixon's morale went up when a Los Angeles political reporter pointed out that Voorhis' vote, 53.5 per cent of the total, was quite a drop from 1944, when he polled 60 per cent.

"Keen political observers . . . thought we ran a darn fine race, and this was the best Republican primary showing in years," Nixon wrote Chairman Day. "Frankly, Roy, I really believe that's true, and it is time some of the rest of the people began to realize it. All we need is a win complex and we'll take him in November."

The general election campaign flared up early in September, much like many others being fought throughout the country that year of meat and housing shortages, labor unrest and general postwar disenchantment. The Republicans were the "outs," and their battlecry was "Had enough?" The theme of the 12th District campaign followed the national pattern in most respects — that is, the incumbent Democrat was branded as a tool of Sidney Hillman's CIO-Political Action Committee, a promoter of controls, and an enemy of free enterprise who would socialize America.

But the Voorhis-Nixon battle developed distinctive nuances of bitterness. The veteran Congressman had never before been confronted by a buzz-saw opponent, and the tenderfoot candidate had never before debated so totally for keeps. Both candidates electioneered on three fronts. Most exciting to them and the voters were five debates. Meanest of the three fronts was a battle of newspaper advertisements and statements. Most strenuous for the candidates were handshaking and coffee-hour tours.

While Voorhis believes, in retrospect, that he would have lost anyway, Nixon believes the turning point for him, as the underdog, was the first debate. "It was tough," Nixon says. "I was the challenger, and he was the experienced incumbent. Once that debate was over, I was on my way to eventual victory." Nixon went into the debates against the wishes of all his advisers except Chotiner. The others feared Voorhis was too experienced and Nixon too green. Chotiner insisted the gamble had to be taken because, at worst, Nixon would lose and, at best, he might strike the spark his campaign needed so badly.

The first debate did just that — thanks to a Political Action Committee endorsement of Voorhis which is still the subject of controversy. There had been a small Nixon advertisement which declared, in part, "A vote for Nixon is a vote against the Communist-dominated PAC with its gigantic slush fund." Voorhis vigorously insisted he had not sought and didn't have the endorsement of the regional Political Action Committee of the CIO. At this Nixon leaped to his feet, drew a paper from his pocket, and read a report in which the Los Angeles chapter of the *national* Political Action Committee recommended that the national group endorse Voorhis. Nixon also read off the names of officers of the national organization's chapter who were also officers of the regional group. Then, dramatically, he thrust the paper at Voorhis.

Shortly afterwards Voorhis issued a long, poignant statement declaring that, while he cherished the support of labor, he didn't have and didn't want the backing of the California CIO because "under present top leadership of the CIO in California, there is at least grave question whether the Communist Party does not exercise inordinate if not decisive influence over state and county organizations."

A few days later he telegraphed the national Political Action Committee demanding that it withdraw its "qualified endorsement" of him.

For the remainder of the campaign Voorhis expended much of his time and energy denying that he was the CIO's errand boy, while Nixon jabbed or punched, as the occasion demanded, with observations about "lip-service Americans" and high officials "who front for un-American elements, wittingly or otherwise, by advocating increasing federal controls over the lives of the people." In mid-October Nixon warned voters against being "fooled" by the "very conservative" tone Voorhis was adopting. "In the last four years, out of forty-six measures sponsored by the CIO and the PAC, my opponent has voted against the CIO and PAC only three times," declared Nixon. "Whether he wants it now or not, my opponent has the PAC endorsement and he has certainly earned it. It's not how a man talks, but how he votes that counts."

The PAC controversy reached its shrill peak three days before the election, when Republican campaign headquarters issued a statement in behalf of a former lieutenant governor accusing Voorhis of "consistently voting the Moscow-PAC-Henry Wallace line in Congress." The statement also mentioned "the insolence of Moscow in telling the American voter to elect PAC candidates, such as Mr. Voorhis," and it pronounced Candidate Nixon to be "a man who will talk American and at the same time vote American in Congress . . . and fight in and out of Congress to perpetuate American ideals and American freedom."

There were, of course, other issues in the campaign, and in the context of those times it is not unlikely that some were more decisive with voters than exchanges about the PAC. There was, for example, the veteran issue. Nixon pointed to his own wartime service (and indirectly to Voorhis' civilian status) in an often-repeated promise "to preserve our sacred heritage, in the name of my buddies and your loved ones, who died that these might endure." For his part, Voorhis referred to his opponent at times as "the Lieutenant Commander" and the "subtlety" escaped no one.

As an "in," Voorhis was compelled to harp on only one positive theme. It was that he had achieved seniority and experience and to turn him out for a newcomer "wouldn't be good sense and would be damaging to popular government in these critical days."

On the other hand, as an "out," with no record to defend, Nixon was free to attack and promise at the same time. Thus he became "thoroughly committed to a program of federal tax reduction" and promised that a Republican Congress would solve the meat, housing, and controls problem.

(It was during this first campaign that Nixon developed the knack of repeating verbatim questions asked of him from the floor. It requires the vocal apparatus to operate on one track while the thinking apparatus operates on another. Nixon does it to give himself time to think of the answer.)

Voorhis had 296 inches of campaign advertising and Nixon 162 inches, in the *Post-Advocate,* the daily newspaper of Alhambra, largest city in the district. It is noteworthy that not one line in a Nixon manifest mentioned the fact that he was a Republican, and none of Voorhis' alluded to his membership in the Democratic party.

Nixon won by a vote of 65,586 to 49,994, and was one of seven Republicans to unseat incumbent Democrats in California. All told, the Republicans picked up fifty-five House seats and won control of the Eightieth Congress. In reflecting on the campaign twelve years later Nixon said the race was, in effect, a contest between a well-known New Dealer and a conservative Republican. "Voorhis lost because that district was not a New Deal district," he said. "Our campaign was a very honest debate on the issues." . . .

At the outset Nixon's favorite work was as a member of a small subcommittee that drafted the Taft-Hartley Labor Law. That was where he became quite friendly with a freshman Democrat from Massachusetts named John F. Kennedy. Nixon and Kennedy were on opposite sides of the Taft-Hartley question, and in the spring of 1947 they went to McKeesport, Pennsylvania, to debate the issue. (Nixon considered Kennedy a good friend; he said "I have a very high regard for him as an able senator and campaigner; he's very attractive and formidable." Kennedy does not now reciprocate those feelings. In fact, his attitude toward Nixon is that he would like very much to run against him for president.)

Meanwhile Nixon's interest in the Un-American Activities Committee was not very great. But it warmed up on August 3, 1948, when Whittaker Chambers, a former Communist, listed among his one-time fellow conspirators a man named Alger Hiss. . . .

4

How I Became a Legislator

Vikenty Narbutovich

People often ask me how I became a deputy to the Supreme Soviet. I find the question hard to answer because it happened so simply and naturally.

I have lived in Gomel all my life. I started work at 14 — this was

Reprinted by permission of *Soviet Life*.

before the 1917 Revolution — as a bricklayer's helper on construction. After the Revolution I learned the trade of fitter. Then I became a boilermaker. Then I got a job as lathe hand at the Gomel Agricultural Machinery plant, and I stayed there.

When I began working in the plant, during the thirties, we were turning out seeders and graders. We thought then that they were terrific machines. But by comparison with the complex machinery our assembly line turns out these days — corn harvesters and beet-digging combines — these early machines look pretty primitive.

I became a machinist, then was promoted to foreman. Now I'm manager of the assembly shop. As a rank-and-file worker I learned the problems of the men and as I advanced in the plant, I kept their friendship and confidence.

All my life had passed before the eyes of my co-workers and fellow townsmen. In 1954 they nominated me as their candidate for deputy to the Supreme Soviet of the USSR, and I was elected by the voters of my district. That was all there was to it.

The job of deputy isn't a simple one. It means not only meeting people and listening to their problems, some of them very difficult to adjust, but getting enough facts and information to make sensible decisions on things I knew nothing about before I was elected. This takes time and energy.

Like most of our deputies, I combine my work as legislator with my job at the plant. I have a secretary, and the allowed thousand rubles a month for clerical help. But aside from that and a per diem allowance while the Supreme Soviet is in session in Moscow, deputies are not paid.

The work of keeping in touch with my constituents is made somewhat easier by the fact that there is an office set aside at the plant for receiving visitors. Saturday is my official visiting day, but I frequently have to take time off during the week to talk to people who can't meet me on Saturday, or to travel to parts of my district where I'm needed.

The plant is in my district also. So that I have obligations there, too. I recently had to solve an interesting problem for a group of people in the shop who wanted to build their own homes.

The way it works is that the state bank will extend a long-term loan at two per cent interest to people who want to build their own homes. The city council — we call it the city Soviet — allocates plots of land for permanent use. Ordinarily, this is routine procedure. But this time there was a hitch.

When I talked to the chairman of the city Soviet, he objected on the ground that the plant had no real housing problem. The people who wanted to build already had apartments. And since the city was suffering from a shortage of building plots and the plant had already been allocated its full quota of housing land, he saw no reason for further grants.

I could see his point, but these were my constituents. They wanted to build homes, and it was my job to help them. We discussed all sorts of possibilities, looked over the whole territory and finally we came up with a reasonable solution.

There was an abandoned quarry not far from the plant. If the land could be graded, it would give building room to spare. It took some talking to persuade the city officials to grade the area. But we did it. We have 40 houses going up there now. I've been invited to two housewarmings already.

Something like this which involves purely local problems is naturally simpler to meet than those which involve larger areas. Gomel, for example, has been having difficulties with its electric-power supply. Although the local power station has doubled its prewar capacity, it still does not produce enough to meet the growing population and industrial needs.

Local people complained to me about restrictions in their use of electricity. They thought it was time something was done about giving Gomel more power.

When I came to Moscow, I went to the Ministry of Power Stations and registered the complaint of my constituents, incidentally putting in a couple of strong words myself. The Ministry promised to send a portable power station. When I got back home, the station had arrived and was waiting on a spur track in the Gomel yards. It hadn't solved the problem completely, but it will help until the big new power station is finished.

As I see it, the function of a deputy is to act as a sort of agent in behalf of the people he represents. If he does a responsible job there, he will be acting in behalf of all the people of the country at the same time. Take the question of pensions, for example. Like all other deputies, I have often had to deal with them in my district.

Our social security system is very broad and embraces all wage and salaried workers and their families. There are no premiums to pay, directly or indirectly. And the benefits are paid by the state. There are no "fine print" clauses containing unexpected exemptions. But still pension legislation needed some up-to-date revision.

For many years it was a whole hodge podge of laws and resolutions that had been passed at different times, and much of it was obsolete. The main trouble was that during the war and the period following it, discrepancies had developed between the wage levels, which were rising, and pensions, which had remained more or less static. Pensions granted to some occupational groups had not been revised since the early thirties and now were too low. Complaints about the pension setup were increasing. That's why a thorough reorganization of the whole system was needed.

It was a complicated problem which affected the national budget. During my two years as a deputy I had learned what balancing the budget meant. In this case it meant raising an additional 13 billion rubles over and above the budget figure of 25 billion rubles that had been allocated for pensions this year. And to accomplish this without increasing taxes at the same time would take some doing.

A solution was found and a new Pension Law was adopted by the Supreme Soviet last July. But it took a great deal of work and thinking, not only by the deputies and the government officials, but by the people generally.

Two months before the July session of the Supreme Soviet, a proposed draft of the new Pension Law was published in the press for discussion throughout the country. Everyone in my district debated the provisions, both at meetings and in conversation. There was general agreement, but, as usual, disagreement as to detail.

This must have been happening everywhere because when the Committees on Legislative Proposals of both houses of the Soviet parliament met, they were faced with 12,000 letters containing amendments and proposals for changes sent in by Soviet citizens. Many were finally adopted, with the result that an additional 500 million rubles had to be added to the budget.

The July session thoroughly discussed various aspects of the pension problem before the legislation was finally adopted.

I was glad to vote for the new Pension Law, a vast improvement over the old one. It guarantees all citizens old age pensions ranging from 50 to 100 per cent of their former earnings, at age 60 for men and 55 for women. For workers engaged in heavy and hazardous jobs, certain office and factory tasks, the age level is five years lower. The new law also provides for disability benefits, including those that arise from non-occupational ailments. Pensions are also paid to widows and children in the event the husband dies.

Upon my return home after the session of the Supreme Soviet, I found my constituents pleased. Many of them told me the new law was exactly what they had suggested. This again showed me that when one meets the demands of his local people, he is also satisfying those of the whole country.

This session of the parliament also considered a number of important international questions. The resolution of the Supreme Soviet on disarmament directed to the parliaments of other countries was approved. The resolution of the Japanese parliament on the prohibition of atomic and hydrogen bomb tests was discussed and a statement adopted noting the unity of viewpoint of both the Japanese and the Soviet legislators on this question.

These are only some of the questions on which I have to speak and vote at sessions of the law-making body of my country, not simply as representative of the people of the whole country. I am one of them and their needs and interests are my own.

III

INTERNAL DETERMINANTS
OF CONGRESSIONAL BEHAVIOR

Congress is, in part, an instrument of society, and societal change is reflected in Congress. Some developments, from the point of view of the individual senator or representative, are not thought about or willed, but simply occur. For example, part of the legislative agenda for Congress at any specific time stems from what is going on in the nation or in the world. Congress did not rationally decide it wanted to face major economic questions after 1929 but the collapse of the economy dictated that it would. Nor did Congress rationally choose to face union and reunion in the mid-nineteenth century, but the onset and playing out of the Civil War necessarily directed its attention toward those issues.

But societal forces are not the only ones that produce change in Congress. Three internal factors at work within the two chambers help to determine the specific legislative output of Congress at any time and simultaneously help determine its general policy stance: (1) those involving the internal distribution of influence in the House and Senate and the informal norms supporting the retention of that distribution; (2) those involving the formal rules of the House and Senate; and (3) those involving the type of member present in Congress and the selective access of those members to positions of influence within the institution.

Critics of Congress usually let their ideology sway their judgments.

A liberal critic tends to see all influence in the hands of senior conservative southern committee chairmen who also have a stranglehold on the use and interpretation of the rules. A conservative critic tends to argue that Congress is in the hands of irresponsible populists who change long-standing rules merely to ensure that their latest whim can be enacted into law. The truth, as usual, is more complicated, and ideology about Congress should not be swallowed whole without a careful look at reality. In part the truth about congressional life is complicated because Congress changes. It has never been a static institution; details have changed constantly and rapidly; its general place and role in the governmental scheme of the United States has changed more gradually. Thus a truth proclaimed about Congress in 1973 might be largely irrelevant by 1977. A proper regard for historical development is useful to those who are addicted to proclamations of truth.

The main competitors for influence inside the House and Senate are the formal party leaders, the most senior committee members (chairmen and ranking minority members), and less senior but still important committee members (typically, subcommittee chairmen and ranking minority members).

The difference in the competition for influence in the contemporary House and Senate is dictated by the size of the two houses: in the Senate almost all members are either subcommittee chairmen or ranking minority members, and hence all senators compete for some share of the institutional influence. In the House, however, leadership and committee positions, and hence the competition for institutional influence, are limited to the senior and experienced members (because the House has more members than positions are available, and experience is the criterion for advancement). The 67-year old freshman congressman from California who did not seek reelection in 1964 because, as he said at the time, he would have to wait longer to develop influence in the House than the laws of nature would be likely to allow, made a wise decision. If he had been a senator, however, he might have developed some small influence in a particular subject matter area in his first few years because he might have been a subcommittee chairman.

At different points in history each of the three main groups of competitors has triumphed, at least in relative terms. Wilson was writing about a period of committee dominance in the late nineteenth century. Huntington portrays the reemergence of that dominance in the early twentieth century after a period of party leader dominance in the closing few years of the nineteenth century and the opening years of the twentieth century. Ripley suggests the ebb and flow of the importance and impact of the party leaders under different kinds of conditions. The Polsby selection underscores the importance of change by concentrating on one recent development: the demise of the "Club" of the 1940's and 1950's in the Senate and its replacement in the 1960's by a wider dispersion of power.

The second cluster of internal determinants of congressional behavior centers on the rules of the House and Senate. The rules can be used for many purposes, although, as Froman points out, they are almost never neutral. In general, they favor those who want to retain whatever the status quo happens to be. Occasionally this is a "liberal" status quo, and its supporters are fending off the forces of conservatism (as, for example, the antiwar senators did in opposing measures they thought would involve the United States in World War I). More often, however, the status quo is "conservative" and the proponents of change are liberals. Thus such devices as the cloture rule in relation to filibusters effectively load the system in favor of the conservatives.

Who comes to Congress and what is the basis for determining their access to positions of influence? Writing about this third cluster of internal factors, Huntington shows that the twentieth century, senior, career-oriented members of the House and Senate have become the rule rather than the exception. Members have also become increasingly devoted to making their careers exclusively in Congress, thus isolating it from other leadership elites in society. One does not have to come to Huntington's conclusions or prescription to accept his data. Indeed, a conservative might well argue that isolating members of Congress is desirable because it does help increase independence from the influence of other elites in society.

During the same time that Huntington discusses, the "seniority rule" — that much abused and much praised artifact of congressional life — became virtually inviolable. As Hinckley argues, it reinforces already existing conservative tendencies in Congress, but it can hardly be held culpable for producing a Congress dominated by conservatives despite eager, aggressive liberal majorities in the House and Senate. By the same token, removal of the seniority rule is not likely to make much difference in the way Congress functions. Thus conservatives and liberals alike place too much importance on its impact; in fact it seems to be a reflection of much deeper institutional patterns and determinants.

5

The Imperious Authority
of the Standing Committees

Woodrow Wilson

The leaders of the House are the chairmen of the principal Standing
Committees. Indeed, to be exactly accurate, the House has as many
leaders as there are subjects of legislation; for there are as many
Standing Committees as there are leading classes of legislation, and
in the consideration of every topic of business the House is guided
by a special leader in the person of the chairman of the Standing
Committee, charged with the superintendence of measures of the
particular class to which the topic belongs. It is this multiplicity of
leaders, this many-headed leadership, which makes the organization
of the House too complex to afford uninformed people and un-
skilled observers any easy clue to its methods of rule. For the chairmen of the Standing Committees do not constitute a cooperative
body like a ministry. They do not consult and concur in the adoption
of homogeneous and mutually helpful measures; there is no thought
of acting in concert. Each Committee goes its own way at its own
pace. It is impossible to discover any unity or method in the dis-
connected and therefore unsystematic, confused, and desultory action
of the House, or any common purpose in the measures which its
Committees from time to time recommend.

And it is not only to the unanalytic thought of the common
observer who looks at the House from the outside that its doings
seem helter-skelter, and without comprehensible rule; it is not at
once easy to understand them when they are scrutinized in their
daily headway through open session by one who is inside the House.
The newly-elected member, entering its doors for the first time, and
with no more knowledge of its rules and customs than the more intelligent of his constituents possess, always experiences great difficulty in adjusting his preconceived ideas of congressional life to

Reprinted by permission of the World Publishing Company from *Congressional
Government* by Woodrow Wilson.

the strange and unlooked-for conditions by which he finds himself surrounded after he has been sworn in and has become a part of the great legislative machine. Indeed there are generally many things connected with his career in Washington to disgust and dispirit, if not to aggrieve, the new member. In the first place, his local reputation does not follow him to the federal capital. Possibly the members from his own State know him, and receive him into full fellowship; but no one else knows him, except as an adherent of this or that party, or as a newcomer from this or that State. He finds his station insignificant, and his identity indistinct. But this social humiliation which he experiences in circles in which to be a congressman does not of itself confer distinction, because it is only to be one among many, is probably not to be compared with the chagrin and disappointment which come in company with the inevitable discovery that he is equally without weight or title to consideration in the House itself. No man, when chosen to the membership of a body possessing great powers and exalted prerogatives, likes to find his activity repressed, and himself suppressed, by imperative rules and precedents which seem to have been framed for the deliberate purpose of making usefulness unattainable by individual members. Yet such the new member finds the rules and precedents of the House to be. It matters not to him, because it is not apparent on the face of things, that those rules and precedents have grown, not out of set purpose to curtail the privileges of new members as such, but out of the plain necessities of business; it remains the fact that he suffers under their curb, and it is not until "custom hath made it in him a property of easiness" that he submits to them with anything like good grace. . . .

Often the new member goes to Washington as the representative of a particular line of policy, having been elected, it may be, as an advocate of free trade, or as a champion of protection; and it is naturally his first care upon entering on his duties to seek immediate opportunity for the expression of his views and immediate means of giving them definite shape and thrusting them upon the attention of Congress. His disappointment is, therefore, very keen when he finds both opportunity and means denied him. He can introduce his bill; but that is all he can do, and he must do that at a particular time and in a particular manner. This he is likely to learn through rude experience, if he be not cautious to inquire beforehand the details of practice. He is likely to make a rash start, upon the supposition that Congress observes the ordinary rules of parliamentary practice to which he has become accustomed in the debating clubs familiar to his youth, and in the mass-meetings known to his later experience. His bill is doubtless ready for presentation early in the session, and some day, taking advantage of a pause in the proceedings, when there seems to be no business before the House, he rises to read it and move its adoption. But he finds getting the floor an arduous and precarious undertaking. There are certain to be others who want it as well as he; and his indignation is stirred by the fact that the Speaker does not so much as turn towards him, though he must have heard his call, but recognizes some one else readily and as a matter of course. If he be obstreperous and persistent in his cries of "Mr. Speaker," he may get that great functionary's attention for a moment — only to be told, however, that he is out of order, and that his bill can be introduced at that stage only by unanimous consent; immediately there are mechanically-uttered but emphatic exclamations of objection, and he is forced to sit down confused and disgusted. He has, without knowing it, obtruded himself in the way of the "regular order of business," and been run over in consequence, without being quite clear as to how the accident occurred. . . .

[I]f he supposes, as he naturally will, that after his bill has been sent up to be read by the clerk he may say a few words in its behalf, and in that belief sets out upon his long-considered remarks, he will be knocked down by the rules as surely as he was on the first occasion when he gained the floor for a brief moment. The rap of Mr. Speaker's gavel is sharp, immediate, and peremptory. He is curtly informed that no debate is in order; the bill can only be referred to the appropriate Committee.

This is, indeed, disheartening; it is his first lesson in committee government, and the master's rod smarts; but the sooner he learns the prerogatives and powers of the Standing Committees the sooner will he penetrate the mysteries of the rules and avoid the pain of further contact with their thorny side. The privileges of the Standing Committees are the beginning and the end of the rules. Both the House of Representatives and the Senate conduct their business by what may figuratively, but not inaccurately, be called an odd device of *disintegration*. The House virtually both deliberates and legislates in small sections. Time would fail it to discuss all the bills brought in, for they every session number thousands; and it is to be doubted whether, even if time allowed, the ordinary processes of debate and amendment would suffice to sift the chaff from the wheat in the bushels of bills every week piled upon the clerk's desk. Accordingly, no futile attempt is made to do anything of the kind. The work is parceled out, most of it to the forty-seven [1] Standing Committees which constitute the regular organization of the House, some of it to select committees appointed for special and temporary purposes. Each of the almost numberless bills that come pouring in on Mondays is "read a first and second time" — simply perfunctorily read, that is, by its title, by the clerk, and passed by silent assent through its first formal courses, for the purpose of bringing it to the proper stage for commitment — and referred without debate to the appropriate Standing Committee. Practically, no bill escapes commitment — save, of course, bills introduced by committees and a few which may now and then be crowded through under a suspension of the rules, granted by a two-thirds vote — though the exact disposition to be made of a bill is not always determined easily and as a matter of course. Besides the great Committee of Ways and Means and the equally great Committee on Appropriations, there are Standing Committees on Banking and Currency . . . on the Judiciary, . . . on Agriculture, . . . and on a score of other branches of legislative concern; but careful and differential as is the topical division of the subjects of legislation which is represented in the titles of these Committees, it is not always evident to which Committee each particular bill should go. Many bills affect subjects which may be regarded as lying as properly within the jurisdiction of one as of another of the Committees; for no hard and fast lines separate the various classes of business which the Committees are commissioned to take in charge. Their jurisdictions overlap at many points, and it must frequently happen that bills are ready which cover just this common ground. Over the commitment of such bills sharp and interesting skirmishes often take place. There is active competition for them, the ordinary, quiet routine of matter-of-course reference being interrupted by rival motions seeking to give very different directions to the disposition to be made of them. . . .

The fate of bills committed is generally not uncertain. As a rule, a bill committed is a bill doomed. When it goes from the clerk's desk to a committee-room it crosses a parliamentary bridge of sighs to dim dungeons of silence whence it will never return. The means and time of its death are unknown, but its friends never see it again. Of course no Standing Committee is privileged to take upon itself the full powers of the House it represents, and formally and decisively reject a bill referred to it; its disapproval, if it disapproves, must be reported

---

[1] At present twenty, with several additional *ad hoc* committees — Eds.

to the House in the form of a recommendation that the bill "do not pass." But it is easy, and therefore common, to let the session pass without making any report at all upon bills deemed objectionable or unimportant, and to substitute for reports upon them a few bills of the Committee's own drafting; so that thousands of bills expire with the expiration of each Congress, not having been rejected, but having been simply neglected. There was not time to report upon them.

Of course it goes without saying that the practical effect of this Committee organization of the House is to consign to each of the Standing Committees the entire direction of legislation upon those subjects which properly come to its consideration. As to those subjects it is entitled to the initiative, and all legislative action with regard to them is under its overruling guidance. It gives shape and course to the determinations of the House. In one respect, however, its initiative is limited. Even a Standing Committee cannot report a bill whose subject matter has not been referred to it by the House, "by the rules or otherwise," it cannot volunteer advice on questions upon which its advice has not been asked. But this is not a serious, not even an operative, limitation upon its functions of suggestion and leadership for it is a very simple matter to get referred to it any subject it wishes to introduce to the attention of the House. Its chairman, or one of its leading members, frames a bill covering the point upon which the Committee wishes to suggest legislation; brings it in, in his capacity as a private member, on Monday, when the call of States is made; has it referred to his Committee; and thus secures an opportunity for the making of the desired report.

It is by this imperious authority of the Standing Committees that the new member is stayed and thwarted whenever he seeks to take an active part in the business of the House. Turn which way he may, some privilege of the Committees stands in his path. The rules are so framed as to put all business under their management; and one of the discoveries which the new member is sure to make, albeit after many trying experiences and sobering adventures and as his first session draws towards its close, is, that under their sway freedom of debate finds no place of allowance, and that his long-delayed speech must remain unspoken. For even a long congressional session is too short to afford time for a full consideration of all the reports of . . . [all the] Committees, and debate upon them must be rigidly cut short, if not altogether excluded, if any considerable part of the necessary business is to be gotten through with before adjournment. There are some subjects to which the House must always give prompt attention; . . . therefore the Committee of Ways and Means and the

Committee on Appropriations are clothed with extraordinary privileges; and revenue and supply bills may be reported, and will ordinarily be considered, at any time. . . . The rest must take their turns in fixed order as they are called on by the Speaker, contenting themselves with such crumbs of time as fall from the tables of the four Committees of highest prerogative. . . .

The House is conscious that time presses. It knows that, hurry as it may, it will hardly get through with one eighth of the business laid out for the session, and that to pause for lengthy debate is to allow the arrears to accumulate. Besides, most of the members are individually anxious to expedite action on every pending measure, because each member of the House is a member of one or more of the Standing Committees, and is quite naturally desirous that the bills prepared by his Committees, and in which he is, of course, specially interested by reason of the particular attention which he has been compelled to give them, should reach a hearing and a vote as soon as possible. It must, therefore, invariably happen that the Committee holding the floor at any particular time is the Committee whose proposals the majority wish to dispose of as summarily as circumstances will allow, in order that the rest of the [other] unprivileged Committees to which the majority belong may gain the earlier and the fairer chance of a hearing. A reporting Committee, besides, is generally as glad to be pushed as the majority are to push it. It probably has several bills matured, and wishes to see them disposed of before its brief hours of opportunity are passed and gone. . . .

These are the customs which baffle and perplex and astound the new member. In these precedents and usages, when at length he comes to understand them, the novice spies out the explanation of the fact, once so confounding and seemingly inexplicable, that when he leaped to his feet to claim the floor other members who rose after him were coolly and unfeelingly preferred before him by the Speaker. Of course it is plain enough now that Mr. Speaker knew beforehand to whom the representative of the reporting Committee had agreed to yield the floor; and it was no use for any one else to cry out for recognition. Whoever wished to speak should, if possible, have made some arrangement with the Committee before the business came to a hearing, and should have taken care to notify Mr. Speaker that he was to be granted the floor for a few moments.

Unquestionably this, besides being a very interesting, is a very novel and significant method of restricting debate and expediting legislative action — a method of very serious import, and obviously fraught with far-reaching constitutional effects. The practices of debate which prevail in its legislative assembly are manifestly of the utmost importance to a self-governing people; for that legislation which is not thoroughly discussed by the legislating body is practically done in a corner. It is impossible for Congress itself to do wisely what it does so hurriedly; and the constituencies cannot understand what Congress does not itself stop to consider. . . .

[T]he debates of Congress cannot, under our present system, have that serious purpose of search into the merits of policies and that definite and determinate party — or, if you will, partisan — aim without which they can never be effective for the instruction of public opinion, or the cleansing of political action. The chief of these reasons, because the parent of all the rest, is that there are in Congress no authoritative leaders who are the recognized spokesman of their parties. Power is nowhere concentrated; it is rather deliberately and of set policy scattered amongst many small chiefs. It is divided up, as it were, into forty-seven seigniories, in each of which a Standing Committee is the court-baron and its chairman lord-proprietor. These petty barons, some of them not a little powerful, but none of them within reach of the full powers of rule, may at will exercise an almost despotic sway within their own shires, and may sometimes threaten to convulse even the realm itself; but both their mutual jealousies and their brief and restricted opportunities forbid their combining and each is very far from the office of common leader.

I know that to some this scheme of distributed power and disintegrated rule seems a very excellent device whereby we are enable to escape a dangerous "one-man power" and an untoward concentration of functions; and it is very easy to see and appreciate the considerations which make this view of committee government so popular. It is based upon a very proper and salutary fear of *irresponsible* power; and those who most resolutely maintain it always fight from the position that all leadership in legislation is hard to restrain in proportion to its size and to the strength of its prerogatives, and that to divide it is to make it manageable. They aver, besides, that the less a man has to do — that is to say, the more he is confined to single departments and to definite details — the more intelligent and thorough will his work be. They like the Committees, therefore, just because they are many and weak, being quite willing to abide their being despotic within their narrow spheres.

It seems evident, however, when the question is looked at from another standpoint, that, as a matter of fact and experience, the more power is divided the more irresponsible it becomes. . . .

In a word, the national parties do not act in Congress under the restraint of a sense of immediate responsibility. Responsibility is spread thin; and no vote or debate can gather it. It rests not so much upon parties as upon individuals; and it rests upon individuals in no such way as would make it either just or efficacious to visit upon them the iniquity of any legislative act. Looking at government from a practical and business-like, rather than from a theoretical and abstractly-ethical point of view — treating the business of government as a business — it seems to be unquestionably and in a high degree desirable that all legislation should distinctly represent the action of parties as parties. I know that it has been proposed by enthusiastic, but not too practical, reformers to do away with parties by some legerdemain of governmental reconstruction, accompanied and supplemented by some rehabilitation, devoutly to be wished, of the virtues least commonly controlling in fallen human nature; but it seems to me that it would be more difficult and less desirable than these amiable persons suppose to conduct a government of the many by means of any other device than party organization, and that the great need is, not to get rid of parties, but to find and use some expedient by which they can be managed and made amenable from day to day to public opinion. . . .

[T]here is within Congress no *visible,* and therefore no *controllable* party organization. The only bond of cohesion is the caucus, which occasionally whips a party together for cooperative action against the time for casting its vote upon some critical question. There is always a majority and a minority, indeed, but the legislation of a session does not represent the policy of either; it is simply an aggregate of the bills recommended by Committees composed of members from both sides of the House, and it is known to be usually, not the work of the majority men upon the Committees, but compromise conclusions bearing some shade or tinge of each of the variously colored opinions and wishes of the committeemen of both parties.

It is plainly the representation of both parties on the Committees that make party responsibility indistinct and organized party action almost impossible. If the Committees were composed entirely of members of the majority, and were thus constituted representatives of the party in power, the whole course of congressional proceedings would unquestionably take on a very different aspect. There would then certainly be a compact opposition to face the organized majority. Committee reports would be taken to represent the views of the party in power, and, instead of the scattered, unconcerted opposition, without plan or leaders, which now sometimes subjects the propositions of the Committees to vexatious hindrances and delays, there would spring up debate under skillful masters of opposition, who could drill their partisans for effective warfare and give shape and meaning to the purposes of the minority. But of course there can be no such definite division of forces so long as the efficient machinery of legislation is in the hands of both parties at once; so long as the parties are mingled and harnessed together in a common organization.

6

Congressional Responses to the Twentieth Century

Samuel P. Huntington

Congress is a frequent source of anguish to both its friends and its foes. The critics point to its legislative failure. The function of a legislature, they argue, is to legislate, and Congress either does not legislate or legislates too little and too late. The intensity of their criticism varies inversely with the degree and despatch with which Congress approves the President's legislative proposals. When in 1963 the 88th Congress seemed to stymie the Kennedy legislative program, criticism rapidly mounted. "What kind of legislative body is it," asked Walter Lippmann, neatly summing up the prevailing exasperation, "that will not or cannot legislate?" When in 1964 the same 88th Congress passed the civil rights, tax, and other bills, criticism of Congress correspondingly subsided. Reacting differently to this familiar pattern, the friends of Congress lamented its acquiescence to presidential dictate. Since 1933, they said, the authority of the executive branch — President, administration, and bureaucracy — has waxed, while that of Congress has waned. They warned of the constitutional perils stemming from the permanent subordination of one branch of government to another. Thus, at the same time that it is an obstructive ogre to its enemies, Congress is also the declining despair of its friends. Can both images be true? In large part, they are. The loss of power in Congress, indeed, can be measured by the extent to which congressional assertion coincides with congressional obstruction.

This paradox has been at the root of the "problem" of Congress since the early days of the New Deal. Vis-à-vis the Executive, Congress is an autonomous, legislative body. But apparently Congress can defend its autonomy only by refusing to legislate, and it can legislate only by surrendering its autonomy. When Congress balks, criticism rises, and the clamoring voices of reformers fill the air with demands for the "modernization" of the "antiquated procedures" of an "eighteenth century" Congress so it can deal with "twentieth-century realities." The demands for reform serve as counters in the legislative game to get the President's measures through Congress. Independence thus provokes criticism; acquiescence brings approbation. If Congress legislates, it subordinates itself to the President; if it refuses to legislate, it alienates itself from public opinion. Congress can assert its power or it can pass laws; but it cannot do both.

LEGISLATIVE POWER
AND INSTITUTIONAL CRISIS

The roots of this legislative dilemma lie in the changes in American society during the twentieth century. The twentieth century has seen: rapid urbanization and the beginnings of a post-industrial, technological society; the nationalization of social and economic problems and the concomitant growth of national organizations to deal with these problems; the increasing bureaucratization of social, economic, and governmental organizations; and the sustained high-level international involvement of the United States in world politics. These developments have generated new forces in American politics and initiated major changes in the distribution of power in American society. In particular, the twentieth century has witnessed the tremendous expansion of the responsibilities of the national government and the size of the national bureaucracy. . . . The expansion of the national government has been paralleled by the emergence of other large, national, bureaucratic organizations: manufacturing corporations, banks, insurance companies, labor unions, trade associations, farm organizations, newspaper chains, radio-TV networks. Each organization may have relatively specialized and concrete interests, but typically it functions on a national basis. Its headquarters are in New

York or Washington; its operations are scattered across a dozen or more states. The emergence of these organizations truly constitutes, in Kenneth Boulding's expressive phrase, an "organizational revolution." The existence of this private "Establishment," more than anything else, distinguishes twentieth-century America from nineteenth-century America. The leaders of these organizations are the notables of American society: they are the prime wielders of social and economic power.

These momentous social changes have confronted Congress with an institutional "adaptation crisis." Such a crisis occurs when changes in the environment of a governmental institution force the institution either to alter its functions, affiliation, and modes of behavior, or to face decline, decay, and isolation. Crises usually occur when an institution loses its previous sources of support or fails to adapt itself to the rise of new social forces. . . .

Congress's legislative dilemma and loss of power stem from the nature of its over-all institutional response to the changes in American society. This response involves three major aspects of Congress as an institution: its affiliations, its structure, and its functions. During the twentieth century Congress has insulated itself from the new political forces which social change has generated and which are, in turn, generating more change. Hence the leadership of Congress has lacked the incentive to take the legislative initiative in handling emerging national problems. Within Congress power has become dispersed among many officials, committees, and subcommittees. Hence the central leadership of Congress has lacked the ability to establish national legislative priorities. As a result, the legislative function of Congress has declined in importance, while the growth of the federal bureaucracy has made the administrative overseeing function of Congress more important. These three tendencies — toward insulation, dispersion, and oversight — have dominated the evolution of Congress during the twentieth century.

AFFILIATIONS: INSULATION FROM POWER

Perhaps the single most important trend in congressional evolution during the twentieth century has been the growing insulation of Congress from other social groups and political institutions. In 1900 no gap existed between congressmen and the other leaders of American society and politics. Half a century later the changes in American society, on the one hand, and the institutional evolution of Congress, on the other, had produced a marked gap between congressional leaders and the bureaucratically oriented leadership of the executive branch and of the Establishment. The growth of this gap can be seen in seven trends in congressional evolution:

1. Increasing tenure of office. In the nineteenth century few congressmen stayed in Congress very long. During the twentieth century the average tenure of congressmen has inexorably lengthened. . . .

2. The increasingly important role of seniority. Increasing tenure of congressmen is closely linked to increasingly rigid adherence to the practices of seniority. The longer men stay in Congress, the more likely they are to see virtue in seniority. Conversely, the more important seniority is, the greater is the constituent appeal of men who have been long in office. The current rigid system of seniority in *both* houses of Congress is a product of the twentieth century. . . .

3. Extended tenure: a prerequisite for leadership. Before 1896 Speakers, at the time of their first election, averaged only seven years' tenure in the House. Since 1896 Speakers have averaged twenty-two years of House service at their first election. Today the Speaker and other leaders of the House and, to a lesser degree, the leaders of the Senate are legislative veterans of long standing. In 1961 fifty-seven House leaders averaged twenty years of service in the House and thirty-four Senate leaders sixteen years of service in the Senate. The top House leaders (Speaker, floor leaders, chairmen and ranking minority members of Ways and Means, Appropriations, and Rules Committees) averaged thirty-one years in the House and nineteen years in leadership positions. The top Senate leaders (President *pro tem.,* floor leaders, chairmen and ranking minority members of Finance, Foreign Relations, and Appropriations Committees) averaged twenty years in the Senate and nine years in leadership positions. . . .

4. Leadership within Congress: a one-way street. Normally in American life becoming a leader in one institution opens up leadership possibilities in other institutions: corporation presidents head civic agencies or become cabinet officers; foundation and university executives move into government; leading lawyers and bankers take over industrial corporations. The greater one's prestige, authority, and accomplishments within one organization, the easier it is to move to other and better posts in other organizations. Such, however, is not the case with Congress. Leadership in the House of Representatives leads nowhere except to leadership in the House of Repre-

sentatives. To a lesser degree, the same is true of the Senate. The successful House or Senate leader has to identify himself completely with his institution, its mores, traditions, and ways of behavior. . . .

5. The decline of personnel interchange between Congress and the administration. Movement of leaders in recent years between the great national institutions of "The Establishment" and the top positions in the administration has been frequent, easy, and natural. . . .

The frequent movement of individuals between administration and establishment contrasts sharply with the virtual absence of such movement between Congress and the administration or between Congress and the establishment. The gap between congressional leadership and administration leadership has increased sharply during this century. Seniority makes it virtually impossible for administration leaders to become leaders of Congress and makes it unlikely that leaders of Congress will want to become leaders of the administration. The separation of powers has become the insulation of leaders. Between 1861 and 1896, 37 per cent of the people appointed to posts in the President's cabinet had served in the House or Senate. Between 1897 and 1940, 19 per cent of the Cabinet positions were filled by former congressmen or senators. Between 1941 and 1963, only 15 per cent of the cabinet posts were so filled. . . .

Movement from the administration to leadership positions in Congress is almost equally rare. . . .

6. The social origins and careers of congressmen. Congressmen are much more likely to come from rural and small-town backgrounds than are administration and establishment leaders. . . .

Of perhaps greater significance is the difference in geographical mobility between congressmen and private and public executives. Forty-one per cent of the 1959 senators, but only 12 per cent of the 1959 corporation presidents, were currently residing in their original hometowns. Seventy per cent of the presidents had moved 100 miles or more from their hometowns but only 29 per cent of the senators had done so. In 1963, over one-third (37 per cent) of the top leaders of Congress but only 11 per cent of administration leaders were still living in their places of birth. Seventy-seven per cent of the congressional leaders were living in their states of birth, while 70 per cent of the administration leaders had moved out of their states of birth. Sixty-one per cent of administration leaders and 73 per cent of political executives had moved from one region of the country to another, but only 19 per cent of congressional leaders had similar mobility.

During the course of this century the career patterns of congressmen and of executive leaders have diverged. At an earlier period both leaderships had extensive experience in local and state politics. In 1903 about one-half of executive leaders and three-quarters of congressional leaders had held office in state or local government. In 1963 the congressional pattern had not changed significantly, with 64 per cent of the congressional leaders having held state or local office. The proportion of executive leaders with this experience, however, had dropped drastically. The congressional leaders of 1963, moreover, were more often professional politicians than the congressional leaders of 1903: in 1903 only 5 per cent of the congressional leaders had no major occupation outside politics, while in 1963, 22 per cent of the congressional leaders had spent almost all their lives in electoral politics.

The typical congressman may have gone away to college, but he then returned to his home state to pursue an electoral career, working his way up through local office, the state legislature, and eventually to Congress. The typical political executive, on the other hand, like the typical corporation executive, went away to college and then did not return home but instead pursued a career in a metropolitan center or worked in one or more national organizations with frequent changes of residence. As a result, political executives have become divorced from state and local politics, just as the congressional leaders have become isolated from national organizations. . . .

7. The provincialism of congressmen. The absence of mobility between Congress and the executive branch and the differing backgrounds of the leaders of the two branches of government stimulate different policy attitudes. Congressmen tend to be oriented toward local needs and small-town ways of thought. The leaders of the administration and of the great private national institutions are more likely to think in national terms. . . .

"Segmental" or "provincial" attitudes are undoubtedly stronger in the House than they are in the Senate. But they also exist in the Senate. . . .

Old ideas, old values, old beliefs die hard in Congress. The structure of Congress encourages their perpetuation. The newcomer to Congress is repeatedly warned that "to get along he must go along." To go along means to adjust to the prevailing mores and attitudes of the Inner Club. The more the young congressman desires a career in the House or Senate, the more readily he makes the necessary adjustments. The country at large has become urban, suburban, and metropolitan. Its economic, social, educational, and technological activities are increasingly performed by huge national bureaucratic organizations. But on Capitol Hill the nineteenth-century ethos of the small-town, the independent farmer, and the small businessman is still entrenched behind the institutional defenses which have developed in this century to insulate Congress from the new America.

• • •

The executive branch has thus grown in power vis-à-vis Congress for precisely the same reason that the House of Representatives grew in power vis-à-vis the Executive in the second and third decades of the nineteenth century. It has become more powerful because it has become more representative. Congress has lost power because it has had two defects as a representative body. One, relatively minor and in part easily remedied, deals with the representation of people as individuals; the other, more serious and perhaps beyond remedy, concerns the representation of organized groups and interests.

Congress was originally designed to represent individuals in the House and governmental units — the states — in the Senate. In the course of time the significance of the states as organized interests declined, and popular election of senators was introduced. In effect, both senators and representatives now represent relatively arbitrarily defined territorial collections of individuals. This system of individual representation suffers from two inequities. First, of course, is the constitutional equal representation of states in the Senate irrespective of population. Second, in the House, congressional districts vary widely in size and may also be gerrymandered to benefit one party or group of voters. The net effect of these practices in recent years has been to place the urban and, even more importantly, the suburban voter at a disadvantage vis-à-vis the rural and small-town voter. In due course, however, the Supreme Court decision in *Wesberry* v. *Sanders* in February 1964 will correct much of this discrepancy.

The second and more significant deficiency of Congress as a representative body concerns its insulation from the interests which have emerged in the twentieth century's "organizational revolution." How can national institutions be represented in a locally elected legislature? In the absence of any easy answer to this question, the administration has tended to emerge as the natural point of access to the government for these national organizations and the place where their interests and viewpoints are brought into the policy-making process. In effect, the American system of government is moving toward a three-way system of representation. Particular territorial interests are represented in Congress; particular functional interests are represented in the administration; and the national interest is represented territorially and functionally in the Presidency. . . .

STRUCTURE: THE DISPERSION OF POWER IN CONGRESS

The influence of Congress in our political system . . . varies directly with its ties to the more dynamic and dominant groups in society. The power of Congress also varies directly, however, with the centralization of power iin Congress. The corollary of these propositions is likewise true: centralization of authority within Congress usually goes with close connections between congressional leadership and major external forces and groups. The power of the House of Representatives was at a peak in the second decade of the nineteenth century, when power was centralized in the Speaker and when Henry Clay and his associates represented the dynamic new forces of trans-Appalachian nationalism. Another peak in the power of the House came during Reconstruction, when power was centralized in Speaker Colfax and the Joint Committee on Reconstruction as spokesmen for triumphant northern Radicalism. A third peak in the power of the House came between 1890 and 1910, when the authority of the Speaker reached its height and Speakers Reed and Cannon reflected the newly established forces of nationalist conservatism. The peak in Senate power came during the post-Reconstruction period of the 1870's and 1880's. Within Congress, power was centralized in the senatorial leaders who represented the booming forces of the rising industrial capitalism and the new party machines. . . .

Since its first years, the twentieth century has seen no comparable centralization of power in Congress. Instead, the dominant tendency has been toward the dispersion of power. This leaves Congress only partially equipped to deal with the problems of modern society. In general, the complex modern environment requires in social and political institutions *both* a high degree of specialization and a high degree of centralized authority to coordinate and to integrate the activities of the specialized units. Specialization of function and centralization of authority have been the dominant trends of twentieth-century institutional development. Congress, however, has adjusted only half-way. Through its committees and subcommittees it has provided effectively for specialization, much more effectively, indeed, than the national legislature of any other country. But it has failed to combine increasing specialization of function with increasing centralization of authority. Instead the central leadership in Congress has been weakened, and as a result Congress lacks the central authority to integrate its specialized bodies. In a "rational" bureaucracy authority varies inversely with specialization. Within Congress authority usually varies directly with specialization.

The authority of the specialist is a distinctive feature of congressional behavior. "Specialization" is a key norm in both House and Senate.

The emphasis on specialization as a norm, of course, complements the importance of the committee as an institution. It also leads to a great stress on reciprocity. In a bureaucracy, specialized units compete with each other for the support of less specialized officials. In Congress, however, reciprocity among specialists replaces coordination by generalists. When a committee bill comes to the floor, the non-specialists in that subject acquiesce in its passage with the unspoken but complete understanding that they will receive similar treatment. . . . Reciprocity thus substitutes for centralization and confirms the diffusion of power among the committees. . . .

Since 1910 in the House and since 1915 in the Senate the overall tendency has been toward the weakening of central leadership and the strengthening of the committees. The restoration of seniority in the Senate and its development and rigidification in the House have contributed directly to this end. So also have most of the "reforms" which have been made in the procedures of Congress. . . . The Budget and Accounting Act of 1921 strengthened the Appropriations Committees by giving them exclusive authority to report appropriations, but its primary effects were felt in the executive branch with the creation of the Bureau of the Budget. During the 1920s power was further dispersed among the Speaker, floor leaders, Rules, Appropriations, Ways and Means chairmen, and caucus chairman. In the following decade political development also contributed to the diffusion of influence when the conservative majority on the Rules Committee broke with the administration in 1937.

The dispersion of power to the committees of Congress was intensified by the Legislative Reorganization Act of 1946. In essence, this act was a "Committee reorganization act" making the committees stronger and more effective. The reduction in the number of standing committees from eighty-one to thirty-four increased the importance of the committee chairmanships. Committee consolidation led to the proliferation of subcommittees, now estimated to number over two hundred and fifty. Thus the functions of integration and coordination which, if performed at all, would previously have been performed by the central leadership of the two houses, have now devolved on the leadership of the standing committees. Before the reorganization, for instance, committee jurisdictions frequently overlapped, and the presiding officers of the House and Senate could often influence the fate of a bill by exercising their discretion in referring it to committee. While jurisdictional uncertainties have not been totally eliminated, the discretion of the presiding officers has been drastically curtailed. The committee chairman, on the other hand, can often influence the fate of legislation by manipulating the subcommittee structure of the committee and by exercising his discretion in referring bills to subcommittees. Similarly, the intention of the framers of the Reorganization Act to reduce, if not to eliminate, the use of special committees has had the effect of restricting the freedom of action of the central leadership in the two houses at the same time that it confirms the authority of the standing committees in their respective jurisdictions. The Reorganization Act also bolstered the committees by significantly expanding their staffs and by specifically authorizing them to exercise legislative overseeing functions with respect to the administrative agencies in their field of responsibility.

The Act included few provisions strengthening the central leadership of Congress. Those which it did include usually have not operated successfully. A proposal for party policy committees in each house was defeated in the House of Representatives. The Senate subsequently authorized party policy committees in the Senate, but they have not been active or influential enough to affect the legislative process significantly. The Act's provision for a Joint Committee on the Budget which would set an appropriations ceiling by February 15th of each year was implemented twice and then abandoned. In 1950 the Appropriations Committees reported a consolidated supply bill which cut the presidential estimates by two billion dollars and was approved by Congress two months before the approval of the individual supply bills of 1949. Specialized interests within Congress, however, objected strenuously to this procedure, and it has not been attempted again. The net effect of the Reorganization Act was thus to further the dispersion of power, to strengthen and to institutionalize committee authority, and to circumscribe still more the influence of the central leadership.

In the years after the Legislative Reorganization Act, the issues which earlier had divided the central leadership and committee chairmen reappeared in each committee in struggles between committee chairmen and subcommittees. The chairmen attempted to maintain their own control and flexibility over the number, nature, staff, membership. and leadership of their subcommittees. Several of the most assertive chairmen either prevented the creation of subcommittees or created numbered subcommittees without distinct legislative jurisdictions, thereby reserving to themselves the assignment of legislation to the subcommittees. Those who wished to limit the power of the chairman, on the other hand, often invoked seniority as the rule to be followed in designating subcommittee chairmen. In 1961 thirty-one of the thirty-six standing committees of the House and Senate had subcommittees and in twenty-four the subcommittees had fixed jurisdictions and significant autonomy, thus playing a major role in the legislative process. In many committees the subcommittees go their independent way, jealously guarding their autonomy and prerogatives against other subcommittees and their own committee chairman. Specialization of function and dispersion of power, which once worked to the benefit of the committee chairmen, now work against them.

The Speaker and the majority floor leaders are, of course, the most powerful men in Congress, but their power is not markedly greater than that of many other congressional leaders. . . . The power base of the central leaders has tended to atrophy, caught between the expansion of presidential authority and influence, on the one hand, and the institutionalization of committee authority, on the other.

At times individual central leaders have built up impressive networks of personal influence. These, however, have been individual, not institutional, phenomena. . . .

FUNCTION: THE SHIFT TO OVERSIGHT

The insulation of Congress from external social forces and the dispersion of power within Congress have stimulated significant changes in the functions of Congress. The congressional role in legislation has largely been reduced to delay and amendment; congressional activity in overseeing administration has expanded and diversified. During the nineteenth century Congress frequently took the legislative initiative in dealing with major national problems. Even when the original proposal came from the President, Congress usually played an active and positive role in reshaping the proposal into law. . . . Since 1933, however, the initiative in formulating legislation, in assigning legislative priorities, in arousing support for legislation, and in determining the final content of the legislation enacted has clearly shifted to the executive branch. All three elements of the executive branch — President, administration, and bureaucracy — have gained legislative functions at the expense of Congress. . . .

Congress has conceded not only the initiative in originating legislation but — and perhaps inevitably as the result of losing the initiative — it has also lost the dominant influence it once had in shaping the final content of legislation. . . . The loss of congressional control over the substance of policy is most marked, of course, in the area of national defense and foreign policy. . . . In domestic legislation Congress's influence is undoubtedly greater, but even here its primary impact is on the timing and details of legislation, not on the subjects and content of legislation.

The decline in the legislative role of Congress has been accompanied by an increase in its administrative role. The modern state differs from the liberal state of the eighteenth and nineteenth centuries in terms of the greater control it exercises over society and the increase in the size, functions, and importance of its bureaucracy. Needed in the modern state are means to control, check, supplement, stimulate, and ameliorate this bureaucracy. . . . In the United States, Congress has come to play a major, if not the major, role in this regard. Indeed, many of the innovations in Congress in recent years have strengthened its control over the administrative processes of the executive branch. Congressional committees responded with alacrity to the mandate of the 1946 Reorganization Act that they "exercise continuous watchfulness" over the administration of laws. Congressional investigations of the bureaucracy have multiplied: each Congress during the period between 1950 and 1962 conducted more investigations than were conducted by *all* the Congresses during the nineteenth century. Other mechanisms of committee control, such as the legislative veto and committee clearance of administrative decisions, have been increasingly employed. . . . In discharging this function, congressmen uncover waste and abuse, push particular projects and innovations, highlight inconsistencies, correct injustices, and compel exposition and defense of bureaucratic decisions.

In performing these activities, Congress is acting where it is most competent to act: it is dealing with particulars, not general policies. Unlike legislating, these concerns are perfectly compatible with the current patterns of insulation and dispersion. Committee specialization and committee power enhance rather than detract from the effectiveness of the committees as administrative overseers. In addition, as the great organized interests of society come to be repre-

SAMUEL P. HUNTINGTON   117

sented more directly in the bureaucracy and administration, the role of Congress as representative of individual citizens becomes all the more important. The congressman more often serves their interests by representing them in the administrative process than in the legislative process. As has been recognized many times, the actual work of congressmen, in practice if not in theory, is directed toward mediation between constituents annd government agencies. . . . This appears to be average. In performing these services congressmen are both representing their constituents where they need to be represented and checking upon and ameliorating the impact of the federal bureaucracy. Constituent service and [administrative] oversight are two sides of the same coin. Increasingly divorced from the principal organized social forces of society, Congress has come to play a more and more significant role as spokesman for the interests of unorganized individuals.

ADAPTATION OR REFORM

Insulation has made Congress unwilling to initiate laws. Dispersion has made Congress unable to aggregate individual bills into a coherent legislative program. Constituent service and administrative overseeing have eaten into the time and energy which congressmen give legislative matters. Congress is thus left in its legislative dilemma where the assertion of power is almost equivalent to the obstruction of action. What then are the possibilities for institutional adaptation or institutional reform?

Living with the Dilemma

Conceivably neither adaptation nor reform is necessary. The present distribution of power and functions could continue indefinitely. Instead of escaping from its dilemma, Congress could learn to live with it. . . . If Congress uses its powers to delay and to amend with prudence and circumspection, there is no necessary reason why it should not retain them for the indefinite future. In this case, the legislative process in the national government would continually appear to be on the verge of stalemate and breakdown which never quite materialize. The supporters of Congress would continue to bemoan its decline at the same time that its critics would continue to denounce its obstructionism. The system would work so long as Congress stretched but did not exhaust the patience of the executive branch and public. If Congress, however, did reject a major administration measure, like tax reduction or civil rights, the issue would be joined, the country would be thrown into a constitutional crisis, and the executive branch would mobilize its forces for a showdown over the authority of Congress to veto legislation.

Reform versus Adaptation: Restructuring Power

The resumption by Congress of an active, positive role in the legislative process would require a drastic restructuring of power relationships, including reversal of the tendencies toward insulation, dispersion, and oversight. Fundamental "reforms" would thus be required. To date two general types of proposals have been advanced for the structural reform of Congress. Ironically, however, neither set of proposals is likely, if enacted, to achieve the results which its principal proponents desire. One set of reformers. . . . urge an equalizing of power among congressmen so that a majority of each house can work its will. . . . Measures of democratization, however, would disperse power among still more people, multiply the opportunities for minority veto (by extending them to more minorities), and thus make timely legislative action still more difficult. The "party reformers," . . . on the other hand, place their reliance on presidential leadership and urge the strengthening of the party organization in Congress to insure support by his own party for the President's measures. In actuality, however, the centralization of power within Congress in party committees and leadership bodies would also increase the power of Congress. It would tend to reconstitute Congress as an effective legislative body, deprive the President of his monopoly of the "national interest," and force him to come to terms with the centralized congressional leadership. . . . Instead of strengthening presidential leadership, the proposals of the party reformers would weaken it.

The dispersion of power in Congress has created a situation in which the internal problem of Congress is not dictatorship but oligarchy. The only effective alternative to oligarchy is centralized authority. Oligarchies, however, are unlikely to reform themselves. In most political systems centralized power is a necessary although not sufficient condition for reform and adaptation to environmental change. At present the central leaders of Congress are, with rare exceptions, products of and closely identified with the committee oligarchy. Reform of Congress would depend upon the central leaders' breaking with the oligarchy, mobilizing majorities from younger and less influential congressmen, and employing these majorities to expand and to institutionalize their own power.

SAMUEL P. HUNTINGTON   119

Centralization of power within Congress would also, in some measure, help solve the problem of insulation. Some of Congress's insulation has been defensive in nature, a compensation for its declining role in the legislative process as well as a cause of that decline. Seniority, which is largely responsible for the insulation, is a symptom of more basic institutional needs and fears. Greater authority for the central leaders of Congress would necessarily involve a modification of the seniority system. Conversely, in the absence of strong central leadership, recourse to seniority is virtually inevitable. Election of committee chairmen by the committees themselves, by party caucuses, or by each house would stimulate antagonisms among members and multiply the opportunities for outside forces from the executive branch or from interest groups to influence the proceedings. Selection by seniority is, in effect, selection by heredity: power goes not to the oldest son of the king but to the oldest child of the institution. It protects Congress against divisive and external influences. It does this, however, through a purely arbitrary method which offers no assurance that the distribution of authority in the Congress will bear any relation to the distribution of opinion in the country, in the rest of the government, or within Congress itself. It purchases institutional integrity at a high price in terms of institutional isolation. . . .

Congressional insulation may also be weakened in other ways. The decline in mobility between congressional leadership positions and administration leadership positions has been counterbalanced, in some measure, by the rise of the Senate as a source of Presidents. This is due to several causes. The almost insoluble problems confronting state governments tarnish the glamor and limit the tenure of their governors. The nationalization of communications has helped senators play a role in the news media which is exceeded only by the President. In addition, senators, unlike governors, can usually claim some familiarity with the overriding problems of domestic and foreign policy.

Senatorial insulation may also be weakened to the extent that individuals who have made their reputations on the national scene find it feasible and desirable to run for the Senate. . . .

Adaptation and Reform: Redefining Function

A politically easier, although psychologically more difficult, way out of Congress's dilemma involves not the reversal but the intensification of the recent trends of congressional evolution. Congress is in a legislative dilemma because opinion conceives of it as a legislature. If it gave up the effort to play even a delaying role in the legislative process, it could, quite conceivably, play a much more positive and influential role in the political system as a whole. Representative assemblies have not always been legislatures. They had their origins in medieval times as courts and as councils. An assembly need not legislate to exist and to be important. Indeed, some would argue that assemblies should not legislate. . . . Representative assemblies acquired their legislative functions in the 17th and 18th centuries; there is no necessary reason why liberty, democracy, or constitutional government depends upon their exercising those functions in the twentieth century. Legislation has become much too complex politically to be effectively handled by a representative assembly. The primary work of legislation must be done, and increasingly is being done, by the three "houses" of the executive branch: the bureaucracy, the administration, and the President.

Far more important than the preservation of Congress as a legislative institution is the preservation of Congress as an autonomous institution. When the performance of one function becomes "dysfunctional" to the workings of an institution, the sensible course is to abandon it for other functions. In the 1930s the Supreme Court was forced to surrender its function of disallowing national and state social legislation. Since then it has wielded its veto on federal legislation only rarely and with the greatest of discretion. This loss of power, however, has been more than compensated for by its new role in protecting civil rights and civil liberties against state action. This is a role which neither its supporters nor its opponents in the 1930s would have thought possible. In effect, the Court is using the great conservative weapon of the 1930s to promote the great liberal ends of the 1960s. Such is the way skillful leaders and great institutions adapt to changing circumstances.

The redefinition of Congress's functions away from legislation would involve, in the first instance, a restriction of the power of Congress to delay indefinitely presidential legislative requests. Constitutionally, Congress would still retain its authority to approve legislation. Practically, Congress could . . . bind itself to approve or disapprove urgent Presidential proposals within a time limit of, say, three or six months. If thus compelled to choose openly, Congress, it may be supposed, would almost invariably approve presidential requests. Its veto power would become a reserve power like that of the Supreme Court if not like that of the British Crown. On these "urgent" measures it would perform a legitimizing function rather than a legislative function. At the same time, the requirement that

Congress pass or reject presidential requests would also presumably induce executive leaders to consult with congressional leaders in drafting such legislation. Congress would also, of course, continue to amend and to vote freely on "non-urgent" executive requests.

Explicit acceptance of the idea that legislation was not its primary function would, in large part, simply be recognition of the direction which change has already been taking. It would legitimize and expand the functions of constituent service and administrative oversight which, in practice, already constitute the principal work of most congressmen. Increasingly isolated as it is from the dominant social forces in society, Congress would capitalize on its position as the representative of the unorganized interests of individuals. It would become a proponent of popular demands against the bureaucracy rather than the opponent of popular demands for legislation. It would thus continue to play a major although different role in the constitutional system of checks and balances. . . .

If Congress can generate the leadership and the will to make the drastic changes required to reverse the trends toward insulation, dispersion, and overseeing, it could still resume a positive role in the legislative process. If this is impossible, an alternative path is to abandon the legislative effort and to focus upon those functions of constituent service and bureaucratic control which insulation and dispersion do enable it to play in the national government.

7

The Seniority System

Barbara Hinckley

The seniority system of Congress has been called by Representative Emanuel Celler "as popular a target as sin itself." The defects of the system have been extensively catalogued for more than two decades with each recurring plea for congressional reform. Yet the seniority

Reprinted from *The Seniority System in Congress,* Barbara Hinckley, © 1971, Indiana University Press, Bloomington. Reprinted by permission of the publisher.

system — basically a device for selecting congressional leaders — has not been systematically examined to determine the kinds of leaders it selects, its specific impact on their selection, or the way it functions within the congressional system. Few institutions have been subject to so much attack and so little appraisal. . . .

KEY CHARACTERISTICS
AND HISTORICAL DEVELOPMENT

The seniority system is a device for selecting the leaders of the standing committees. It is a way of ranking members, by party, according to their years of consecutive service on the committee. Parties add or drop members only at the lowest rankings. The seniority system, then, designates the top-ranking member of each party. The senior member whose party gains control of Senate or House becomes the chairman; the senior member from the other party becomes the ranking minority member.

The seniority system is unique to the United States Congress. No other national legislative assemblies, no state legislatures use seniority as the sole criterion for choosing leaders. . . .

The "seniority rule" is a custom, not a formal rule of Congress. The rules simply dictate that House or Senate shall determine committee membership and chairmen. . . . Yet despite its lack of formal status, in recent American history exceptions have been made only in extraordinary circumstances. . . .

The rule is strongly reinforced by the tradition of respect for seniority in Congress. It is part of the "seniority-protégé-apprentice system," to use Richard Fenno's phrase, for minimizing conflict over who shall exercise influence and who shall not. This affects all congressmen, not merely those in line for chairmanships. Respect for seniority affects the choice of committee assignments, assignment of office space, recognition on the floor and in committee hearings, as well as committee chairmanships.

The historical development of the seniority system in House and Senate throws further light on the present situation. To summarize only the highlights, in the nineteenth century seniority was only one of a number of criteria governing the selection of chairmen. The seniority rule grew stronger as legislation became more complex, leading to pressures for specialization and "professionalization"; at the same time House and Senate careers were growing longer. One can find a firm seniority principle at work in the Senate between 1885 and 1895, although it had become a generally accepted rule even before the Civil War. Despite a slower growth in the junior chamber, there was an erratic but continuing increase in the number of times seniority was followed in the selection of House chairmen from 1881 through 1910. The seniority principle gained strength as the Speaker's control over appointments was undermined with the Republicans in 1910 and with the Democrats in 1919, and after the House's unsuccessful experimentation with more centralized leadership seniority emerged as the single automatic criterion for selecting chairmen. . . .

SCOPE AND LIMITS OF THE STUDY

This study, then, attempts a systematic analysis of the seniority system with particular attention to its capacity to select leaders who are representative of their congressional party. It attempts to extricate the effects of the system, particularly the requirement of long congressional service, from other influences affecting the kind of chairmen selected. The strategy for analysis is as follows. First, the four congressional parties are examined to see what kind of action may be expected at a given time in a given congressional party, not simply what may be expected from the Southern Democrats who happened to hold chairmanships in the past two decades. Second, within each party, committee leaders are compared with the full congressional party membership, the "senior" membership, and the "committee seniors," in an attempt to isolate points of influence on the final selection of chairmen.

The main focus of attention is on the chairmen and ranking minority members (the "shadow chairmen") — altogether the 40 Senate Democrats, 51 House Democrats, 46 Senate Republicans, and 71 House Republicans who headed the standing committees of Congress during the twenty-year span from 1947 through 1966. Ranking minority members are sufficiently secure electorally speaking to allow them a place in the comparison. A "senior" will be defined by length of consecutive congressional service, the definition varying with the congressional party. No one definition of seniority can meaningfully be applied across the four congressional parties. A "committee senior" will be defined as a congressional senior who either stayed on at least one committee of initial appointment or, if elected before 1946, stayed on at least one committee he was appointed to following the 1946 Legislative Reorganization Act's revision of the committee structure. . . .

These data provide a reliable description of various patterns of representation in Congress. Members of Congress are classified by their age and congressional seniority; by the electoral "safeness" and regional and demographic characteristics of their constituencies; by their support for party and presidential programs; and by the "liberalism" or "conservatism" of their voting records. These diverse classifications permit considerable flexibility in comparing the four congressional parties and in pinpointing possible different kinds of influence in the selection of chairmen.

The period chosen, 1947–1966, covers almost the full span of the modern committee structure set by the 1946 Reorganization Act. One major part of the investigation is based on patterns formed over the full time span, since we are dealing with a process that occurs over time, and since a shorter time span would rule out analysis of the Senate, whose full membership is subject to change only once in six years. Separate investigations for single Congresses are included where relevant. Brief accounts of patterns existing before 1946 are included for comparative purposes.

Some limits of the study should be made clear at the outset. The concept of "representativeness" raises a host of problems of definition, of evidence, and of interpretation. "Representativeness" is here defined simply as *proportionality,* a correspondence in distribution between two or more groups. The ideal is assumed to be an exact correspondence between the thing represented and the representative as in the "one-man-one-vote" standard for apportionment. Although the group to be represented by the chairmen is not made explicit in the commentaries, it is taken in this study to refer to the members of the congressional party. The assumption is that all that can be expected of an ideally representative group of chairmen is that they reflect the proportions of their congressional party membership in certain important respects. If the Republicans can elect no Southerners to the Senate, Republican Senate chairmen cannot be expected to "represent" the South.

While the salient characteristics selected as a necessary first step in this investigation — such as age, safeness of the seat, region, support of the President, and liberal or conservative voting — may not tell the whole story of a chairman's "representativeness," they are stressed in the traditional criticism and are perceived by congressmen themselves to be important. Note criticisms of the "Southern-biased" seniority system or attempts to "liberalize" the Democratic Steering Committee or Rules Committee.

Neither measurement nor interpretation is easy, however. How much deviation from a one-to-one correspondence can be permitted?

How much is "unrepresentative"? The point is important, for no one measure can be exclusively relied on without creating rigid categories which would distort the results. Further, some of the strongest evidence may come from the kind of situation that is not susceptible to precise measurement at all. . . .

THE IMPACT OF THE SENIORITY SYSTEM

Perhaps the single most important finding of this study is that the effect of the seniority system on the kind of committee chairmen selected by Congress is at most a limited one. Democratic committee chairmen or ranking minority members, taken as a group, reflect with fair accuracy the composition of the Democratic members in Congress, and the Republican leaders even more accurately reflect their party's membership. Thus Southerners have filled more than 50 per cent of the Democratic committee chairs in the past two decades, and Southerners have usually comprised more than 50 per cent of the Democratic membership of the House and Senate.

The effect of the seniority system is limited because its requirement of continuous service in House or Senate can be met by a majority of congressmen. The majority of House and Senate seats are safe for the incumbents. Indeed, there are more congressmen qualified by long congressional service for committee chairs than there are chairs to be filled; hence factors other than congressional seniority, such as original committee assignments, and subsequent reassignments, can and do influence the selection of chairmen.

While the seniority system reflects the distribution of members, the reflection may be subject to some distortion. The congressional seniority requirement does screen out the small number of states and districts which switch party frequently. And at times of majority party upsets, the committee leadership may in the short run, be noticeably unrepresentative of Congress as a whole. Thus the increase of Midwestern strength in the congressional Democratic parties since the late 1950's has only recently begun to show up in the geographical redistribution of chairmanships. Because of this time lag, the seniority links congressional leadership not to the party as it is but to the party as it used to be. Actually, the difference is usually not large because of the stability of voting preferences.

The seniority system also provides a magnifying effect: it gives a bonus to the majority faction in the party, whether majorities are reckoned on a basis of North versus South, rural versus urban, or liberal versus conservative. Critics have stressed that the seniority system benefits those kinds of congressmen who have been in office longest. But in practice, the group with the longest tenure has tended also to be the largest and strongest group. The present analysis has shown that the group, geographical or other, with the largest number of members of Congress nearly always turns out to have the largest number of chairmanships (or ranking minority members). The one exception is the overrepresentation of rural districts among House Democrats.

Since the effects of congressional seniority on the selection of chairmen are marginal at most, the seniority system permits considerable variation in the way chairmanships are distributed. Republicans, but not Democrats, exhibit an extremely close fit between leaders and all members of the congressional party. The degree of unrepresentativeness within the parties also varies. This suggests that factors other than length of congressional service, such as patterns of committee assignments and reassignment, might be studied further for their influence on the selection of chairmen.

On the basis of these findings, it may be interesting to reconsider the traditional criticism of the seniority rule.

Basically, there is no evidence that application of this rule results in regional bias. The geographical distribution of the members of Congress is reproduced in the leaders on a regional and even more clearly on a state-by-state basis. Some advantage in Democratic chairmanship accrues to both the South and the West. Congressional seniority can help to explain Southern, but not Western, overrepresentation.

Democratic members from rural districts are overrepresented by committee chairmen and those from all other districts (not merely metropolitan districts) are underrepresented. But this is not true of Republicans. The rural overrepresentation among Democratic chairmen cannot be explained by the congressional seniority requirement, nor fully explained by rural-urban differences in committee changes. While committee seniority appears to play some part in benefiting the rural congressmen, again the luck or discretion involved in original committee assignments may influence the results.

Nor are small states (by population) overrepresented in the Senate. No systematic misrepresentation of states by population is observable for either party.

As to policy stands, Democratic committee chairmen show some conservative bias, and some bias against support for their party or President; Republicans do not. The Republican committee leaders followed almost exactly the same pattern as all Republican members of Congress in roll-call voting. The leaders were no more conservative than the Republican membership. The bias for conservatism and against party and President is found among Northern as well as Southern Democrats. While these effects are traceable in part to the congressional seniority requirement, all stages in the process of selecting chairmen — congressional seniority, original committee assignments, committee changes — appeared to contribute to the conservative cast of the Democratic chairmen.

THE SENIORITY SYSTEM AND THE CONGRESS

How does the seniority rule affect the operation of Congress? Congress differs from many other organizations in that it does not control the selection of its own members. Members of Congress are elected by the voters. The seniority rule, then, provides a key organizational link between the party system and Congress and between the members of Congress and its leaders. Under the system, leaders are chosen from among the senior members, those who know well the organization's rules and customs. And they are chosen in a way that reinforces the main areas of strength, the established interests in the majority party in Congress. The process reflects fairly accurately the composition of the party in Congress as it has been formed over time. Where it distorts, it does so by giving the majority faction in the congressional party an increased advantage. It thus reinforces traditional areas of party strength. It helps the political parties to organize the Congress in a way that ensures that established *party* interests and established *congressional* interests will not conflict, and in a way that strengthens them both.

The seniority rule rewards age and continuous service in a body that prides itself on its long traditions and continuity. The average age in Congress is the highest in any major Western legislature. The seniority rule builds a time lag into the selection of leaders of a body well known for other time lags. It gives some slight advantage to intraparty groups and factions in Congress that were already strong and usually already dominant, in the membership. Hence, when bills are obstructed in committee, there is often reason to believe that if reported out, they would be obstructed on the floor. Graham Barden, foe of federal aid to education, used every obstructionist device available to a chairman and some improvisations of his own to stop aid bills in committee. After Barden's retirement and the elevation of liberal Adam Clayton Powell to the chairmanship of House Education and Labor, aid to education bills were stopped by the Rules

Committee or defeated on the floor. The seniority system reflects and reinforces a deeper congressional conservatism.

Moreover, it helps to reinforce the decentralized character of leadership in Congress, which protects the diverse interests of the members and strengthens Congress's independence of the Presidency. Power centralized in the hands of party leaders could be more easily controlled from the outside than power dispersed among many centers. The seniority system helps Congress to defend itself against outside control by preventing lines of influence from forming between Congress and the White House. It strengthens the Congress in its well-known desire to be independent of the Presidency. As Roger Davidson and colleagues remark:

> The influence of Congress is enhanced . . . because seniority leaders represent "immovable" objects with which the executive branch must contend. . . . Many members who are troubled over the decline of Congress take comfort from the belief that, however irksome a chairman may seem to his colleagues, he may be even more so to executive-branch officials.

The seniority system clearly strengthens the particularistic, centrifugal tendencies in the Congress. By multiplying centers of power down to the level of committee chairmen, it contributes to the fragmentation of power which frequently makes any attempt to form a governing majority impossible.

Finally, and crucially important in a Congress which is characterized by plural, decentralized leadership and multiple interests, and in which the political process requires the forming and reforming of coalitions, the seniority system offers stability in the distribution of influence. It offers *predictability* concerning who has power in what area. Such predictability would seem a necessary prerequisite for carrying on political business. Thus the seniority system offers something valuable to leaders — both party and committee leaders — and members alike, as well as to interested parties outside Congress.

One of the most intriguing phenomena in the study of political institutions is the way systems perpetuate themselves, create and nourish subsystems that reinforce the parent system. Both leaders and ordinary members of Congress are attached to the seniority system because they profit by the stability, predictability, and maintenance of traditional power alignments which it fosters. And by contributing this stability, predictability, and support of decentralized leadership, the seniority system helps to support the larger congressional system which has produced and is nourishing it.

An exception to these remarks are, of course, the opponents of the system, who constitute a small minority of congressmen, supported by some outsiders. But these opponents seek change. They seek a more centralized distribution of influence in Congress which would be more sensitive to presidential leadership, not tendencies reinforcing decentralization and congressional independence. These opponents clearly seek a different kind of Congress, which, in view of the stable, mutually reinforcing tendencies described above, will not easily be effected. Indeed, the present study suggests that if change *is* to be effected, it will come not through altering the seniority rule or defeating Speakers of the House, but through gradual changes in the membership of Congress, brought about by the voters in elections.

For in one sense, the critics are quite correct. The seniority system is a profoundly conservative institution — not because it biases the kind of leaders selected, but because it reinforces the conservatism already present in Congress.

8

Goodbye to the Inner Club

Nelson W. Polsby

At the opening of the 91st Congress in January [1969], Senator Edward M. Kennedy (D-Mass.) challenged Senator Russell Long (D-La.) for the position of Senate Democratic Whip. Long, chairman of the powerful Finance Committee and a Senator for 20 years, had held the Whip post nearly as long as Kennedy had been in the Senate.

The position is elective, by secret ballot in the caucus of Democratic Senators at the opening of each Congress, and, as readers of newspapers could hardly avoid noticing, Kennedy won handily.

A few days later, Senator Robert P. Griffin (R-Mich.) left the Committee on Labor and Public Welfare for an opening on the relatively low-ranked Committee of Government Operations, and Senator Eugene F. McCarthy (D-Minn.) voluntarily left the prestigi-

From Nelson W. Polsby, "Goodbye to the Inner Club," *The Washington Monthly* (August 1969), pp. 30–34.

ous Foreign Relations Committee to take up a place on the same committee. His public explanation of the move consisted of a Delphic quote from Marshall McLuhan: "Operations is policy." When Senator Lee Metcalf (D-Mont.) removed himself from the Finance Committee that same week, in order to stay on Government Operations, he explained that the Finance Committee had become "just a rubber stamp for the House Ways and Means Committee. No matter what the Finance Committee or the Senate does," he said, "when we come back from conferences with the House we have given in to Wilbur Mills. He runs both committees." In part, Metcalf was protesting a decision of the Democratic Steering Committee, which had forced him to reduce his committee responsibilties from three to two (while permitting more senior Senators to hold three assignments). The Steering Committee also reduced the size of the Appropriations and Foreign Relations Committees in a move widely interpreted as an attempt to staunch the flow of power from senior to junior Senators who might otherwise have been able to go a long way toward outvoting the chairmen of these two committees.

To a generation of followers of the U.S. Senate, these were peculiar goings-on. Whoever heard of Senators leaving important committees to go on unimportant ones — voluntarily? Or committee chairmen worried about uprisings of the peasants? Or an agreeable young man of negligible accomplishments, one eye cocked on the Presidency, knocking off a senior Southern chairman running for a job tending the inner gears of the institution?

If this sort of thing can happen in broad daylight these days on Capitol Hill, there must be something seriously the matter with the ideas that have dominated conversation about the Senate for the last 15 years. For at least since the publication of William S. White's *Citadel: The Story of the U.S. Senate* (1956), the common assumption has been that the Senate has been run by an "inner club" of "Senate types." "The Senate type," White wrote, "is, speaking broadly, a man for whom the Institution is a career in itself, a life in itself, and an end in itself." Although others might belong to the inner club, "At the core of the Inner Club stand the Southerners, who with rare exceptions automatically assume membership almost with the taking of the oath of office."

"The Senate type," White continued, "makes the Institution his home in an almost literal sense, and certainly in a deeply emotional sense. His head swims with its history, its lore. . . . To him, precedent has an almost mystical meaning. . . . His concern for the preservation of Senate tradition is so great that he distrusts anything out of the ordinary. . . . As the Southern members of the Inner Club make the ultimate decisions as to what is proper in point of manner — these decisions then infallibly pervading the Outer Club — so the whole generality of the Inner Club makes the decisions as to what *in general* is proper in the Institution and what *in general* its conclusions should be on high issues."

White conceded, of course, that the Senate had its "public men," who made their way by inflaming or instructing public opinion. But he argued that it was not these grasshoppers but rather the ants of the Inner Club who got their way in the decision-making of the Senate.

Since the publication of *Citadel,* commentators on Senate affairs have routinely alluded to the Inner Club as though to something as palpable as an office building. No senatorial biography — or obituary — is now complete without solemn consideration of whether the subject was in or out. Discussions of senatorial business can hardly compete with dissections of the Inner Club's informal rules, tapping ceremonies, secret handshakes, and other signs and stigmata by which members are recognized. One writer, Clayton Fritchey in *Harper's,* took the further step — in 1967 — of actually naming names.

By far the most zealous promoter of the whole idea was someone whose opinion on the matter must be given some weight. This is the way Joseph S. Clark described a lunch that Majority Leader Lyndon B. Johnson gave for Clark's "class" of freshman Democrats in 1957:

> As we sat down to our steaks at the long table in the office of Felton M. (Skeeter) Johnston, Secretary of the Senate, . . . we found at our places copies of *Citadel: The Story of the U.S. Senate,* autographed "with all good wishes" not only by its author William S. White . . . but by the Majority Leader as well. During the course of the lunch, which was attended by the other recently re-elected leaders, Senator Johnson encouraged us to consider Mr. White's book as a sort of *McGuffey's Reader* from which we could learn much about the "greatest deliberative body in the world" and how to mold ourselves into its way of life.

These days, somehow, the mold seems to have broken. Ten years after the Johnson lunch Clayton Fritchey's *Harper's* article named Russell Long as a "full-fledged member" of the Inner Club. Of Edward M. Kennedy, Fritchey said: "On his own, the amiable Teddy might some day have become at best a fringe member of the Club, but he is associated with Robert F., who like John F., is the archetype of the national kind of politician that the Club regards with suspicion. It believes (correctly) that the Kennedy family has always looked on the Senate as a means to an end, but not an end in itself." And yet, only two years later, Kennedy unseated Long.

POWER IN THE SENATE

Some time ago, in *Congress and the Presidency* (1964), I argued that the notion of an inner club misrepresented the distribution of power in the Senate in several ways. First, it vastly underplayed the extent to which *formal* position — committee chairmanships, great seniority, and official party leadership — conferred power and status on individual Senators almost regardless of their clubability. Second, it understated the extent to which power was spread by specialization and the need for cooperative effort. Fritchey's list bears this out; of the 92 nonfreshman Senators in 1967, he listed 53 as members or provisional members of the Inner Club. This suggests a third point: the existence of an inner club was no doubt in part incorrectly inferred from the existence of its opposite — a small number of mavericks and outsiders. The Senate has always had its share of these, going back at least as far as that superbly cranky diarist, Senator William Plumer of New Hampshire, who served from 1803 to 1807. But the undeniable existence of cranks and mavericks — uncooperative men with whom in a legislative body it is necessary (but impossible) to do business — does not an Inner Club make, except, of course, by simple subtraction.

To dispute that there is an all-powerful Inner Club is not, of course, to claim that no norms govern the behavior of Senators toward one another, or that this body of adults has no status system. Any group whose members interact frequently, and expect to continue to do so on into the indefinite future, usually develops norms. All groups having boundaries, a corporate history, a division of labor, and work to do may be expected to have folkways and an informal social organization. What was opened to question was whether, in the case of the U.S. Senate, the informal social organization was as restrictive or as unlike the formal organization as proponents of the Inner Club Theory believed.

To these observations I would now add a number of others, the most important of which would be to suggest that the role of the Senate in the political system has changed over the last 20 years in such a way as to decrease the impact of norms internal to the Senate on the behavior and the status of Senators.

NELSON W. POLSBY   133

One possible interpretation of what went on at the opening of the current Congress is that the Senate today is far less of a citadel than when William S. White first wrote it. It is a less insular body, and the fortunes of Senators are less and less tied to the smiles and frowns of their elders within the institution.

WHY OPERATIONS?

What is the great attraction, for example, of the Committee on Government Operations? It reports little legislation, has oversight over no specific part of the executive branch. Rather, it takes the operations of government in general as its bailiwick, splits into nearly autonomous sub-committees, and hold investigations. In short, it has the power to publicize — both issues and Senators. It takes less of a Senator's time away from the increasingly absorbing enterprise of cultivating national constituencies on substantive issues.

The claim that lack of ambition for the Presidency distinguishes members of the Inner Club could not have been correct even 20 years ago, considering the Presidential hankerings of such quintessentially old-style Senate types as Robert A. Taft of Ohio, Richard B. Russell of Georgia, and Robert Kerr of Oklahoma. Today, Presidential ambition seems to lurk everywhere in the Senate chamber.

Over the course of these last 20 years, the Senate has obviously improved as a base from which to launch a Presidential bid, while other bases — such as the governorships — have gone into decline. There has certainly, since World War II, been a general movement of political resources and of public attention toward Washington and away from local and regional arenas. Growth of national news media — especially television — has augmented this trend. The impact upon the Presidency of this nationalization of public awareness has been frequently noted. To a lesser extent, this public awareness has spread to all national political institutions. But of these, only the Senate has taken full advantage of its increased visibility. In the House, Sam Rayburn refused to allow televised coverage of any official House function, and Speaker John W. McCormack has continued this rule. The executive branch speaks through the President or an occasional Cabinet member, and the Supreme Court remains aloof. Thus, only Senators have had little constraint placed on their availability for national publicity. Senate committee hearings are frequently televised. Senators turn up often on the televised Washington quiz shows on Sunday afternoons. House members, even the powerful committee chairmen, rarely do. National exposure does not seem to be as important a political resource for them.

As senatorial names — Kefauver, McCarthy, Kennedy, Goldwater — became household words, Governors slipped into relative obscurity. Where once the Governor's control of his state party organization was the single overwhelming resource in deciding who was Presidential timber at a national party convention, television and the nationalization of resources began to erode gubernatorial power. Early Presidential primaries, with their massive national press coverage, made it harder and harder for the leaders of state parties to wait until the national party conventions to bargain and make commitments in Presidential contests. Proliferating federal programs, financed by the lucrative federal income tax, were distributed to the states, in part as senatorial patronage. Governors were not always ignored in this process, but their influence was on the whole much reduced. Meanwhile, at the state level, services lagged and taxes were often inequitable and unproductive. Responsible Governors of both parties have often tried to do something about this problem, but it has led to donnybrooks with state legislatures, great unpopularity, and, on some occasions, electoral defeat.

This decline of Governors and the shift of public attention to national politics and national politicians goes some distance in explaining how the Senate, in its role as an incubator of Presidential hopefuls, seems to have made it increasingly hard for a Senate inner club to monopolize power. As the stakes of the senatorial game have changed, so has the importance of informal norms and folkways internal to the Senate, in the life space of Senators.

TWO ACCIDENTS

In my view, two historical accidents also played a part. The first was the majority leadership of Lyndon B. Johnson. Ambitious for the Presidency, immensely skilled, Johnson sedulously perpetuated the myth of the Inner Club while destroying its substance.

If the idea of the Inner Club was collegiality among the fellowship of the elect, the essence of Johnson's Senate operation was the progressive centralization of power in the hands of the Majority Leader. By the time Johnson left the Senate, after eight years as Majority Leader, the "Inner Club" could command little of the power attributed to it. It had too long been merely a facade for Johnson's own activity — a polite and palatable explanation for the exercise of his own discretion in committee appointments, legislative priorities, and tactics. Under the loose rein of Majority Leader Mike Mansfield, the Senate has again become a much more collegial body whose corporate work has been pretty much determined by Presidential programs and priorities. But it has not recaptured the sense of cohesion, community, and separateness that is supposed to have existed "in the old days." Younger men have come in, and in the last few years liberal majorities on legislation mobilized by the executive departments were by no means uncommon.

The second historical accident that shaped the contemporary Senate was the style of service hit upon by several post-war Senators, but most notably pioneered by the late Arthur Vandenberg of Michigan, and, in the 1950's and 1960's, brought to full flower by Hubert Humphrey. This new style combined the concerns over national issues — formerly attributed mainly to outsiders — with patience and a mastery of internal procedure and strategy. Like Johnson, Humphrey entered the Senate in 1949. Unlike Johnson, Humphrey had a large and varied stock of interests in, and commitments to, public policy. These attuned him to demands from outside the Senate. Through his phenomenally retentive mind, insatiable curiosity, and unquenchable optimism, Humphrey could learn enough to hold his own on any issue. Invariably his name went on the bills that reached out for new national constituencies.

Much earlier than most members of his generation, Humphrey sensed the possibilities in the Senate for long-range political education. He spent the Eisenhower era incubating ideas that, in a better climate, could hatch into programs. In the early 1950's a flood of Humphrey bills (many of them co-sponsored by other liberal Senators) on civil rights, Medicare, housing, aid to farm workers, food stamps, Job Corps, area redevelopment, disarmament, and so on died in the Senate. A little over a decade later, most of them were law, and Humphrey had in the meantime become a political leader of national consequence.

. By reconciling acceptance within the Senate with large public accomplishments, Humphrey set a new style — and it is a style that has grown in popularity among younger Senators as the role of the Senate as an appropriate place in the political system for the incubation of new policy and the building of national constituencies emerges more sharply.

9

Majority Party Leadership in Congress

Randall B. Ripley

. . . In the twentieth century, the primary general task of the majority party leaders is mediating between the President's legislative posture (and, by extension, the legislative posture of the executive branch) and the legislative posture of members of Congress, singly, collectively, and organized in standing committees. . . .

THE TYPES OF MAJORITY

The mediating role played by the majority leaders, regardless of situational details, suggests a way of classifying Congress in terms of the type of majority party leadership that is present. Four categories emerge. Two involve a situation in which the President and the majorities of both houses are of the same party and the President, viewing himself as the single most significant legislative leader, attempts to have Congress enact his legislative preferences into law. Here the majority party leaders in Congress head what can best be termed a presidential majority. At least such a majority is potentially able to work for presidential positions and programs, even if it is not uniformly willing to do so.

A further distinction is necessary. Some presidential majorities appear to be partisan in nature and some appear to have a more bipartisan cast to them. This distinction, although not always sharp, is based on the nature of the habitual appeals for legislative support made by the President and by the leaders of his party in the House and Senate.

If the President and the congressional leaders of his party concentrate almost exclusively on seeking the support of their own party members, then the majority is termed *presidential-partisan*. If, on the other hand, the President and his congressional leaders often seek minority party support for their legislative position, the majority is termed *presidential-bipartisan*. The bipartisan element is usually quite limited. Most Presidents and congressional leaders would prefer to carve majorities out of their own party exclusively, except perhaps on matters involving foreign policy. But in some Congresses it is necessary to appeal to the minority party on certain domestic matters because the majority party is not united enough to win legislative victories by itself. It may also be possible to attract some minority votes, usually because of splits in the minority party.

Type of Majority	Party Control of White House and Congress	Attitude of President toward his Legislative Role	Nature of Appeal for Support
Presidential-bipartisan	Same	Active	Bipartisan
Presidential-partisan	Same	Active	Partisan
Congressional	Same	Passive	Either bipartisan or partisan
Truncated	Mixed	Either active or passive	Either bipartisan or partisan

A third category covers the situation in which the President and the majority of both houses are of the same party but the President is more willing to let Congress set many of its own legislative priorities. The President here still makes recommendations to Congress, but the volume of recommendations is smaller than in the first two situations, the recommendations are less detailed, and presidential activity on their behalf is less vigorous. This situation is designated as a *congressional* majority. The congressional leaders themselves can expect to state legislative preferences that are in part different from, or at least independent of, those of the President and can expect to get action on them. They can also anticipate more control over the details of scheduling and tactics. Obviously, the dividing line between the two presidential categories and the congressional category is somewhat ambiguous. Yet the judgments of both historians and journalists on the legislative role of the various Presidents in the twentieth century seem both clear and consistent enough to make the necessary distinction.

The fourth category is easier to define. It covers situations in which the majority of at least one house of Congress is not of the President's party. The term *truncated* majority seems best to describe this situation. Here the majority in either the Senate or the House is not complete because it does not possess the man who has the potential of being the chief legislator.

The criteria for classifying majorities may be summarized in tabular form [above.]

THE LEADERS AND THE PRESIDENT

Both the President and the leaders have a choice of alternatives in structuring their relations with one another. Presidents can (1) work with the leaders (usually with close consultation and advance planning), (2) avoid the leaders by appealing directly to rank-and-file members or to the public, (3) work against the leaders, or (4) be legislatively inactive.

The leaders can (1) work with the President and use his help (usually with advance planning, (2) remain apathetic to what the President wants or does legislatively, (3) oppose the President, or (4) initiate their own legislation (which usually involves telling a relatively inactive President that his priorities are not as important as theirs).

If the President chooses to work with the leaders and the leaders choose to work with the President and use his help, the basic character of the leader-President relationship is *cooperation*. . . .

If the President elects to work against the leaders and the leaders elect to oppose the President, the basic character of their relationship is *opposition*. . . .

When the President chooses to avoid the leaders or to be inactive and the leaders decide either to remain apathetic to presidential desires or initiate legislation, their relationship is marked by *unsupported initiation*. . . .

There are four possible variations to this relationship of unsupported initiation. First, initiation can come from the President but be ignored by Congress. . . . Second, both the President and the congressional leaders can initiate on the same issues, without ever supporting (or opposing directly) each other's initiatives. . . . This variation is, of course, closely related to a relationship of opposition. Third, both the President and the congressional leaders can be inactive and allow initiation to come from outside the organs of government. . . . Fourth, the congressional leaders can initiate and the President can remain largely inactive. . . .

The general character of the relations between the majority party leaders and the President on domestic matters in the ten representative Congresses is summarized in the table [below].

	Congress	Years	Character of Relations	President
Presidential Majorities	59th	(1905–07)	Mixed (mostly opposition and unsupported initiation; some cooperation)	T. Roosevelt
	88th	(1963–64)	Cooperation	Kennedy; Johnson
	63rd	(1913–15)	Cooperation	Wilson
	73rd	(1933–34)	Cooperation	F. Roosevelt
Congressional Majorities	67th	(1921–23)	Mixed (mostly unsupported initiation; some cooperation and opposition)	Harding
	69th	(1925–27)	Mixed (mostly unsupported initiation; some cooperation and opposition)	Coolidge
	83rd	(1953–54)	Mixed (mostly unsupported initiation and cooperation; some opposition)	Eisenhower
Truncated Majorities	62nd	(1911–13)	Mixed (mostly opposition in House; mostly unsupported initiation in Senate)	Taft
	80th	(1947–48)	Opposition	Truman
	86th	(1959–60)	Opposition	Eisenhower

Leader-President Relations in a Presidential Majority

In four of the Congresses the party leaders in the majority faced a President of their own party who believed in an active legislative leadership role for himself. Both Roosevelts, Wilson, Kennedy, and Johnson all held an activist view of the presidency in the legislative process but varied their approach to Congress in terms of exactly what response they expected. Wilson both assumed and demanded that he have a loyal Democratic party behind him. Franklin Roosevelt assumed his following would be loyal, mainly because the majorities were so large. Theodore Roosevelt, Kennedy, and Johnson all saw the necessity of appealing at least on some occasions for help from the minority party members.

The responses of the congressional leaders of the majority party to the demands, expectations, and attitudes of these Presidents differed. But the differences seem to follow a trend through time: the more recent leaders, faced with an active and demanding legislator in the White House, have come to view themselves almost unquestioningly as lieutenants of their President. Their fellow senators and representatives, the press, and the interested part of the general public have also begun to see the role of loyal lieutenant as the natural one for a congressional leader of the President's party.

Speaker Cannon and Senator Aldrich in the Fifty-ninth Congress were immediate heirs to a tradition that allowed them to view themselves as at least equal to the President when discussing and planning legislative activities. Furthermore. they inherited a tradition of inactive, conservative Republican Presidents and firmly controlling, conservative Republican leaders in Congress. When faced with an active, somewhat progressive Republican President, who was willing to cooperate with them on many matters but willing also to fight them, if they did not cooperate, on a few major matters, Cannon and Aldrich reacted in different ways.

Cannon, on the major bills, usually remained at least passively compliant to what the President wanted, even if he did not actively work for legislative success in all cases. On some matters he did work actively and swiftly to achieve the President's general purposes. Aldrich was a far more haughty and proud personality than Cannon. He was usually opposed to the major Roosevelt initiatives, at least passively. On a few occasions he fought him openly.

In the Sixty-third Congress the Democratic leaders assumed from the outset that they would be the loyal co-workers of President Wilson. Wilson began consulting them long before he was even inaugurated, and they were given a direct and personal stake in the legislative success of Wilson's program, which had also become their own program. When there was disagreement between the party platform and the President, the leaders felt that they still had the freedom and even the duty to stand by the platform and reject the President's violation of it.

In the Seventy-third Congress the economic situation in the country at large, coupled with Franklin Roosevelt's insistence on action to remedy it, mobilized the Democratic leaders in Congress behind him. From the beginning they were loyal and unquestioning lieutenants.

In the Eighty-eighth Congress it was simply assumed, both in the White House and on the Hill, that the congressional leaders of the President's party would be his lieutenants and work for the enactment of his legislative program.

Leader-President Relations
in a Congressional Majority

In three of the Congresses the President neither assumed that he had the central role to play in the legislative process, even though his party controlled Congress, nor did he assume that he had no role to play. All three had views of the proper constitutional balance between the President and Congress that inhibited their legislative activity.

The degree of activity of these three varied, and the response of the congressional leaders also varied. President Harding wanted to return legislative power to Congress but, on a few occasions, had specific legislative demands of his own that he pressed vigorously. The leaders of his party in Congress were quite happy with his desires to return legislative power to them, and they were willing to take that power. They were less happy with the few demands that he did make. When his preferences on scheduling and theirs clashed, they let it be known that they would make such decisions. Harding acquiesced. When Harding became insistent on prompt congressional action with which they disagreed, some of the leaders opposed him publicly. When Harding's preferences and the leaders' preferences coincided, the leaders were quite content to be thought of as staunch administration spokesmen. But they refused to be lieutenants to a President who was captain. Many times Harding was, in effect, their lieutenant.

Coolidge presented even less of a challenge to the congressional supremacy viewpoint of the Republican leaders in Congress. He held the same beliefs they did about the place of Congress and did not trouble them often with specific requests and certainly never with demands. The congressional leaders were delighted with Coolidge's views on presidential-congressional relations, with the sparseness of his legislative requests, and the content of the few requests he did make. The Republican leaders under Coolidge usually appeared to be loyal administration spokesmen, but they clearly felt themselves, not the President, to be in command. On some issues, some of the leaders felt it necessary to be at least partially independent from the administration position.

In the Eighty-third Congress a slightly different situation emerged. President Eisenhower had many of the same beliefs as Harding and Coolidge, but he was also institutionally buttressed by an extensive Executive Office that Harding and Coolidge had not possessed, so that without even trying he seemed to be the Great Initiator. As Richard Neustadt has pointed out:

> We tend to measure Truman's predecessors as though "leadership" consisted of initiatives in economics, or diplomacy, or legislation, or in mass communication. If we measured him and his successors so, they would be leaders automatically. A striking feature of our recent past has been the transformation into routine practice of the actions we once treated as exceptional. A President may retain liberty, in Woodrow Wilson's phrase, "to be as big a man as he can." But nowadays he cannot be as small as he might like.

In his first year in office, Eisenhower was not prepared to take the commanding role as proposer of legislation, and he had to spend a good portion of his time opposing what seemed to him unwise initiatives from Congress. But in the second session of the Eighty-third Congress he prepared and initiated a far-reaching legislative program, although his success with it was limited. He also organized a legislative liaison office in the White House that surpassed the efforts of his predecessors. Thus Eisenhower was far more active and far more important legislatively than Harding or Coolidge, although many of his personal predispositions were similar. But because of the institutional aspects of the presidency he inherited — and because of the institutions that will buttress every President in the foreseeable future — a congressional majority on the pattern of the Sixty-seventh and Sixty-ninth Congresses was impossible. This option has been partially closed to Presidents and majority partly leaders alike.

In the Eighty-third Congress the attitudes of the leaders varied widely. Speaker Martin accepted the legitimacy of the President's legislative leadership role and wanted more direction from the President than Eisenhower was willing to provide. On the other hand, Senate Majority Leader Knowland clashed openly with the administration. That the Majority Leader should be the administration's loyal lieutenant, however, was firmly enough implanted in Knowland's mind that he tried to differentiate between his individual senatorial role and his role as leader.

In the Eighty-third Congress, as the relations between Eisenhower and his congressional leaders developed, it became clear that the congressional leaders could not control Eisenhower as the congressional leaders had controlled Coolidge and Harding. Ways and Means Chairman Reed made the most concerted effort to do so but in the end failed because Eisenhower and the central House leaders united against him.

Congressional majorities have moved closer to presidential majorities in many respects. The thought of autonomous congressional leaders of the President's party is shocking to the contemporary observer of Congress and probably to the congressional leaders themselves, even if not to all of the members of House and Senate. Senate leaders have retained a greater degree of independence in both presidential and congressional majorities than House leaders.

Leader-President Relations
in a Truncated Majority

The majority party leaders in the three truncated majorities all reacted similarly: they cooperated with the President on foreign matters but generally opposed him on domestic matters in such a way as to gain political credit for the next presidential and congressional election. In one sense the majority party leader of a truncated majority has the most freedom of all: he can ignore the President's views about his place as a legislative leader if he can keep his fellow partisans solidly united behind him. He can decide for himself what part of the President's program he will accept or reject. Nevertheless, his actions are circumscribed by the broad necessity of cooperating on foreign policy and making political points on domestic policy. The leader of a truncated majority has great room for maneuver in the tactics of opposition and embarrassment on the domestic front, if his followers are willing to go along with him, but he must necessarily remain partially frustrated by his inability to accomplish much of his own program domestically. The succeeding election must be the vindication and fulfillment of his actions for the preceding two years.

To succeed legislatively with their own program, the leaders of a truncated majority need to command the votes to override the potent weapon of the veto. Only in the Eightieth Congress could the majority party leaders do this with any frequency on major legislation. In the Eighty-sixth they tried and failed, and in the Sixty-second they did not try. To attain success, the leaders also need to be able to appeal to public opinion on their own or at least to have a President who is temporarily ineffective in mobilizing public opinion. In the Eightieth Congress Truman tried to rouse public opinion but had little success. Thus Taft, Martin, and the congressional Republicans had increased chances for success. But in the Eighty-sixth Congress, Eisenhower was quite successful in getting a favorable response from the public to his campaign to keep government spending in check.

Frustrations also seem inevitable for a truncated majority because once the leaders have announced a legislative program, that program immediately becomes split among the various standing committees. Consequently, it is not seen as a whole nor thought of as a single program. The President's program is also split in this way, but he has the advantage of being able to call the program to the attention of the public by periodically submitting lists of "must" legislation and reminding the public of the nature and scope of his program. Subsequent reminders of this nature by congressional leaders are not often made and receive minimum attention even when made.

THE LEADERS AND THE MEMBERS

The Techniques of Leadership

The leaders of both houses in any type of majority have a number of techniques they can employ to gain the support of their members for specific legislative ends. The basic choice the leaders must make is how active and enterprising to be in applying these techniques.

In general, the leaders of a presidential majority are highly active in the use of techniques. They have more definite legislative goals than the leaders of congressional or truncated majorities, and these goals motivate them to act vigorously. The leaders of a truncated majority are somewhat less active. They tend to be motivated to act with some vigor because of their clear political goals of capturing the White House and retaining control of Congress. The leaders of a congressional majority are the least active. They are motivated mainly by their rhetoric that Congress should outshine the President in the legislative process. In practice, however, the motivation of rhetoric proves to be far weaker than the motivation of clear legislative or political goals.

A brief summary of the main techniques open to the leaders of the majority party shows the range of what has been done and suggests the options that face present and future majority party leaders.

First, the most consistently used technique has been personal (including telephone) contact. Regardless of other conditions or type of majority, House and Senate leaders have gone to their members in person or on the phone to ask specific actions of them. They ask not only for favorable roll call votes, but often for other favors, such as voting in committee, speaking on the floor, or being absent from or present on the floor. Only occasionally will a leader stay aloof from his members and not engage in much personal contact. Senator Knowland in the Eighty-third Congress and Senator Lodge in the Sixty-seventh Congress avoided personal contacts with their fellow partisans. But they are exceptions.

Second, the leaders have at times been able to effect changes in the rules, procedures, or practices of the House or Senate. The leaders of presidential majorities have been the most innovative in this regard. In the Sixty-third Congress, for example, the Democratic leaders in the House operated under relatively new procedures of their own shaping. In the Senate they wrote new rules that made the committees reliable from the President's viewpoint. In the Seventy-third Congress, the House leaders made no formal rules changes. But they did make greater use of the Rules Committee resolution as a device for tightly controlling the action on the floor to the benefit of the President's legislative program. In the Eighty-eighth Congress the leaders solidified a gain they had made in the preceding Congress by permanently increasing the size of the Rules Committee to make it a reliable arm of the leadership.

Leaders of congressional majorities attempted no notable changes in rules, practices, or procedures; leaders of truncated majorities were moderately active in using this technique. In the Sixty-second Congress the Democratic House leaders developed new procedures for operating. In the Eightieth Congress, Senate Majority Leader Taft used a new party organ, the Policy Committee, to keep his narrow majority firmly behind him. The Democratic leaders in the Eighty-sixth Congress were less innovative, missing a chance to reform or "stack" the Rules Committee in the House.

Third, virtually all majority party leaders in both houses in all of the Congresses studied sought to have some influence over the assignments to standing committees. This influence ranged from the absolute control of Speaker Cannon in the Fifty-ninth Congress to the spot influence of Speaker McCormack in the Eighty-eighth Congress.

Fourth, the leaders have often encouraged the standing committee contingents from their party to develop unanimous positions before reporting a bill to the floor. In this way, the majority party can resolve potentially disruptive differences of opinion among its own members before exposing itself to the attack of the minority party. Leaders of the three kinds of majority parties have used this technique. It seems to be a fundamental method for assuming some measure of party control over legislation.

A variation and extension of this technique is restricting the real bargaining sessions of conference committees to members of the majority party so that the minority is prevented from exploiting potentially disruptive differences between the two houses. Prevailing standards of fairness to the minority in the Senate and House currently prohibit most uses of this variation in conference. It is still used in standing committees in both houses, although the minority party may protest.

Fifth, a technique that is employed mostly by leaders of presidential and truncated majorities, and little or rarely by leaders of a congressional majority, is taking an official party position to solicit loyal behavior from party members. A statement on the floor, a letter to all members of the party, a statement by a policy or steering committee, or a position adopted in a party caucus can be used to convey the party position.

Sixth, in some presidential majorities the leaders have sought to gain critical support from their members by co-opting a few important members into the leadership in the struggle over specific bills. By choosing with care whom they co-opt, the leaders can probably influence personal friends or ideological comrades of the co-opted man to follow him in supporting the leaders.

Seventh, some leaders, especially in presidential majorities, have sought to channel specific demands from individuals, blocs, groups, or state delegations within their own party so as to gain support for important measures. An effective use of this technique necessitates a sizable effort by the leaders to know the mood of their members. How much they know depends in part on the personal relations of the leaders with the rank-and-file members of their party and in part on the quality of the information-gathering network or machinery that the leaders have.

Leaders of a presidential majority usually have better information than leaders of congressional majorities. For example, Cannon relied heavily on the soundings of his five or six top lieutenants. Senator Aldrich relied on his own contacts with his fellow Republican senators as his primary source of information about their desires. In the Sixty-third Congress Kern in the Senate and Underwood in the House relied a great deal on caucus debate to keep them abreast of the sentiments of the party members.

In the Seventy-third Congress the House leaders used two new organizations — the Steering Committee and the whip organization — as information gatherers. The whip organization proved more reliable and useful. It occupied a prominent place in the Democratic scheme of leadership in the Eighty-eighth Congress.

In the Sixty-seventh and Sixty-ninth Congresses the leaders seemed to have been hampered by an imperfect grasp of the wants of their fellow Republicans. The Senate leaders in both Congresses seemed somewhat removed from their membership, and the Senate often appeared almost leaderless. In the House in the Sixty-seventh Congress Mondell used the clumsy device of the Steering Committee to help him get some picture of the temper of the Republican side of the House. Longworth in the Sixty-ninth Congress discarded the Steering Committee and used three close lieutenants as his additional eyes and ears.

Senate leaders have been more content than the House leaders to let personal relationships determine the extent of their knowledge. House leaders have more often felt the urge and necessity to rely in part on some information-gathering machinery, either formal or informal. Thus when a Senate leader, such as Knowland in the Eighty-third Congress, has cool relationships with many of his members, he is not likely to know much about the mood of the majority party in the Senate. But when a leader such as Johnson in the Eighty-sixth Congress cultivates personal relations, he is likely to have a detailed grasp not only of the mood of the majority party but also of the individuals in it.

Eighth, in some Congresses, particularly presidential majorities, the leaders have used the technique of offering tangible rewards to the loyal and withholding them from the disloyal. These rewards have included federal patronage, buildings, and projects. The leaders have also used electoral aid in the form of money (coming either from a congressional campaign committee or from contributions of individual wealthy contributors close to the leaders) or campaigning by the leaders for individual members in their states or districts.

Ninth, leaders in both houses in the three kinds of majorities have used the technique of controlling at least some of the flow of information to the members on the substance and on the schedule of legislation. By making themselves the principal source of such information, the leaders have sought to enhance their stature in the members' eyes.

Tenth, the leaders of presidential-bipartisan and truncated majorities have made at least minor concessions to, and compromises with, the minority party. Presidential-bipartisan leaders often need minority aid to achieve their ends. Truncated leaders often need minority aid if they want to obtain the President's signature and especially if they want to override a veto.

Finally, the majority party leaders can control the floor proceedings, particularly in the House, to their own benefit. They can schedule matters at the most propitious time (a technique also open to the majority leaders in the Senate), arrange for influential speakers, manage the pattern of voting to their own advantage, and provide for overall control of time and amendments through rules from the House Rules Committee. Leaders of all three kinds of majorities have used this technique.

Patterns of Leadership

The majority party leaders can choose, within the limits of tradition, immediate past practice, and personal ability, how they will organize themselves to effect their legislative preferences. Patterns of leadership are differentiated by the way party leaders most consistently make important decisions about legislative strategy and tactics. . . .

In the Senate a presidential-bipartisan majority tends to follow the Floor Leader as the primary leader. In the House a presidential-bipartisan majority tends to follow the Speaker as the primary leader. Here the majority party turns to centralized leadership in order to afford maximum help to the President who is looking primarily to them for aid.

In the Senate a presidential-partisan majority tends to look to the President (or, secondarily, the Floor Leader) for leadership. In the House a presidential-partisan majority also tends to look to the President (or, secondarily, the Floor Leader) for leadership. The majority members are generally willing to follow almost anywhere the President leads. The appeal of the President to his own fellow partisans is strong enough that he usually does not have to worry about attracting minority party support. Majorities of this mentality often are willing to let the President himself be the chief congressional leader. If they choose one of the other patterns of leadership, they are most likely to fix on highly centralized patterns in which the leaders can be of maximum help to the President.

In the Senate a congressional majority tends to use a collegial group for leadership. In the House a congressional majority tends to use a collegial group or the Speaker for leadership. If the majority party decides to keep a substantial amount of power for itself and tries to reduce the President's legislative role, it will not do so by uniting behind a single strong leader in each house. Rather it usually finds it necessary to share the hoarded power. Ironically, this sharing of power is likely to make the majority party less able to perform quickly and surely the legislative tasks it has set for itself.

Majority parties that want to aid the President of their own party do so by trying to provide strong, centralized, loyal leadership of their own. Majority parties that do not particularly care about following the legislative wishes of a President of their own party attempt to initiate their own legislative product by following a decentralized leadership. They make their task even more difficult than it normally would be, a circumstance suggesting that the majority party in Congress is at its most efficient, even if not always at its happiest, when attempting to work closely with a President of the same party. When the majority party tries to save power for itself and deny it to the President, it becomes less efficiently organized. But less efficient organization may be satisfying in some situations, especially if the legislative goals of the congressional leaders are modest.

In the Senate a truncated majority tends to look to the Floor Leader for leadership. In the House a truncated majority tends to look to the Floor Leader or Speaker for leadership. Here the impact of politics is clearly seen: facing a President of the opposition party motivates the majority party in the House and Senate to look to centralized leadership that can give it at least some campaign material, if not legislation.

THE RESULTS OF LEADERSHIP ACTIVITY

Judged on the basis of the ten Congresses selected for close study, the presidential majorities were the most successful legislatively, the congressional majorities had only moderate success, and the truncated majorities had only slight success. All four of the presidential majority parties could claim legislative success based on their own promises, expectations, and preferences. The three congressional majority parties scored some successes, but they also met a number of defeats. Of the three truncated majorities, only that in the Eightieth Congress had much legislative success, and it was a political failure. The other two truncated majorities could claim only political success.

CHARACTERISTICS OF THE TYPES OF MAJORITY

The foregoing discussion of the relations between types of majorities, leader-President relations, leader-member relations, and legislative success may be summarized in tabular form. . . .

Type of Majority	Character of Leader-President Relations	Degree of Innovation in Use of Techniques	Degree of Centralization in Leadership Pattern		Degree of Legislative Success
			House	Senate	
Presidential	Cooperation	High	High	High	High
Congressional	Mixed (mostly unsupported initiation)	Low	Varied	Low	Low
Truncated	Opposition	Varied	High	High	Low

HOUSE-SENATE DIFFERENCES

In addition to systematic differences between the types of majority, a general difference between the House and the Senate emerges. Regardless of the type of majority in a given Congress, party leadership is likely to be more centralized, organized, effective in producing legislative results, and more meaningful to individual members in the House. Because the Senate is smaller, individual senators are likely to be more visible and more powerful than individual members of the House. Thus the chances that individual senators will willingly submit to, or demand, active party leadership is decreased. Furthermore, because senators serve on a number of committees and subcommittees, they can find a niche for themselves without the aid of the central leaders. In the House each member typically is on only one committee. He can certainly not afford to offend the chairman of that committee. If the chairman is close to the central leaders, he cannot afford to offend the central leaders either. He usually needs their good will for the advancement of his career.

The size of the two bodies has also resulted in firmer leadership control over the scheduling of floor business in the House. A member who offends the Speaker stands a chance of being punished by the Speaker's refusal to schedule his bills for floor action. An aggressive Senate leader has some ability to do this, but typically chooses not to. Instead, most Senate leaders have been content to schedule whatever bills standing committees report.

WHY MAJORITIES DIFFER: CONDITIONS FOR LEGISLATIVE SUCCESS

If the majority in Congress is presidential, chances for legislative success, as defined by the President and the congressional leaders themselves, are far greater than in the other two types of majority. This should not be interpreted to mean that Congress, in order to be productive, has to abdicate its creative legislative powers in favor of the President and the executive branch and merely approve what they propose. Congress and its leaders can be creative in legitimating, amending, and criticizing the proposals of an active President. Some congressional initiation, although probably not by the leaders themselves, can also occur in this setting, although the executive is likely to take or receive credit for it. Experience in this century suggests that active, important legislative leaders in Congress can co-exist successfully with an active, important legislative leader in the White House. The examples of Aldrich and Cannon in the Fifty-ninth Congress and Theodore Roosevelt, Underwood and Kern in the Sixty-third Congress and Wilson, and the Democratic triumvirate in the House in the Eighty-eighth Congress and Johnson underline this point.

Furthermore, some of the least active and effective congressional leaders appeared when some of the least active and effective Presidents were in office, suggesting that congressional leaders do not become "strong" only when there is a "weak" President but rather that legislative weakness in the White House breeds legislative weakness on the Hill. For example, Taft, Harding, Coolidge, and Eisenhower all were willing to let Congress exercise a great deal of power. Yet the Senate in each case responded by naming as its principal leader a man either unwilling or unable to exercise forceful leadership: Gallinger, Lodge, Curtis, and Knowland.

Many complex factors produce a given type of majority party and also determine the level of performance within each type. The data in this [selection] lead to no absolute explanation of why different types of majority leadership emerge or why different results emerge from

Congresses of the same type. However, the data do support four concluding generalizations about conditions for success. The greater the number of conditions that are met, the more likely that a Congress will be legislatively successful.

First, within a presidential majority the larger the majority (especially in the House), the greater are the chances for success. In general, the Sixty-third and Seventy-third Congresses were more uniformly successful than the Fifty-ninth and Eighty-eighth Congresses. They possessed larger majorities in the House.

There has also been some speculation that an extremely large majority disintegrates. Before the Eighty-ninth Congress (1965-66) met (with the Democrats controlling the House 294 to 141 and the Senate 68 to 32) and began to pass important pieces of legislation desired by the President and the House and Senate leaders, many newspapers and magazines predicted disintegration. The Seventy-fifth Congress (1937-38), in which the Democrats had 331 House seats to the Republicans' 89, and 76 Senate seats to the Republicans' 16, was the classic case of a majority supposedly unmanageable because of size. Despite this overwhelming majority and his own personal triumph in the 1936 election, President Franklin Roosevelt suffered a number of major defeats. However, factors other than size of majority explain these defeats. For example, Roosevelt had generally poor liaison with Congress. He had also made many members especially angry at the outset with his court-packing proposal.

If the majority is congressional or truncated, size of majority does not seem to be a key limit on, or spur to, leadership activity and accomplishment.

Second, within all three types a new majority is likely to have more legislative success than an established majority. . . .

New majorities, regardless of type, display more enthusiasm for their legislative task than established majorities. They may be less expert at accomplishing their goals smoothly, but inexperience does not hamper them seriously. A long-standing majority is smooth but more detached and less enthusiastic unless re-energized by dynamic leadership, either from the White House or from within the House or Senate. The Fifty-ninth and Eighty-eighth Congresses, for example, succeeded largely because Presidents Roosevelt and Johnson could either overwhelm or energize the leaders.

The Eighty-ninth Congress was a partial exception to this generalization. Although the Democrats had been in the majority for ten years in both houses, they were still able to cooperate with President

Johnson in 1965 to produce an abundance of important new legislation. But, in a sense, the sweeping Democratic electoral triumph of 1964 produced a majority new in mood and spirit, even if not new to majority status.

Third, in both presidential and congressional majorities the chances of legislative success are enhanced if the President is active in helping the House and Senate leaders plan the detailed tactics of legislative combat. Wilson with the Sixty-third, Roosevelt with the Seventy-third, and Johnson with the Eighty-eighth were more interested in working out details than Roosevelt with the Fifty-ninth and Kennedy with the Eighty-eighth. They also were more successful legislatively. In a congressional majority Eisenhower was more active in planning details than Harding, who in turn was more active than Coolidge. The degree of success again corresponded to the degree of activity.

Fourth, in all three kinds of majority, leaders who are more innovative are more successful. In the Sixty-third Congress Underwood and Kern both experimented heavily with the binding caucus. In the Seventy-third Congress Robinson experimented with a caucus, and the House leaders turned to a new whip organization and a new Steering Committee to aid them. These leaders were more consistently successful than the less innovative (although still active) leaders of the Fifty-ninth and Eighty-eighth Congresses.

In the Eighty-third Congress the House leaders who were aggressive in containing unfriendly committee chairmen helped to produce a higher degree of success than that achieved by the relatively unimaginative leaders of the Sixty-seventh Congress. Longworth in the Sixty-ninth Congress was somewhat innovative, but the lack of Republican leadership in the Senate nullified part of his impact.

In the Eightieth Congress Taft installed a Steering Committee and made it important. In the Sixty-second Congress Underwood in the House began to use the binding caucus. These efforts brought them more success than the majority leaders of the Eighty-sixth Congress, who were willing to use only the techniques they had been using.

No one of these four conditions is sufficient to predict legislative success or failure; if several of the conditions are pointing the same way, the chances of success are greater. The most successful majority party is likely to be a presidential majority with a large majority, newly come to power, with a President actively involved in legislative tactics, and with innovative leaders. The least successful is likely to be a congressional majority with a small majority, concluding a long tenure in the majority, with a hostile President, and with complacent and unimaginative leaders.

10

Congressional Rules

Lewis A. Froman, Jr.

It may now be appropriate . . . to discuss some over-all effects of rules and procedures in Congress and the conditions under which changes in the rules can take place. This will help give us some idea of the possibilities of congressional reform and what is involved when attempts to change the rules are made.

First, few rules and procedures are neutral, politically, in their effects. That is, rules and procedures define the conditions under which the "game" will be played. When there is conflict among the players in the game, as there is in most important pieces of legislation in Congress, the rules and procedures lay out the conditions for the conflict and provide certain processes, sometimes alternative processes, under which proponents and opponents may "make moves" in the "game." But some rules and procedures will favor one side, some rules and procedures will favor the other side. Strategies and tactics will be built around the rules and procedures which will be most favorable to one side or the other.

For example, the cloture rule in the Senate obviously gives an enormous advantage to any intense minority. A filibuster can be used by conservatives, moderates, or liberals, but in each case it is a protection for those who are against change. Filibusters are used, for example, by Southern Democrats against those who wish to regulate race relations. It is also used by Northern Democrats against those who may wish to change certain decisions by the Supreme Court (in the field of state legislative apportionment, for example). Since it is the liberals who are most in favor of change and the conservatives who are least in favor of change, the filibuster rule, in balance, favors conservatives. But in any case it favors those who favor the legislative *status quo*.

The argument favoring retention of the present cloture rule is that although it is all right to have a system of majority rule, it must be tempered with some provision to protect minorities against the majority. Minority rights, in other words, as well as majority rule, must be preserved and protected. Requiring two-thirds to end debate simply means that nothing can be done to the minority unless an extraordinary majority can be formed.

The argument in favor of changing Rule XXII suggests that the majority, when it is ready to act, should be allowed to act. If the majority is not allowed to act, then, in effect, the minority wins. A justification that the minority should win over the majority, and that the filibuster rule allows such an event to happen, promotes a system of minority rule, not majority rule.

The two arguments, then, directly conflict. To help us around the conflict it would be useful to make a distinction between kinds of majorities and minorities. Robert Dahl suggests, for example, that when there is a conflict between an *intense* minority and an *apathetic* majority, it is probably a good idea to let the minority win. If a majority is going to impose an extreme hardship on the minority, then the majority should at least be intense too. The alternative is to allow apathetic majorities to prevail over intense minorities, a practice which may lead to dissatisfaction and instability. The cloture rule does allow minorities to win cases where they are opposed by apathetic majorities.

But let us take the difficult case, an intense minority opposed by an equally intense majority. Who should win in this case? All other things being equal (and in this case intensity is assumed to be roughly equal), democratic principles would prescribe majority rule. To allow the alternative to occur would be to allow a minority to prevail with no other justification than that the minority is "right" and the majority "wrong." The cloture rule does allow intense minorities in opposition to apathetic or intense majorities. . . .

The cloture rule, then, does not distinguish between intense minorities in opposition to apathetic or intense majorities. In each case the minority can win. How, then, can one set up a rule which would allow intense minorities to win over apathetic majorities but not over intense majorities? Establishing a two-thirds rule is not the answer. A two-thirds rule clearly favors the minority in cases where each is equally intense. It would be extremely difficult and impractical to develop, independently, a measure of intensity which would distinguish between apathetic and intense majorities.

We are left, apparently, with the dilemma with which we began. It is probably a good idea for there to be some provision for intense minorities to win over apathetic majorities. But it is not a good idea for intense minorities to prevail over intense majorities. The cloture rule allows intense minorities to win in both cases, and no rule can be provided which, independently, could distinguish between intense and apathetic majorities.

The proponents of majority rule argue, however, that there are other safeguards against apathetic majorities winning over intense minorities. The entire congressional system is so complicated and involves so many steps that *status quo* proponents will always be favorably situated in at least one of these many steps. Then, too, the Senate is not the only legislative body, and Congress is not the only governmental institution. There are the federal courts, the President, administrative agencies, independent regulatory commissions, state and local governments, and special districts which also make public policy. That is, to argue that the Senate, any more than any other institution, needs a rule to prevent a majority from tyrannizing over a minority seems a little far-fetched. Also, in Congress the bargaining process probably favors intense minorities rather than apathetic majorities. It is only when the majority is intense that it might prevail over an intense minority.

It is probably the case, then, that intense minorities are quite adequately protected through other mechanisms. To add to these mechanisms Rule XXII is to increase the likelihood that intense minorities will also prevail over intense majorities. There are some factors which mitigate the effects of the two-thirds cloture rule, but these factors are hardly justification for such a system.

Similarly, rules in the House of Representatives are of significant advantage to those who want to maintain the *status quo*. The requirement of 218 signatures for a discharge petition gives considerable advantage to committees and committee chairmen who stall legislation proposing change. In some cases those who benefit from the *status quo* will be liberals, as, for example, with the so-called Quality Stabilization Bill which would allow national price-fixing by manufacturers whose goods travel in interstate commerce. More often than not, however, this rule works to the advantage of conservatives who are able to prevent liberal legislation from reaching the floor. Two hundred eighteen signatures are very difficult to get, not only because most issues do not have an already formed intense majority to support them, but also because the norm of reciprocity works against its use.

The fact that rules and procedures generally favor those who are resisting change has a number of important implications. One is that those congressmen and senators who wish to change the *status quo* are forced, by the rules, to do a considerable amount of bargaining, not only on the differences which occur among themselves but also with those who favor the *status quo*. The alternative to bargaining will often be defeat, since those who wish to protect the *status quo* are often numerous, intense, and in strategic positions. It is possible, under some conditions, to avoid bargaining with those who favor the *status quo* by invoking special rules and procedures which may by-pass the opposition, but often even some members of the coalition that favor change will desert the coalition on such procedural issues. Again, the factor of reciprocity looms as an important reason why this would be the case.

A second implication of the fact that rules and procedures, generally speaking, favor those who prefer the *status quo* over change, has to do with attempts to change the "rules of the game." Looking at rules and procedures as not being neutral in the congressional contest, proposals to change the rules, in many cases, are attempts to change the ability of certain members, and hence certain interests, to prevail in future contests. In other words, changes in the rules may change the advantage of one group of players over others. In this sense, some rules changes redistribute power. Because this is so, certain proposals to change the rules are the most bitterly fought contests in congressional politics.

Not all rules changes, however, can be considered to be redistributive. Some rules changes simply increase or decrease the alternatives of the players without redistributing power. These kinds of changes are not necessarily easy to pass, but they are easier than rules changes which redistribute power. Rules changes which are regulatory in their effects involve a considerable amount of bargaining, especially compromises among those who feel most directly affected by the new regulations. Such changes take place as a result of changes in the work loads or functions of the members over long periods of time.

Two such regulatory changes . . . occurred in the Senate in 1964. One rule change allowed Senate committees to meet during the morning hour. Previously, committees were not allowed to meet when the Senate was in session except by unanimous consent. Since no important business is usually conducted during the morning hour, and since committee work-loads are increasing, it was felt by a large group of senators that such a change would be desirable.

A second change concerned the question of germaneness of debate. Previously, debate in the Senate did not have to be germane to the pending business. A senator could talk on any topic at any time.

Some members found this to be an inconvenience and proposed that debate be germane for four hours after the close of the morning hour. This figure was cut back to three hours and agreed to.

Although both changes in the Senate rules were fought by a significant minority they were not bitterly fought. This was primarily because a redistribution of power was not involved in either case. These changes were simply regulatory changes producing what some members felt was a more convenient schedule, given their enormous work-loads. It is significant to note, in fact, that the most intense debate took place over Senator Clark's amendments to these two changes in the rules which would have had redistributive consequences. Senator Clark wanted to allow a majority of the Senate, without debate, to allow committees to sit anytime during a Senate session, not just during the morning hour, and he wished to allow a majority of the Senate, again without debate, to be able to require that debate be germane for any period of time. Both of these proposed changes would have allowed majority decisions without debate. For this reason, each proposal would have had some effect on the ability of senators to filibuster, and hence were strongly opposed by Southern Democrats and Republicans, as well as many Northern Democrats. Part of the strategy of a filibuster is to force a halt to all work in the Senate, thereby holding up all bills. This, it is felt, might have the effect of increasing the pressure on those who want to turn to other things. If the strategy works, the bill is withdrawn or, at the minimum, significantly modified along the lines desired by the filibusterers. Allowing committees to meet at any time by a non-debatable majority vote would interfere with this strategy.

Similarly, Senator Clark's proposal to allow the Senate to determine, by a non-debatable majority vote, that all debate must be germane would also interfere with a filibuster, since filibusterers sometimes may want to speak non-germanely. Since both of Clark's proposals were viewed as affecting another very important rule which distributes power in a certain way, both were strongly opposed and both were defeated.

The House of Representatives, on the other hand, has had a number of recent successes in changing rules which significantly redistribute power in favor of the more liberal members. In 1961 the size of the Committee on Rules was changed from 12 to 15 members. In 1965 the House made three rules changes, previously discussed. One rule change provided for a 21-Day Rule, a second rule change allows a majority to send a bill to conference with the Senate rather than requiring a rule from the Committee on Rules, and the third change prevents the objection of a single member demanding an engrossed copy of a bill from delaying a vote on final passage of a bill. In each case the changes in the rules redistributed advantages from the conservatives to the liberals. It is clear, however, that such changes would not have been possible without the extraordinary Democratic majority after the 1964 election and without the help of a small, but crucial, group of Republicans. It is entirely possible, as happened in 1951 after the 1949 adoption of the 21-Day Rule, that a future Congress, not so heavily populated by Northern Democrats, will reverse one or more of these decisions. The rule most likely to be changed is the 21-Day Rule since this is the rule most seriously objected to by the more conservative members of Congress. [The 21-Day Rule was in fact repealed by the Ninetieth Congress.]

IV

EXTERNAL PRESSURES ON CONGRESS

Congressional policy results not only from the wisdom and motivations of its own members but also from the constant interaction of outside actors with Congress. Three classes of these outside forces are particularly important: the members' own constituencies, interest groups, and the executive branch — both the bureaucracy and the presidency.

No one of these forces dominates Congress constantly, and their relative influence varies from time to time and issue to issue. But, in general, routine matters (for example, small alterations in various crop allotments) tend to be decided in accord with agreements reached in close cooperation between key members of Congress (usually senior committee and subcommittee members), key representatives of interest groups, and key bureaucrats. More visible matters (for example, a new program of aid to education) tend to be open to a great measure of presidential influence. Constituency influence is potentially present on many kinds of issues, but in a much more subtle way than is widely understood.

Stokes and Miller demonstrate in their article about constituency influence that voters' knowledge is limited about the identity of their congressman, the policy stands of individual congressmen, the identity of the majority party in Congress, and similar matters. Stokes and Miller conclude that, given the widespread policy ignorance of the voting constituents, the mass electorate has only a very marginal impact on the policy behavior of members. That they have an impact is undoubted — after all every contest has a winner and at least one loser — but their policy effect is limited. Because no readily identifiable stream of policy views flows from the mass population to their congressmen — with the exception of a vocal few — congressmen have a great deal of leeway and freedom in determining what policies they will pursue in Washington.

Dexter reinforces this notion of freedom, suggesting that members are basically free to select the constituents they will listen to and the messages from them that they will hear. Members can generally find a way to obtain additional confirmation of opinions they already hold.

Despite the findings of Stokes and Miller and Dexter, however, the influence of constituents and even local parties cannot be written off entirely. Even though most voters lack information on a broad range of issues, certainly in nearly all districts a few constituents are both well informed on at least a few issues of vital importance to them and also possess resources important to the member — for example, potential campaign contributions, favorable coverage in a newspaper, endorsement in an important local union, and so on. These constituents have an almost automatic claim on a member's time and ear and, in some cases, perhaps on his vote in Congress. Members certainly may have a great deal of freedom but when their influential constituents (which may include some local party leaders) have opinions they are unlikely to ignore these preferences altogether.

Also, despite good social science evidence that suggests congressmen have every reason to feel free and relaxed, in fact some do not feel that way. Indeed, perhaps on the slimmest of objective grounds, at least some members feel under constant pressure from constituents and in constant danger of election defeat — even though they may routinely win over 60 per cent of the vote year after year.

Constituency influence of this sort is perhaps more diluted in the Senate than in the House but is certainly not completely absent. Most senators also are likely to have a few selected voices they hear and listen to. They are also likely to seek some constituent favor assiduously as a hedge against their forays into the world of electoral politics every six years.

Lowi, Surrey, and Wolman and Thomas all discuss interest group activities in different fields operating under different conditions. Agriculture, about which Lowi writes, has almost become an area of self-government that includes both public and private officials (members of the Department of Agriculture, some members of Congress, farm organization representatives) while excluding nearly everyone else, including most of Congress (agriculture committee members and agricultural appropriations subcommittee members are not excluded) and the president and his top advisers. Most of what gets done in agriculture happens quietly and without interference by anyone outside the system itself.

The tax policy-making system also allows room for impact of interest groups and influential individuals seeking relief from some specific provision of the tax code, as Surrey describes. But unlike agriculture, the tax area has no well-established system of self-government that deals with recurring problems; rather, each problem tends to be unique. And, unlike the highly predictable attitudes and stances of the officials involved in agriculture (relevant committee members in Congress and employees of the Department of Agriculture), the attitudes of those involved in tax matters (members of the House Ways and Means Committee and the Senate Finance Committee and Treasury employees) are somewhat less predictable. Also, general tax policy differs significantly depending on which party controls Congress and the executive branch, whereas agriculture policy — despite some party posturing about parity and free enterprise — varies much less.

Wolman and Thomas look at housing and education and ask how a relatively new interest group tries to work with existing institutions and officials. They conclude that the influence of black groups is limited in these fields for many reasons endemic both to the existing patterns of interactions and interests and to the black groups themselves.

The president and the bureaucracy seek to influence congressional policy in four major ways. First, the president personally makes public appeals to Congress for a few high priority items. Too often casual observers of American politics conclude that such public exhortations comprise the main element of presidential participation in legislative policy making, and that legislative success is the inevitable result of vigorous public appeals. Such a view overlooks the many additional functions a president must perform in pursuit of legislative success.

Second, an elaborate set of presidential proposals — subsuming the most visible ones — must be put together and advanced, which is beyond the competence of any individual. The procedures, practices, and interactions of the presidency and bureaucracy that Neustadt describes for the Eisenhower years continue to be used.

Third, specific proposals for authorizing legislation need the attentive and diligent work of the president and his staff. Lyndon Johnson describes one such case of hard work from his perspective as
a former president: his three-year effort to obtain a tax increase in
the closing years of his administration.

Fourth, specific programs that have been approved in principle
also have to be funded. Most often, this is a matter of relatively in-
visible bargaining and negotiations between small bureaucratic units
and congressional appropriations subcommittees. Wildavsky describes some of that interaction.

Party and Constituency

11

Party Government
and the Saliency of Congress

Donald E. Stokes and Warren E. Miller

Any mid-term congressional election raises pointed questions about
party government in America. With the personality of the President
removed from the ballot by at least a coat-tail, the public is free to
pass judgment on the legislative record of the parties. So the civics
texts would have us believe. In fact, however, an off-year election
can be regarded as an assessment of the parties' record in Congress
only if the electorate possesses certain minimal information about
what that record is. The fact of possession needs to be demonstrated,
not assumed, and the low visibility of congressional affairs to many
citizens suggests that the electorate's actual information should be
examined with care.

How much the people know is an important, if somewhat hidden,
problem of the normative theory of representation. Implicitly at least,

From Donald E. Stokes and Warren E. Miller, "Party Government and the Saliency of Congress," *Public Opinion Quarterly,* 26 (Winter 1962), pp. 532–46.

the information the public is thought to have is one of the points on which various classical conceptions of representation divide. Edmund Burke and the liberal philosophers, for example — to say nothing of Hamilton and Jefferson — had very different views about the information the public could get or use in assessing its government. And the periods of flood tide in American democracy, especially the Jacksonian and Progressive eras, have been marked by the most optimistic assumptions as to what the people could or did know about their government. To put the matter another way: any set of representative institutions will work very differently according to the amount and quality of information the electorate has. This is certainly true of the institutional forms we associate with government by responsible parties. A necessary condition of party responsibility to the people is that the public have basic information about the parties and their legislative record. Without it, no institutional devices can make responsibility a fact.

To explore the information possessed by those who play the legislative and constitutent roles in American government, the Survey Research Center of the University of Michigan undertook an interview study of Congressmen and their districts during the mid-term election of Eisenhower's second term. Immediately after the 1958 campaign the Center interviewed a nationwide sample of the electorate, clustered in 116 congressional districts, as well as the incumbent Congressmen and other major-party candidates for the House from the same collection of districts. Through these direct interviews with the persons playing the reciprocal roles of representative government, this research has sought careful evidence about the perceptual ties that bind, or fail to bind, the Congressman to his party and district. We will review some of this evidence here for the light that it throws on the problem of party cohesion and responsibility in Congress.

THE RESPONSIBLE-PARTY MODEL
AND THE AMERICAN CASE

What the conception of government by responsible parties requires of the general public has received much less attention than what it requires of the legislative and electoral parties. The notion of responsibility generally is understood to mean that the parties play a mediating role between the public and its government, making popular control effective by developing rival programs of government action that are presented to the electorate for its choice. The party whose program gains the greater support takes possession of the government and is held accountable to the public in later elections for its success in giving its program effect.

Two assumptions about the role of the public can be extracted from these ideas. First, in a system of party government the electorate's attitude toward the parties is based on what the party programs are and how well the parties have delivered on them. The public, in a word, gives the parties *programmatic* support. And, in view of the importance that legislative action is likely to have in any party program, such support is formed largely out of public reaction to the legislative performance of the parties, especially the party in power.

Second, under a system of party government the voters' response to the local legislative candidates is based on the candidates' identification with party programs. These programs are the substance of their appeals to the constituency, which will act on the basis of its information about the proposals and legislative record of the parties. Since the party programs are of dominant importance, the candidates are deprived of any independent basis of support. They will not be able to build in their home districts an electoral redoubt from which to challenge the leadership of their parties.

How well do these assumptions fit the behavior of the American public as it reaches a choice in the off-year congressional elections? A first glance at the relation of partisan identifications to the vote might give the impression that the mid-term election is a triumph of party government. Popular allegiance to the parties is of immense importance in all our national elections, including those in which a President is chosen, but its potency in the mid-term congressional election is especially pronounced. This fact is plain — even stark — in the entries of Table 1, which break down the vote for Congress in 1958 into its component party elements. The table makes clear, first of all, how astonishingly small a proportion of the mid-term vote is cast by political independents. Repeated electoral studies in the United States have indicated that somewhat fewer than 1 American in 10 thinks of himself as altogether independent of the two parties. But in the off-year race for Congress only about a twentieth part of the vote is cast by independents, owing to their greater drop-out rate when the drama and stakes of the presidential contest are missing.

Table 1 also makes clear how little deviation from party there is among Republicans and Democrats voting in a mid-term year. The role of party identification in the congressional election might still be slight, whatever the size of the party followings, if partisan allegiance

	Party Identification [a]			
	Democratic	*Independent*	*Republican*	*Total*
Voted Democratic	53 [b]	2	6	61
Voted Republican	5	3	31	39
Total	58	5	37	100

[a] The Democratic and Republican party identification groups include all persons who classify themselves as having some degree of party loyalty.

[b] Each entry of the table gives the percentage of the total sample of voters having the specified combination of party identification and vote for the House in 1958.

sat more lightly on the voting act. But almost 9 out of every 10 partisans voting in the off-year race support their parties. Indeed, something like 84 per cent of *all* the votes for the House in 1958 were cast by party identifiers supporting their parties. The remaining 16 per cent is not a trivial fraction of the whole — standing, as it did in this case, for 8 million people, quite enough to make and unmake a good many legislative careers. Nevertheless, the low frequency of deviation from party, together with the low frequency of independent voting, indicates that the meaning of the mid-term vote depends in large part on the nature of party voting.

THE SALIENCY OF THE PARTIES' LEGISLATIVE RECORDS

If American party voting were to fit the responsible-party model it would be *programmatic* voting, that is, the giving of electoral support according to the parties' past or prospective action on programs that consist (mainly) of legislative measures. There is little question that partisan voting is one of the very few things at the bottom of our two-party system; every serious third-party movement in a hundred years has foundered on the reef of traditional Republican and Democratic loyalties. But there is also little question that this voting is largely nonprogrammatic in nature. A growing body of evidence indicates that party loyalties are typically learned early in life, free of ideological or issue content, with the family as the main socializing agency. Certainly the findings of adult interview studies show that such loyalties are extremely long-lived and, summed across the population, give rise to extraordinarily stable distributions. The very persistence of party identification raises suspicion as to whether the country is responding to the parties' current legislative actions when it votes its party loyalties.

That this suspicion is fully warranted in the mid-term election is indicated by several kinds of evidence from this research. To begin with, the electorate's perceptions of the parties betray very little information about current policy issues. . . .

How little awareness of current issues is embodied in the congressional vote also is attested by the reasons people give for voting Republican or Democratic for the House. In view of the capacity of survey respondents to rationalize their acts, direct explanations of behavior should be treated with some reserve. However, rationalization is likely to increase, rather than decrease, the policy content of reasons for voting. It is therefore especially noteworthy how few of the reasons our respondents gave for their House votes in 1958 had any discernible issue content. The proportion that had — about 7 per cent — was less even than the proportion of party-image references touching current issues.

Perhaps the most compelling demonstration of how hazardous it is to interpret party voting as a judgment of the parties' legislative records is furnished by the evidence about the public's knowledge of party control of Congress. When our 1958 sample was asked whether the Democrats or the Republicans had had more Congressmen in Washington during the two preceding years, a third confessed they had no idea, and an additional fifth gave control of the Eighty-fifth Congress to the Republicans. Only 47 per cent correctly attributed control to the Democrats. These figures improve somewhat when nonvoters are excluded. Of those who voted in 1958, a fifth did not know which party had controlled Congress, another fifth thought the Republicans had, and the remainder (61 per cent) correctly gave control to the Democrats. However, when a discount is made for guessing, the proportion of voters who really *knew* which party had controlled the Eighty-fifth Congress probably is still not more than half.

It would be difficult to overstate the significance of these figures for the problem of party government. The information at issue here is not a sophisticated judgment as to what sort of coalition had *effective* control of Congress. It is simply the question of whether the country had a Democratic or a Republican Congress from 1956 to

1958. This elementary fact of political life, which any pundit would take completely for granted as he interpreted the popular vote in terms of party accountability, was unknown to something like half the people who went to the polls in 1958.

It is of equal significance to note that the parties' legislative record was no more salient to those who *deviated* from party than it was to those who voted their traditional party loyalty. It might be plausible to suppose that a floating portion of the electorate gives the parties programmatic support, even though most voters follow their traditional allegiances. If true, this difference would give the responsible-party model some factual basis, whether or not the greater part of the electorate lived in darkness. But such a theory finds very little support in these data. In 1958 neither the issue reasons given for the congressional vote nor the awareness of party control of the Eighty-fifth Congress was any higher among those who voted *against* their party identification than it was among those who voted *for* their party. . . .

Nor do the perceptions of party control of Congress that *are* found supply a key to understanding the congressional vote. Whatever awareness of control the electorate had in 1958 was remarkably unrelated to its support of candidates for the House. . . .

The conclusion to be drawn from all this certainly is not that national political forces are without *any* influence on deviations from party in the mid-term year. Clearly these forces do have an influence. Although the fluctuations of the mid-term party vote, charted over half a century or more, are very much smaller than fluctuations in the presidential vote or of the congressional vote in presidential years, there is *some* variation, and these moderate swings must be attributed to forces that have their focus at the national level. Even in 1958 one party received a larger share of deviating votes than the other. Our main point is rather that the deviations that *do* result from national forces are not in the main produced by the parties' legislative records and that, in any case, the proportion of deviating votes that can be attributed to national politics is likely to be a small part of the total votes cast by persons deviating from party in a mid-term year. This was specifically true in 1958.

If the motives for deviations from party are not to be found primarily at the national level, the search moves naturally to the local congressional campaign. A third possibility — that deviations are by-products of state-wide races — can be discounted with some confidence. Despite the popular lore on the subject, evidence both from interview studies and from aggregate election statistics can be used to show that the influence of contests for Governor and Senator on the outcome of House races is slight in mid-term elections, although these contests can have an immense influence on turnout for the House. In our 1958 sample, a majority of those who deviated from party in voting for the House *failed* to deviate also at the state level; more often than not, what had moved them into the other party's column at the House level was dissociated from the contests for Governor or Senator in which they voted. Moreover, the fact that an elector deviates from his party in voting both for the House and some office contested on a state-wide basis is not conclusive evidence that the state race has influenced his choice for the House, rather than the other way around. When the possibility of *reverse* coat-tail effects is allowed for, the reasons for believing that the state-wide race is a potent force on the House vote seem faint indeed. As we search for the motives for deviation from party, analysis of the local congressional race pays greater dividends.

THE SALIENCY
OF CONGRESSIONAL CANDIDATES

By the standards of the civics text, what the public knows about the candidates for Congress is as meager as what it knows about the parties' legislative records. Of the people who lived in districts where the House seat was contested in 1958, 59 per cent — well over half — said that they had neither read nor heard anything about either candidate for Congress, and less than 1 in 5 felt that they knew something about both candidates. What is more, these remarkable proportions are only marginally improved by excluding nonvoters from the calculations. Of people who went to the polls and cast a vote between rival House candidates in 1958, fully 46 per cent conceded that they did so without having read or heard anything about either man. What the other half *had* read or heard is illuminating; we will deal with its policy content presently. Many of our respondents said they knew something about the people contesting the House seat on the basis of very slender information indeed.

The incumbent candidate is by far the better known. In districts where an incumbent was opposed for re-election in 1958, 39 per cent of our respondents knew something about the Congressman, whereas only 20 per cent said they knew anything at all about his nonincumbent opponent. The incumbent's advantage of repeated exposure to the electorate is plain enough. In fact, owing to the greater seniority and longer exposure of Congressmen from safe districts, the public's awareness of incumbents who were unopposed for re-election in 1958 was as great as its awareness of incumbents who had had to conduct an election campaign that year.

The saliency of a candidate is of critical importance if he is to attract support from the opposite party. However little the public may know of those seeking office, any information at all about the rival party's candidate creates the possibility of a choice deviating from party. That such a choice occurs with some frequency is shown by the entries of Table 2, whose columns separate party identifiers in contested districts in 1958 according to whether they were aware of both candidates, the candidate of their own party or the other party only, or neither candidate. The condition of no information leads to fairly unrelieved party-line voting, and so to an even greater degree does the condition of information only about the candidate of the voter's own party. But if partisan voters know something about the opposition's man, substantial deviations from party appear. In fact, if such voters know *only* the opposition candidate, almost half can be induced to cast a vote contrary to their party identification. In the main, recognition carries a positive valence; to be perceived at all is to be perceived favorably. However, some *negative* perceptions are found in our interviews, and when these are taken into account the explanation of deviation from party becomes surer still. For example, if we return to Table 2 and select from the third column only the voters who perceived the candidate of the other party *favorably,* a clear majority is found to have deviated from party al-

Table 2

**Percentage Voting for Own Party Candidate
and Other Party Candidate for House in 1958,
by Saliency of Candidates in Contested Districts**

	Voter Was Aware of			
Voted for Candidate	*Both Candidates (N = 196)*	*Own Party Candidate Only (N = 166)*	*Other Party Candidate Only (N = 68)*	*Neither Candidate (N = 368)*
Of own party	83	98	60	92
Of other party	17	2	40	8
Total	100	100	100	100

legiance in casting their votes. And if we select from the first column only the handful of voters who perceived the candidate of their own party *negatively* and of the opposite party *positively,* almost three-quarters are found to have deviated from their party loyalty in voting for the House.

What our constituent interviews show about the increment of support that accrues to the salient candidate is closely aligned to what the candidates themselves see as the roots of their electoral strength. Our interviews with incumbent and nonincumbent candidates seeking election to the House explored at length their understanding of factors aiding — or damaging — their electoral appeal. In particular, these interviews probed the candidates' assessment of four possible influences on the result: traditional party loyalties, national issues, state and local contests, and the candidates' own record and personal standing in the district. Caution is in order in dealing with answers to questions that touch the respondent's self-image as closely as these. Specifically, we may expect some overstatement of the candidate's own importance, particularly from the victors, and we may expect, too, that too large a discount will be applied to party allegiance, since this "inert" factor, having little to do with increments of strength, is so easily taken for granted.

After these allowances are made, it is still impressive how heavy a weight the incumbent assigns his personal record and standing. The Congressman's ranking of this and the other factors in the election is shown in Table 3. As the entries of the table indicate, more

Table 3

**Relative Importance of Factors in Re-election
as Seen by Incumbent Candidates in 1958 (in percentages)**

Perceived as	Personal Record and Standing	National Issues	Traditional Party Loyalties	State and Local Races
Very important	57	26	25	14
Quite important	28	20	21	19
Somewhat important	9	20	24	27
Not very important	3	27	18	19
Not important at all	3	7	12	21
	100	100	100	100

than four-fifths of the incumbents re-elected in 1958 felt that the niche they had carved out in the awareness of their constituents had substantial impact on the race, a proportion that exceeds by half the percentage who gave as much weight to any of the three other factors. This difference is more than sheer puffing in the interview situation, and the perceptual facts it reveals deserve close attention. Among the forces the Representative feels may enhance his strength at the polls, he gives his personal standing with the district front rank.

In view of the way the saliency of candidates can move the electorate across party lines, great stress should be laid on the fact that the public sees individual candidates for Congress in terms of party programs scarcely at all. Our constituent interviews indicate that the popular image of the Congressman is almost barren of policy content. . . . By the most reasonable count, references to current legislative issues comprised not more than a thirtieth part of what the constituents had to say about their Congressmen. . . .

CONCLUSION

What the public knows about the legislative records of the parties and of individual congressional candidates is a principal reason for the departure of American practice from an idealized conception of party government. On the surface the legislative elections occurring in the middle of the President's term appear to be dominated by two national parties asking public support for their alternative programs. Certainly the electorate whose votes they seek responds to individual legislative candidates overwhelmingly on the basis of their party labels. Despite our kaleidoscopic electoral laws, the candidate's party is the one piece of information every voter is guaranteed. For many, it is the only information they ever get.

However, the legislative events that follow these elections diverge widely from the responsible-party model. The candidates who have presented themselves to the country under two party symbols immediately break ranks. The legislative parties speak not as two voices but as a cacophony of blocs and individuals fulfilling their own definitions of the public good. Party cohesion by no means vanishes, but it is deeply eroded by the pressures external to party to which the Congressman is subject.

The public's information about the legislative record of the parties and of Members of Congress goes far toward reconciling these seemingly contradictory facts. In the congressional election, to be sure, the country votes overwhelmingly for party symbols, but the symbols have limited meaning in terms of legislative policy. The eddies and cross-currents in Congress do not interrupt a flow of legislation that the public expects but fails to see. The electorate sees very little altogether of what goes on in the national legislature. Few judgments of legislative performance are associated with the parties, and much of the public is unaware even of which party has control of Congress. As a result, the absence of party discipline or legislative results is unlikely to bring down electoral sanctions on the ineffective party or the errant Congressman.

What the public's response to the parties lacks in programmatic support is not made up by its response to local congressional candidates. Although perceptions of individual candidates account for most of the votes cast by partisans against their parties, these perceptions are almost untouched by information about the policy stands of the men contesting the House seat. The increment of strength that some candidates, especially incumbents, acquire by being known to their constituents is almost entirely free of policy content. Were such content present, the Congressman's solidarity with his legislative party would by no means be assured. If the local constituency possessed far greater resources of information than it has, it might use the ballot to pry the Congressman away from his party quite as well as to unite him with it. Yet the fact is that, by plying his campaigning and servicing arts over the years, the Congressman is able to develop electoral strength that is almost totally dissociated from what his party wants in Congress and what he himself has done about it. The relevance of all this to the problem of cohesion and responsibility in the legislative party can scarcely be doubted.

The description of party irresponsibility in America should not be overdrawn. The American system *has* elements of party accountability to the public, although the issues on which an accounting is given are relatively few and the accounting is more often rendered by those who hold or seek the Presidency than by the parties' congressional delegations. Especially on the broad problem of government action to secure social and economic welfare it can be argued that the parties have real differences and that these have penetrated the party images to which the electorate responds at the polls.

Nevertheless, American practice does diverge widely from the model of party government, and the factors underlying the departure deserve close analysis. An implication of the analysis reported here is that the public's contribution to party irregularity in Congress is not so much a matter of encouraging or requiring its Representatives to deviate from their parties as it is of the public having so little information that the irregularity of Congressmen and the ineffectiveness of the congressional parties have scant impact at the polls. Many of those who have commented on the lack of party discipline in Congress have assumed that the Congressman votes against his party because he is forced to by the demands of one of several hundred constituencies of a superlatively heterogeneous nation. In some cases, the Representative may subvert the proposals of his party because his constituency demands it. But a more reasonable interpretation over a broader range of issues is that the Congressman fails to see these proposals as part of a program on which the party — and he himself — will be judged at the polls, because he knows the constituency isn't looking.

12

The Representative and His District

Lewis A. Dexter

We talk frequently of a Representative or Senator "representing" or "failing to represent" his constituents. This is shorthand. The fact is the congressman represents his image of the district or of his constituents (or fails to represent his, or our, image of them). How does he get this image? Where does it come from?

On numerous important policy matters, he hears nothing from his constituency. But whether he hears anything on an issue, what he hears, whom he hears from, or how he interprets what he hears all vary depending upon the kind of person he is, the kind of associations he has had and has in the constituency and in Washington, the public image of his interests and concerns, and the background information or misinformation which he possesses. . . .

From Lewis A. Dexter, "The Representative and His District," *Human Organisation*, 16:1. Reprinted by permission of the author as copyright holder. In Lewis A. Dexter, *Sociology and Politics of Congress* (Chicago: Rand McNally, 1970), the article is revised and incorporated in a larger discussion of attention in politics.

A good many congressmen believe that their districts feel very strongly on this, or the other issue, and that they are constrained therefore to vote a certain way. The more sophisticated realize, of course, that legislative procedures and processes are so complex that it is more often than not possible to go through the motions of conforming to such views without helping to enact them, when they believe the public preference to be wrong. On most issues, out of a desire to serve the district or from indifference, many congressmen do go along with any view which they believe "the district" holds strongly. When the chips are down, and they have to declare themselves, some will vote against their convictions and for their constituents' (presumed) preferences.

This situation has led to a series of classical utterances on the moral problem of the representative: *Should he sacrifice his judgment to his constituents' inclinations as he conceives them or not?* It would be more accurate to emphasize the ways in which representatives' beliefs about constituent preference are functions of the channels of communication and the special processes of transaction between constituents and representatives rather than of anything else.

If this is in fact so, more students of representation and representatives would concur with Congressman Veteran's interpretation of the representative-constituent picture. The latter has for years been at the center of the legislative issues which provoke the most comment by critics of "pressure," and he told me early in my study of reciprocal trade:

> You know I am sure you will find out a congressman can do pretty much what he decides to do and he doesn't have to bother too much about criticism. I've seen plenty of cases since I've been up here where a guy will hold one economic or political position and get along all right; and then he'll die or resign and a guy comes in who holds quite a different economic or political position and he gets along all right too. That's the fact of the matter.

The first difference between some congressmen and others is how (consciously or unconsciously) they define their responsibilities.

Many of the congressmen interviewed about both tariff and defense matters referred to a personal conception of what they owe their job, of what in some circles would be called "professional obligation." A few made explicit and many apparently hold implicit theories of representation. These theories of representation were not, except for a few instances, so far as I could tell, directly derived from philosophical or academic sources. They resulted from the experiences of men facing the actual moral complexities of a job.

Some members expressed themselves in terms of their obligation to select the right course, regardless of the views of their constituents. For instance, Congressman Stubborn has for a good many years represented a district which (according to interviews with business interests in the district and from an economic analysis of its industrial situation) is inclined to favor the reciprocal trade program. Nevertheless he says:

> Oh, knowing my stubborn characteristics, no one ever thinks he can change me, you know . . . some of my people say, "You may not agree with this man, 'Stubborn,' but you know where he stands."

Mr. Stubbborn agreed that if fate were to select as his successor a Clarence Randall type "free trader," such a man would be able to vote for a reciprocal trade program without much difficulty, but Stubborn interrupted an effort to probe this point further by declaring:

> That's because they (my constituents) do not really understand the matter. During the twenty-one years reciprocal trade has been in effect, it has had . . . [and he named various alleged or actual consequences which he regards as evil] . . . There isn't any use trying to change me!

Congressman Emphatic on the other hand voted the same way as Mr. Stubborn on the Reciprocal Trade Extension Act of 1955 because of a quite different definition of his responsibility. He said:

> My first duty is to get reelected. I'm here to represent my district. . . . This is part of my actual belief as to the function of a congressman. . . . What is good for the majority of districts is good for the country. What snarls up the system is these so-called statesmen–congressmen who vote for what they think is the country's interest . . . let the Senators do that. . . . They're paid to be statesmen; we [members of the House] aren't. (This was said sarcastically, but without humorous intent.)

Mr. Leader, as strong a supporter of reciprocal trade as Mr. Stubborn is an opponent of it, comes fairly close to Mr. Stubborn in his attitude towards constituent opinion. Said Leader:

> You're not identifying me on this of course? It's strictly confidential? Always bear in mind there are those in Congress who lead their districts and those who are led by them. . . . It makes a lot of difference. . . . The "ruanga" growers of my district never opposed me

on reciprocal trade. . . . The answer is government stockpiling for them. . . . I think I have convinced these men that a program of high tariffs would not assist them and I think my viewpoint has gained general acceptance from them.

Several times he spoke of himself as having "straightened out" people who had seen the matter "wrongly." . . .

Mr. Fourth represents a district in which there is vociferous anti-reciprocal trade sentiment. This district also has strong economic reasons for supporting reciprocal trade and a particularly influential number of intellectuals predisposed toward reciprocal trade. Mr. Fourth showed how a portion of the district can influence a man when he said:

My impulses when I came down here were in favor of trade not aid, until I started to hear all sorts of things from my district. . . . So, actually, when you stack all these things together, well you're in favor of trade not aid, but, goodness, there comes a time . . . if trade means wholesale layoffs in your district. . . . I've got any number of letters against it . . . carpets, imported rugs . . . there've been around 300 layoffs in a local bicycle plant . . . textiles . . . chemicals . . . electrical equipment . . . glass salesmen. It's difficult to get figures. I assume the Randall Commission report has them. . . . I haven't had time to read it. I don't know. . . . I assume that the people I hear from exaggerate the seriousness of the situation but still that it is serious.

Mr. Fourth ultimately voted against reciprocal trade on the key votes; the decisive factor appears to have been his unwillingness to separate himself from several members from his state, also of junior status, who were definite in their opposition to reciprocal trade. Mr. Fourth, according to his colleagues, was wavering as late as two hours before the vote. Had the Chairman of his state delegation (who strongly supported reciprocal trade) personally requested his support, he might well have voted the other way. But he was obviously uncertain, *on the reciprocal trade issue,* whether to adopt the role of servant of his district (as he conceived its desires) or to think in terms of the ideology, implied by the phrase "trade not aid." How he would vote was therefore completely unpredictable. Had he stumbled into any one of three congressmen with strong pro-reciprocal trade views in the lobby or the corridors just before the vote, he might have voted the other way.

Congressman Fourth's vote was unpredictable because on this particular issue he does not have a clear conception of what his obligations are. On some issues — flood control or taxes affecting the major agricultural product of the district — one can predict that he would see his responsibility as being almost exclusively to the district. On others — particularly those under consideration by the very important subcommittee of which he is a member — he would be strongly inclined to emphasize national interest in some form as against district concern.

Congressmen tend to see their obligations as being either to the nation or to their constituency — other equally possible obligations are seemingly not considered.

Obligation seemed to be conceived as national interest versus district interest (district interest was often, as in the case of Mr. Emphatic, related to reelection and therefore to self-interest). No congressman interviewed indicated any feeling of moral obligation to our allies or to any other country, although our allies are regarded instrumentally as means. This is contrary to a theory sometimes expressed that Americans tend to adopt some favorite foreign country as "theirs." Also, reference to representing a region (the South, the West, New England) was very slight. . . .

A congressman's conception of his district confirms itself, to a considerable extent, and may constitute a sort of self-fulfilling prophecy.

Early in my study of reciprocal trade, Congressman Veteran told me:

> You know I am sure you will find out a congressman can do pretty much what he decides to do and he doesn't have to bother much about criticism.

Within the limits of the morally and sociologically conceivable (no congressman from Alabama in 1942 could have advocated integration for instance!), a congressman has a very wide range of choices on any given issue, *so far as his constituency is concerned!* His relationships in the House or Senate and with party leadership, of course, limit these choices severely. It is a fact, however, that there is no district viewpoint as such to be represented on the overwhelming majority of issues. A few will care one way and a few the other, but the issue will be insignificant or unknown to the great majority. Indeed, in many districts, only a fraction of the voters know the name of their congressman, let alone how he voted on a particular issue.

A congressman of my acquaintance took about 100 letters which he received on a particular issue and checked the registration of the writers. He found that almost three-quarters of them were not registered in his district. What difference then would their views make with respect to his prospects for reelection? Mr. Emphatic who insisted that he was representing his district's desires, was led nevertheless, by my questions, to admit that more than likely none of the workers presumably represented by him actually knew how he had voted. . . .

Actually, most of the letters Mr. Emphatic received and most of the comments he heard originated in three large plants in the district and they represented less than 7% of the voters of the district. These plants are organized by national unions which, ironically enough, in chalking up Mr. Emphatic's score in 1956, were inclined to regard his vote against reciprocal trade as an anti-labor vote. Fortunately for him, his stand on other matters and his personal contacts offset this factor. Of the groups in the district, only members of the League of Women Voters wrote to him in favor of reciprocal trade. "They aren't," he averred, "God knows, a potent political force; and all their letters are damn stilted, right out of the same handbook." Actually, however, it was likely that the League members would remember in 1956, and perhaps again in 1958, how he voted. And, because of the "racial" and academic composition of the district, League members may have some influence outside their own membership. It would have been perfectly possible for Mr. Emphatic to take the reverse position favoring reciprocal trade and still to regard himself as representing his district — particularly since the area also has a strong port interest. . . .

A congressman has great difficulty in deciding what the viewpoint of the district is even on such an issue as reciprocal trade. Most persons with an interest or belief in the tariff will have interest or beliefs in other issues as well. Thus, the most effective representation of their overall interests may necessitate concessions on some matters, in order to get along with party leadership, colleagues, or prominent committee members in Congress. "Joe Martin and Charlie Halleck in their heart of hearts," said a prominent Republican, "certainly go along with us, not with the White House on this; and they can swing twenty-five votes, at least, anytime they want; we lost by less than twenty-five votes, so they beat us." Martin is the Republican leader; Halleck is his likely successor as Republican leader or Speaker when he steps down. Is a congressman doing a better job of representing his district when he keeps in the good graces of such powerful men (and thereby helps to get a bridge or a new post office or a dam for his district) or when he opposes them on an issue, the details of which no one will remember six months later? The Republican who told me this is one of the most persistent enemies of reciprocal trade in the party and he is probably the most effective in a quiet way. He is opposed to reciprocal trade in part because of its "harmful" effect on his district. However, he cheerfully admitted, "It wouldn't make any difference what my congressman does on this matter," insofar as his re-election is concerned. Afterwards he qualified this by saying that perhaps the incumbent ought not stick his neck out strongly *for* reciprocal trade, but there is no call for activity of any kind.

A congressman hears most often from those who agree with him.

A congressman's relationships with his district tend to be maintained through a small group whom he knew before he was elected or through a group who have since then worked closely with him. Generally speaking, the views of those whom he knew prior to his election tend to be more like his than do the views of the "average" voter. It is a well-known fact that we tend to be like the people with whom we associate and vice versa. Also, most of the people who have worked closely with the congressman since his election — because he is a congressman — have a particular axe to grind. They will naturally tend therefore to stress agreement with him on issues about which they are not concerned — just as salesmen typically do not disagree with their customers on politics. For several years, I wondered about the unfavorable references congressmen frequently made to the League of Women Voters and several times to delegations from labor unions. Ultimately, it occurred to me that these two groups are probably the only ones which seriously, on a face-to-face basis, year after year, go over with a congressman the issues on which they disagree with him. Because their efforts cannot be entirely discounted as "politics," they make congressmen uncomfortable. . . .

Some men automatically interpret what they hear to support their own viewpoints.

Mr. First of New Hungary does not think he hears much about foreign imports. Mr. Second, coming from the same sort of district in the same city, says:

> It's either the first or second most important issue with me. Unemployment is the other. And, of course, they're really the same thing.

The last sentence is the clue to why Mr. Second hears so much more than Mr. First about foreign imports. When Mr. First hears about unemployment, he hears just about the invidious differential effect which accelerated amortization and certain other tax provisions have had on industry in the area. In fact, when I talked to him about the tariff, he advised me that I really ought to study accelerated amortization. Mr. Second, however, interprets almost any statement about unemployment as a plea for relief from foreign imports. Sometimes it is, but sometimes it isn't. So, seeing the same men and hearing the same things said, Mr. Second will "hear" about tariff matters. Mr. First will not. (Mr. Third, their colleague from an adjoining district, is vitally interested in wilderness preservation, hunting, and fishing. He sees many of the same men, but they are likely to talk to him about his interests, and if they do talk to him about unemployment, he is less likely to draw any special conclusions from the talk.) . . .

In more general terms, what congressmen hear and how they interpret what they hear depends on who they are.

Conventional discussion of the relationship between congressmen and constituents assumes that the kind of man the congressman is does not influence what he hears from the district and that the question is whether he follows or contravenes district sentiment. The notion of the congressman representing "the" district at least needs restatement *in terms of a particular congressman* who represents what he hears from the district as he interprets it. And his interpretation results from his being the particular kind of person he is and is reputed to be. . . .

Pressure is how you see it.

"Pressure" and "pressure politics" are regarded by most "sophisticated" people today as "explaining" a great deal that happens. But it was frequently impossible to find any admission of or apparently any awareness of "pressures." That was not because shrewd and worldly politicians were concealing what really goes on from this naive and innocent interviewer and his naive and innocent colleagues.

The reason is explained by Senator Service's assistant:

> There are very few people actually pressuring us, even if you count all we hear about all issues. Seriously, the sense of being pressured is a matter of reaction. Other people who get no more mail than we do in this office would say, "See how much pressure is on me." We don't feel it. . . . Sure, you get mail. It's just that so-and-so makes more 'phone calls than somebody else. The result is purely physical. It isn't a representation of what or how or when people are going to vote in elections. My personal opinion is that members of most organizations make up their minds on what they read in the papers without reference to organizations.

With this theory of voting behavior, Senator Service's assistant naturally will not be too much worried by a good deal of effort to get him or his boss to change politics — he simply will not regard it as pressure.

Congressman Widesight amusingly illustrated the point made by Service's assistant. Mr. Widesight has moods when he reaches way out into left field looking for things to worry about, things which might possibly defeat him. One day, discussing reciprocal trade, he said that things were very bad indeed. His reason was that he was getting "so much" mail against it. "I, whom they never used to bother at all." When I checked with his secretary later, I found he couldn't possibly have received more than 50 letters (representing glass, electrical equipment, and 2 or 3 bicycle interests) opposing reciprocal trade. This was only a fraction of the mail Senator Service receives on the same matter. It was also a fraction of what Congressman Widesight himself has several times heard on other matters such as postal pay increases. However, Widesight is accustomed to communications on that issue and he wasn't accustomed to them on the reciprocal trade issue. . . .

Even where there is a considerable amount of what the outsider would consider pressure, the point made by Senator Service's assistant is entirely valid. What you call pressure . . . or what you feel to be pressure . . . depends on how thick your skin is. Mr. Second, for instance, told me that he had been subject to no "pressures — that is, no threats." To many men in politics threats alone represent the only real pressure because they know very well that few votes are actually lost on any one given issue such as reciprocal trade. But, of course, what is a threat to one man is not a threat to another. (For comparison, we should have studied some explosive issues like "McCarthyism" or *humane slaughtering* or perhaps some issues in which the profit-and-loss relationship is clearer like the question of pay increases for postal employees.)

The most strongly felt kind of pressure on the reciprocal trade issue came, apparently, from Speaker Rayburn and the Democratic leadership against the potentially recalcitrant Democrats. Speaker Rayburn attended a breakfast for freshmen congressmen shortly before the vote and said, in effect, that he'd discovered that those who go along, get along. One new member regarded this as pressure — a threat. Another new member (actually probably more vulnerable in terms of his factional position and his position within the delegation) did not. Both of them failed to "go along." Aside from this speech, most of the "pressure" on the doubtful members seems to have come through the grapevine or from their own apprehensions as to what might happen if they bolted the party leadership.

One reason why fairly few members seem to have felt pressure on this matter is to be explained in terms of their background and associations in local politics. In many states, "pressure" on matters like highway contracts or patronage or even for or against gubernatorial programs, must be relatively heavy — that is, threats are far more common at the state level than they are in Washington. Many congressmen come from such a background and a good many are still involved in local conflicts about patronage, contracts, etc. As a result, Washington to them seems very mild.

Nagging may also be called pressure, whether done by mail or in person. When a congressman has definitely announced his stand and does not intend to switch it, he resents being bothered by avoidable pleas (pressures) to change. The resentment point, obviously, is highly individual so one man's pressure is another man's routine.

The Interests

13

How the Farmers Get What They Want

Theodore J. Lowi

In his Farm Message of January 31, President Johnson proposed that Congress establish a bipartisan commission to investigate the concentration of power in the food industry. In the same message the President called for new legislation to strengthen farmer cooperatives, to encourage their expansion through merger and acquisition, and to provide them with further exemptions from the antitrust laws.

This was the beginning of the "Johnson round" in agriculture. It is part of a familiar pattern. An attack on the food industry's market power, coupled with proposals for expanded and stronger farm co-

From Theodore Lowi, "How Farmers Get What They Want," *The Reporter* (September 14, 1954), pp. 34–37.

operatives, is obviously not an attack on concentration itself. Rather it is an attack on the intervention of non-agricultural groups into strictly agricultural affairs.

That agricultural affairs should be handled strictly within the agricultural community is a basic political principle established before the turn of the century and maintained since then without serious reexamination. As a result, agriculture has become neither public nor private enterprise. It is a system of self-government in which each leading farm interest controls a segment of agriculture through a delegation of national sovereignty. Agriculture has emerged as a largely self-governing federal estate within the Federal structure of the United States.

President Johnson recognized these facts within three weeks of his accession when he summoned a conference of agriculture leaders to formulate a program by which agriculture should be served and regulated. The most recent concession to agriculture's self-government was the wheat-cotton bill. Because cotton supports were too high, the cotton interests wrote a bill providing for a subsidy of six to eight cents a pound to mills in order to keep them competitive with foreign cotton and domestic rayon without touching the price supports. On the other hand, wheat supports were too low because wheat farmers last year in referendum overwhelmingly rejected President Kennedy's plan to provide some Federal regulation along with supports. The wheat section of the new act calls for a program whereby wheat farmers may voluntarily comply with acreage reduction for subsidies of up to seventy cents a bushel but without the Federal supply regulations. The press called this a major legislative victory for Mr. Johnson, but the credit is not his. That the press could see this as a victory for anyone but organized cotton and wheat is a testimonial to the total acceptance by President, press, and public of the principle that private agriculture interests alone govern agriculture and should do so.

The reasons for agriculture's self-government are deep-rooted, and the lessons to be drawn are important to the future of American politics. For a century agriculture has been out of step with American economic development. Occasional fat years have only created unreal expectations, to be undercut by the more typical lean years.

Quite early, farmers discovered the value of politics as a counterweight to industry's growth and concentration. Land-grant and homesteading acts were followed by governmental services in research and education. Continuing distress led to bolder demands.

First there were efforts to effect a redistribution of wealth in favor of agriculture. As a debtor class, farmers saw inflation as the solution, and Bryan was their spokesman for cheaper money and cheaper credit. The monopolies, the railroads, the grain merchants and other processors, the banks, and the brokers were to be deprived of power over the market by dissolution or by severe restraints. Next, farmers sought solutions by emulating the business system: the co-operative to restrain domestic trade and international dumping over high tariff walls and to restrain international trade. Yet all these mechanisms either were not enacted or did not live up to expectations.

With the coming of the New Deal and with its help, organized agriculture turned to self-regulation. The system created during the 1930's has endured to this day, and with only a few marginal additions and alterations is accepted almost unanimously by farm leaders. Self-regulation might have taken several forms, the most likely one being a national system of farm-leader representation within a farmers' NRA. Instead, a more complicated system of highly decentralized and highly autonomous subgovernments developed, largely for Constitutional reasons. Agriculture was the most "local" of the manufacturing groups the Federal government was trying to reach. The appearance if not the reality of decentralizing Federal programs through farmer-elected local committees helped avoid strains on the interstate commerce clause of the Constitution. But this avoidance of Constitutional troubles created very special political difficulties.

THE LOCAL COMMITTEES

The Federal Extension Service shows how the system works. It is "co-operative" in that it shares the job of farm improvement with the states, the land-grant colleges, the county governments, and the local associations of farmers. The county agent is actually employed by the local associations. In the formative years, the aid of local chambers of commerce was enlisted, the local association being the "farm bureau" of the chamber. In order to co-ordinate local activities and to make more effective claims for additional outside assistance, these farm bureaus were organized into state farm bureau federations. The American Farm Bureau Federation, formed at the Agriculture College of Cornell University in 1919, was used as a further step toward amalgamation. To this day there is a close relationship between the farm bureaus, the land-grant colleges, and the Extension Service. This transformation of an administrative arrangement into a political system has been repeated in nearly all the agricultural programs during recent decades. The Extension Service exercises few controls from the top. There are cries of "Federal encroachment" at the mere suggestion in Washington that the Department of Agriculture should increase its supervision of the extension programs or co-ordinate them with other Federal activities.

As the financial stakes have grown larger, the patterns of local self-government remains the same. Price support — the "parity program" — is run by the thousands of farmer-elected county committees that function alongside but quite independently of the other local committees. Acreage allotments to bring supply down and prices up are apportioned among the states by the Agricultural Stabilization and Conservation Service. State committees of farmers apportion the allotment among the counties. The farmer-elected county Stabilization and Conservation Committees receive the county allotment.

These committees made the original acreage allotments among individual farmers back in the 1930's; today, they make new allotments, work out adjustments and review complaints regarding allotments, determine whether quotas have been complied with, inspect and approve storage facilities, and perform as the court of original jurisdiction on violations of price-support rules and on eligibility for parity payments. The committees are also vitally important in the campaigns for the two-thirds vote required to fix high price supports. Congress determines the general level of supports, and the Secretary of Agriculture proclaims the national acreage quotas for adjusting the supply to the guaranteed price. But the locally elected committees stand between the farmer and Washington.

Most other agricultural programs have evolved similarly. Each is independent of the others, and any conflicts or overlapping mandates have been treated as nonexistent or beyond the jurisdiction of any one agency. The Soil Conservation Service operates through its independent soil-conservation districts, of which there were 2,936 in 1963, involving ninety-six per cent of the nation's farms. Each district's farmer-elected committee is considered a unit of local government. The Farmer Co-operative Service operates through the member-elected boards of directors of the farm co-ops. In agricultural credit, local self-government is found in even greater complexity. The Farm Credit Administration exists outside the Department of Agriculture and is made up of not one but three separate bodies politic, a triangular system mostly farmer-owned and totally farmer-controlled.

THEODORE J. LOWI   187

TEN SYSTEMS AND POLICIES

The ten principal self-governing systems in agriculture, in fiscal 1962, disposed of $5.6 billion of the total of $6.7 billion in expenditures passing through the Department of Agriculture. During the calendar year 1962, $5.8 billion in loans was handled similarly. This combined amount represents a large portion of the total of Federal activity outside national defense.

Each of the ten systems has become a powerful political instrumentality. The self-governing local units become one important force in a system that administers a program and maintains the autonomy of that program against political forces emanating from other agricultural programs, from antagonistic farm and nonfarm interests, from Congress, from the Secretary of Agriculture, and from the President. To many a farmer, the local outpost of one or another of these systems *is* the government.

The politics within each system is built upon a triangular trading pattern involving the central agency, a Congressional committee or sub-committee, and the local district farmer committees (usually federated in some national or regional organization). Each side of the triangle complements and supports the other two.

The Extension Service, for example, is one side of the triangle completed by the long-tenure "farm bureau" members of the Agriculture Committees in Congress and, at the local level, the American Farm Bureau Federation with its local committees. Further group support is provided by two intimately related groups, the Association of Land Grant Colleges and Universities and the National Association of County Agricultural Agents.

Another such triangle unites the Soil Conservation Service, the Agriculture subcommittee of the House Appropriations Committee, and the local districts organized in the energetic National Association of Soil Conservation Districts. Further support comes from the Soil Conservation Society of America (mainly professionals) and the former Friends of the Land, now the Izaak Walton League of America.

Probably the most complex of the systems embraces the party program. It connects the Agricultural Stabilization and Conservation Service with the eight (formerly ten) commodity subcommittees of the House Agriculture Committee and the dozens of separately organized groups representing the various commodities. (Examples: National Cotton Council, American Wool Growers Association, American Cranberry Growers Association.) These groups and congressmen draw support from the local price-support committees wherever a particular commodity is grown.

THE FARMER HAD HIS WAY

These systems have a vigorous capacity to maintain themselves and to resist encroachment. They have such institutional legitimacy that they have become practically insulated from the three central sources of democratic political responsibility. Thus, within the Executive branch, they are autonomous. Secretaries of Agriculture have tried and failed to consolidate or even to co-ordinate related programs. Within Congress, they are sufficiently powerful to be able to exercise an effective veto or create a stalemate. And they are almost totally removed from the view, not to mention the control, of the general public. (Throughout the 1950's, Victor Anfuso of Brooklyn was the only member of the House Agriculture Committee from a non-farm constituency.)

Important cases illustrate their power:

In 1947, Secretary of Agriculture Clinton P. Anderson proposed a consolidation of all soil-conservation, price-support, and FHA programs into one committee system with a direct line from the committees to the Secretary. Bills were prepared providing for consolidation within the price-support committees. Contrary bills provided for consolidation under soil conservation districts. The result: stalemate. In 1948, a leading farm senator proposed consolidation of the programs under the local associations of the Extension Service. Immediately a House farm leader introduced a contrary bill. The result: continuing stalemate.

In Waco, Texas, on October 14, 1952, Presidential candidate Eisenhower said: "I would like to see in every county all Federal farm agencies under the same roof." Pursuant to this promise, Secretary Ezra Taft Benson issued a series of orders during early 1953 attempting to bring about consolidation of local units as well as unification at the top. Finally, amid cries of "sneak attack" and "agricrat," Benson proclaimed that "any work on the further consolidation of county and state offices . . . shall be suspended."

From the very beginning, Secretary Benson sought to abandon rigid price supports and bring actual supports closer to market prices. In 1954, as he was beginning to succeed, Congress enacted a "commodity set-aside" by which $2.5 billion of surplus commodities already held by the government were declared to be a "frozen reserve" for national defense. Since the Secretary's power to cut price supports depends heavily upon the amount of government-owned surplus carried over from previous years, the commodity set-aside was a way of freezing parity as well as reserves. Benson eventually succeeded in reducing supports on the few commodities over which he had authority. But thanks to the set-aside, Congress, between fiscal 1952 and 1957, helped increase the value of commodities held by the government from $1.1 billion to $5.3 billion. What appeared, therefore, to be a real Republican policy shift amounted to no more than giving back with one hand what had been taken away by the other.

President Eisenhower's first budget sought to abolish farm home-building and improvement loans by eliminating the budgetary request and by further requesting that the 1949 authorization law be allowed to expire. Congress overrode his request in 1953 and each succeeding year, and the President answered Congress with a year-by-year refusal to implement the farm housing program. In 1956, when the President asked again explicitly for elimination of the program, he was rebuffed. The Housing subcommittee of the House Banking and Currency Committee added to the President's omnibus housing bill a renewal of the farm housing program, plus an authorization for $500 million in loans over a five-year period, and the bill passed with a Congressional mandate to use the funds. They were used thereafter at a rate of about $75 million a year.

On March 16, 1961, President Kennedy produced a "radically different" farm program in a special message to Congress. For the first time in the history of price supports, the bill called for surplus control through quotas placed on bushels, tons, or other units, rather than on acreage. An acreage allotment allows the farmer to produce as much as he can on the reduced acreage in cultivation. For example, in the first ten years or so of acreage control, acreage under cultivation dropped by about four per cent, while actual production rose by fifteen per cent. The Kennedy proposal called for national committees of farmers to be elected to work out the actual program. This more stringent type of control was eliminated from the omnibus bill in the Agriculture Committee of both chambers and there were no attempts to restore them during floor debate. Last-minute efforts by Secretary Orville L. Freeman to up the ante, offering to raise wheat supports from $1.79 to $2.00, were useless. Persistence by the administration led eventually to rejection by wheat farmers in 1963 of all high price supports and acreage controls.

The politics of this rejected referendum is of general significance. Despite all the blandishments and inducements of the administra-

tion, the farmer had his way. The local price-support committees usually campaign in these referendums for the Department of Agriculture, but this time they did not. And thousands of small farmers,
eligible to vote for the first time, joined with the local leadership to
help defeat the referendum. It is not so odd that wheat farmers would
reject a proposal that aims to regulate them more strictly than before.
What is odd is that only wheat farmers are allowed to decide the matter. It seems that in agriculture, as in many other fields, the regulators
are powerless without the consent of the regulated.

Agriculture is the field where the distinction between public and
private has been almost completely eliminated, not by public expropriation of private domain but by private expropriation of public
domain. For more than a generation, Americans have succeeded in
expanding the public sphere without giving thought to the essential
democratic question of how each expansion is to be effected. The creation of private governments has profoundly limited the capacity of
the public government to govern responsibly and flexibly.

14

Black Interests, Black Groups, and Black Influence in the Federal Policy Process: The Cases of Housing and Education

Harold L. Wolman and Norman C. Thomas

Few would disagree that American politics is characterized by bargaining, negotiation, compromise, and mutual accommodation. But
some have argued that these characteristics, rather than indicating
consent . . . indicate instead that dissent is being suppressed and that
the political system is stable *because* of that suppression. . . .

All interests do not become translated into group demands, it is
argued, because certain segments of the population lack the re-

From Harold L. Wolman and Norman C. Thomas, "Black Interests, Black
Groups, and Black Influence in the Federal Policy Process," *Journal of Politics,*
32 (November 1970), pp. 875–97.

sources for effective group participation. Studies of participation have shown that lower-class people in particular, possessing little education and low political efficacy, are less likely to join groups than are their middle- and upper-class counterparts. . . .

Moreover, the critics contend, decision makers are likely to be much less receptive to certain types of groups, particularly those that put stress on the social system by pushing for change. The decision makers do not dispassionately weigh the relative forces of the contending groups and then register a decision. In many cases the decision makers can determine who has effective access on the basis of their own values. . . .

The "Negro revolt" of the past decade provides an important and appropriate setting for an investigation of the relevance of some of the criticisms that have been made of the pluralist description of American politics. To the extent that black Americans do share common interests, how successful have they been in achieving effective access to federal decision makers and in helping to shape national policy to conform with those interests? The "Poor People's Campaign" of 1968 provided a dramatic indication that black participation in federal policy processes has not been satisfactory in the view of many black groups and their leaders.

Studies that we conducted during 1967–68, independently but in close contact with each other, of the process of formulating national policies in the areas of housing and education, have provided us with evidence that black participation in national policy processes is not as effective or as extensive as the pluralist description suggests it should be. (We are assuming the existence of relatively greater unmet demands, i.e., felt needs, among black Americans than among the rest of the population.) Specifically, we examined the federal policy-making processes to discover which groups had access and where, and at what points in the policy process that access occurred. We found an absence of black access and effective black participation at crucial stages in the process. It is our purpose in this paper to present that evidence, to suggest explanations for it, and to assess its significance in relation to the pluralist description of American politics.

METHODOLOGY

In studying national policy making in housing and education we employed the conceptual framework of a policy system. The policy systems, as we defined them, included key individuals located in the bureaucracy (the departments of Housing and Urban Development and Health, Education and Welfare and their principal operating agencies in the areas of housing and education), Congress (the relevant legislative and appropriations committees), organized clientele or special interest groups in each policy area, and persons whom we have designated as "public-interest representatives" (influential persons in related professions, in the general community, or affiliated with general or non-clientele interest groups). We distinguished between clientele-group representatives and public-interest representatives because the former have a sustained professional concern over the policy areas through an organization created for that purpose while the latter are involved either as individuals or as members of groups with a broader focus, e.g., labor unions or business associations. The members of the two policy systems were quite similar in terms of their institutional affiliations, positions, or resource bases. (See Table 1.) . . .

Table 1

Membership in the Housing and Education Policy Systems by Institution/Position/Resource Base

	Housing	*Education*
Congress: Members	19	18
Congress: Staff	7	7
Bureaucracy	14	18
Executive Office of the President	8	6
Clientele groups	12	16
Public interest representatives	8	10
Total	68	77

At the final stage of data gathering, we conducted interviews with 62 members of the housing and 71 members of the education policy systems. The interview instruments employed primarily open-end questions. We asked similar, but not identical, questions in the two areas regarding the representation and access of various groups in the different stages of the policy process. Because our interview procedures were eclectic, as elite studies tend to be, the data are non-quantitative and our analysis is conducted in qualitative terms. Where we do discuss data, it is not precisely comparable between the two policy areas. . . .

BLACK GROUPS AND PARTICIPATION
IN POLICY MAKING

How do groups representing black interests attempt to influence public policy at the national level? Do they take advantage of the multiplicity of access points available in the education and housing policy processes? To answer these questions, we first considered the major black groups on the assumption that each represented interests held by some portion of the black community.

Historically, the NAACP has been the black organization most active in attempting to influence public policy. The principal thrust of the NAACP's efforts has been towards achieving integration, particularly in the area of education. It has employed litigation as the principal means to this end. But the NAACP has neither engaged in any form of long-range policy planning for education nor made organized efforts to influence federal policy at the innovative or formulative stages.

A substantial amount of litigation is also initiated by the Legal Defense and Education Fund, a legally independent organization associated with the NAACP. It has been concerned primarily with the enforcement of Title VI of the Civil-Rights Act of 1964 which requires state and local governments to comply with federal desegregation guidelines in order to participate in various federally funded programs.

The NAACP's concentration on educational integration has rendered it nearly quiescent in other areas. From 1963 until 1968 it had no particular housing program and no staff member to deal with matters of housing policy — an area that is surely one of major concern to members of the black community. Prior to 1963, the NAACP's housing program, as might be expected, was concerned mostly with segregation in the housing market.

The NAACP, through its lobbyist Clarence Mitchell, does make efforts to influence policy at the legislative consideration stage. Mitchell often directs his efforts through the vehicle of the Leadership Conference of Civil Rights, an umbrella group consisting of 112 organizations whose purpose is to "advance the cause of civil rights through the enactment of legislation." The Conference acts primarily as a coordinator; its influence derives from the resources possessed by its most important constituents groups — the NAACP, the Industrial Union Division of the AFL-CIO, and the National Council of Churches.

The Leadership Conference is primarily concerned with securing the passage of civil-rights laws such as the Civil-Rights Act of 1964 and the Voting-Rights Act of 1965. The Conference — and Mitchell in particular — is credited with playing a major role in the passing of the federal open-housing law in 1968. The Leadership Conference's major efforts, however, have been directed towards civil-rights legislation in the strict sense; its involvement in other areas of concern to black people — such as education and housing — is on an ad hoc basis, usually to meet an overt threat related to civil rights. Like the NAACP, the Leadership Conference has been almost completely uninvolved in housing legislation. Generally, in areas other than civil rights, the Conference's involvement in the policy process does not occur soon enough to influence substantially the shape of the final product. Rather, it reacts to threats and emergencies. . . .

The National Urban League is involved in operational programs, particularly in housing at the local level, but it makes no major effort as an organization to affect national policy other than through *pro forma* testimony before congressional committees. Like the Legal Defense and Educational Fund, it is forbidden to lobby because of its tax-exempt status. Even so, Whitney Young, the [late] Urban League's Executive Director, [was] very active personally in the innovation and formulation stage of the housing policy-making process. Young emphasize[d] desegregating the housing market and providing governmental resources to private enterprise so that the supply of low- and moderate-income housing may be increased. It seems clear that Young's influence [was] due to his reputation and his personality — and particularly to the high respect that President Johnson held for him — rather than the resources of the Urban League.

The Congress of Racial Equality (CORE) has made little attempt to influence policy at the national level, although its leaders have, from time to time, testified before congressional committees. Neither has it developed a coherent national program for either housing or education. CORE's position, as reflected in congressional testimony, has emphasized the following: the need to provide the resources from which private enterprise can increase the supply of low-income housing; the desirability of establishing housing co-ops; and the necessity for black control of decision-making processes at the local level. The Student Non-Violent Co-ordinating Committee (SNCC) makes no attempt either to influence policy or to formulate a program at the national level other than to say that "the U.S. Government ought to give massive amounts of money directly to black communities with no strings attached."

The Southern Christian Leadership Conference does not lobby in the normal sense of the word, but the late Dr. Martin Luther King, Jr., frequently used public confrontation to gain access to the mass media in order to influence decision makers in the legislative-consideration stage through moral suasion. King employed this strategy most successfully on civil-rights issues that were publicly perceived as "moral" issues.

In summary, black groups have directed most of their efforts to influence national policies on issues involving civil rights. These have been largely formal and visible activities, e.g., lobbying and litigation, that occur fairly late in the policy process, particularly at the stages of legislative consideration and implementation. At those stages certain actions can be prevented and marginal changes in policy outputs affected, but the major thrust of policies cannot substantially be altered, for they have been shaped in the earlier innovative and formulative stages when the basic agenda is set.

BLACK GROUPS
AND ACCESS TO THE POLICY-MAKING ELITE

The pattern of black participation in the policy-making process is quite similar in housing and education. Very few blacks were found in the policy-making elites that we studied. In housing there were only two black members of the elite, including, of course, Robert Weaver who as the first Secretary of Housing and Urban Development was also the first black member of the Cabinet. While not the major concern of this paper, the nature and significance of Weaver's involvement in the housing policy system is a matter of some controversy. On the one hand, there are those, including some of our respondents, who believe that he exercised a steady, persuasive influence from his key position and that his influence was of considerable value to the black community. On the other hand, his critics, who included not a few black leaders, some journalistic commentators, and a number of our respondents, depreciated his impact on two counts: that he was an inept administrator and an ineffectual politician, and that he thought and acted like a white person. We can only note but not settle the debate. In the education policy system, only one black participant was involved and he was associated with organized labor.

But did the organized groups representing black interests have effective access to members of the policy-making elite? The evidence indicated that they did not. We asked the members of the education policy system: "What are the two or three groups or forces outside the government that have the most impact on federal policy involving elementary and secondary education?" and "higher education?" Not one of the 71 respondents cited a civil-rights organization or any other element in the black community. . . . We also asked the education respondents, "Outside your immediate office, who are the ten people whom you see most frequently, formally or informally, with respect to matters that involve federal educational policy?" None of the 71 respondents cited a representative of a civil-rights organization or any other black leader as a person whom they consulted. This is fairly impressive negative evidence of the absence of black access to the national educational policy-making elite. Members of the policy-making elite had neither reference groups nor personal contacts in the black community.

We obtained at least some positive evidence of the same phenomenon by asking 59 of the respondents: "Do you feel that all relevant and concerned groups have adequate opportunity to express their views concerning federal educational policies?" Thirty-six of those who responded to the question believed that certain groups did not have adequate access to the policy process in education. These groups included four distinct categories: the Negro-urban poor; various educational interests, including vocational education, independent schools, and private liberal-arts colleges; teachers, students, and parents; and state and local education officials. . . .

Some explanations of these phenomena are suggested by examining the location of the respondents in the policy process. Only one of 16 congressionally affiliated respondents in comparison with two of 18 bureaucrats and eight of 25 persons located outside the federal government were of the opinion that the Negro-urban poor lacked adequate access. These differences are substantial if not striking. It is possible that for members of Congress and their staffs the Negro-urban poor are not a meaningful constituency. Indeed, they are but a recently invented constituency with relevance for persons outside the federal government and, to a lesser degree, for bureaucrats. It is also probable that the presence of highly visible black lobbying on Capital Hill kept most congressional respondents from citing the black community or its organization as groups lacking effective access. . . .

It is difficult to reach a clear and confident interpretation of these responses. On the one hand, it is notable that more of the respondents cited the Negro-urban poor as lacking adequate access than any other group. On the other hand, it is impressive that so few mentioned the lack for black groups. We can conclude that there is some concern over the lack of black access (expressed by one in five respondents) and substantial concern over the adequacy of access for *all* relevant groups including the blacks (expressed by three in five). . . .

In housing, the pattern of responses was substantially the same. . . .

In sum, the responses indicate that black access to the policy-making elites is limited in terms of the reference groups and personal contacts with the influential policy makers and that a sizeable, but not substantial, number of those who are influential believe that black people lack adequate access to the process.

VIRTUAL AND INDIRECT REPRESENTATION

Although our findings strongly indicate that black groups on the whole do not possess effective access to the major centers of decision making in the domestic policy-making process, it does not follow that black interests are ignored by the policy-making elite. Indeed, members of the elite themselves may share these interests. Thus, when housing decision makers were questioned about their agreement with the policy positions of the four major black organizations, 34 of the 42 who responded either generally agreed or agreed very strongly with the NAACP or Urban League, while 13 answered similarly for SNCC and CORE. . . .

More specifically, certain units within the executive branch were institutionally structured and certain officials took it upon themselves to represent the interests of the black community — or at least some of the interests of some parts of the black community. In HUD, the Office of Community Development and the Office of Equal Opportunity, both headed by blacks, provided such representation, particularly in the implementation stage. Neither of these units, however, was a major center of policy making. Within HEW the Commissioner of Education and the Special Assistant to the Secretary for Civil Rights assumed a special responsibility for the interests of black people. At the time of this inquiry, the commissioner was a white man while the Civil-Rights Assistant was a black woman. The commissioner's record as a champion of civil rights had earned him the antipathy of most Southern congressmen. The Civil-Rights Assistant was concerned primarily with Title VI compliance and she did not participate in the overall development of educational policies except as they related to civil-rights matters. The U.S. Office of Education (USOE) also maintained an Office of Programs for the Disadvantaged which had the responsibilitiy of receiving and processing suggestions and complaints from poor people about the operation of federal education programs.

Federal institutions outside the main policy system also represented some black interests. Demands from these institutions acted as inputs to the policy-making system from within the Administration. The Office of Economic Opportunity (OEO) in particular argued the case for black interests, although much more effectively in education than in housing. In education, the OEO administered two programs, Headstart (later transferred to USOE) and Upward Bound, oriented towards helping black children overcome cultural, economic, and educational obstacles. Through these programs, OEO was able to influence other programs that affect black children.

Probably the most important form of indirect representation of black interests came from demands on the policy-making elite made by certain non-governmental groups such as the Urban Coalition, the National Council of Churches, and the AFL-CIO. Of these groups, organized labor has clearly been the most important. Despite the fact that many rank-and-file unionists did not appear to support black-oriented policies, labor leadership consistently pushed for legislation favorable to moderate black interests. The fight to pass a federal open-housing law in 1968 is a prime example. According to a survey of the AFL-CIO membership conducted by the Joseph Kraft polling organization in January 1967, a majority of the membership opposed labor's stand in favor of the federal law. Yet a year later, labor lobbyists were in the forefront of the fight to pass the legislation.

Labor, or at least its leaders, apparently has fairly explicit working relations with the black civil-rights groups. . . .

There are a number of other ways in which black "representation" is achieved in the policy process. Perhaps the most important in the minds of the policy-making elite, which tends to believe that there *should* be black representation, is the practice of consulting a few well-known black leaders or enlisting them in formal and highly visible advisory capacities. One respondent called this "the Whitney Young approach" in reference to the frequent inclusions of the prestigious Executive Director of the Urban League on advisory councils, public commissions, and other study groups. The other aspect of this form of black representation is consultation with intellectuals and experts, e.g., educators, urbanologists, etc. who tend to be affiliated with universities, foundations, and research institutes. . . .

Although black interests are not excluded from any of the stages of the policy-making process, serious deficiencies do exist in efforts at interest articulation through indirect representation. The most obvious is that groups or institutions attempting to represent black interests are often restrained by their own constituencies from fully representing those interests. Thus, although labor may support open-housing, the building-trade unions strongly oppose efforts to allow Negro residents to work on housing rehabilitation projects in their neighborhoods, since this requires using non-union labor. . . .

More important, however, is the question of which black interests get articulated through indirect representation. Obviously the black community is not monolithic; various segments within it do have interests that differ, and in some cases quite markedly. In the extreme case are large numbers of blacks who view integration as a major and important policy goal while a smaller but highly articulate number of blacks espouse racial separation. It is quite apparent that the black interests articulated through indirect representation are those that are popularly termed moderate. The more militant interests only come to the attention of the decision makers, if at all, through the mass media, which have recently focused much attention on militant black spokesmen. . . .

Finally, at this point in history, the very existence of indirect representation — regardless of how adequate that representation may be — is unacceptable to many blacks. No matter how noble the intentions of liberal white groups, blacks frequently perceive white efforts to aid the black cause as paternalistic and patronizing. Blacks tend to regard such efforts as a continuation of the master-subordinate relation implicit in the history of race relations in America. Whites may unwittingly reflect this relation even as they seek to improve racial harmony. . . .

ANALYSIS

Both pluralists and most of their critics have assumed that rational men who hold common interests will organize into groups in order to achieve their goals. Mancur Olson has recently argued, however, that exactly the opposite is true. The rational individual will not make the sacrifices — such as time, energy, money — necessary to join a large voluntary group. He reasons that his participation will not make any measurable difference in the group's accomplishments, yet he will benefit from the group's accomplishments whether he is a member or not. Successful groups are, by Olson's persuasive logic, necessarily small groups or groups that are "fortunate enough to have an independent source of selective incentives. Thus, in order to receive the AMA journal, which keeps them informed on recent advances in medicine, doctors must belong to the American Medical Association. Unfortunately for black groups no similar incentives provide an effective means of coercing black people to join and contribute to them.

The consequent lack of resources has meant that black groups have had to make hard choices about where to concentrate their energies. Because almost all of the black groups at the national level are no more than coalitions of local groups, there is a natural reluctance to expend already scarce resources at the national level. Instead, efforts have been concentrated on influencing policies at the local level where the problems and processes may be less complex, and where the payoffs will, in all probability, be more tangible and visible.

The emerging ideology of black power, shared to some extent by nearly all black groups, reinforces the tendency to focus on local politics. Local activity is consistent with an emphasis on direct citizen participation, which seems to form an integral part of the ideology. In addition, the more militant version of the ideology holds that it is pointless to work with or thrrough a "racist white power structure" at the federal level. . . .

The lack of special incentives and the concentration of effort at the local level means that black groups suffer from a severe lack of resources when they do attempt to influence policy at the national level. . . .

The lack of technical expertise among black groups has been a major problem. On the whole, black organizations have not been able to develop coherent programs in either housing or education. . . .

Probably a more serious lack has been the inability of black groups to develop more lobbyists of the quality of Clarence Mitchell. . . . The reason for this lack may be that the kind of temperament characteristic of a good lobbyist is not readily found in members of most black groups and particularly not in militant ones. . . . Most black groups . . . have emphasized a highly moral and emotional approach better aimed at the mass public than at the policy-making elite. For whatever reasons, however, there is widespread agreement that most black groups do not have a good understanding of the operations of the policy process. . . .

In addition, black groups face a number of specific problems in securing access simply because they are black groups. The concentration of black people in the urban North and the rural South limits the willingness of many congressmen to pay them much heed since they are not major factors in their constituencies. Another problem is that relatively few black leaders have sufficient personal prestige or professional status to guarantee their inclusion, formally or informally, at the innovative and formulative stages. Aside from Whitney Young in housing and Kenneth Clark in education and a handful of others of similar stature, few blacks are actively consulted by the White House, the agencies, or the key congressional leaders. Nor do they have easy access to influential policy makers in those places. Finally, it may be that access is severely restricted by certain members of the elite who do not view some of the black groups — particularly the more militant ones — as legitimate participants in the political process.

SUMMARY AND IMPLICATIONS

The major reason for the ineffectiveness of black participation appears to be a severe lack of resources and a decision to concentrate most activity at the level of local communities. The result is that the few efforts made by black groups to influence national policy suffer from insufficient expertise, with respect to both the complexities of policy and the workings of the policy process. Black participation and representation occurs primarily in the legislative-consideration and the implementation stages of the policy process. Black organizations and leaders have made little attempt to influence policy development at the innovative and formulative stage where meaningful choices between long-range alternatives are for the most part made.

The policy goals that black groups have pursued have been short-run, direct, and highly visible: principally to attack overt racial discrimination and to promote integration. Only recently have black groups begun to direct their efforts towards problems of black poverty rather than towards the lack of legal equality. Most black participation has been aimed at the courts and Congress through litigation and legislative lobbying.

Black interests are represented indirectly in the policy-making process through a variety of mechanisms. Probably the most important of these is that certain members of the decision-making elite may already share some attitudes of some black groups. Outside the elite, organized labor has often represented black interests to decision makers. But indirect representation is often incomplete and ineffective, and many blacks perceive it to be a demeaning survival of the paternal master-slave relation between blacks and whites.

It appears that the pluralist description of the American political system is not entirely adequate. Our research has shown that black interests and black groups do not, on the whole, possess effective access to the centers of decision making in federal education and housing policy. This lack of influence is not, however, due primarily to the causes that most critics of pluralism have suggested. Contrary to their analyses, channels of access do appear to be relatively open and most decision makers seem willing to listen to any groups who use them. The extremely limited use of the channels by groups with the most manifest set of unmet demands reveals a flaw in the pluralist analysis. As Mancur Olson has pointed out, the main assumption of the pluralists — that rational men sharing interests will form groups in order to accomplish their ends — is defective. This applies not only to the black community, but to other interests as well — for example, housewives, students, commuters or, more generally, consumers, as opposed to producers, of goods and services.

Furthermore, there are defects in the pluralist assumption that the response of the decision-making elite will normally be satisfactory. Without examining specific policy outcomes, it seems obvious that the response of federal policy makers to black demands, whether they are articulated by marginal black participation or indirect white representation, is inadequate. . . .

15

How Special Tax Provisions Get Enacted

Stanley S. Surrey

Recently there has been considerable criticism directed against the existence in our tax laws of provisions granting special treatment to certain groups or individuals. The purpose of this article is to consider the question of why the Congress enacts these special tax provisions.

From Stanley S. Surrey, "The Congress and Tax Lobbyists: How Special Tax Provisions Get Enacted," *Harvard Law Review* 70:1145 (1957). Copyright 1957 by The Harvard Law Review Association.

SOME MAJOR FACTORS

High Rates of Tax

The high rates of the individual income tax and of the estate and gift taxes, are probably the major factor in producing special tax legislation. This is, in a sense, a truism, for without something to be relieved of, there would be no need to press for relief. The point is that the average congressman does not basically believe in the present rates of income tax in the upper brackets. When he sees them applied to individual cases, he thinks them too high and therefore unfair. Any argument for relief which starts off by stating that these high rates are working a "special hardship" in a particular case or are "penalizing" a particular taxpayer — to use some words from the tax lobbyist's approved list of effective phrases — has the initial advantage of having a sympathetic listener.

Tax Polarity

The existence of two rate structures in the income tax and of two types of taxes on the transfer of wealth permits a congressman to favor a special group by placing its situation under the lower rate structure or the less effective tax. Thus, the presence of the twenty-five-per-cent capital-gains rate enables Congress to shift an executive stock option from the high rates applying to executive compensation to the lower capital-gains rate. If there were no special capital-gains rate, or if we did not tax capital gains at all, this shift could not be made, since a congressman would not completely exempt the stock option. Similarly, the presence of a gift tax permits certain transfers of wealth, such as transferred life insurance, to be shifted from the higher estate tax to the lower gift tax. As a consequence, given this congressional tendency, we reach the paradox that having a gift tax as well as an estate tax may, given the present lack of proper co-ordination of the two taxes, result in less effective taxation of certain transfers of wealth than if we relied only on an estate tax.

Technical Complexity

The high rates of tax, the complexities of modern business, the desires of the wealthy and middle-income groups for clear tax charts to guide their family planning, the Government's need for protection against tax avoidance, the claims of tax equity, and various other factors have combined to make the income, estate, and gift taxes exceedingly complex in technical detail. These technicalities involve the drawing of countless dividing lines. Consequently, a case on the high-tax side of a line may closely resemble the cases on the other side receiving more favorable tax treatment. The result is a fertile ground for assertions of inequity and hardship as particular taxpayers desire legislation to bend the dividing lines and thereby extend the favorable treatment to their situations. Also, faulty tax planning, ill-advised legal steps, or transactions concluded in ignorance of tax law can produce severe tax consequences. These "tax penalties" could have been averted under an informed tax guidance that would have taken the taxpayer safely through the technical tax maze. In these circumstances, the taxpayer facing severe monetary hurt because of a "mere technicality" (to use the phrase that will be pressed on the congressman) is quite likely to evoke considerable sympathy for his plight.

History and Politics

The accidents of tax history also play a major role in the existence of special provisions. Tax-exempt securities in large part achieved their favored status through the vagaries of constitutional interpretation and not through any special desire to relieve the wealthy. Percentage depletion for oil and gas and the deduction of intangible drilling expenses have their roots in legislative compromises and administrative interpretation which for the most part do not appear to have been planned as special-interest relief. It is only later that the extent of the tax generosity inherent in such provisions is comprehended. But by then they are in the law, the problem of the group benefited is one of defense rather than attack, and the strategic advantages are all with that group. This is especially so when the area involved touches on major political matters, as in the case of percentage depletion and tax-exempt securities.

Political considerations naturally overhang this whole area, for taxation is a sensitive and volatile matter. Any major congressional action represents the compromises of the legislator as he weighs and balances the strong forces constantly focused on him by the pressure groups of the country. Many special provisions — capital gains, for one — are caught in these swirling pressures.

Separation of Executive
and Legislative Branches of Government

But many of the tax provisions we are considering do not lie at this political level. They are simply a part of the technical tax law. They are not of major importance in their revenue impact. But they are of major importance to the group or individual benefited and they are glaring in their departure from tax fairness. The inquiry, therefore, must here be directed toward some of the institutional features in the tax-legislation process which may be responsible for special provisions of this technical variety.

Congress occupies the role of mediator between the tax views of the executive and the demands of the pressure groups. This is so whether the tax issue involved is a major political matter or a minor technical point. The Congress is zealous in maintaining this position in the tax field.

The Congress regards the shaping of a revenue bill as very much its prerogative. It will seek the views of the executive, for there is a respect for the sustained labors of those in the executive departments and also a recognition, varying with the times, of the importance of presidential programs. But control over the legislation itself, both as to broad policies and as to details, rests with the Congress. Hence a congressman, and especially a member of the tax committees, is in a position to make the tax laws bend in favor of a particular individual or group despite strong objection from the executive branch. Under such a governmental system the importance to the tax structure of the institutional factors that influence a congressman's decision is obvious.

SOME INSTITUTIONAL FACTORS

The Congressman's Desire To Be Helpful

A congressman's instincts are to be helpful and friendly. If it were otherwise, he would not be in Congress. When a constituent, or some other person who is in a position to claim attention, seeks legislative action, the congressman likes to respond within reason. If the proposal presented to him is at all rational he will, in all probability, at least introduce it in bill form so as not to offend the constituent. If the congressman is not a member of one of the tax committees, that may end the matter — but it may not, for the proposal has been launched and lies ready to be pushed ahead by whatever pressures may be generated in its behalf.

Lack of Congressional Appreciation
of Departure From Fairness

In many cases the congressman considering a special tax provision may not realize that tax fairness is at all involved. He sees only the problem of the particular constituent or group concerned. The case in this focus may be very appealing, for human beings are involved with human problems. The income tax, always an impersonal, severe, monetary burden, becomes an oppressive force bearing down on men in difficulty. The congressman may therefore not even appreciate that arguments of over-all fairness and equity have any relation to the question, or may very well think them too intangible and remote. Provisions for the relief of the blind and the aged are perhaps illustrations. Or the congressman, moved simply by a desire to help a constituent, may not understand the ramifications of the proposal. He is not a tax technician and he may view the proposal in isolation rather than perceive its relationship to the intricate technical structure of the revenue code. The proposal, so viewed, becomes merely a "little old amendment" which helps a constituent and does no harm. His brother congressmen are quite willing to be good fellows and go along, especially if the congressman urging the proposal is well-liked. After all, they too from time to time will have "little old amendments" to propose. Thus, in 1955 the Ways and Means Committee decided that in the initial consideration of members' bills dealing with technical matters it would allow each member one bill to be considered and then reported by the full committee if the bill met with unanimous agreement.

The Treasury Department's Presentation

The congressman's failure to recognize that tax fairness is at all involved may often be due to the inadequacy of the Treasury Department's presentation of the issues. This is not said critically, but by way of explanation. The problem facing the Treasury in these matters is formidable. The interested constituents or groups are generally skillful in presenting their cases in appealing form. Their energies are concentrated on one matter; they have time and money to devote to it; they may have the advantage of personal acquaintance, directly or through intermediaries, with the congressman; they can obtain skilled counsel informed on the ways of the Congress. The Treasury's tax staff must tackle all of these problems; its members are usually not chosen for skill in the presentation of issues or in handling congressmen; although on the whole remarkably good, considering the compensation, they are rarely among the ablest in the tax field, nor do they usually have the needed experience.

Lack of Omniscience on the Part of the Treasury

The treasury tax staff is not omniscient. Yet understanding approaching omniscience is needed to do its job. A lack of knowledge on any particular matter, a failure of skill at any moment, can be fatal. The approach of the average congressman is to hear the private group, find out in general what it wants, react sympathetically for a variety of reasons, and then ask the Treasury whether there is any objection to the proposal. If the Treasury is off its guard and acquiesces, the proposal becomes law. If the Treasury is unprepared and presents a weak case, the proposal becomes law. Equally serious is the in-between situation in which the Treasury acknowledges that some hardship is present in the particular situation, but points out that the difficulty is but a phase of a general problem and that it has not yet been able fully to analyze the general area. It therefore urges that the particular proposal be postponed until further study is given to the whole matter. But recognition of some hardship and of some merit in his particular proposal is all that the congressman needs. His constituent wants relief from that admitted hardship now, and not years later when the whole matter has been thought through and his case fitted into a solution appropriate for many cases. Hence the congressman will seek approval of the proposal in the limited form necessary to solve the particular problem presented to him — and a special tax provision is thereby born.

Lack of Opposition apart from the Treasury Department to Proponents of Special Tax Provisions

The critical importance that attaches to the level of treasury competence and the fatal consequences of any slip on its part derive from its unique position in tax legislation. The question, "Who speaks for tax equity and tax fairness?," is answered today largely in terms of only the Treasury Department. If that department fails to respond, then tax fairness has no champion before the Congress. Moreover, it must respond with vigor and determination, and after a full explanation of the matter it must take a forthright stand on the issues. A Treasury Deparrtment that contents itself with explaining the issues and then solemnly declaring the matter to be one for the policy determination of Congress abdicates its responsibility. The congressman understands aggressiveness and a firm position. He is often in the position of the small boy inwardly seeking parental bounds for his conduct while outwardly declaiming against them. He may not accept policy guidance from the treasury policy spokesman, but he wants it presented. He will invariably interpret a treasury statement that the matter is one for his own policy decision as a victory for the seeker of the special provision.

Thus, in the tax bouts that a congressman witnesses the Treasury is invariably in one corner of the ring. Assuming the Treasury decides to do battle, which is hardly a safe assumption at all times, it is the Treasury versus percentage depletion, the Treasury versus capital gains, the Treasury versus this constituent, the Treasury versus that private group. The effect on the congressman as referee is inevitable. He simply cannot let every battle be won by the Treasury, and hence every so often he gives the victory to the sponsors of a special provision. Moreover, the Treasury is not an impersonal antagonist — it is represented before the Congress by individuals. These individuals are constantly forced to say that enactment of this proposal will be unfair, and the same of the next, and the next. The congressman, being only human is bound from time to time to look upon these individuals as the Cassandras of the tax world. To avoid this dilemma, the Treasury in a close case will sometimes concede the issue if the proposal can be narrowly confined. It feels compelled to say "yes" once in a while simply to demonstrate that it maintains a balanced judgment and possesses a sense of fairness. A special provision is thus enacted simply because it happens to have somewhat more merit than the numerous other special proposals before the committees and because an affirmative answer here by the Treasury will protect negative responses to the other proposals.

The Congressional Tax Staff

The description of the Treasury as the principal and often the sole defender of tax fairness calls for a consideration of the role of the congressional tax staff. Most of the congressional tax technicians are members of the staff of the Joint Committee on Internal Revenue Taxation and as such serve both the House Ways and Means Committee and the Senate Finance Committee. There are a few technicians attached to the separate committees, and the clerks of the committees can play a very important role if they are personally so inclined. But institutionally the chief guidance given to Congress by its own employees cames from this joint committee staff.

The members of this staff work closely with the treasury tax technicians. Their work on the details of proposals and drafts is highly important, but the task of policy formulation and policy guidance to the congressmen appears to be reserved exclusively to the chief of that staff. His role is a difficult and unenviable one. Many congressmen pass along to him the tax proposals that they are constantly receiving from their constituents. Undoubtedly, the Chief of Staff discreetly but effectively blocks many of these proposals from proceeding further. But he also, whatever his inclinations may be, cannot in his situation always say "no." Perhaps inevitably on the crucial issues his role tends to be that of the advocate of the congressman advancing a particular proposal on behalf of a special group. The special-interest groups cannot appear in the executive sessions of the committees, and the congressman sympathetic to their point of view is not technically equipped to present their case; he tends to look to the Chief of Staff to assume that task. Further, he looks to the Chief of Staff to formulate the technical compromises which will resolve the dispute between the special-interest group and the Treasury. The Chief of Staff must therefore work closely with the congressmen and be "brilliantly sensitive to their views." He must necessarily be able to gauge the degree of interest that a congressman may have in a proposal and weigh that in the consideration of the guidance he will give.

Because of these institutional pressures the Chief of Staff is very often the opponent of the Treasury Department before the tax committees. As a result, the difficulties for the average congressman on the tax committees become even greater. The issues get more and more complex as the "experts" disagree, and the congressman can hardly follow the technical exchanges. He is quite often content to fall back on the comfortable thought that, since the congressional expert appears to disagree with the treasury experts, there is adequate technical justification for voting either way. Hence the congressman is free to be guided by his own sympathies and instincts. Since generally these sympathies are in favor of the private groups, their proposals obtain his vote.

Unfortunately agreement between the congressional Chief of Staff and the Treasury can sometimes present just as difficult a problem. When the two disagree, at least the congressman who is seeking to discover the real issues may find them exposed at some time through this disagreement of experts. But if the experts agree, the effect is often to foreclose any real committee consideration of the issues. The congressman may be lulled into thinking that no significant issues are involved, and the proposal therefore becomes law. But if the government experts have erred, or if they have incorrectly gauged the congressional sentiment, special benefits may well result which the congressman would not have sanctioned had he understood what was involved.

Lack of Effective Aid from the Tax Bar

The lack of any pressure-group allies for the Treasury in its representation of the tax-paying public could have been remedied in part by effective aid from the tax bar. Yet for a good many years the vocal tax bar not only withheld any aid but very often conducted itself as an ally of the special pressure groups. Many a lawyer representing a client seeking a special provision could without much difficulty obtain American Bar Association or local-bar-association endorsement for his proposal. He could then appear before Congress and solemnly exhibit the blessing of the legal profession. In fact, the activity of the Bar Association in this respect became so obvious that it seemingly boomeranged — many a congressman began instinctively to smell mischief when presented with a Bar Association tax proposal or endorsement.

Lack of Public Knowledge of Special Tax Provisions

Perhaps the most significant aspect of the consideration of special tax provisions by the Congress is that it usually takes place without any awareness of these events by the general public. Almost entirely, these matters lie outside of the public's gaze, outside of the voter's knowledge. The special provisions which are enacted lie protected in the mysterious complex statutory jargon of the tax law. This technical curtain is impenetrable to the newspapers and other information media. The public hears of debate over tax reduction or tax increase and it may learn something about the general rate structure. But it seldom learns that the high rates have no applicability to much of the income of certain wealthy groups. Nor does it understand how this special taxpayer or that special group is relieved of a good part of its tax burden. All of these matters are largely fought out behind this technical curtain. Hence the congressman favoring these special provisions has for the most part no accounting to make to the voters for his action. He is thereby much freer to lend a helping hand here and there to a group which has won his sympathy or which is pressiing him for results.

The Relationship of Special Tax Provisions to Private-Relief Bills

Some of these special provisions represent simply private-relief claims for the particular individual benefited. While phrased as amendments to the tax law, they are only money claims against the Government based on the equities asserted to exist. Thus, it is said of a senator skilled in congressional ways that he would ask the legislative draftsman preparing the draft of a particular tax provision to make the amendment as general in language and as specific in application as was possible. The tax committees and the Treasury have not solved the problem of how to handle these special bills. Curiously enough, some tax situations do come through the judiciary committees as private-relief bills along with other private-relief bills involving claims against the Government. These bills may involve, for example, a removal of the barrier of the statute of limitations in cases thought equitable, or the recovery of funds spent for revenue stamps lost in some fashion. Here they are subject to the criteria developed over the decades by those committees in the handling of private-claims bills. These criteria are reasonably strict, and few of the bills pass the Congress. Of those that do succeed, a number are vetoed, and a veto is customarily regarded as a final disposition of the bill.

Many situations come before the tax committees that are quite comparable, in that the tax proposal is equivalent to a money claim against the Government, equal to the tax to be saved, sought for a specific taxpayer on equitable grounds. This is especially true in the case of proposals of a retroactive character. In the tax committees these special proposals tend to take on the coloration of an amendment to the tax code of the same character as all the various substantive tax matters before these committees. In essence, all amendments to the tax laws that private groups push on their own behalf are designed to lower taxes for the proponents and thereby relieve them from a tax burden to which they are subject. The special proposals thus become simply one more amendment in the long list of changes to be considered. The proponents of these special proposals are thereby able to cloak the fact that they are presenting private-relief claims against the Government. This is especially so when the proposal is considered as merely one more item in a

general revenue bill. Here it is also protected from the threat —
and fate — of a presidential veto. Even when the proposal is considered as a separate bill, the fact that it is merely one of the bills
before a tax committee that is considering a great many substantive
bills involving amendments to the tax code generally produces the
same result. The committee will tend to focus on the proposal as
curing a substantive defect in the law and lose sight of the fact that
the special proposal is essentially a private-relief bill.

The Executive Branch

16

Planning the President's Program

Richard E. Neustadt

Early in 1954, President Dwight D. Eisenhower presented to the Congress — and the country and his party — some 65 proposals for new
legislation, over and above appropriations. This presentation was a
massive affair. First came six weeks of well-publicized preliminaries:
cabinet deliberations, congressional briefings, press conferences, and
a fireside chat. Then, in three annual messages to Congress — a
State of the Union Address, a Budget Message, and an Economic
Report — the President set forth his bundle of proposals, elaborat-
ing certain aspects, outlining the rest. Along with these came seven
supplementing special messages, each filling in details on some particular: Taft-Hartley, farm price supports, social security, health,
housing, atomic energy, foreign aid, and trade. And following the
messages Administration-approved bills, conveyors of the ultimate
details, were introduced in Congress.

Throughout, one theme was emphasized: here was a comprehensive and coordinated inventory of the nation's current legislative

From Richard E. Neustadt, "Planning the President's Program," *American Political Science Review*, 49 (1955), pp. 113–26.

needs, reflecting the President's own judgments, choices, and priorities in every major area of Federal action; in short, his "legislative program," an entity distinctive and defined, its coverage and its omissions, both, delimiting his stand across the board. And — quite explicitly — this stand was being taken, this program volunteered, in order to give Congress an agenda, Republicans a platform, and voters a yardstick for 1954.

Thus, one year after his inaugural, Eisenhower espoused a sweeping concept of the President's initiative in legislation and an elaborate mechanism for its public expression; developments which no one seemed to take amiss. Both in governmental circles and in the press, the whole performance was regarded almost as a matter of course, a normal White House response to the opening of Congress. The pattern, after all, was quite familiar; the comprehensive program expressed in ordered sequence, with some sort of publicized preliminaries and detailed follow-up, had been an annual enterprise in Truman's time. Indeed, while Eisenhower had undoubtedly improved upon the earlier mechanics, his 1954 procedure seemed expressive less of innovation than of reversion to accustomed practice. In 1953, he had been criticized in many quarters for failing to produce a defined program of this kind; now that "failure" was made good, a general expectation satisfied in the "customary" way.

Customary, perhaps; yet as recently as 1946 an informed observer had remarked, accurately enough, on the "absence of cohesion in the legislative program of the chief executive — absence, in fact, of a program clearly designated as such." Presidential reports and recommendations to Congress were as old as the Constitution; presidential sponsorship of specific measures, highlighted in special messages and spelled out in Administration bills, had been a commonplace in Franklin Roosevelt's time and by no means unknown much earlier. But the elaborate paraphernalia of a comprehensive and specific inventory, contents settled and defined as regards substance no less than finance, *presented in detailed fashion and packaged form at the opening of each session of Congress* — this was a "custom" scarcely nine years old, a postwar phenomenon evolving under Truman and now carried forward under Eisenhower.

Here is an institutional development of no mean proportions, with a great preparatory effort obviously involved in advance of every session. Three questions are suggested: First, currently, what are the mechanics of this program preparation; how is the job done and by whom? Second, historically, what gave rise to such institutionalization in the postwar decade; how did it evolve and how did it survive the change of Administration? Third, prospectively — and specu-latively — what may the whole development imply regarding powers, opportunities, of President and presidency in the legislative process? This paper attempts answers to these questions; its starting point is the making of the Eisenhower program of 1954.

PREPARING THE EISENHOWER PROGRAM OF 1954

"The presentation of a legislative program," wrote Truman in his farewell message to the Congress, "falls properly to my successor, not to me . . . and I would not infringe upon his responsibility to chart the forward course." This was easier said by the outgoing President than done by the incoming, with his first Congress already in session (courtesy the Twentieth Amendment). In 1953, for the first time in years, there was no "legislative program," no charting of the course in the specific sense conveyed by Truman's words and prior practice.

At the outset, Eisenhower did present to Congress his own report on the State of the Union, but he chose throughout that address to keep most of his legislative references general to the point of homily. The new regime, while reducing appropriations requests — as in the case of the Air Force — forebore to present a complete new budget document and message; while revising some economic policies — as in the case of credit and controls — it attempted no new Economic Report. During the spring of 1953, a number of Administration stands on legislation were developed and expressed, piecemeal, in special messages or bills, or both. But for the most part these en-compassed only inescapable necessities — like foreign aid, taxation, reciprocal trade — where scheduled expirations of authority forced the presidential hand. More characteristic were the surveys, investi-gations, and study groups brought forward by the President or his subordinates in lieu of action recommendations on numbers of great issues, foreign and domestic.

What accounts for this lack of firm programming in the congres-sional session of 1953? . . .

[W]hatever Eisenhower's personal position, there seems no doubt that certain members of his entourage were then distinctly predis-posed against a comprehensive program presentation along any-thing like Truman's lines. "We always meant to have a program," appears a considerable overstatement, at least if "we" refers to the whole White House entourage in 1953. Conciliating Congress was the order of the day; by some, apparently, this was interpreted as *not* doing whatever Truman might have done. Moreover, some of the new White House aides appear to have been seriously concerned about the constitutional proprieties; others disturbed about the range of Democratic intervention in domestic spheres; still others doubtful of the need for further emphasis on lawmaking, per se. Such attitudes as these add up to general bearishness toward widespread volunteering of firm presidential stands on current or prospective legislation — especially when controversial. "Let Congress struggle with it; keep us out." Here was, reportedly, an often-sounded White House theme through most of the first session of the 83rd Congress.

Yet scarcely five months after that session's close, there came the Eisenhower legislative program of 1954. Whether as an outcome of deliberate plans, or of changed attitudes, or both, this represents a distinct alteration in approach from one session of Congress to the next. How did it come to pass? How was the newness tempered, the bearishness reduced, the program put together?

In May, 1953, the Bureau of the Budget sent to the multilith machines — in preparation for June 30 distribution — its annual call for estimates from Federal agencies, in this case for fiscal 1955. Included in that document as an instruction to each agency was section 86, entitled "Legislative Program":

> A statement will be submitted [September 15] describing the preliminary legislative program of the agency for the forthcoming session of Congress. This statement should include *all* items of legislation [other than appropriations] which the agency contemplates proposing during the ensuing twelve months. . . .
>
> The statement should be in three parts:
>
> 1. Those items in the President's legislative program which have not yet been enacted . . . limited to proposals . . . specifically identified by the President as part of his program, or specifically held [by Budget through central clearance] to be "in accord with the program of the President."
> 2. Legislative proposals not included in part 1 . . . which would cause no increase in budgeting requirements.
> 3. Legislative proposals not included in part 1 . . . which would cause an increase in budgeting requirements . . . arranged to reflect relative priority among items on the list and also . . . with respect to other portions of the budget. . . .
>
> With respect to each item of proposed legislation, this statement should set forth (1) the subject matter . . . together with a summary statement of the objectives . . . and the need . . . (2) the state of readiness of legislative drafts and other supporting material; (3) a reference to the numbers of pertinent bills and . . . reports [in recent

sessions] . . . together with a brief appraisal . . . (4) a forecast of both the appropriations and the expenditures required . . . and (5) the names of other [interested] departments and agencies. . . .

This language was identical with that included in the 1952 call for estimates issued a year earlier before the close of Truman's term. Indeed, section 86 and its requirements had been a feature of each Budget call since 1949. Their renewal in 1953 marks not an Eisenhower innovation but a bureaucratic continuum, an attempted restoration of routines, an action taken on the Budget's own initiative without advance assurance as to either agency response or ultimate White House reaction.

This was a venture with no guarantees attached; it was, however, something more than a leap in the dark. The Budget Bureau's renewal of section 86 was powerfully reinforced by two other acts of initiative, one preceding, one following preparation of the new call for estimates.

The first of these involved the agencies. As early as January, 1953, the new Budget Director, Joseph M. Dodge, had corralled cabinet colleagues, one by one, for orientation briefings by his career aides. In a number of cases these sessons were held even before Inauguration Day, providing several cabinet members-designate their first glimpse from inside into the complexities of their new assignments. And at each briefing Budget staffers took occasion, with Dodge's assent, to inform the department head about "his" legislative program (compiled the preceding fall), its existence in form and fact, its usefulness for orientation, its potential for planning and control, its liability to renewal on Budget's call.

Thereby, a piece of left-over machinery idling in the departmental depths was impressed on the consciousness of new department heads at a uniquely favorable moment. This had its due effect; by late summer 1953, when lower-level bureaucrats began preparing agency responses to Budget's new call, their top superiors, in almost every case, were reasonably well acquainted with the departmental "program," quite acclimated to its presence as a fact of departmental life, and quite prepared to oversee its renovation and renewal in advance of 1954.

Meanwhile the Budget had taken a further act of initiative, this time involving the White House. Early in July, 1953 President Eisenhower had voiced some concern about means to bring together, well in advance, data and suggestions for his January, 1954 State of the Union message. Budget aids were asked to brief him on his predecessor's practice; they took the opportunity to urge some White House recognition for the programming requirement in section 86 of the new call for estimates. In Truman's time it had been customary for the President to write each agency in early autumn, requesting message data and, at the same time, reiterating over his own signature the main terms of section 86. Message and program requests had long been joined; that was made clear to the new President.

The result was an identical letter to each cabinet officer over Eisenhower's signature and bearing signs of his own dictation. Dated July 30, 1953 — a month after formal issuance of Budget's call — the letters asked for substantive ideas appropriate to the State of the Union Message, these ideas to be based on a "thorough rethinking of the mission of your department and the . . . means to achieve it." And, quite explicitly, that review was to "complement attention you are giving the 1955 budget and the formulation of a carefully planned, specific legislative program."

If there were any doubts remaining at top departmental levels about the propriety — and the priority — of Budget's legislative call, this missive from the President appears to have resolved them. By mid-September, 1953, agency legislative programs were flowing to the Budget. By early October, departmental message memoranda were en route to the White House, many of them referencing or appending these programs to concretize suggested points of emphasis. The President had called for a "thorough rethinking." Here, in this double-barrelled presentation, was the visible response.

Cumulatively, it was an astonishing response, at least to those White House staffers disinclined toward executive initiatives in legislation. For here were departmental declarations of intent to sponsor literally hundreds of measures great and small, *most of which the President was being asked to make his own by personal endorsement in a message.* And among these were dozens of proposals, espoused now by one or another of Eisenhower's own department heads, closely resembling — in general purpose, if not always precise form — predecessor measures urged in Truman's time and bearing then a Fair Deal label: an expansion of social security, an increased minimum wage, a revision of immigration laws, a broadening of unemployment compensation, and many more. Mostly these represented improvements in going programs long advocated by career administrators (and their clientele) to modernize or clarify the application of public policies in their charge. Agency legislative programs in 1953 were not sheer replicas of those in 1952 and earlier — some items were stricken, others added, still others revised — but their content makes plain that mixed with the rethinking from on high was a good deal of educating from below.

For eight years past — save only 1953 — there had been a presidential charting of the course in Truman's terms: an executive inventory of specifics (agenda and yardstick both) for action by the Congress. Now, in October, 1953, these agency submissions forecast that some such executive charting would be done in 1954 — if not by Eisenhower comprehensively, then by his cabinet members piecemeal; if not in his name, then in theirs. At his own invitation they had defined their ambitions, drawn their plans, and these now turned out to encompass controversial innovations of national concern, inextricably involving the President's position and prestige. Were he therefore to influence scope, scale, priorities, and presentation, he needs must act upon their requests for endorsement, thereby asserting his own rule in program-making, *his* plans, *his* charting of the course as against theirs.

The implications were not lost for long upon the presidential staff. . . .

Within the White House . . . there was no escaping action upon agency submissions. By mid-October it was generally conceded that whatever major issues they might raise would have to be acknowledged in some form or fashion — negatively, at the very least — by or before Eisenhower's annual messages. This necessitated first of all a close look at the contents of the pile well in advance of message preparation. And by early November, such examination was preoccupying half the members of the White House entourage.

Their initial "look-see" became a rather elaborate affair. Under the aegis of the Assistant to the President, Sherman Adams, with his deputy, Wilfred E. Persons, and the then Special Counsel, Bernard M. Shanley, actively in charge, anywhere from six to ten members of the entourage — depending on subject-matter — joined in an item-by-item review around the conference table; over a two-week period this involved some 12 meetings of two to three hours apiece. . . .

[From mid-October through December of 1953, program-making went through various stages, briefly summarized here. With the help of Roger Jones, career chief of the Budget Bureau's Office of Legislative Reference, the staff sorted through some 33 "major" proposals, pros and cons of each were sought from congressional and "outside" sources and priorities among the proposals were established. From late November through mid-December several cabinet presentations were made, consensus was sought, with Eisenhower actively participating. This served educative and co-ordinative purposes and also as a dress rehearsal for what was to be many cabinet members' first full-scale approach to a legislative committee.]

In the course of these various proceedings late in 1953 — staff reviews, presidential briefings, cabinet presentations, and attendant negotiations — the White House grew increasingly committed to an Eisenhower legislative program, the more so as its practicable scope and character came clear. By the end of November there was no longer any question that a program would ensue, or that it should appear in annual messages, or that it should be at once comprehensive and concrete. Amidst the concentration on specifics, these things came to be taken for granted. In part, this is attributable to the sheer momentum of those staff and agency proceedings once started on their way. In part, it seems related to the intra-party power struggle in which Senator McCarthy had engaged with increasing directness since the death of Senator Taft the preceding summer. On December 2 and on December 16 the President at press conference took pains to assert that his own forthcoming program, *not* McCarthy's chosen issue, would measure Republican performance in the election year of 1954; this hard upon the Senator's press statements to the contrary. The presidential program, once, perhaps, a questionable undertaking or a necessary chore, was now become a prime political imperative, its relative readiness a godsend, one expects, to the regime. . . .

On December 17, 18, and 19, 1953, Eisenhower formally unveiled his program to the Republican congressional leadership, in an unprecedented series of carefully staged briefings at the White House. With the President presiding, these ran a full eight hours daily, covering a subject-matter agenda fixed in advance and rigidly enforced from the chair. The Vice-President, the Speaker, the Majority Leaders, and the Whips were in attendance at all times, as were most members of the cabinet and the White House entourage. Committee chairmen and their ranking (Republican) associates participated when their subjects were discussed, arriving and departing on a pre-determined schedule; so did a number of executive officials below cabinet rank. In deference to Eisenhower's own communiques, issued each afternoon, and honoring his personal request, those moving in and out avoided detailed comment to the press; thereby, the White House got ideal publicity in presidential terms — headlines about Eisenhower and his program but no scoops on particulars. . . .

Less than three weeks intervened between these leaders' meetings in December, 1953 and the President's State of the Union Address to Congress; it was a busy season for the message drafters. In policy terms there was by this time little left to be decided, but the contents of the several messages remained to be coordinated, their relative scope and coverage fully defined, specific drafts agreed upon — or, indeed, written — and final language snarls worked out. In carrying these matters forward, actual drafting of the Budget Message was left largely to the Budget Bureau, the White House checking mainly general tone and precise wording of concrete proposals. Similarly, drafting of the Economic Report remained largely in the hands of the Economic Council chairman, himself a prime participant in earlier staff consultations. But for the psychologically most important annual message, the President's personally delivered State of the Union Address, the drafting was from first to last a White House undertaking. . . . The first consolidated State of the Union draft was so crowded with specifics that it would have taken some three hours to deliver. In consequence, large portions were pulled out to form the first five of Eisenhower's 1954 special messages, his personal address becoming in the end a sort of preparatory note and table of contents for the supplementing documents to follow.

Meanwhile, the departments concentrated on bill drafting in order that each definite proposal conveyed by these messages might be backed promptly by a detailed draft of legislation bearing an Administration label and ready for transmission (formally or not) to Congress. . . .

Neither by content nor tone were documents like these well suited to the task of dramatizing for the country and his party the President's own personality and purposes. Yet if there was but little drama in the messages themselves, there was, perhaps, much to be gained by focussing attention on their presentation as a collectivity, seeking dramatic impact in the sheer fact of "program," aside from the nature or the statement of its parts. To this the White House — President and staff together, it appears — devoted a great deal of thought and care during December, 1953.

In the five weeks before the State of the Union Address, there emanated from the White House a steady stream of press communiques and dope stories concerning the program's preparation. Specific plans were guarded rather carefully — the aim, no doubt, to generate suspense — but generalized official comments on the special cabinet sessions, and in particular the legislative leaders' meetings, were arranged and facilitated by the White House press office with all the fanfare usually reserved for first-rank international conferences. After the conclusion of those meetings, December 19, the President removed to Georgia over Christmas, whence came almost daily stories of last-minute conferences on the impending messages with officials flown down from Washington. On January 4, 1954, all this was capped by a radio and television address to the nation, in which Eisenhower plugged his program and urged everyone's attention to its imminent unveiling. In dramatic appeal this discourse was scarcely an unqualified success; trying to reach the country in the evening hours without depriving Congress of its first crack at details, he avoided scooping his congressional address at the expense of over-generalizing. Nevertheless, the notion that something portentous impended, Eisenhower's own, received top billing once again in news-casts and the press.

On January 5, the President met minority legislative leaders at the White House for a courtesy preview of his recommendations; thereby the press got one last "program" story before the opening of Congress. Then on Thursday, January 7, came the President's State of the Union Address to the Congress, another radio and television presentation, if at noon. There followed on three successive Mondays and Thursdays no less than seven of his supplementing messages, spaced for optimum press play and in a sequence obviously intended to strengthen the impression of a vast executive creation, highlight its most generally appealing features, blur the rest: Taft-Hartley and farm messages sent up at the same time on the same day (with a Korean defense treaty sent the Senate simultaneously); social security, health, and housing messages each featured in a separate package on a separate day; housekeeping and limited-interest requests buried by the dozen in the Budget Message; tax reduction dominant in the Economic Report. . . .

LEGISLATIVE PROGRAMS
AND PRESIDENTIAL LEADERSHIP

Traditionally, there has been a tendency to distinguish "strong" Presidents from "weak," depending on their exercise of the initiative in legislation. The personal appearances in the hall of the House, the special messages, the drafted bills, the public appeals, so characteristic of contemporary program presentation, have all been represented in the past — no farther back than Franklin Roosevelt's time — as signs of a President's intention or capacity to "dominate" the Congress. If these were once relevant criteria of domination, they are not so today. As things stand now they have become part of the regular routines of office, an accepted elaboration of the constitutional right to recommend; as such, no more indicative of presidential domination than the veto power, say, in Herbert Hoover's time.

Indeed, from the congressional point of view, "service," not domination, is the reality behind these presidential undertakings. In practical effect, they represent a means whereby Congress can gain from the outside what comes hard from within: a handy and official guide to the wants of its biggest customer; an advance formulation of main issues at each session; a work-load ready-to-hand for every legislative committee; an indication, more or less, of what may risk the veto; a borrowing of presidential prestige for most major bills — and thus a boosting of publicity-potentials in both sponsorship and opposition.

That Congress wants these things and finds them useful for its purposes may be judged from the almost total absence nowadays of vocal criticism or surprise at annual presentations of the President's program; an indicator reinforced by irritated comments, privately expressed on both sides of the aisle, when Eisenhower stayed his hand in 1953. Outcries against "dictatorship" and "speeches-from-the-throne" have long been stilled in responsible quarters. In 1947, Senator Taft told a Budget aide that as a matter of orderly procedure Republican committee chairmen *ought* to have the Democratic President's own views across-the-board and in detail, else the committees would lack solid ground from which to gauge the pleadings of departments and their clientele. In 1953, the very senior chairman of a major House commititee reportedly admonished an Administration witness, "don't expect us to start from scratch on what you people want. That's not the way we do things here — *you* draft the bills and *we* work them over."

As that remark suggests, the Congress deals not in abstract ideas but in bills. It comes to grips with substance in terms of phraseology. The process cannot start without a draft. And since executive expertise is often indispensable, while executive wishes are data to be weighed — though quite conceivably ignored — a "downtown" draft has tangible advantage as the starting point. But more than drafting service is provided by contemporary presidential programs. Annual programming serves also to identify, to render timely, in effect to choose, most *legislative* issues on which serious attention is to center at a session; the President becomes agenda-setter for the Congress, the chief continuing initiator of subject-matter to reach actionable stages in committee and on the floor, whether or not ultimately passed. Of course, as Lawrence Chamberlain and others have made plain, most major measures are the product of long germination, much cross-fertilizing. Quite so; the service of contemporary Presidents has been less creativity than crystallization; a matter less of seeding new terrain than of tracing new lines in old ground, thereby to mark the field for current cultivation.

In this respect, the presidency is performing for the Congress a task apparently beyond that body's institutional capacity to carry on its own account. When one looks at the legislative record of the last decade, the major controversial measures brought to focus, debate, and near-passage, or enactment on congressional initiative *alone,* are small scatteration relative to those highlighted by — or with assistance from — the President: most prominently, perhaps, the Taft-Hartley Act, the two McCarran Acts, and the perennial Bricker Amendment.[1] Of these, at least Taft-Hartley may be ascribed actually to a reverse sort of presidential initiative — Truman choosing *not* to propose action in an area where momentary public sensitivity was certain to evoke response of some sort from the 80th Congress. . . . Presidential silences no less than statements may serve to delineate the actionable issues.

But note that setting an agenda is not the same thing as enforcing it; selecting issues for consideration is not equivalent to having bill enacted into law. For evidence one has but to review the course of any recent congressional session. As a matter of fact, the most institutionalized aspects of the President's involvement in the legislative process are precisely those least concerned with actual campaigning for his program once presented: legislative programming and legislative clearance, *not* legislative in-fighting and signal-calling, day-by-day. To be sure, periodic White House meetings with congressional party leaders have become the norm; agendas prepared for the President in Truman's time; minutes kept as well in Eisenhower's. And Eisenhower has established in his entourage an Army-type liaison operation, its several staff aides covering each corner of the Hill on regular patrols. But formal leaders' sessions tend to be ambassadorial encounters; organized liaison tends to create its own

---

[1] Other items which reached the point of passage include the tax reduction measures of 1947 and 1948, the first tidelands bill in 1947, and the natural gas and basing point bills of 1949. Of course, there have been infinite numbers of amendments to, adjustments in — and sheer denials of — Administration proposals, over the years, as matters of distinct congressional initiative, oppositional to presidential purposes or claimed intent. But these are in a different category. The fact that Presidents are now so largely raisers of the issues does not signify that they are safe from penalties for having done so; quite the contrary, both in and out of Congress.

chores, if not, indeed, to confuse liaisoners' loyalties. So far as one can judge from the outside, it remains true in Eisenhower's time — as in Truman's and F.D.R.'s before him — that when the chips are down, there is no substituting for the President's own footwork, his personal negotiation, his direct appeal, his voice and no other's on the telephone. Naturally, such methods cannot guarantee success; to overwork them would be self-defeating; to institutionalize them may well be impossible. Yet these, not programming devices, must bear the weight, provide the test, of presidential "domination" over Congress.

Indeed, a presidential purpose to control the congressional *product* may actually be impeded, not advanced, by legislative programming as presently evolved. Those massive, annual presentations have a tendency to blur the public impact of particulars, scatter attention, divert interest — as with Eisenhower's messages of 1954, or Truman's, year by year. Regularized repetition tends to dilute the dramatic, focussing effects of personal appearance and appeal. White House sponsorship spread wide tends to reduce the import of each presidential label. Manifold commitments tend to complicate the task of striking particular bargains. Multi-item programs tend to encourage score-keeping by parties, press, and public, ordinarily with the result of stressing losses over gains on a strict by-the-numbers basis. . . .

But whether or not always advantageous in those terms, the annual presidential inventory and its attendant mechanics have now become so rooted in responsibilities of office, so customary in the view of press and public, so satisfactory to the Congress, so institutionalized in the executive, that major alteration of the present pattern, much less its permanent abandonment, would appear no light matter for a President, nor likely. . . . And these are backed now by accustomed practices each year becoming more entrenched — not only as responses to congressional and public expectations, but as prime means to policy decision and control in the executive. To disavow them now might be to trade more flexibility with Congress for fewer hand holds on departments — this difficulty among others.

17

Budgetary Strategies

Aaron Wildavsky

Budgetary strategies are actions by governmental agencies intended to maintain or increase the amount of money available to them. Not every move in the budgetary arena is necessarily aimed at getting funds in a conscious way. Yet administrators can hardly help being aware that nothing can be done without funds, and that they must normally do things to retain or increase rather than decrease their income.

Our major purpose in this chapter is to describe in an orderly manner the major budgetary strategies currently being employed and to relate them to the environment from which they spring. In this way we can, for the first time, describe the behavior of officials engaged in budgeting as they seek to relate their requirements and powers to the needs and powers of others. Strategies are the links between the intentions and perceptions of budget officials and the political system that imposes restraints and creates opportunities for them. When we know about strategies we are not only made aware of important kinds of behavior, we also learn about the political world in which they take place.

Strategic moves take place in a rapidly changing environment in which no one is quite certain how things will turn out and new goals constantly emerge in response to experience. In this context of uncertainty, choice among existing strategies must be based on intuition and hunch, on an "educated guess," as well as on firm knowledge. Assuming a normal capacity to learn, however, experience should eventually provide a more reliable guide than sheer guesswork. When we discover strategies that are practiced throughout the entire administrative apparatus, we suspect that officials have discovered paths to success which may not be wholly reliable but

From *The Politics of the Budgetary Process,* Aaron Wildavsky, pages 63–100. Copyright © 1964 by Little, Brown and Company (Inc.). Reprinted by permission.

which have proved to be more advantageous than the available alternatives.

UBIQUITOUS AND CONTINGENT STRATEGIES

What really counts in helping an agency get the appropriations it desires? Long service in Washington has convinced high agency officials that some things count a great deal and others only a little. Although they are well aware of the desirability of having technical data to support their requests, budget officials commonly derogate the importance of the formal aspects of their work as a means of securing appropriations. Budget estimates that are well prepared may be useful for internal purposes — deciding among competing programs, maintaining control of the agency's operations, giving the participants the feeling they know what they are doing, finding the cost of complex items. The estimates also provide a respectable backstop for the agency's demands. But, as several informants put it in almost identical words, "It's not what's in your estimates but how good a politician you are that matters."

Being a good politician, these officials say, requires essentially three things: cultivation of an active clientele, the development of confidence among other governmental officials, and skill in following strategies that exploit one's opportunities to the maximum. Doing good work is viewed as part of being a good politician.

Strategies designed to gain confidence and clientele are ubiquitous; they are found everywhere and at all times in the budgetary system. The need for obtaining support is so firmly fixed a star in the budgetary firmament that it is perceived by everyone and uniformly taken into account in making the calculations upon which strategies depend.

"Contingent" strategies are particular; they depend upon conditions of time and place and circumstance; they are especially dependent upon an agency's attitude toward the opportunities the budgetary system provides for. Arising out of these attitudes, we may distinguish three basic orientations toward budgeting in increasing order of ambition. First, defending the agency's base by guarding against cuts in old programs. Second, increasing the size of the base by moving ahead with old programs. Third, expanding the base by adding new programs. These types of strategies differ considerably from one another. An agency might cut popular programs to promote a restoration of funds; it would be unlikely to follow this strategy in adding new programs. We shall take up ubiquitous and contingent strategies in turn.

CLIENTELE

Find a Clientele

For most agencies locating a clientele is no problem at all; the groups interested in their activities are all too present. But for some agencies the problem is a difficult one and they have to take extraordinary measures to solve it. . . .

Serve Your Clientele

For an agency that has a large and strategically placed clientele, the most effective strategy is service to those who are in a position to help them. "If we deliver this kind of service," an administrator declared, "other things are secondary and automatic." . . .

Expand Your Clientele

In order to secure substantial funds from Congress for domestic purposes, it is ordinarily necessary to develop fairly wide interest in the program. . . .

Concentrate on Individual Constituencies

After the Census Bureau had made an unsuccessful bid to establish a national housing survey, Representative Yates gave it a useful hint. The proposed survey "is so general," Yates said, "as to be almost useless to the people of a particular community. . . . This would help someone like Armstrong Cork, who can sell its product anywhere in the country . . . but will it help the construction industry in a particular area to know whether or not it faces a shortage of customers?" Later, the Bureau submitted a new program that called for a detailed enumeration of metropolitan districts with a sample survey of other areas to get a national total. Endorsed by mortgage holding associations, the construction material industry, and Federal and state housing agencies, the new National Housing Inventory received enthusiastic support in Congress. . . .

Secure Feedback

Almost everyone claims that his projects are immensely popular and benefit lots of people. But how do elected officials know? They can only be made aware by hearing from constituents. The agency can do a lot to ensure that its clientele responds by informing them that contacting Congressmen is necessary and by telling them how to go about it if they do not already know. In fact, the agency may organize the clientele in the first place. The agency may then offer to fulfill the demand it has helped to create. Indeed, Congressmen often urge administrators to make a show of their clientele. . . .

Divided We Stand

The structure of administrative units may be so arranged as to obtain greater support from clientele. It may be advantageous for a department to create more bureaus or subunits so that there are more claimants for funds who can attract support. . . .

United We Fall

The Weather Bureau is an example of an agency that did rather poorly until it took the many suggestions offered by its supporters in Congress and established a separate appropriation for research and development. The new category was the glamorous one and it was easier to attract support alone; being lumped in with the others hurt its appeal. . . .

Advisory Committees Always Ask for More

Get a group of people together who are professionally interested in a subject, no matter how conservative or frugal they might otherwise be, and they are certain to find additional ways in which money could be spent. . . .

Do Not Admit Giving in to "Pressure"

> Civil Aeronautics Board official: . . . One of the reasons there has been such substantial expansion in local airline service, believe it or not, is largely due to the members of Congress.
> Representative Flood: I hope you are talking about Hazleton, Pa.
> CAB official: I am talking about Pennsylvania as well as every other state. I do not want to leave the impression here that there has been undue pressure or that we have been unduly influenced by members of Congress, but we have tried to cooperate with them.
> Representative Flood: I do not care what the distinction is.

But if They Press Make Them Pay

> CAB official: . . . Senator . . . if there are any members of Congress apprehensive about the increasing level of subsidy, this has not been evident to the Board. . . . I cannot think of any local service case in which we have not had at least 15, 20, or 25 members of Congress each one urging an extension of the local service to the communities in his constituency as being needed in the public interest. . . . We felt that they, if anyone, knew what the public interest required . . . as to local service . . . with full knowledge that this would require additional subsidy.

Avoid Being Captured

The danger always exists that the tail will wag the dog and the agency must exercise care to avoid being captured. Rival interests and Congressmen may be played against each other. New clientele may be recruited to replace the old. The President and influential Congressmen may be persuaded to help out. Or the agency may just decide to say "no" and take the consequences. . . .

I do not mean to suggest that getting constituency support is all that counts. On the contrary, many agencies lay down tough criteria that projects must meet before they are accepted. The point is that there are ordinarily so many programs that can be truly judged worthwhile by the agency's standards that its major task appears to be that of gaining political support. Priorities may then be assigned on the basis of the ability of the program and its sponsors to garner the necessary support.

CONFIDENCE

The sheer complexity of budgetary matters means that some people need to trust others because they can check up on them only a fraction of the time. . . . If we add to this the idea of budgeting by increments, where large areas of the budget are not subject to serious questions each year, committee members will treat an agency much better if they feel that its officials will not deceive them. Thus the ways in which the participants in budgeting try to solve their staggering burden of calculation constrain and guide them in their choice of means to secure budgetary ends.

Administrative officials are unanimously agreed that they must, as a bare minimum, enjoy the confidence of the appropriations committee members and their staff. . . . How do agency personnel seek to establish this confidence?

Be What They Think They Are

Confidence is achieved by gearing one's behavior to fit in with the expectations of committee people. Essentially, the desired qualities appear to be projections of the committee members' images of themselves. Bureaucrats are expected to be masters of detail, hard-working, concise, frank, self-effacing fellows who are devoted to their work, tight with the taxpayer's money, recognize a political necessity when they see one, and keep the Congressmen informed. . . .

Play It Straight!

Everyone agrees that the most important requirement of confidence, at least in a negative sense, is to be aboveboard. . . . A lie, an attempt to blatantly cover up some misdeed, a tricky move of any kind, can lead to an irreparable loss of confidence. . . .

Integrity

The positive side of the confidence relationship is to develop the opinion that the agency official is a man of high integrity who can be trusted. He must not only give but must also appear to give reliable information. He must keep confidences and not get a Congressman into trouble by what he says or does. He must be willing to take blame but never credit. Like a brand name, a budget official's reputation comes to be worth a good deal in negotiation. . . . The crucial test may come when an official chooses to act contrary to his presumed immediate interests by accepting a cutback or taking the blame in order to maintain his integrity with his appropriations subcommittee. It must not be forgotten that the budget official often has a long-term perspective and may be correct in trying to maximize his appropriations over the years rather than on every single item. . . .

Make Friends: The Visit

Parallel in importance to the need for maintaining integrity is developing close personal relationships with members of the agency's appropriations subcommittee, particularly the Chairman. The most obvious way is to seek them out and get to know them. . . .

I'd Love to Help You but...

Where the administrator's notion of what is proper conflicts with that of a Congressman with whom it is desirable to maintain friendly relations, there is no perfect way out of the difficulty. Most officials try to turn the Congressman down by suggesting that their hands are tied, that something may be done in the future, or by stressing some other project on which they are agreed. . . .

Give and Take

At other times some compromise may be sought. Secretary of Commerce Averell Harriman was faced with the unpalatable task of deciding which field offices to eliminate. He first used internal Department criteria to find the lower one-third of offices in point of usefulness. Then he decided which to drop or curtail by checking with the affected Congressmen, trying to determine the intensity of their reactions, making his own estimate of whom he could and could not afford to hurt. Harriman's solution was a nice mixture of internal and political criteria designed to meet as many goals as possible or at least to hold the Department's losses down.

Truth and Consequences

In the end, the administrator may just have to face the consequences of opposing Congressmen whose support he needs. Even if he were disposed to accommodate himself to their desires at times, he may find that other influential members are in disagreement. He may play them off against one another or he may find that nothing he can do will help. The best he may be able to do is to ride out the storm without compounding his difficulties by adding suspicions of his integrity to disagreements over his policies. He hopes, particularly if he is a career man, that the Congressmen will rest content to damn the deed without damning the man.

Emphasis

The administrator's perception of Congressional knowledge and motivation helps determine the kind of relationships he seeks to establish. The administrator who feels that the members of his appropriations subcommittees are not too well informed on specifics and that they evaluate the agency's program on the basis of feedback from constituents, stresses the role of supporting interests in maintaining good relations with Congressmen. He may not feel the need to be too careful with his estimates. The administrator who believes that the Congressmen are well informed and fairly autonomous is likely to stress personal relationships and demonstrations of good work as well as clientele support. Certain objective conditions may be important here. Some subcommittees deal with much smaller areas than others and their members are likely to be better informed than they otherwise would be. Practices of appointment to subcommittees differ between House and Senate and with passing time. Where Congressmen are appointed who have direct and important constituency interests at stake, the information they get from back home becomes more important. If the composition of the committee changes and there are many members without substantial background in the agency's work, and if the staff does not take up the slack, the agency need not be so meticulous about the information it presents. This situation is reflected in the hearings in which much time is spent on presenting general background information and relatively little on specifics.

Subcommittee and Other Staff

Relationships of confidence between agency personnel and subcommittee staff are also vital and are eagerly sought after. Contacts between subcommittee staff and budget officers are often frequent, intensive, and close. Frequency of contacts runs to several times a day when hearings are in progress, once a day when the bill is before the committee, and several times a month during other seasons. This is the principal contact the committee staff has with the Executive Branch. Even when the staff seeks information directly from another official in the agency, the budget officer is generally apprised of the contact and it is channeled through him. Relationships between ordinary committee staff members and Budget Bureau personnel are infrequent, although the people involved know one another. The top-ranking staff members and the Budget Bureau liaison man, however, do get together frequently to discuss problems of coordination (such as scheduling of deficiency appropriations) and format of budget presentation. At times, the BOB uses this opportunity to sound out the senior staff on how the committee might react to changes in presentation and policy. The staff members respond without speaking for the committee in any way. There also may be extensive contact between committee staff and the staff attached to individual Congressmen, but there is not a stable pattern of consultations. House and Senate Appropriations Committee staff may check with one another; also, the staff attached to the substantive committees sometimes may go into the financial implications of new bills with appropriations staff.

When an agency has good relations with subcommittee staff it has an easier time in Congress than it might otherwise. The agency finds that more reliance is placed on its figures, more credence is given to its claims, and more opportunities are provided to secure its demands. Thus one budget officer received information that a million-dollar item has been casually dropped from a bill and was able to arrange with his source of information on the staff to have the item put back for reconsideration. On the other hand, a staff man can do great harm to an agency by expressing distrust of its competence or integrity. Asked if they would consider refusing to talk to committee staff, agency officials uniformly declared that this refusal would be tantamount to cutting their own throats.

CONGRESSIONAL COMMITTEE HEARINGS

The observer who knows that Congressmen and bureaucrats frequently engage in mutually profitable transactions during the year may make the mistake of discounting the hearings as mere ritual. In some cases it is true that the conclusions have been arrived at in advance and that the hearings serve only to create a record to convince others to support the committee's action. But most of the time hearings do have an importance of their own so that what happens may have an effect on the committee's decision. Some agencies are rather wary of too close a relationship with Congressmen; their top officials may lack a gift for the personal touch; they prefer to make their case in the open at the hearings. Even when personal relationships are close and continuous the pressure of time on the parties concerned may mean that prior consultation has been kept to a minimum. Not all items have previously been discussed and it may be necessary to muster support for them at the hearings. Not every Congressman on an appropriations subcommittee may have been included in personal visits and these votes may be needed when the subcommittees go into the mark-up session. Confidence may rapidly be dissipated by a poor performance. No one wants to trust incompetents. . . .

RESULTS

Confidence rests to some extent on showing the Budget Bureau and Congress that the programs are worthwhile because they lead to useful results. The word "results" in this context has at least two meanings, which must be disentangled. In one sense it means that some people feel they are being served. In a second sense it means that the activity accomplishes its intended purposes. This sense of "result" itself involves a basic distinction. There are programs that involve a product or a service that is concrete, such as an airplane, and others that involve activities that resist measurement, such as propaganda abroad. The demonstration of results differs in both cases, as do the strategies employed.

Serve an Appreciative Clientele

The best kind of result is one that provides services to a large and strategically placed clientele, which brings its satisfaction to the attention of decision makers. (The clientele may be producers of services, as in the case of defense contractors.) The kinds of strategies involved have been discussed under "clientele," and we shall go on to others in which the second sense of "result" is implicated.

It Works: The Problem of Criteria

Outside of overwhelming public support, there is nothing that demonstrates results better than tangible accomplishment. The Polaris does fire and hit a target with reasonable accuracy; a nuclear submarine actually operates; a range-reseeding project makes the grass grow again. Interpretation of accomplishments as being worthwhile depends on finding criteria and on how tough these criteria are permitted to be. The Nike-Zeus missile may be fine if it is only supposed to knock down a few missiles or half of an enemy's missiles; it may be utterly inadequate if the criterion is raised to all missiles or most missiles or is changed to include avoidance of decoys. There is great temptation to devise a criterion that will enable a project's supporters to say that it works. At the same time, opponents of a project may unfairly propose criteria that cannot be met. And there are times when men reasonably disagree over criteria because no one knows what will happen. We hope and pray to avoid nuclear war. But if it comes, what criteria should a civil defense program have to meet? If one argues that it must save everyone, then no program can show results.

Suppose, however, that one is willing to accept much less — say half or a third or a fifth of the population. Then everything depends on estimates which can surely be improved upon but which nobody can really claim to be reliable as to likely levels of attack, patterns of wind and radiation, and a multitude of other factors. . . .

STRATEGIES DESIGNED TO CAPITALIZE ON THE FRAGMENTATION OF POWER IN NATIONAL POLITICS

The separation of powers and the internal divisions of labor within Congress and the Executive Branch present numerous opportunities to play one center of power off against another.

Compensation

Supporters of a program who have superior access to one house of Congress may seek to raise the program's grant to allow for bargaining with the other branch. If they can get their way or arrange to split the difference in the Conference Committee, they are that much ahead. . . . The Senate may get its friends to prepare questions and answers in the House hearings and floor debates in anticipation of trouble with the other chamber.

Cross Fire

Although the presence of differing interests and degrees of confidence in the House and Senate may provide the agency with room to maneuver, it may also subject it to a withering cross fire from which there is no immediate escape. . . .

Both Ends Against the Middle

The separation between appropriations and substantive committees creates another opportunity to exploit differences between dual authorities. Appropriations committees often refuse funds for projects authorized by substantive committees. And substantive committees, with or without agency backing, sometimes seek to exert influence over appropriations committees. A familiar tactic is the calling of hearings by substantive committees to dramatize the contention that an authorized program is being underfinanced or not financed at all. Knowing that the appropriations committees have the final say, the substantive committees can afford to authorize any project they deem good without too much concern for its financial implications. Appropriations committees sometimes seek to write legislation into appropriations bills; this effort may lead to a conflict with the substantive committee that spills over onto the floor of the houses of Congress. Participants believe that there is now greater awareness, particularly on the part of staff members, of the need to maintain contact between the two kinds of committees in regard to the financial implications of legislation and the legislative implications of appropriations.

Agencies stand to gain by exploiting these conflicts to their own advantage. They try to use an authorization as a club over the head of the appropriations committees by pointing to a substantive committee as a source of commitment to ask for funds. . . .

18

Congress and the Presidency

Lyndon B. Johnson

For twenty-nine years Capitol Hill was my home. In all those years I thought I knew Congress fairly well, understood its many moods, grasped its essential nature. But like other Presidents with previous experience on Capitol Hill, I found that once I reached the White House the Congress appeared far less familiar. However close we might remain, I knew that our relationship could never be the same. . . . What follows is one scene in a play of many acts. It is the story of my long struggle with the Congress to obtain a tax surcharge, a struggle that reveals the sources of conflict between the President and the Congress.

In the days of the Old Economics federal spending was generally regarded, in congressional rhetoric, as close to sin — unless it was for

Condensed from Chapter 19 "Bite the Bullet" from *The Vantage Point* by Lyndon Baines Johnson. Copyright © 1971 by HEC Public Affairs Foundation. Reprinted by permission of Holt, Rinehart and Winston, Inc.

your own constituency. A budget surplus was the height of virtue, a deficit the symbol of shame. Political figures regularly compared the federal budget to a family budget and warned of disaster if it remained in the red for long. Recessions and depressions were the unavoidable evils of a business cycle in which expansion and decline followed one another as winter follows autumn.

With the triumph of the New Economics in the enactment of the tax cut of 1964, most of these stereotypes seemed to be laid to rest. Many inhibitions against direct governmental intervention to stimulate or brake the economy were apparently lifted. The Legislative and the Executive branches seemed finally to have reached a "meeting of the minds" on taxation. But stimulation proved easier than braking, and the meeting of the minds proved temporary.

True to its sponsors' promise, the tax cut brought our economy close to full employment. It stimulated economic expansion, increased production, and strengthened consumer markets. Unemployment fell to its lowest level in eight years. But this achievement was short-lived. Our sluggish economy had indeed been stimulated, but with the rising cost of the war in Vietnam on top of growing consumer demand, the economy was dangerously close to overheating late in 1965. We tried to cool it down, but with each passing month inflation rose. . . .

One major source of conflict between the Legislative and Executive branches is the difference in constituency. The President is concerned with the economic well-being of the entire nation. Congress, by contrast, is the product of 50 state and 435 local constituencies, each representing only one piece of the national jigsaw puzzle. Many Congressmen and Senators understood my concern for the economy as a whole, but each legislator had one overriding need — to make a record with the people who sent him to office. On the subject of taxes, the people were extremely vocal. Mail on the Hill was running heavily against a tax increase. On many days in 1966 one or another Congressman would call me to say that he was with me in spirit — he understood my predicament and sympathized with me, but it would be political suicide for him to support a tax increase.

A second area of conflict is the difference in information. On economic questions, I had the opinions of a wide range of experts in the Council of Economic Advisers, the Treasury, and the Bureau of the Budget. By 1966 these advisers were united in both their diagnosis of the economic problem and their prescribed remedy. In their judgment, inflation was being created by a high level of income which was forcing prices up because demand was outpacing the capacity to produce. The remedy: a tax increase to hold demand to acceptable levels.

While a President has a large number of experts and statisticians available, the individual Congressman must rely on a personal staff of three or four and a committee staff of half a dozen or less. Consequently, he must either accept our facts, which he often dislikes doing, or find his own sources of information. Those sources were readily available. Though most economists agreed that a tax increase was needed to combat inflation, a significant minority disagreed, and their arguments did not go unheeded.

Throughout most of the struggle a majority of the members of the House Ways and Means Committee, which is responsible for writing tax bills, operated from a different reading of the economy than ours. In their judgment, inflation was caused not by excessive demand but by producers passing on higher costs, especially wages, as higher prices. Other members of Congress believed that the solution was to reduce government spending. There was little agreement on which items of the budget should be cut. In fact, it was difficult to hold back the Appropriations Committee and the Congress as a whole from increasing the amounts in my budget. Senator William Proxmire of Wisconsin, a member of the Joint Economic Committee, held still another view. He agreed that "in a booming, bursting, zooming economy a tax increase is the right medicine to stop inflationary pressure." But he did not believe that our economy was booming. On the contrary, he thought that the principal trouble was excessive cost, not excessive demand, and that demand for most products was actually deficient. If this were true, a tax increase would only make things worse by reducing demand even further.

These were all honest differences of opinion based on conflicting evaluations, varying sources of information, and contradictory diagnoses of the problem. It is no wonder, in such circumstances, that conflict arose over the best remedy.

A third source of traditional Executive-Legislative conflict is the difference in time perspective. The President and the Congress run on separate clocks. The occupant of the White House has a strict tenancy. He has, at most, two terms of four years each to reach his goals. Consequently, the Presidency is geared to force decisions and actions. . . . In contrast to the President's limited tenancy in the White House, a careful Congressman can make a home for life on Capitol Hill. While the President must live with crises and deadlines, a Congressman can cultivate the art of delay and refrain from commitment — especially if the commitment is to increase everybody's taxes.

As Chairman of the Ways and Means Committee, Representative Wilbur Mills had a different constituency than I. His leadership would be judged by his Arkansas electorate and his colleagues in the House. In building his reputation, Chairman Mills followed a basic principle. He wanted to report a bill to the floor when he felt there was a good chance of passing it. Over the years he developed great skill in estimating votes in the committee and the House. When the votes were lacking, he preferred to wait rather than risk the reputation of his committee and the image of his leadership.

In the tax fight Mills was particularly sensitive about his reputation. On one occasion I remember he suffered a rare defeat. A debt-ceiling bill reported out by his committee was rejected by the House as a whole. Mills did not relish such occasions. He was determined to proceed with maximum caution. By contrast, I felt the need for maximum speed. When the economy shows signs of faltering, prompt countermoves are absolutely essential.

These differences — in constituency, information, and time perspective — are built-in conflicts. They provide tension enough to satisfy the most demanding constitutional system. But in America we are blessed with a watchdog press, often ready to improve on the work of the Founding Fathers as well as the President. The tax issue was an ideal subject. The conflict between Chairman Mills and the President provided headlines. The press enjoys a fight between the White House and Capitol Hill. With each newspaper report, our disagreements escalated. First Mills was reported to be hurt because I had not consulted him on the tax bill. Soon he felt utterly neglected. Before long he was downright angry. In all this, no mention was made either of the many long White House sessions in which Mills participated in the initial drafting of the tax message or of the dozens of hours the Secretary and Under Secretary of the Treasury spent with him throughout the entire legislative struggle.

Actually, Mills was an extremely skillful Congressman and a man of integrity. I liked him, and I enjoyed a close working relationship with him. Yet a myth repeated often enough soon becomes accepted truth. Before long, in some strange way the dignity of our offices became involved, making natural compromise more difficult.

Far more important on most issues are the sources of cooperation that bring the President and Congress together and enable them to work in tandem to advance the public interest. In the politics of taxation, not the least of my troubles in 1967 was that the ordinary forces of cooperation were severely strained.

In many instances, party philosophy serves as a loose cement that binds together the President and many members of Congress, but in the case of the tax bill the Democratic party was split. On the one hand, many conservative Democrats were saying to me: "We'll go with you on the tax increase, but only if you wrap it in the American flag as a wartime measure and use the revenue solely for military expenditures and not for your Great Society programs." On the other hand, several liberals were saying: "We'll go with you, but only if you use all the revenue to build the Great Society programs, not for any of your military efforts." Other liberals insisted on tax reforms as part of any tax bill. And everyone was saying: "We've got elections and we just don't want any new taxes." . . .

Following Gardner Ackley's recommendations in his memo of December 1965, I began to move against inflation early in 1966. My first actions were carefully measured. I knew the obstacles we faced. I had to take one step at a time, hoping to bring the Congress along with me. I began in the State of the Union message delivered on January 12, 1966, with a call for a temporary restoration of automobile and telephone excise taxes and for accelerating collection of corporate and personal tax payments. These measures would add $6 billion in federal revenue, an important start. Two months later Congress responded with the Tax Adjustment Act of 1966.

As soon as the first act was signed, I began exploring the possibilities of a second. In his next memo to me on March 12, 1966, Gardner Ackley pointed out: "We are not facing an explosive situation. A little inflation won't be fatal. But inflationary psychology and inflationary symptoms are taking root. If they do get firmly established, it will be hard to uproot them and hard to resist pressures for overly restrictive action." Early in 1966 I discussed a possible tax increase with my Cabinet officers. I asked for their opinions. Only one Cabinet member, Secretary of Commerce John Connor, spoke in favor of higher taxes. A vote showed the Cabinet to be in overwhelming opposition.

On March 30, 1966, I invited more than 150 leading businessmen to a dinner at the White House. After dinner, I outlined our economic situation and asked them:

> How many of you would recommend tomorrow a tax increase to the Congress for the purpose of restraining our economy? Those of you that would, I wish you would raise your right hand.

Not a single hand went up. Not one of those businessmen supported a tax increase to dampen the rising inflation. A few weeks later I met with a group of labor leaders. I posed a similar question. I got a similar answer. . . .

I sounded out the congressional leadership on a tax increase, and their answer was painfully clear. The House leadership reported late in the spring of 1966 that of twenty-five members on the Ways and Means Committee, the most support I could then expect was four votes. Chairman Mills's vote was not among them. In the highly charged preelection atmosphere, I was advised that I was lucky to be able to count on even four votes.

On August 30, 1966, House Majority Leader Carl Albert told Larry O'Brien bluntly: "The tax bill will be extremely difficult, if not impossible to pass and certainly will mess up other programs." We were forced to settle for second best: a bits-and-pieces revenue package passed in September that suspended the 7 per cent investment credit, curtailed federal agency borrowing from the private market, and scaled down prospective expenditures. At the same time, we had to try to restrain wage and price increases, using every opportunity to express our concern to leaders of business and labor. . . .

The fiscal and monetary measures we carried out in 1966 had some effect. . . . In spite of losing forty-seven Democratic seats in the House in the 1966 elections, we seemed to have some chance of success in 1967 — compared with almost no chance in 1966.

Early in 1967 we estimated that a 6 per cent tax surcharge, to become effective the following July, would slow inflation without risking a recession. I urged the Congress again to pass a surcharge in my State of the Union message on January 10, 1967. We could not get action on it for the first six months of that year, since the combination of monetary restraints and the repeal of investment credit had produced a serious pile-up of inventories and the temporary threat of recession.

By July 1967, however, the economy was moving up again, and it was clear that even a 6 per cent surcharge would not be enough. But if not 6 per cent, what should the figure be — 8 per cent? 9 per cent? 10 per cent? Should corporations pay a higher surcharge than individuals? Should citizens with low incomes be exempted? On these and other details I consulted with the Congress through Wilbur Mills. He was in steady contact with the White House throughout the drafting session late in July.

Long experience — from the National Youth Administration to the U.S. Senate — had taught me the value of such consultation. When Congress helps to shape projects, they are more likely to be successful than those simply handed down from the Executive branch. With Chairman Mills, we worked on the draft of the tax message as if we were marking up a bill in Executive session or in conference. . . .

Before the message was sent to the Hill, I asked for a survey of the initial reactions of key committee members and interest groups to the proposed bill. This checklist was compiled by members of the White House congressional liaison staff, the appropriate Cabinet members, and agency staff men. On the tax issue, Secretary of the Treasury Fowler and Under Secretary Joe Barr were responsible for checking the House Democrats; Commerce Secretary Alexander Trowbridge coordinated the check on business and labor; and agency staff men contacted Republican Senators and Congressmen. There is nothing mysterious about this technique. Each man received a list of people to contact and was expected, within one or two days, to describe the attitudes and opinions of those consulted. Taken together, the individual readings gave us a rough estimate of the congressional feeling on the issue at stake.

The key to accurate head counts is personal knowledge or trust and the ability to probe beneath the surface to see what individuals are really thinking and feeling. If a liaison man knew his contacts well — if he knew who was irritated about what, who had a tough election ahead, and who had ambitions for higher office — he could judge their reactions in one conversation or phone call. But if he did not know his men well, he might never be able to interpret tone, nuance, and spirit. Without this kind of preparation, checks on specific legislation are of little use.

In the Ways and Means Committee attitudes were split. Approval was unlikely without the strong support of Chairman Mills. By this time reactions from business and labor were somewhat more favorable, though both groups had qualifications. Business leaders argued that the tax increase should be accompanied by significant spending cuts; labor leaders argued for taxing corporations at twice the rate charged for individuals.

But more than surveys were needed. Throughout my Presidency I insisted that we brief the Congress fully before our messages were sent to the Hill. We made many mistakes, but failure to inform and brief the Congress was not one of them. . . .

On the morning of August 3, 1967, the day the tax proposal went up, I held a briefing for about seventy Congressmen, including the House leadership, the assistant whips, the House committee chairmen, and the members of the Ways and Means Committee and the Appropriations Committee. I wanted to give them an advance look at the document. Getting a look ahead of others may seem unimportant, but if it helps a Congressman's ego a little bit, it may make all the difference. In dealing with such complex legislation, it was especially important for the President to give Congressmen all the information he had. In the weeks that followed we held a dozen similar briefings, eventually inviting every Democrat and almost half of the Republicans to the White House, where I explained the problem the nation faced and answered all questions. We knew the risks of putting information in the hands of the potential opposition. But I felt that even if some members used our own information against us, at least the debate would be based on fact.

Merely placing a program before Congress is not enough. Without constant attention from the administration, most legislation moves through the congressional process at the speed of a glacier. . . .

One of the President's most important jobs is to help the Congress concentrate on the five or six dozen bills that make up his legislative program. For this reason, I insisted that appropriate members of the administration be ready with strong testimony when congressional hearings began on August 14, 1967. Here, as throughout the entire two-year struggle, Secretary Fowler exhibited an extraordinary combination of good judgment, persistence, dedication, and courage. Between August 1967 and January 1968 he took an active part in three full sets of congressional hearings on the tax bill.

From the outset, Chairman Mills insisted on substantial cuts in government spending. We had serious problems with this. The budget submitted in January 1967 was already lean. It represented the considered judgment of my best advisers, and we were deeply concerned that further cuts would endanger critical social programs.

But I sensed the mood of the House, and I recognized that compromise was essential. Late in September 1967 we informed the Ways and Means Committee that we would make significant spending cuts, but only after the regular appropriations bills had passed and we knew what Congress had already cut. We promised to review each appropriation bill once it was enacted. Only then, when we knew what and how much it contained, could we determine further cuts. To specify the cuts first, as the Ways and Means Committee requested, would have been like tailoring a suit before knowing the dimensions of the cloth. We could not cut something out that was not in, and we would not know what was in until the bills were passed.

My problems and preferences were not the only issues. Without the approval of Representative George Mahon, Chairman of the House Appropriations Committee, Mills's formula for reducing spending had little chance of survival. Chairman Mahon was in no mood to weaken the authority of his powerful committee by permitting the Ways and Means Committee to determine expenditures. To accept the latter's demand for an overall spending cut might be interpreted, in effect, as making Mills chairman of both Ways and Means and Appropriations. The argument over who should cut first, Congress or the President, soon began to sound like the chicken-or-egg dilemma. While the Congress stalled, prices continued to rise and the inflationary spiral became an increasingly important factor in wage settlements.

It was late in November before we got a workable compromise approved by both Mills and Mahon. By that time Congress had passed twelve of the fourteen appropriations bills and Director Charles Schultze and his specialists in the Bureau of the Budget were able to work out a plan for the expenditure cuts. Our compromise was embodied in a two-part legislative proposal: the first title incorporated the 10 per cent surtax and the second title spelled out a formula for spending reductions. We were not happy with the size of these cuts; nor was the House Appropriations Committee. But once again the situation demanded compromise.

As autumn turned to winter and the 1967 congressional session drew to a close, the tax bill remained locked up in the Ways and Means Committee. My willingness to compromise had sharpened the appetites of those who saw in this struggle a long-awaited chance to slash the Great Society programs. Every time we neared agreement on spending cuts, the ante was raised — from $2 billion to $4 billion to $6 billion. Something had to be done to break the stalemate, something outside ordinary bargaining channels.

When traditional methods fail, a President must be willing to bypass the Congress and take the issue to the people. By instinct and experience, I preferred to work from within, knowing that good legislation is the product not of public rhetoric but of private negotiations and compromise. But sometimes a President has to put Congress' feet to the fire. The tax surcharge battle was a case in point. For months I had worked through the leaders on the Hill. I had negotiated and compromised as fully and as fairly as I could, but the bill remained firmly locked in the Ways and Means Committee.

I decided to take the issue to the people. I expressed my concern in every appropriate forum, including the 1968 State of the Union address, the budget message, and the consumer message, urging — almost pleading — for a tax bill. The issue was never whether the American people should like the tax or not. Of course they would not like it; I did not like it either. The issue was whether they would dislike it as much as the consequences of *not* enacting the tax. Those consequences would be exorbitant prices, unparalleled interest rates, and dangerous budget and balance-of-payments deficits.

Somehow, I never got those dangers across to the public or the Congress. For one thing, I failed to explain clearly enough that the surcharge was not a 10 per cent increase in the income tax rate but rather a tax on a tax, or ten extra cents on every dollar of taxes — ten cents to buy an insurance policy against damaging inflation. Another thing I failed to get across was my deep concern about the state of the economy and the relation of the dollar to the world economy. At the time I was pleading for the tax bill, several newspapers increased our difficulties by speculating that I did not really want a tax increase, that deep down I hoped it would fail.

Sometimes it seemed that the only way to reach the papers and the people was to pick a fight with the Congress, to say mean words and show my temper. The most widely publicized statement I made in the fall of 1967 was of this character. A reporter at my November 17 press conference remarked that "there are increasing statements from Capitol Hill that say that your tax bill is dead for this session of Congress." In reply I said:

> I think one of the great mistakes that the Congress will make is that Mr. Ford [the House Republican leader] and Mr. Mills have taken this position that they cannot have any tax bill now. They will live to rue the day when they made that decision. Because it is a dangerous decision. It is an unwise decision.

The impact of such a statement is mixed. It may serve to galvanize support in the Congress and the country, but it may also shorten tempers and polarize thought and emotion. Both happened after my "They will live to rue the day" speech. Representative Mills and the Republican leadership were reported to be furious. Predictions came from the Hill that I would "rue the day" that I had made such a statement; that I had killed chances for a tax bill once and for all. At the same time, it seemed that my fighting spirit had aroused many previously apathetic supporters to action.

I sometimes felt that Congress was like a sensitive animal — if pushed gently it would go my way, but if pushed too hard it would balk. I had to be aware constantly of how much Congress would take and of what kind of mood it was in. As winter turned to spring, my worries about how far and how fast to push the Congress were submerged by deepening financial problems in the international market. . . . Our legislative stalemate over taxes was interpreted abroad as a failure of the democratic process and a clear indication that America had neither the will nor the ability to keep its economic affairs under control.

The international crisis had done what we could not do: arouse the American public and many congressional leaders to the need for decisive action. But frequently an aroused public brings on a heightened sense of partisan politics. The nearer we came to the Presidential primaries in the spring of 1968, the more partisanship grew and the more I feared that many Republicans would oppose the tax bill so they could campaign in the midst of galloping inflation and blame it on my "reckless spending and fiscal irresponsibility." . . .

The whole situation weighed heavily on my mind in the critical weeks of March as I came to my decisions on Vietnam and prepared to deliver my March 31 speech. Next to peace in Southeast Asia and the world, I believed the tax surcharge was the most urgent issue facing the country. I increasingly felt that on both of these issues my position as standard bearer of the Democratic party would be a serious impediment to further movement. I prayed that my decision to refuse the nomination would turn the tide. On March 31 I expressed these thoughts in the plainest language I knew:

> . . . tonight we face the sharpest financial threat in the postwar era — a threat to the dollar's role as the keystone of international trade and finance in the world.
>
> . . . We must have a responsible fiscal policy in this country. The passage of a tax bill now, together with expenditure control that the Congress may desire and dictate, is absolutely necessary to protect this nation's security, to continue our prosperity, and to meet the needs of our people. . . .
>
> These times call for prudence in this land of plenty. I believe we have the character to provide it, and tonight I plead with the Congress and with the people to act promptly to serve the national interest, and thereby serve all of our people.

The first response to my plea came from an unexpected quarter, the U.S. Senate. Although the Constitution requires that the House initiate tax legislation, the Senate can amend a bill passed by the House. The Senate is very different from the House; it has its own traditions, procedures, precedents, and rules. The Senate's smaller size allows it to operate in a more leisurely fashion, without the strict limitations required in the House. Any subject may be discussed on the floor at any time, simply by moving that an amendment be made to pending business.

On March 22, in the midst of a debate on a bill the House had passed to extend automobile and telephone excise taxes, two Senators decided to take advantage of this flexibility in Senate procedure. George Smathers of Florida, a Democrat, and John Williams of Delaware, a Republican, jointly proposed a package of amendments to the excise bill. Included were two critical additions: our 10 per cent surcharge and a formula for cuts in spending. On April 2, two days after my public plea, the Senate passed the excise bill with the amendments.

We were concerned about the spending formula, which required us to cut outlays by $6 billion. We also anticipated a House claim that this Senate action represented an "invasion of sacred prerogatives." But we had come to believe that positive Senate action was essential to prod the House into movement. We felt that it was the only hope we had for passage.

I greeted with relief the news that the Senate had passed the excise bill, amendments and all. The stage was set for a battle in the conference committee, where the two different bills would somehow have to be meshed into one. The key to compromise was the size of the spending reductions. The Senate was on record for a cut of $6 billion, but the administration, a majority of the liberals in both houses, and most members of the House Appropriations Committee remained firmly committed to a maximum cut of $4 billion. Our only hope was to bring pressure on the Senate from the House conferees and to compromise at $5 billion. Once again, Wilbur Mills held the key to the compromise. On April 11 I had a long talk with him about these matters.

I told Chairman Mills that I had tried every way I knew to find an acceptable compromise and had even forsworn another term, thinking that might help. "But," I said, "I think the situation is as bad now as it was before." I told him that whether he realized it or not, the country's economy was about to go down the drain and we had to write a tax bill that we could both live with. Mills seemed to understand my concern completely. He remarked that although he didn't have the problem in his district, the plight of the cities was critical. He said he knew I could not cut back the budget for urban affairs and that I might even have to ask for more money. Notes I made at the time show that Mills then said he thought he could "get by" with the $5 billion figure as spending limitation. With those words, our long-sought compromise was finally in sight. We parted in high spirits for the first time in the long surcharge struggle. I began to relax.

In a few days, however, Chairman Mills evidently decided that he would not compromise at $5 billion. Word came from the conference committee that the House conferees, like their Senate counterparts, would insist on a $6 billion reduction. I met with Mills again on April 30 in the Cabinet Room. I had assembled some of the leaders who I thought might help me sway Mills — Speaker McCormack and Representatives Carl Albert, George Mahon, and Hale Boggs. Art Okun, the new Chairman of the Council of Economic Advisers, was also with us, as was Charles Zwick, the new Director of the Bureau of the Budget, and J. Barefoot Sanders, Jr., who had replaced Larry O'Brien as chief of my legislative liaison staff.

Mills appeared to be backing away from the $5 billion compromise, and again we tried to reason with him. As I remember, it was Speaker McCormack who asked him pointedly what his actual position was, and faced with such a blunt and direct question, Mills appeared to relent in our favor.

But at any figure — $4 billion, $5 billion, or $6 billion — the conference committee seemed in no hurry to act. In fact, it appeared to some that the Ways and Means Committee was jealously guarding its prerogative of initiating tax measures, but was not initiating any legislation. As the stalemate continued day after day, I decided once again to appeal directly to the people. In a nationally televised press conference on May 3, I stated:

> I want to make it perfectly clear to the American people that I think we are courting danger by this continued procrastination, this continued delay.
> . . . I think the time has come for all of the members of Congress to be responsible and, even in an election year, to bite the bullet and stand up and do what ought to be done for their country.

That statement aroused a certain amount of anger on Capitol Hill, but it made headlines all over the country and helped break the logjam. On May 1 the House Appropriations Committee approved a resolution to cut budget expenditures for the fiscal year 1969 by at least $4 billion. Only after this action did the Ways and Means Committee approve a resolution on May 6 recommending a 10 per cent tax surcharge and a cut in spending of at least $4 billion. And on May 9 the Senate-House conferees finally announced their agreement on including the 10 per cent surcharge in the excise tax bill. To our disappointment, they insisted on a reduction of $6 billion in federal spending in fiscal 1969. Apparently, Mills felt that he had left himself an escape hatch when his committee called for "at least" $4 billion in cuts.

The liberals were disappointed with Chairman Mills. So was the House leadership, and so was I. Although he had very strong sentiment that supported him, Mills's insistence on a $6 billion cut had polarized the issue and destroyed all hope of easy compromise. Within hours the $6 billion figure became a rallying cry among liberals to defeat the conference committee's report. The AFL-CIO, the National Education Association, the National Council of Churches, the U.S. Conference of Mayors, the Urban Coalition, and other groups began to lobby against the report. . . .

Despite these impassioned pleas to hold our ground, I knew there was no conceivable way I could get a tax increase without accepting some compromise in expenditure reductions. But it was not entirely up to me. The Congress was deadlocked too. The liberals were refusing to go along with spending cuts. We needed a viable strategy to bring them along. We knew one critical element of that strategy. Unless we could get a vote on the $4 billion figure, the liberals would feel they were letting down their constituents, the poor and the blacks, and would probably vote against the conference report. But if a special vote could be taken to register their "conscience" publicly and openly, then perhaps the door to later compromise would remain open.

This was one of many occasions when our Tuesday leadership breakfasts proved invaluable. Those breakfasts gave us the chance to talk frankly with congressional leaders. They provided a forum for debating possible solutions to complicated legislative problems. At a leadership breakfast on May 21, 1968, we agreed to sponsor a motion on the House floor to send the conferees back with instructions to reduce the spending cutbacks from $6 billion to $4 billion. Speaker McCormack and Majority Leader Albert said they would figure out the details with the House parliamentarian and find someone to introduce the motion.

I decided to hold a series of private sessions in the White House for the liberal Democrats to explain our strategy and my position. In the confidence of the Cabinet Room, I told them that I hated the thought of the $6 billion cut and hoped against hope for passage of the $4 billion motion, but that if it failed I did not feel I could let the tax bill die. "It will take a great deal of pulling to squeeze that $6 billion out without hurting key domestic programs," I said. "But if we have to cut that much, I am determined not to let those programs suffer."

On May 29 the motion to reduce the cut to $4 billion was introduced by Democratic Representative James A. Burke of Massachusetts. The votes were tallied, and our fears confirmed. The House rejected the motion overwhelmingly, by a vote of 259 to 137. With this defeat, the unpleasant choice was painfully clear. Either we accepted the $6 billion cut or we would lose the tax bill. I thought about our budget and the difficulty of cutting $6 billion out of it, but I could not let the tax bill fail. Far too much depended on its passage.

One major question remained. Even if we agreed to the $6 billion cut, would a majority of the House accept the conference report? This was where the head count became our most critical tool.

With so many factors at work, we knew that an accurate head count would be very difficult. But my liaison staff had been gathering information on the tax bill for eighteen long months, and the final head count was simply a distillation of that intelligence. In this last survey the members of Congress were asked not simply how they intended to vote but under what conditions they would vote yes or no. And on the basis of their answers — "I'm all for it, but unless the Detroit delegation votes for it as well, I cannot go with you" . . . "I can be swung over but only if I get a chance to see what's going to happen to the programs for the cities" . . . "I am uncommitted and will remain so until the last moment" . . . "I am against it, I've been against it for months, and I don't intend to change my mind" . . . "I will wait in the well and vote yes if, and only if, it's crucial" . . . "I'll go with you but only if the House leadership actively encourages me" — the members were divided into five categories: "with us," "probably with us," "uncommitted," "probably against," and "against."

With the head count as our blueprint, the enormous job of individual persuasion began. We concentrated on the "uncommitteds" and those "probably against," attempting to develop an individual approach to meet the needs of each member. Wild images have been concocted to describe this process of persuasion. A great deal of mystery surrounds the President's role. But the real task of persuasion is far less glamorous than the imagined one. It is tough, demanding work. For despite the stereotyped Presidential image, I could not trade patronage for votes in any direct exchange. If word spread that I was trading, everyone would want to trade and all other efforts at persuasion would automatically fail. To say this is not to say that rewards (such as White House tours, invitations to social functions, birthday greetings, and Presidential photos) do not go to faithful Congressmen. But these are generally delivered by the White House staff after the fact, and on the basis of a pattern of voting, not by the President personally in exchange for a specific vote.

Nor could I rely on the "big threat" or direct reprisal to produce compliance. It is daydreaming to assume that any experienced Congressman would ignore his basic instincts or his constituents' deepest concerns in quaking fear of the White House. My best hope was to make a good, solid, convincing case for the administration's position.

I tried in every possible way to make a convincing case on the surcharge to the Hill. First, we had to mobilize support in the outside community to ease the path for Congressmen willing to join our effort. In the final days of May, with Secretary Fowler's help, a dozen organizations undertook active support of the surcharge. They included the American Bankers Association, the American Farm Bureau's Federation, the National Association of Manufacturers, and the Chamber of Commerce. In addition, a group of five hundred business leaders, headed by such able men as Henry Ford, was organized specifically to stimulate support for the surcharge. These national leaders in turn contacted their local business representatives, asking each to speak to the Congressman in his own district and let him know that the overwhelming preponderance of responsible businessmen strongly favored the conference report as the only source of sound fiscal policy. These last-minute visits and calls proved especially valuable in helping to sway many Republicans to our side.

Trying to sitmulate traditional Democratic support was more difficult. For many months labor leaders had been deeply concerned about the impact of budget cuts on the Great Society programs. It was no surprise when the AFL-CIO spoke out publicly against the conference committee's report. Once again I understood their anger, but I knew that if labor lobbyists were to stalk the Hill, warning Congress that a vote for the tax bill would be a vote against labor, the liberals would have little choice but to vote against the bill. The Burke motion helped a great deal. So did a special meeting with labor leader George Meany. We talked the problem out. Several days later the labor lobbyists quietly lowered their voices.

I knew how hard it was, especially for those heading the domestic agencies, to accept deep budget cuts as the price for the tax bill. Budget Director Zwick and his staff worked day and night to find a way to absorb the $6 billion cut with as little damage as possible to the Great Society programs. At our Cabinet meeting on May 29 I outlined that package and the dimensions of our choice. I described my judgment that in this case we had to take the lesser of two evils and find a way to cut the extra $2 billion. I assured the Cabinet officers that I hated the cut as much as they did, but I added: "It won't be anything like the headache or anything like as bad as saying to the world that we have no fiscal responsibility and we will not pass the tax bill. Therefore I want to ask for something I've never asked a Cabinet to do before. I want to see how much muscle we've got left — if any! I would like you to sit down with these 250 men [Democratic Senators and Congressmen] that you've been associated with, most of them for the last eight years, and see which ones you're willing to sit down and talk with. And say that our country is in trouble and here's why, and you hope they can accept this report, and, if they do, it will not tear their program to pieces."

I knew that in spite of their personal feelings the Cabinet officers would respond to the nation's interests. That same afternoon, they began canvassing the Hill. The following day I made my position public at a press conference:

> So the only choice remaining now is whether the need for a tax increase is so urgent that we must accept a $6 billion reduction. I believe that the need for a tax increase is that urgent. If the Congress will vote for the conference report containing the tax increase and the $6 billion expenditure cut, I shall approve it.

With these words, the struggle entered its final phase. Once again the head count became critical. In such a situation personal contact from the President can be decisive, but generally only with key members whose votes will have a multiplying effect on the votes of many others. So I had my own list of men to contact.

When I made these phone calls, I had no set script. Sometimes I would start with: "What's this I read about your opposing my bill?" Other times I would ask: "What do you think of this bill?" Or: "Say, Congressman, I haven't seen you around in a while, just wondering how you've been." But a common theme ran through these talks — friendship and respect. If I were to name the one factor above all others that helped me in dealing with the Congress, I would say it was the genuine friendship and rapport I had with most Congressmen and Senators. I understood and respected men who dedicated their lives to elective office. Most politicians are men of principle dedicated to the national interest. I believed that I, as President, had the responsibility to appeal to that dedication, to outline what I considered the national interest required, to lay out the alternatives, and to hope that a reasonable man would understand and accept his duty.

Finally, the day of the vote arrived — June 20, 1968. We did not expect the tally to take place until late in the afternoon or early in the evening. In the middle of the day a large number of administration leaders and supporters left the Capitol to attend a luncheon on the other side of town in honor of Representative Albert. About one o'clock H. R. Gross, Iowa's actively partisan Republican, unexpectedly took the House floor. He moved that the House return the conference report to the Senate without action, on the grounds that the bill was unconstitutional because it had originated in the Senate. Gross's proposal was a privileged motion — that is, one allowing time for only an hour's debate. An urgent summons was sent to the congressional luncheon and the members rushed back, worried that they might not reach the House in time. But we were lucky. The tally was still in progress when the luncheon crowd arrived to cast their votes and defeat Gross's motion.

The final roll call on the bill began at 7:05 P.M. At that time, I was attending a reception for foreign educators at the State Department. Several reporters rode back with me to the White House after the reception was over, and we sat in the car talking for twenty minutes or so. Just before 8 P.M. one of my aides came out to the car and handed me a message: "Mr. President: The House has just adopted the conference committee report — with the 10 per cent surcharge." The vote was 268 to 150, reflecting substantial support from all quarters, conservatives and liberals, Republicans and Democrats. The staff had estimated correctly — we'd either win big or not at all. I returned immediately to the Oval Office to make a statement:

> The House of Representatives today declared itself for a responsible fiscal policy. Its voice will be heard around the world. Our democracy has passed a critical test. . . . I am very hopeful and confident that the Senate will promptly complete legislative action on this matter.

The next day, June 21, the Senate adopted the conference report, and the 10 per cent surcharge became the law of the land with my signature on June 28. . . .

V

CONGRESS AS AN INSTRUMENT
OF GOVERNMENT

In the early 1960's, former Seneator Joseph Clark asserted that Congress had become "the sapless branch" of government. Much of this saplessness was characterized by an inability of Congress to challenge executive dominance. The materials in this section help to illustrate the question of the vitality of Congress.

To analyze a complex institution like Congress, it is necessary to take it apart and examine all its pieces. But eventually the parts have to be put back together if we are ever to appreciate Congress as a single instrument of government, as surely it is. The parts can only be understood within the larger scheme.

Case studies are almost indispensable for an appreciation of such a complex institution as Congress. And political science is rich in the case literature. An editor's problem is more one of elimination than discovery. However, each case study or case analysis is unique in some aspects, and that is precisely its virtue. Concentration on a single decision or problem has the advantage of providing the nuance of political dynamics. But nuance is gained at a price, and that price expresses itself in an agony of concern over the representativeness of each case.

The uniqueness of the single case can be bypassed in two ways. One way is to have a theory of politics that provides guidance and criteria for classifying cases — to help define what case is a case *of*.

Both editors have done a great deal of professional research and writing on this problem and know just enough about it to avoid introducing the complexities of a theoretical approach in an introductory book of readings.[1] Fortunately, a second route away from the uniqueness of the single case is effective and serviceable although not as good in the long run as theory. This route is of course simply providing several cases rather than a long single case.

Our cases include a great variety of subjects, from atoms and suburbs to top brass and Vietnamese hamlets. Committees of very different status, power, and orientation are involved. Clientele groups range from scientists to the ghetto poor; and issues vary from intense moral confrontations to the most ignoble pork barrel. Almost the whole universe of political strategies can be identified, because our cases exhaust most of the possible ways Congress can be used as an instrument of power: passing statutes, passing resolutions, exercising review by committee oversight, influencing the executive through expert staff, influencing public opinion by high-level debate and low-level investigatory techniques, control of diplomacy through the power to reject treaties, and the potent but problematic control by manipulating the purse strings.

The cases provide the student with more varieties of political experience than he could ever get by direct exposure in Washington. But they present such a variety of experience that he will almost have to become his own theorist. We aim to confuse as much as to guide, because the educated person will never explore unless he is confused to start with. Enough materials are provided for responsible generalization. And good dialogue can take place, because within all this variety the cases nevertheless provide a common universe of discourse.

To get such a discourse under way, one final observation seems appropriate. If one conclusion can be carried away from the cases in this section, plus particularly the Cooper-Church debate, it is that the separation of powers is still alive, though ailing. The separation of powers is the adrenal gland of the system. When the branches confront each other, at the top or through committees and agencies, they do so with energy, publicity, and a good bit of common rationality. Why Congress so often seems eager to avoid confrontation is a mystery we continue to ponder. But even without the answer we can continue to hail confrontation as a virtual prerequisite for a healthy

[1] See, for example, Theodore Lowi, "Four Systems of Policy, Politics, and Choice," *Public Administration Review* (July-August, 1972); and Randall B. Ripley, *Public Policies and Their Politics* (New York: Norton, 1966), pp. vii–xviii.

legislative politics U.S.A. Perhaps if we hail it strongly enough, loudly
enough, and often enough, a few more congressmen might hear about
it.

Policy Formulation

19

Rules and Power:
The Depressed Areas Act

John F. Bibby and Roger H. Davidson

An omnipresent feature of the legislator's environment is the complicated set of rules and procedures under which he must operate. Congress is no different from any other complex organization in its need
for regularized procedures, and the Constitution clearly provides that
"each House may determine the rules of its proceedings." [1] In a
legislative body, rules and procedures are intimately related to the
political conflicts among individuals and interests. That is, the rules
are not neutral but rather work to encourage certain types of actions
and discourage others. Mastery of the rules can give a member a
formidable resource in the "legislative struggle," and constitutes a part
of the mystique of a Sam Rayburn, a Richard B. Russell, or a Howard
W. Smith.[2]

From *On Capitol Hill: Studies in the Legislative Process* by John Bibby and
Roger Davidson. Copyright © 1967 by Holt, Rinehart and Winston, Inc. Reprinted by permission of Holt, Rinehart and Winston, Inc.
    [1] Article I, Section 5.
    [2] Rayburn, Speaker of the House (1940–46, 1949–52, 1955–61), was a mod-
erate Democrat from Texas; Russell, a conservative Democrat from Georgia,
served for years as chairman of the Senate Armed Services Committee; and
Judge Smith, an extremely conservative Democrat from Virginia, literally ran
the House Rules Committee during the 1950's and early 1960's when the Rules
Committee was maiming and killing civil rights and other social legislation.
Their mastery of parliamentary law and maneuver indeed had a great deal to do
with their power. — Eds.

Some of the differences between the House and the Senate are reflected in the development of their rules. Both houses derive their procedures from three sources: *Jefferson's Manual* of parliamentary laws, the rules of each house, and precedents derived from rulings of the chair in each house. The House of Representatives has forty-three complicated rules, supplemented by *Hinds' and Cannon's Precedents,* an eleven-volume compendium of interpretations by various speakers and chairmen of the "Committee of the Whole House." For the average congressman, the 500-page synopsis, *Cannon's Procedure in the House of Representatives,* is sufficient for daily needs. The operation of the House is necessarily more complex than that of the Senate, because of the former's size. It has therefore evolved a tight system of procedures that leaves little room for dilatory tactics. Yet, during debate on most bills flexibility is obtained by resolving the House into the Committee of the Whole House. Under this device, debate is actually regulated by agreement between the managers of the bill and the chief opponents. This procedure will be discussed more fully below.

In the smaller and more leisurely Senate, the rules are simpler and more lenient. The last general revision of the forty rules was done in 1884. Debate is typically fixed by unanimous consent, and, as in the House, the standard practice is to divide and control time between proponents and opponents of the bill by prior agreement. The Senate cherishes its privilege of free and unfettered debate. . . . [In a recent reform effort] the Senate adopted a "rule of germaneness," which directed that debate after the "morning hour" (the daily period prior to consideration of pending legislation) must be relevant to the business at hand. Attempts at compliance have met with confusion and anguish, and the rule has not so far altered the pace of senatorial business.

Detailed description of congressional rules would be a tedious and, for the most part, pointless endeavor. (Fortunately for most members and their legislative aides, a call to the parliamentarian will clarify most entanglements with the rules.) The role of procedures in legislative politics can be illustrated by the case history of the Area Redevelopment Act of 1961. During the six years prior to its passage, this measure encountered most of the procedural hurdles common to social-welfare legislation of the 1950's and 1960's. In this sense, the story of the Area Redevelopment Act serves a concrete illustration of the frustrations of congressional liberals. . . . The following account is not the *whole* story of the enactment of Public Law 87–27; it is a synopsis of its legislative history, focusing on congressional rules and procedures as the principal variables.

COMMITTEE REFERRAL

The original depressed areas legislation was hastily introduced in the summer of 1955 by Senator Paul H. Douglas (D. Ill.) and was designed to implement the policy dictum of the 1946 Employment Act: "It is the continuing policy and responsibility of the Federal Government to use all practicable means . . . to promote maximum employment, production, and purchasing power." In spite of general postwar prosperity, it soon became apparent that long-term unemployment in certain declining industries and localities was creating persistent "pockets of poverty." This hard-core unemployment was especially visible during periods of economic slack, and with the 1954–1955 recession depressed-areas legislators began prodding the Eisenhower Administration to devise a solution for the problem. Concerned over the plight of southern Illinois' depressed coal regions, Douglas introduced a $390-million package-proposal for financial and technical aid — including prefential treatment in government contracts, technical assistance, vocational retraining, and loans and grants to help communities lure new industry.

Six months later, the Eisenhower Administration sponsored a modest $50-million bill. Republican leaders continued to give lukewarm support to the Administration's proposal, but the focal point of discussion during the next six years remained "the Douglas bill," in its various and evolving forms.

A combative liberal with a mercurial temperament, Douglas typified the Senate "outsider." His theory was that he would have influence *on* Congress later, if not *in* it now; and his heroes (their pictures adorned his office walls) were such legislators as George W. Norris and Robert M. LaFollette, Sr. He was used to having the rules used against him; and when the Area Redevelopment Act became law in 1961, it was the first law to bear his name in his twelve years as a senator.

Yet Douglas was strategically positioned to lead the fight for his legislation: in addition to being rotating chairman of the Joint Economic Committee (which does not handle legislation), he held a seat on two Senate committees: Banking and Currency and Labor and Public Welfare. As it turned out, the former committee had the best claim for considering the measure, but for several reasons the bill, S. 2663, was referred to Labor and Public Welfare. In the Labor Committee Douglas chaired his own subcommittee, and committee Chairman Lister Hill (D. Ala.) allowed him free rein. Liberal majorities in both the subcommittee and full committee were favorable and ultimately passed the Douglas bill over to the floor with only minor changes. The other claimant for jurisdiction over the measure, the Senate Banking and Currency Committee, presented no such bright prospect. Douglas did not have a subcommittee there, and the committee's membership seemed less favorable to such "welfare" measures as S. 2663.

Thus, it seemed merely good politics when Douglas requested, and was granted, referral of his bill to Labor and Public Welfare. On jurisdictional grounds, however, referral to Labor and Public Welfare was questionable. On the other side of Capitol Hill, the House Banking and Currency Committee had taken charge of the legislation. Senate Rule XXV seemed to confirm this decision: Banking and Currency shall have jurisdiction over "financial aid to commerce and industry, other than matters relating to such aid which are specifically assigned to other committees. . . ." It was not long before this rule began to raise trouble for Douglas.

On January 5, 1956, Banking and Currency Chairman J. William Fulbright (D. Ark.) [3] wrote Chairman Hill and warned that his committee would be "compelled to reserve the privilege of requesting an opportunity to consider the bill." The letter apparently went unanswered, and Fulbright refrained from playing his hand until June 28, the day after Hill's committee reported S. 2663. At that time Fulbright wrote Majority Leader Lyndon Johnson (D. Tex) that he intended to ask that the bill be referred to Banking and Currency. At such a late date in the session, this action could only kill the bill. "I felt that it was necessary . . . to raise this question," Fulbright explained later, "because I believe it is my duty to protect the jurisdiction of that committee under the rules." Fulbright's real motives, however, lay deeper: as a southerner, he regarded the area redevelopment bill as an effort to preserve "old and worn-out" industrial regions at the expense of such expanding areas as his own state of Arkansas. A jurisdictional dispute could serve as a lever to halt the Douglas bill, or at least to force its revision. . . .

Fulbright's move caught the Douglas forces at an inopportune moment. Douglas had just resigned from Labor and Public Welfare to take a long-coveted seat on Finance, and Douglas' old subcommittee was no longer active. Moreover, there was no way to sidestep Fulbright's impeccable parliamentary position so late in the congressional session. Majority Leader Johnson and Chairman Hill therefore arranged for Senator John F. Kennedy (D. Mass.), now ranking member

[3] Senator Fulbright shifted to the chairmanship of Foreign Relations as soon as a vacancy and his seniority on that committee provided him the opportunity — Eds.

of Douglas' old subcommittee, to bargain with Fulbright. At a series of meetings, staff aides hammered out a series of three amendments favoring rural areas of unemployment and designed to render the bill more acceptable to southern senators. Accepted "reluctantly" by Kennedy during the brief floor debate, the amendments were Fulbright's "price" for dropping his jurisdictional objections. In addition, Fulbright received assurances that his committee would assume jurisdiction over the bill in the future. The deal having been consummated, S. 2663 passed the Senate easily, by a vote of sixty to thirty.

This incident illustrates the importance of "the politics of referral and jurisdiction." In most cases referral is routine and thus removed from the legislative struggle. But complex or "border-line" bills may straddle several committees, making the matter of referral an important tactical consideration. A miscalculation, as in this case, may have costly consequences.

THE END-OF-THE-SESSION SQUEEZE

While Fulbright was exacting his concessions in the Senate, the bill's advocates in the House were waging a hopeless battle against time. At the center of the controversy was the House Rules Committee, which, through exercise of its broad scheduling powers, stands between the legislative committees and the House floor.[4] For controversial measures that cannot be disposed of by more automatic parliamentary devices, the Rules Committee must grant a "rule" under which the bill is considered on the House floor. When a rule is requested by the legislative committee, Rules must first decide whether to hold hearings; if this is granted, it may then vote on whether to grant the rule.[5] As will be seen, a negative action by Rules (refusal to schedule hearings, or a negative vote on granting a rule) usually serves to kill the bill, because the methods of circumventing the Rules Committee are cumbersome and time-consuming. Under the time limitations accompanying the end of the legislative session, alternative procedures become even more difficult to apply.

As early as June 29, the depressed-areas bill had been reported by Banking and Currency, but the Rules Committee, working through the

[4] For a thorough analysis of the operations of the Rules Committee, see James A. Robinson, *The House Rules Committee* (Indianapolis: Bobbs-Merrill, 1963).

[5] The type of rule granted may also have important consequences for the bill's fate on the floor. "Open rules" permit floor amendments; "closed rules" either prohibit them or allow only specialized types of amendments. Some rules waive points of order against bills where there may be some parliamentary objection. In addition, rules typically specify a time limit for debate.

end-of-session log jam, showed no inclination to clear the bill for floor debate. To further complicate the situation, the bill was caught in the crossfire of a feud between Rules and Banking and Currency over housing legislation. At the insistence of the Democratic leadership and friendly Rules members, a hearing was finally held on July 21 — six days before adjournment! The committee merely voted to defer action on granting a rule, apparently killing the bill for the Eighty-fourth Congress.[6]

One last chance remained for House passage that session. With adjournment imminent, the House was operating under an agreement whereby the Speaker would recognize members to move passage of bills under suspension of the rules (such a motion requires a two-thirds vote). According to precedent, the Speaker will recognize a member to move the suspension of the rules only with the consent of both majority and minority floor leaders. Speaker Rayburn and Majority Leader John McCormack (D. Mass.) agreed to allow the depressed-areas bill to be called up; but Minority Leader Joseph Martin (R. Mass.) said he would have to consult with Administration officials "downtown."

The Senate sent S. 2663 to the House early on the afternoon of July 26. The devious process of extracting a definitive answer from the Administration occupied the remainder of that day, and most of the next. Finally, Representatives Ivor Fenton and James Van Zandt, Pennsylvania Republicans who had authored depressed-areas bills of their own, were enlisted to obtain the Administration's approval. It soon became apparent that the White House was leaving the decision to the Commerce Department. Secretary Sinclair Weeks, who was known to be skeptical about the legislation, dispatched Assistant Secretary Frederick H. Mueller to the Capitol to negotiate with Fenton and Van Zandt. After two hours of discussion, during which congressional supporters even offered to substitute the Eisenhower bill, the two Pennsylvanians emerged to inform their colleagues that the Administration was opposed to having any bill whatsoever brought to the floor. In view of the Administration's position, there was no hope for last-minute passage of the bill.

This story was repeated publicly by Democrats throughout the 1956 presidential campaign. For their part, Administration spokesmen never bothered to deny the incident. Running on the slogan of "peace and prosperity," they were content to let the issue ride.

---

[6] Votes in the Rules Committee are seldom recorded. It appeared that, had a final vote been recorded, the bill would have lost by a six to five vote.

Administration officials argued privately, however, that they had been victimized by a trap play: had they consented to House passage of the President's bill, the Douglas forces would have used the House-Senate conference as leverage to restore the provisions of the original S. 2663 — thus driving the Administration into an even more awkward position. Needless to say, their suspicions were not without foundation. The lesson of this incident was that the end of the session places a premium on time, if the niceties of the rules are to be observed. If the rules are to be sidestepped, there must often exist an interparty comity not obtainable where controversial legislation is involved. Thus a special challenge faces legislative tacticians.

POWER PLAY IN COMMITTEE

Early in 1957, Douglas reintroduced the depressed-areas bill as S. 964. This time it was referred to Fulbright's Banking and Currency Committee and Douglas' newly acquired Production and Stabilization Subcommittee. For more than a year, the bill was stalled, confirming the sponsors' original fears about Banking and Currency. (The alignment on the committee is shown in Table 1.) Douglas charged that his subcommittee was "stacked" against him, while Fulbright insisted that nothing of the kind had been intended. The only hope lay in bringing the bill to the full committee, and this could be done either through an informal agreement with Fulbright or a formal vote of the full committee.

Table 1

**The Banking and Currency Committee
on the Douglas Bill, 1957–1958**

	Against	*For*	*Doubtful*
Subcommittee	Fulbright (D)	Douglas (D)	
	Frear (D)	Sparkman (D)	
	Capehart (R)		
	Bricker (R)		
	Bush (R)		
Total	5	2	0
Full committee	Robertson (D)	Monroney (D)	Payne (R)
	Bennett (R)	Clark (D)	Beall (R)
		Proxmire (D)	Case (R)
Total	7	5	3

For a time, Douglas failed to perceive the solution to his dilemma, preferring futile neogtiations with Fulbright on dislodging the bill from the subcommittee. These negotiations were perfunctory, for the two men had never been close associates. For his part, Fulbright was still suspicious that the bill would disadvantage the new industrial areas, which depended on low wages to lure industries from the older, heavily unionized areas. Moreover, he was not generally disposed to favor federal intervention in such problems.

The impasse broke in early 1958 when Senator Frederick Payne (R. Me.) let it be known that he was available for a compromise. Payne faced a tough re-election fight that fall in a state in which hard-core unemployment in the Saco-Biddeford-Sanford textile region was a major issue. Douglas and Payne quickly reached an accord: Payne would introduce a new bill, which would be substituted in full committee for the Douglas bill. Senators Clifford Case (R. N.J.) and J. Glenn Beall (R. Md.) would go along to make the eight-seven majority.

On March 11 Payne introduced his bill, S. 3447, in what he called "a sincere effort to compromise the differences between the Douglas and Administration bills. . . ." Beall and Case were cosponsors, along with Senator Margaret Chase Smith (R. Me.). The bill was, of course, referred to Banking and Currency; and Payne asked Fulbright to schedule S. 3447 for early action by the full committee.

The step of placing Payne's bill on the full committee's agenda was accomplished a week later, when hearings opened on Fulbright's own antirecession measure, the ill-fated community facilities bill (S. 3497). According to plan, as soon as Fulbright called the meeting to order Payne moved that the committee go into executive session. Fulbright refused to bring the motion to a vote, and for thirty minutes witnesses waiting to testify were treated to a rare display of verbal fireworks.[7] Payne led off by observing that, in view of the speedy consideration accorded Fulbright's own bill, the depressed-areas proposal ought to be considered promptly. Fulbright countered by reminding the committee that Douglas was chairman of the subcommittee and "in no way inhibited from holding a meeting of his subcommittee at any time he wants to, and submitting the matter to a vote." Instead, he asserted — glaring at Douglas — "You only talk about it."

[7] Transcripts of hearings, as well as floor debates, are "revised" by Members and their staffs before publication — ostensibly to clear up grammatical errors, but often for more extensive alterations. Even the "sanitized" version of this incident makes zesty reading, however. See U.S. Senate, Committee on Banking and Currency, *Community Facilities Act of 1958* (Washington: 1958), pp. 1–13.

To this Douglas retorted that he had not dared bring the issue to a vote "in view of the membership . . . selected for that subcommittee by the Senator from Arkansas." Moreover, he had been trying to negotiate with Fulbright; but the latter's "unyielding determination to kill the bill" had forestalled agreement. Fulbright elaborately denied both charges.

An acrimonious free-for-all ensued. Douglas called Fulbright a "deep-freeze artist," and the latter replied that Douglas was "derelict in his duty." Soon the entire committee was hopelessly entangled in parliamentary procedure. Then Payne inquired whether his own bill, S. 3447, had been referred to a subcommittee. It was discovered that it had not; that is, the bill was still technically before the full committee. Douglas then moved that the bill be declared the "pending order of business" of the full committee. After some further haggling Douglas' motion was adopted, by a vote of eight to five.[8]

Having forged a winning coalition in the committee, Douglas and Payne had employed a power play to breach their bill's major obstacle in the Senate. The "clean bill" (a new bill embodying the original bill and the proposed alterations) — so favorable to Douglas' goals that he refused to call it a compromise — soon cleared the full committee. The unhappy incident in the committee illustrated that a chairman's prerogatives may border on the arbitrary, and that to control the exercise of these prerogatives may require a determined majority willing to risk the costs of forcing a confrontation. Fulbright could not have been expected to make concessions until Douglas had enough votes in full committee to pass the bill. Once his bipartisan coalition had been fashioned, Douglas could force Fulbright to back down, either through informal agreement or a committee showdown. The fact that the latter course was followed was probably a function of the somewhat tenuous relationship between the two men.

[8] Senator Bennett (R. Utah), who would have voted with the minority, was absent. Senator Frear (D. Del.) was subject to cross-pressures and voted "present." The following colloquy illustrated his dilemma:

Frear: "I am in favor of following the rules of the committee. I am in favor of having the chairman . . . exercise the rules. I have no objection, personally, to having the full committee act on the bill of the Senator from Maine but I do not desire to place myself in the position of voting against what the chairman has the authority to do. Nor do I want to vote against the Senator from Illinois (Douglas), because I think he has a right to ask that. I therefore ask I be excused from voting."

Robertson: "With all due deference, I do not think the gentleman is correct. I was in the same position. I did not want to go against the chairman, and had no personal feeling, but I voted and I think you should too. You have no personal reason except a little embarrassment."

JUDGE SMITH ENTERS

Once out of the Senate Banking and Currency Committee, the Douglas-Payne compromise readily passed the Senate by a forty-six to thirty-six vote. The House Banking and Currency Committee trimmed the bill somewhat and reported it on July 1, 1958. This shifted the arena to the often troublesome House Rules Committee. And as in 1956, the end-of-the-session problem began to loom ahead.

With an eye to the fall congressional elections, House Democratic leaders let it be known that they wanted the Douglas-Payne bill brought to the floor. They reasoned that President Eisenhower might be induced to sign the bill as a "bipartisan" solution to the depressed-areas problem. If he vetoed the bill, Democrats would have a ready-made campaign issue. A midyear economic recession added urgency to the situation.

After some delay, Rules Chairman Howard W. Smith (D. Va.) scheduled a hearing, during which his committee forced the bill's sponsors to agree to offer a floor amendment eliminating a direct Treasury borrowing ("backdoor financing") provision. (Strongly favored by Douglas and the liberal advocates of the bill, this feature would have allowed the agency to draw authorized funds directly from the Treasury, rather than submitting expenditures to the annual appropriations process. Liberals argue that this device permits agencies to make long-range financial commitments, while many legislators — especially in the House — view it as a threat to the prerogatives of the appropriations committees.) The Rules Committee forced the deletion of backdoor financing and then cleared the bill by a six-five vote on August 7, nearly six weeks after Banking and Currency had reported it. By this time it was late in the session; and under pressure of time Judge Smith's prerogatives might be sufficient to prevent debate. Following the vote, Smith told reporters that "a rule was ordered reported on the depressed-areas bill." Smith had three legislative days in which to file his report; then, seven more legislative days might elapse before the rule was called up on the floor. If the Judge did neither of these things within the prescribed time, further delays would ensue. Any of these could be fatal to the bill in the closing days, and even hours, of the session.

Since adjournment was set for Labor Day, Representative Daniel Flood (D. Pa.) led a delegation of congressmen to Judge Smith's Alexandria, Virginia, home. By agreeing to delete a section of the bill providing subsistence allowances for unemployed workers while they were being retrained, the group was able to get Judge Smith to promise he would report the rule by August 12. Smith was as good as his word, and the Douglas-Payne bill — complete with the amendments Smith had extracted — passed by a standing vote. On the eve of adjournment, the revised bill was sent to the White House.

Even when operating within the confines of the rules, such holders of institutionalized power as Judge Smith have considerable latitude of action. These prerogatives may be enhanced by time shortages at the close of each session. As we have seen, costs may have to be incurred in such cases to assure that the rules are meticulously observed.

CALENDAR WEDNESDAY

President Eisenhower vetoed the Douglas-Payne bill — a move that some commentators held partially responsible for Republican losses in the congressional elections that fall. (Senator Payne himself was defeated for re-election.) Both the Administration and the Douglas camp introduced new bills as the Eighty-sixth Congress convened, and by the end of March the Senate had passed the Douglas version (S. 722). Two months later, the House Banking and Currency Committee reported the bill. This brought the measure again into the hands of the Rules Committee, where it languished for a full year.

The "depressed-areas congressmen," now bolstered by the newly formed liberal Democratic Study Group, attempted to enlist Speaker Rayburn's help in dislodging the bill from Rules. Faced with a troublesome Rules Committee, Rayburn had to exercise caution by not expending credit on hopeless legislative ventures. The task of the depressed-areas coalition was to convince the Speaker that the bill was needed in their districts, that it would have favorable consequences for the Democratic party, and — perhaps most important — that it had enough votes to pass on the House floor. The late Clem Miller (D. Calif.), then a freshman congressman and an active member of the Democratic Study Group, has provided an engaging account of the confrontation with Rayburn:

> Groups cluster in the big antechamber outside his "official" office just off the floor of the House. Six or eight of us crowd about, ushered into the half of a railway car by his quite correct and unassuming aides. The Speaker is very friendly. The mouth, so downcurved for public ceremony, turns up readily and warmly in private. We range ourselves on the edges of chairs and sofas. The conversation begins all brisk and rapid-fire, about this and that and the other. The Speaker answers easily, and in good humor. His eye flicks over the

group. He is a coachman for a poorly harnessed team. When will we begin? As I am the only freshman, he singles me out for special comment. This is simply delightful. Finally, a senior member of the group says, "Now, Mr. Speaker, about the Depressed Areas Bill."

The joviality evaporates. But just as easily as before, the Speaker responds, "When are you boys going to do something about them upstairs?" He gestures towards the ceiling, above which the Rules Committee has its rooms.

"That's what we came to see you about." The Speaker tries another tack. "With everything going well in the country . . . this bill . . . I don't see any great need for it." At once a chorus of anguish. We are ready for him on this. In rapid salvos everyone present, each experienced in the science of telling words, fires off bits — his reasons why this bill is needed now. There is even a scattering of shot — about aircraft shutdowns in Texas. We had received reports of the Speaker's doubts about the urgency of this bill, and to be forewarned is to be forearmed. So many problems of Congress are of such long standing that, many times, the basic issues get clouded with the passage of time. Everyone had presumed that the Speaker knew the facts about the depressed areas legislation. He had heard the story retold over so many years. Actually, his information was out-of-date.

'Round the room we went, each adding a fast reappraisal of the need for this legislation.

The Speaker saw this was no group to go through the center with, so he tried his first move again. When were we going to do something with the Democratic members of the Rules Committee? And what could we do, we asked? We were asking the help of the Speaker with the gentlemen upstairs. The ball remained in midfield. The interview limped to a close.

Had there been achievement? Perhaps. Perhaps a fresh understanding by the Speaker of a perplexing national disgrace. Perhaps a word would go out "upstairs." Perhaps he would not put in a fatal objection should we try something on our own. The question, as always, boiled down to an appraisal — did we have the votes? Yes, the Speaker was interested in the currency of the problem itself. He was interested in the connection between chronically depressed areas and the areas of automation and technological change. But — but, he asked, could we produce the needed votes when and if we got to the Floor?

To this, we had chorused assent. Yes, we had the votes by a wide margin if we could only go to a test.[9]

[9] Clem Miller, *Member of the House,* John W. Baker, ed. (New York: Scribner, 1962), pp. 90–91.

Rayburn promised help but seemed in no hurry: since Eisenhower had already vetoed a bipartisan bill, there was no reason to press the House for a more liberal measure until the 1960 presidential campaign was closer at hand. It was not until March of 1960 that Rayburn induced Judge Smith to hold hearings; on April 21, the committee turned down the rule by a six-six vote. (When he had the necessary votes to withhold a rule, Judge Smith was a particularly tenacious opponent.)

The leadership now had to settle on a means of circumventing the committee. Of the available alternatives, suspension of the rules (see the section on The End-of-the-Session Squeeze, above) was out of the question because the consent of the Minority Leader, Charles Halleck (R. Ind.), could not be secured. A more feasible method, the discharge petition, was considered but discarded. Under the rules, any committee that refuses to report a piece of legislation may be discharged of its responsibility by a motion signed by a simple majority of the House (218 signatures). If the petition is successful, the bill is printed on the Discharge Calendar and taken up on the second and fourth Mondays of each month. House norms discourage discharges, because they represent a vote of "no confidence" in the committee system. Only two laws in modern times have been enacted via the discharge route.[10] Seven days after the Rules vote, therefore, Majority Leader McCormack notified the House that S. 722 would be brought to the floor under a third procedure, Calendar Wednesday.[11]

In this procedure, the names of standing committees are called alphabetically by the clerk each Wednesday. The chairman of a committee desiring immediate action on one of its bills before Rules may call up the bill when his committee's name is reached. Action on such a bill must be completed by the end of the calendar day, under a two-hour limit for general debate. This feature of the rule makes users of Calendar Wednesday vulnerable to delaying tactics by the opposition. Because of this hazard, the procedure is normally dispensed with by unanimous consent, and the most recent use had been ten years before, in 1950.

[10] The Wage and Hour Act of 1938 and the Federal Pay Raise Act of 1960.

[11] Another device for circumventing the Rules Committee, the so-called "21-day rule," was not operative during the period of this case study. First enacted by the Democratic 81st Congress in 1949, the rule provided that, if the Rules Committee had reported adversely on a bill, or if it had failed to report favorably within 21 days, the Speaker might recognize the chairman of the legislative committee to call up the bill for House consideration. The rule was repealed in 1951 but was reinstated in 1965 at the instigation of Speaker McCormack and a liberal coalition.

On Wednesday, May 4, an objection to dispensing with Calendar Wednesday by unanimous consent was to have launched the festivities. But, at 12:02 P.M., when the final "Amen" of the chaplain's invocation had hardly been uttered, one of the two "sentries" stationed on the floor by Republicans and southern Democrats opposed to the bill — John C. Davis (D. Ga.) — raised a point of no quorum and the quorum bells rang out. Twenty-one minutes were spent calling the roll, and 379 members were found present.[12] Then the Speaker moved that "further proceedings [rounding up all absentees] under the roll call be dispensed with" by uanimous consent. When the anticipated objection was heard from John Bell Williams (D. Miss.), McCormack moved to dispense with further proceedings and called a "previous question" on his motion. Davis countered by moving to table McCormack's motion of previous question and demanding a roll call. Davis' motion was defeated after a twenty-three-minute roll call. Similar roll calls to approve McCormack's two motions (previous question, then the main motion) took another half hour. By this time the House had consumed one hour and thirty-eight minutes in satisfying everyone that a quorum was present.

Rayburn now moved to dispense with reading of the journal — normally a routine means of facilitating business. On this afternoon, however, Davis insisted on a full reading. Members were heard to groan audibly as they disappeared for lunch. Four minutes later Davis, noting that the chamber was emptying, made a point of no quorum. Twenty-two minutes were required to reassemble a quorum, after which the round-robin of roll calls began again. Three roll calls were completed. Up to this point, the House had spent three hours and fifteen minutes on quorum calls.

The clerk resumed the reading of the journal while members drifted away once more. Twenty minutes later Williams looked around at the empty chairs and raised a point of no quorum. And so it went for most of the afternoon.

In the end Davis and Williams relented to allow the House to consider the bill. After the journal was approved, Speaker Rayburn ordered the call of the committees under the Calendar Wednesday procedure. When the clerk reached Banking and Currency, Chairman Brent Spence (D. Ky.) called up S. 722 for consideration. Minority Leader Charles Halleck (R. Ind.) ordered a test vote on the bill by demanding a roll call on whether the House wanted to consider it. The

[12] A quorum of the House is a simple majority, or 218. For the Committee of the Whole, a quorum is only 100 — one reason this device is so convenient for substantive debate.

motion carried comfortably, 221 to 171. With this vote the House was automatically transformed into a "Committee of the Whole." This relatively informal procedure has the effect of easing the fight against dilatory tactics, since only 100 members are required for a quorum and time-consuming roll calls are prohibited. When substantive debate finally commenced at 5:08 P.M., the House had consumed almost four and one-half hours calling the roll twelve times.

Only two hours were devoted to general debate, but even then dilatory tactics were employed by the bill's opponents. When Chairman Spence offered an amendment to substitute a committee-approved $251-million measure for the Senate's $389.5-million bill (S. 722), Congressman James Haley (D. Fla.) forced a thirty-minute reading of the thirty-two-page substitute. When Representative William Widnall (R. N.J.) offered the Administration's $53-million version, it too had to be read verbatim. The committee substitute was accepted, but the Widnall version was rejected by a 152 to 77 standing vote. The decisive vote — on a motion to recommit the bill to committee — came at 9:30 P.M., and the margin was 223 to 162 against recommittal. The Committee of the Whole then dissolved and reported its decision to the full House so that the House could vote final passage of the bill.

The obstruction of the southern sentries, Davis and Williams, demonstrated the risky nature of Calendar Wednesday, since the rules specify that it may consume no more than a single day. The majority's victory in this case depended not entirely upon the exhaustion of the minority's dilatory weapons, but also on the minority's deliberate decision to relent. Since the depressed-areas bill obviously had the necessary votes, the southern Democratic opponents decided that the better part of wisdom was to avoid carrying their obstructionism to the extreme. No doubt they did not want to be responsible for depriving the Democratic party of a useful campaign issue, in light of the assumption that Eisenhower would veto the measure. Nevertheless, a price must be paid when extraordinary legislative channels are invoked. The price for passage of S. 722 under Calendar Wednesday was the bothersome and time-consuming series of roll calls.

CONFERENCE COMMITTEE POLITICS

As predicted, President Eisenhower vetoed the 1960 depressed-areas bill — thus presenting the Democrats with a prime campaign issue. Conveniently, a recession had set in during mid-1960 and the issue of unemployment was a salient one in the depressed areas of New England, Appalachia, and the Midwest. The new Democratic Administration, which assumed office in January, was committed to the passage of a Douglas-type bill for the relief of such areas. As a senator, Kennedy had been a cosponsor of area redevelopment legislation from its inception; and his campaign in the West Virginia primary of 1960 had left an indelible impression of the joblessness and poverty he found there.

The passage of a Douglas-type bill was thus a foregone conclusion. The six-year impasse between a Republican Administration and Democratic majorities on Capitol Hill was at an end. Negotiation now focused on several important details of administering the program. Douglas lost several of these skirmishes, the chief one being a fight over where the new agency would be located in the executive structure. Douglas favored creation of a new, independent Area Redevelopment Administration that would presumably be free of the "vested interests" embodied in the regular departments. He was especially suspicious of the Eisenhower Administration's insistence on placing the program in the Commerce Department, since he feared that its "business clientele" would sabotage the program. When the Kennedy Administration came out for this alternative, Douglas realized he was "surrounded" and accepted defeat.

A second major skirmish centered around the perennial issue of backdoor financing. Douglas had always favored Treasury financing over the customary annual appropriations process in order to permit the agency to make long-range financial commitments. It was not clear, however, what position the Administration would take. In fact, two depressed-areas bills introduced in 1961 could claim to have Administration "sponsorship." One was Douglas' own bill, which had been recommended by a pre-Inaugural "Task Force on Unemployment" appointed by President-elect Kennedy and chaired by Douglas. This bill had been awarded the honor of being numbered S. 1 and, in accordance with Douglas' thinking, included Treasury financing. The actual Administration bill (H.R. 4569), prepared downtown in February, was obligingly introduced by Chairman Spence under his own name. It called for financing by appropriations.

Douglas successfully steered the Treasury financing provision of S. 1 through the Senate. But the House, always more sensitive than the Senate toward the appropriations committees' prerogatives, accepted the Spence bill without even a test vote on the financing issue.

When the two chambers pass different versions of the same bill, a conference must be held to resolve the discrepancies before the measure can go to the President. Conference politics are as complex as any on Capitol Hill, and are undoubtedly least understood of all the aspects of congressional procedure. Conferences had been involved earlier in the history of depressed-areas legislation, in 1958 and 1960; but an ingenious twist in parliamentary maneuvering made the 1961 conference particularly noteworthy.

First, White House aides sent word to Chairman Spence that the Administration would prefer Treasury financing — an obvious gesture to appease Douglas. With ill-concealed feeling, Spence remarked to his fellow House conferees that he wished the White House would make up its mind. But Spence would remain loyal to the Administration's wishes, as would the rest of the House Democratic conferees: Wright Patman (Tex.), Albert Rains (Ala.), and Abraham Multer (N.Y.)

The problem then became how to induce the House to accept Treasury financing. As chairman of the conference, Douglas gave considerable thought to the question and came up with an adroit parliamentary maneuver. Since the House had acted upon the legislation most recently, it was the Senate's decision whether to ask for a conference.[13] The Senate did so, and the House acquiesced. The distinction was important, for if precedent were to be honored, "a conference report is made first to the house agreeing to the conference," in this case, the House of Representatives.[14] If the House were allowed to pass on the conference report first, it would undoubtedly decline to approve the backdoor-financing feature and send its conferees back to the bargaining table, probably with instructions not to "recede" on that issue.

But *Cleaves' Manual* governing conferences is based on precedent and not on rule. Accordingly, Douglas directed the Legislative Reference Service to prepare a lengthy memorandum outlining his rights as conference chairman and citing relevant precedents. Several precedents were turned up that were at variance with normal practice. Armed with this information, and with the consent of the House Democratic conferees, Douglas refused to turn over the conference papers (records) to the House conferees and instead delivered the report directly to the Senate floor, where it was approved.

The House was thus confronted with a take-it-or-leave-it choice: It had to accept the report with Treasury financing, or there would be no bill at all. It chose to pass the bill, 223 to 193; observers estimated

[13] "The request for a conference must always be made by the house in possession of the papers." *Cleaves' Manual*, section 3.

[14] *Cleaves' Manual*, section 35.

that only about twenty-five votes were lost because of the financing provision. But the incident provoked an outburst from Appropriations Chairman Clarence Cannon (D. Mo.). "What a way to run a business — any business from a peanut stand to a bank," he exclaimed. "And yet that is the way we are running the greatest government on earth. Let us close the back door."

Douglas was very proud of his victory. Like many liberals, he had long viewed the rules as silent partners of the conservative bloc. Now he felt the weight of the rules on his own side. With a mastery of the rules — and the connivance of relevant persons — much is possible on Capitol Hill. Without these resources, little can be accomplished.

EPILOGUE

In the end, Douglas' master tactical stroke was of doubtful value. In the final bill of the 1961 session, a supplemental appropriations bill, a piqued Clarence Cannon and his colleagues wiped out backdoor financing for the Area Redevelopment Administration simply by appropriating it $170.75 million for fiscal 1962. On September 27, the House debated the bill (P.L. 87–332), approved it, and then adjourned for the year.

Even as the House was acting, the Senate was debating the appropriations bill; and when the Senators discovered that the House had adjourned, they were enraged. Even such fiscal conservatives as Everett Dirksen (R. Ill.) and Karl Mundt (R. S.D.) decried this "affront to the Senate." "An outrage is being perpetrated on the Senate," Minority Leader Dirksen declared. "Are we a coordinate branch of the legislative establishment, or are we not?" Though the Senators sullenly approved the bill, they indicated that the interhouse dispute had not ended. This incident contributed substantially to the spectacular 1962 feud between the House and Senate appropriations committees.

On the other hand, observers noted that the House bill included all the funds ARA had requested. It was conceded that Douglas' earlier coup may have served the negative function of inducing Cannon to exercise caution in overruling the conferees' decision.

The lesson to be gleaned from this epilogue is that the arenas for legislative maneuvering are numerous and continuous, and that tactical defeats of the moment may be turned into victories in another arena and at another time. Or, as in this case, a tactical advantage may be nullified by subsequent action. In commonplace idiom, "He who laughs last, laughs best."

CONCLUSIONS: THE RULES AND LEGISLATIVE POLITICS

The Area Redevelopment Act of 1961 (P.L. 87–27) was signed into law by President Kennedy on May 1, 1961 — the first major legislative accomplishment of the "New Frontier." Thus ended a seven-year struggle for depressed-areas assistance on the part of an unwieldy coalition of liberal legislators, trade unions, economists, city planners, and farm progressives. There are many "nooks and crannies" in the history of P.L. 87–27 that are of interest to students of politics. The foregoing account has not done justice to this history, since our purpose has been the narrower one of illustrating the role of rules and procedures in legislative politics.

In the light of this objective, several themes have recurred throughout this analysis:

1. "The rules" have influence over legislative outcomes. They are resources, and mastery of them is a form of power in Congress. Senator Douglas' absence from the Senate floor while southerners speedily referred the 1956 civil rights bill to the Judiciary Committee, a traditional graveyard for such legislation, was an unfortunate miscalculation that resulted in a pigeon-holing of the bill within the rules. Douglas' actions as chairman of the 1961 conference committee on the depressed-areas bill, on the other hand, constituted a shrewd use of the rules for his own advantage.

2. Yet the rules are not independent of the power struggle that lies behind them. There is very little that the houses cannot do under the rules — so long as the action is backed up by votes and inclination. Yet votes and inclination are not easily obtained; and the rules persistently challenge the proponents of legislation to demonstrate that they have both resources at their command. Thus, there is little to prevent obstruction at every turn except the tacit premise that the business of the house must go on.

3. The rules cannot always be invoked with impunity. If they are resorted to indiscriminately or flagrantly, there is the risk that they will be redefined and the prerogative taken away or modified. Fulbright was made to realize this during the 1958 Banking and Currency Committee fight; Judge Smith certainly understood this in the 1958 incident, though repeated flirtations with the marginal extremes of his authority in 1960 led to its redefinition in 1961, when Speaker Rayburn was able to "pack" the Rules Committee.[15]

[15] The House voted to increase the size of the Rules Committee, making it possible for Rayburn to add moderates and liberals who could outvote Rules Committee Chairman Smith and his allies. — Eds.

4. A corollary principle is that rules and precedents often develop a life of their own. They may be valued for their own sake, and may not be subject to cynical machinations of the moment. There are two reasons for this. First, routinization itself has value in a conflict-laden body such as a legislature, for it confines conflict and settles many questions that might otherwise be troublesome. Secondly, a member who breaches the rules today may expect to have them used against him at some future date. It is this ghost that haunts senators when they are confronted with the issue of cloture and that reinforces the congressional folkway of deference to the rules.

20

The Model Cities Program

Randall B. Ripley

The problem of urban decay has plagued this nation for decades. Many observers believe that the problem is an inescapable consequence of industrial and technological achievement — the price we must pay for "being civilized." Others believe that urban decay is too high a price to pay for progress and that we might well escape this consequence of technology if we but tried hard to do so; to them civilization means rising out of squalor, not descending into it.

For over twenty years the federal government has — with varying degrees of success — involved itself in efforts to combat the problems of urban areas. Another front in this continuing war was opened in 1966 when Congress passed the Demonstration Cities and Metropolitan Development Act (DCMDA). Its central feature was a three-year $1.2 billion authorization to carry out President Johnson's demonstration cities [1] proposals. The object of the proposals was to rebuild decayed neighborhoods in selected cities by coordinating a wide array

From *The Politics of Economic and Human Resource Development* by Randall B. Ripley, copyright © 1972, by The Bobbs-Merrill Company, Inc., reprinted by permission of the publisher.
[1] Following a summer of urban riots in 1966 "demonstration cities," Johnson's original term, was quietly changed to "model cities."

of existing federal, state, local, and private efforts, as well as utilizing innovative approaches. The new program aimed at the social, economic, and physical problems of the blighted neighborhoods. . . .

POLICY SUBSTANCE AND POLICY PROCESS

Background and Agenda-Building

. . . In 1965 the Democratic party in Congress contained many liberals who were dissatisfied with the substance of existing federal programs for the cities, especially in housing, and the Republican party contained many conservatives who were dissatisfied with the procedures and patterns of responsibility in these programs. Many executive branch officials and state and local officials shared these twin concerns. Thus, the "demands" that led to the model cities formula emanated not only from the national government in Washington and its field establishments elsewhere but also from state and local governments and public housing authorities.

The unrest and rioting in American cities that began on a large and continuing scale in the summer of 1964 helped to call a whole range of urban problems to the attention of the Johnson administration and to reenforce the attention and priority the administration was already giving some of the problems. President Johnson designated a special Task Force on Urban Problems in late 1965. He appointed as its chairman Robert C. Wood, who subsequently became the first Under Secretary of the Department of Housing and Urban Development. This task force advocated the use of demonstration programs to show what the federal government could do to alleviate the plight of the cities by working closely with local officials, agencies, and residents and by coordinating the efforts of a large number of federal agencies already involved in "city aid" in one capacity or another. The principal recommendations of the task force's report were adopted by the Johnson administration and sent to Capitol Hill in the form of bills early in 1966.

A Brief History of the Program

. . . The principal thrust of events in 1966 was to provide congressional legitimation of a policy statement formulated by the administration.

In 1967 the administration sought congressional legitimation of a further policy statement about the level of financing for the program.

Congress authorized less than half of the funds requested, thus restricting the policy actions that could subsequently take place. Limited policy actions were taken in 1967 with the selection of the first cities to receive planning funds.

In 1968 policy actions by the Model Cities Administration (MCA) continued with the designation of more cities to receive planning grants. By the end of the year the funding for the first nine cities was approved. Congress again approved only a portion of the funds requested for further policy actions.

In 1969 the new Republican administration retained the program but reoriented it in a series of policy statements and actions that theoretically widened its scope of activity but did not immediately add funds to undertake those activities. The first nine grants were suspended and reinvestigated, but by late spring money began to flow to recipient cities for implementation of the plans. By January 1970 more than one-third of all the designated cities were receiving funds to implement their five-year plans.

During 1970 the Nixon administration, through its policy statements and actions, continued to shift the program away from its Great Society aura toward a Republican "new federalism" image. With its stress on local initiative, local control, and program coordination the Model Cities program was viewed by HUD officials in the Nixon administration as being even more central to the federal government's attack on urban problems than it was in the Johnson administration. In both administrations, however, procedural commitments and goals have been more important at the operating levels of government than substantive commitments and goals.

In 1971 the Nixon administration made it clear that it had little place for the Model Cities program in its planning for the future. In the winter and spring the administration took three actions that made its intentions clear. First, it threatened to cut off all commitments to designated cities after the end of calendar 1971. A wave of opposition from city officials led it to retract this action. Second, the President proposed the elimination of Model Cities as a separate program so that the resources allocated to it could be included in his revenue-sharing program for urban community development. Consequently, the administration asked for no new budgetary authority for the program. Third, in May the administration had available $1.107 billion in unexpended appropriations for Model Cities but firmly planned to spend only $375 million. The Office of Management and Budget had impounded $583 million; the fate of the remaining $149 million was unclear.

Policy Statements

Throughout the history of the Model Cities program its principal policy makers have resided in the executive branch. The Wood task force formulated the initial proposals in 1965. President Johnson adopted its recommendations and sent them to Congress in early 1966. In the remaining two Johnson years any funding requests came from preliminary groundwork done by the Department of Housing and Urban Development, the Bureau of the Budget, the White House staff, and occasionally the President himself. . . .

The formulators of the Model Cities program saw it as a program that — by consciously manipulating social conditions in their favor — would have an impact on even the poorest residents of American slums. They sold the program to others in two ways: in speaking to liberals they advocated it for what it was, namely, a program of social manipulation; but in speaking to conservatives they portrayed it as a program of subsidy.

The administration figures most visible during the early stages of the policy statement process were Secretary Robert C. Weaver, Under Secretary Robert C. Wood, and Assistant Secretary H. Ralph Taylor, all of HUD. Both Wood and Weaver appeared in congressional hearings on the Model Cities bill and testified for it. Taylor was active on the banquet route, drumming up support among local officials who would be affected by the legislation.

Within Congress the three most visible advocates were Wright Patman (D., Tex.), Chairman of the House Banking and Currency Committee, William Barrett (D., Pa.), Chairman of the House Subcommittee on Housing, and Edmund Muskie (D., Me.), a member of the Senate Banking and Currency Committee and floor manager for the bill.

Achieving congressional legitimation of the Johnson administration's program of social manipulation was a difficult task from the outset and never became any easier along the way. Although Congress had long viewed the technique of subsidy with favor, it was less favorably disposed to the technique of social manipulation in behalf of the poor. Significant opposition to the program developed in Congress. Within both the House and Senate Banking and Currency Committees most Republicans opposed it. Republican opposition was equally vocal on the floor of both chambers, especially in the House. The four most outspoken opponents, all Republicans, were Congressmen Paul Fino of New York and William Brock of Tennessee and Senators John Tower of Texas and Bourke Hickenlooper of Iowa. Each was a member of the Banking and Currency Committee in his chamber. While the Republicans proposed no comprehensive alternative plan, they did offer several amendments that would have fundamentally changed the President's bill. The bill that finally emerged from Congress was considerably modified from the original version.

Congressmen Fino introduced a substitute bill in late February. The Republican bill duplicated many of the administration's proposals regarding program and financial criteria, but it departed sharply from the administration's version in its substitution of a federal information officer for the federal coordinator and its insistence on language expressing the sense of Congress that the demonstration projects were not to detract "in any way" from the powers of the local governments to control and administer existing federal grant-in-aid programs. The major differing provisions in the Fino bill were toned down and incorporated into the administration's bill. The requirement that a federal coordinator be stationed in the city was dropped, and cities were given the option of asking for a "metropolitan expediter."

Another modification of the administration's bill was the elimination of provisions requiring model cities to have racial integration as a goal of their plans; in fact, an amendment was adopted that dropped school-bussing requirements as a condition for assistance. Other amendments broadened the scope of the program to include small cities, reduced the federal share of Model Cities grants from 90 percent to 80 percent, and dropped the requirement that cities establish a separate agency specifically designed to administer the Model Cities program.

Despite these changes in the bill, congressional and administration supporters still had great difficulty steering the bill through Congress. Senator Muskie proved himself adept at building a winning coalition in the Senate, where the bill passed by a comfortable margin (53–22), but the House proved less receptive to the measure. Following intensive lobbying by the administration and the U.S. Conference of Mayors and a sizable cut in the size of the federal commitment, the House authorized the program by a vote of 178 to 141.

Few substantive amendments have been considered since the 1966 authorization. The Nixon administration sponsored an amendment in 1969 to prohibit the use of labor contracts that hampered the use of modern housing techniques such as prefabricated housing in the Model Cities program. Under strong union pressure Congress limited the applicability of this amendment to HUD's experimental "Operation Breakthrough" and did not apply it to the Model Cities program.

Another important amendment proposed by the Nixon administration in 1969 also encountered defeat in Congress. The proposal would have given Model Cities and many other urban programs an "open-ended authorization"; that is, no ceiling would be set on their appropriations, and the administration would be free to request funds as necessary.

Congress has been increasingly generous in authorizing funds for the Model Cities program. Table 1 summarizes the authorizations granted. One should keep in mind that the effect of the supplementary grants is greater than the level of funding might suggest since they maximize the ability of local governments to meet the matching requirements of other grant-in-aid programs.

Table 1
Authorizations for Model Cities, 1968–71

Category	Fiscal Year (figures in millions)			
	1968	1969	1970	1971
Supplementary grants	$400	$ 500	$1,000	$1,312.5 [c]
Urban renewal funds	250	500 [a]	[b]	[b]
Total	$650	$1,000	$1,000	$1,312.5

Note: Amounts do not include planning funds.

[a] Includes a $150 million carry-over.

[b] Urban renewal funds earmarked for the Model Cities program were transferred to another account. In 1969 Congress required that 35% of urban renewal funds in fiscal 1970 and fiscal 1971 be earmarked for "neighborhood development programs."

[c] Includes a $712.5 million carry-over.

Apart from the flurry of partisanship surrounding the initial authorization for the Model Cities program, both congressional parties have consistently supported the program. By 1969 the program was considered safe enough that no roll-call votes were taken on amendments to the program in the House, and the entire bill (which authorized many other HUD programs in addition to Model Cities) passed in the House 339–9, with only 5 Republicans voting against it. It passed in the Senate on a voice vote. . . .

Policy statements made by Model Cities administrators and supporters underwent a . . . marked transformation following the change of administrations in 1969. . . . Under Johnson administration officials the themes stressed most often included:

— the model cities approach as the ultimate federal tool for eradicating urban blight and poverty;
— concentrating the planning and implementation efforts on limited areas of selected cities, known as target neighborhoods;
— emphasizing citizen participation in the planning and implementation of the program, but not at the expense of the established local government's role;
— the centrality of the mayors' role in the program, and the bolstering of local government in general;
— improving the "delivery systems" for existing federal programs for the cities.

Some critics during the Johnson administration believed that the Model Cities program was being oversold — that it was promising more than it could deliver given the budgetary limitations upon it and the keen competition for scarce resources. Cities were urged to be comprehensive in their plans, and as a result they often submitted plans that were overly ambitious rather than realistically attainable.

The program was retained, although not warmly embraced, by the Nixon administration in 1969 and 1970. One reason that President Nixon may be reluctant to talk publicly about Model Cities is that the program still retains too much of the flavor of its Great Society heritage. However, HUD Secretary Romney, Under Secretary Richard Van Dusen, and Assistant Secretary for Model Cities Floyd Hyde have all given the program their support, and they have labored hard to give it a more Republican orientation. These HUD administrators have sought to deemphasize some of the themes stressed by the previous administration, to reemphasize others, and to add a few of their own. They have:

— emphasized making the program more responsive to local needs and less susceptible to federal management;
— made strong commitments to supporting the local governments and giving the mayors a stronger role in the program;
— deemphasized the citizen participation aspects of the program, especially in administration;
— announced that the scope of the program would be increased to include entire cities rather than just target neighborhoods;
— toned down the promises of results, trying to make expectations realistic by promising only what is deliverable;

— stressed the need for a more unified interpretation of administrative policies at all levels of administration.

In addition, HUD officials have announced their desire to give cities in the future almost complete control of mobilizing and coordinating resources, moving away from a federal review of cities' compliance with federal standards and toward a goal of allowing cities to set their own standards, monitored federally only by audits to determine whether cities are spending their federal dollars according to the terms of their contract. Also in an experimental vein HUD officials have expressed the hope that in the Model Cities program they can soon begin to award block grants instead of the narrow categorical grants that are now awarded.

Policy Actions

In the Johnson years policy actions (other than appropriations) related to establishing guidelines for planning, evaluating applications for planning grants, awarding grants for planning, and articulating the administrative philosophy of the program. No program grants were made until the last month of President Johnson's term in office.

Guidelines sent to the cities stated that the individual programs: should be comprehensive and encompass all of the social and environmental problems of the neighborhood; should concentrate efforts on a limited area (10 percent or less of the population, or up to 15,000 in smaller cities); should utilize new and imaginative approaches; and should make a substantial impact on the conditions of life and the quality of the environment.

The first call for applications to the Model Cities program brought 193 responses by the May 1967 deadline. The task of deciding which applicants would receive planning grants fell to a committee of representatives from the five departments and one autonomous agency that concern themselves with urban problems: Commerce (Economic Development Administration); Justice (Community Relations Service); Labor; Health, Education, and Welfare; Housing and Urban Development; and the Office of Economic Opportunity. This unusual way of selecting applicants reflected the spirit of coordination that the program was designed to foster.

Controversy arose soon after the November 1967 announcement awarding planning grants. Charges of partisan politics were made by some congressmen (particularly Florence Dwyer, a New Jersey Republican). A relationship was alleged between the voting on certain amendments to the poverty program and the awarding of grants twelve hours later. The basis for these charges was that all of the planning grants except two were awarded to districts whose representative in the House had supported the antipoverty authorization bill twelve hours earlier and that only eight of the sixty-three grants went to districts represented by Republicans. Partisan considerations appeared to play a smaller role in the second round of selections, with about one-third of the awards going to districts represented by Republicans (many of whom had previously opposed the program).

As the program began to be administered from Washington in the latter half of the Johnson administration four themes received particular stress:

1. The mayor was to be the central figure in the program, and the established authorities in the cities were to be bolstered and obeyed. The existing institutional structure at the local level was assumed to be the backbone of the program. One of the principal aims of the program was to strengthen this machinery — and not merely for the more specific purpose of carrying out and achieving the aims of the Model Cities program itself. . . .

2. Citizen participation is to be encouraged, but never at the expense of the authority of the city government. . . .

3. The central purpose of the program is to improve "delivery systems" for existing federal programs for the cities. Existing federal, state, and local programs should, in the view of the administrators, be combined in a more efficient and effective effort at delivery. The content of the goods delivered took second place to the efficiency of the delivery itself.

4. The states must also be accorded a place in the Model Cities program. . . .

Tension between Washington and the "field" (that is, federal employees in the eligible cities) was built into the administration of the program during the Johnson years, however. . . .

Under the Nixon administration actions have been taken to follow through on most of its policy statements.

HUD officials have enforced a unified interpretation of administrative policy at local and regional levels, an interpretation that had not emerged before Johnson left office. This interpretation stresses the centrality of the mayor's role in administration and reenforces the structures of local government. At the same time citizen participation has been deemphasized, and there is no longer any hint of citizen control. The residents still have a share in the planning, but HUD officials have made clear that final responsibility and authority lie in the mayor's office, not with citizens' groups.

To increase the mayors' support for and understanding of the program and to illustrate its potential impact for them, HUD Assistant Secretary Floyd Hyde, himself a former mayor, held three conferences for model city mayors in mid-1969. The mayors represent a potentially long-term stable constituency for Model Cities and all of HUD, and officials are eager to cultivate the relationship. Model Cities is the first HUD program that operates to support city governments directly. Other federal grant-in-aid programs have a fragmenting effect on the power of local governments because funds are disbursed to many nongovernmental agencies or governmental agencies in addition to the cities themselves.

A significant policy action occurred in the spring of 1970 when a proposal was being circulated inside the government to divert up to 87 percent of Model Cities' $575 million appropriation to a special Presidential program to assist school districts undergoing desegregation. HUD officials, the mayors, and some members of Congress successfully lobbied against the proposal, and on 14 May President Nixon assured Secretary Romney that no funds would be diverted from Model Cities' money. The lobbying effort also increased the support of some mayors who had previously been only lukewarm toward the program.

Other HUD policy actions since Nixon's accession to the presidency have included eliminating the size restriction on target neighborhoods so that entire cities may come into the program, and eliminating some of the federal red tape in the program. A Task Force on Model Cities, chaired by Professor Edward Banfield of Harvard reported that "some of the Model Cities administration's regulations have been greatly simplified and reduced; planning guidelines have been cut from about 40 single-spaced pages (with appendices) to eight pages; the cities are no longer under pressure to be 'comprehensive' in their proposals." These changes are aimed at continued decentralization of the program's operation and administration.

One facet of administration that has troubled HUD under both the Johnson and Nixon administrations has been its statutory authority to coordinate the spending of other departments for programs that affect model cities. The authority to coordinate looks attractive on paper, but in practice HUD has encountered interdepartmental rivalries, jealousies, and a persistent reluctance to earmark funds for programs in model cities. HUD had expected more generous support than has been forthcoming from other departments operating programs in model cities. In fiscal 1970 the Office of Economic Opportunity set aside $17 million and had three men involved in coordination. The Labor Department set aside only $27 million and has only one man working on model cities coordination. The concentration of manpower programs in model cities that was expected at the beginning of the program never materialized, and Labor's contribution to Model Cities has remained small. HEW has been more generous in earmarking funds — $98 million was set aside in fiscal 1970 — and twenty-five men work on coordinating HEW involvement in model cities. However, HEW is also attempting to replace HUD as the principal agency for all human resources programs in the Model Cities program, a move hardly calculated to endear it to HUD.

Table 2

Congressional Action on Administration Requests for Model Cities Appropriations (figures in millions of dollars)

Fiscal Year	Category	Administration's Request	House Figure	Senate Figure	Final Figure	Percentage of Request Granted
1968	Supplemental grants	400	150	400	200	50
	Urban renewal funds	250	75	125	100	40
	Total [a]	650	225	525	300	46
1969	Supplemental grants	500	400	500	312.5	63
	Urban renewal funds [b]	500	100	500	312.5	63
	Total	1,000	500	1,000	625.0	63
1970	Supplemental grants	675	500	600	575	85
1971	Supplemental grants	575	575	575	575	100

[a] Does not include $12 million in planning funds.

[b] Urban renewal funds for model cities were transferred from the Model Cities program to another account after fiscal 1969.

Congress has entered the policy action arena for Model Cities chiefly in the realm of appropriations. The congressional response to funding requests that the Model Cities program has enjoyed since its original authorization is one indication of its support in Congress (see Table 2). In 1967, the first year that the appropriations were made (for fiscal 1968), the Model Cities program was in serious jeopardy. As with the authorization, the House generally and House Republicans particularly took a conservative position toward funding the program. The Senate, however, was more liberal, with the result that the Senate Appropriations Committee restored a major portion of the program funds the House had deleted.

The first conference committee report ended in disagreement, with the House and Senate conferees instructed to return to their separate chambers for further instructions. The administration reduced the opposition to Model Cities by relaxing its efforts to obtain favorable congressional action on the rent supplements program.

The debate during 1967 focused on whether or not the program should be funded at all. Wary of the experimental nature of the Model Cities program, the conservatives in the House came very close to killing the program altogether. Only the defection of a conservative Republican, Louis Wyman of New Hampshire, in the subcommittee and again on the floor enabled the bill to pass. Lobbying activities by mayors of cities vying for funds, by leading "national" businessmen (mostly Republican), and by local civic and business interests aided the administration's cause.[2] Enough Republicans seemed to be attracted by the local benefits and local control in the program to allow it to continue life.

The second conference report in 1967 agreed on a figure 50 percent lower than the administration's request. This agreement, as well as the nature of its supporting coalition, helped to determine that in the future Model Cities would be sold by its proponents and viewed by almost all policy makers as a program of subsidy rather than a program of major manipulative or redistributive import. This switch represented a major shift away from what the program's formulators originally envisioned for Model Cities, but it very likely also represented the only way the program could survive.

During the appropriations process for fiscal 1969 Congress again made a substantial cut in the administration's request but nonetheless appropriated $625 million, more than twice the amount allocated for fiscal 1968. One-half of the funds were earmarked for urban renewal projects within model cities, and conservatives now seemed willing to live with it as a program of subsidy.

The upward trend in appropriations continued in 1969. With the prospect of a limited number of cities entering the execution phase of the program, President Johnson's 1970 budget envisioned $750 mil-

[2] See *Congressional Quarterly Almanac,* 1967, pp. 478–79.

lion dollars going to Model Cities. With the earmarked urban renewal funds having been transferred out of the Model Cities budget, the figure represented a 50 percent increase over the previous year's request. The Nixon figure for fiscal 1970 was more conservative — $675 million — and the amount appropriated by Congress was $100 million less.

In 1970 President Nixon still showed no interest in expanding Model Cities; in fact, he was willing to see it shrink. The amount of his request was the same amount appropriated the previous year, $575 million. Congress did not cut that request.

Analysis of appropriations behavior for Model Cities indicates somewhat dwindling administration support and gradually increasing, though not overwhelming, congressional support. Table 3 shows that in absolute terms the administrations' requests for Model Cities funds have increased for every year except fiscal 1971. In terms of the percentage of the total authorization requested, the Johnson administration was much more supportive of the program (100 percent of the authorization requested for both 1968 and 1969) than the Nixon administration has been (67 percent and 44 percent, respectively, for 1970 and 1971). Table 2 shows that Congress has steadily granted a greater share of the administrations' requests in percentage terms, although the absolute amounts may technically have decreased since fiscal 1969 (reflecting the transfer of urban renewal funds to another account). Congressional support has been largely bipartisan since the initial funding debates. In the Senate 98 percent of the Democrats and 100 percent of the Republicans voted for the appropriations bill for fiscal 1971 (which also funded other HUD programs and independent offices). In the House 99 percent of the Democrats and 95 percent of the Republicans voted for the bill.

Table 3

Administration Appropriations Requests in Relation to Authorizations for Model Cities

Fiscal Year	Authorization (in millions)	Appropriations Request (in millions)	Percentage of Authorization Requested as Appropriations
1968	$ 400	$400	100
1969	500	500	100
1970	1,000	675	67
1971	1,312.5	575	44

In summary, at its inception, the Model Cities program was envisioned by its formulators as a vehicle for the manipulation of social conditions and the redistribution of economic rewards. It was to be a demonstration project for a small, limited number of cities that would eradicate blight and create monuments of true urban renewal. The manipulative aspects of the program were too unpopular with Congress to remain unaltered, and at the end of the legitimation phase the policy that emerged was more subsidy than social engineering. The number of demonstration cities was expanded to 150, and strengthening the hand of city governments and mayors was emphasized.

The Model Cities program has continued under the Nixon administration, but its focus and emphasis under Republican aegis has shifted to its procedural and administrative features, stressing decentralization and the role of the mayor. Budgetary support in dollar terms has declined.[3] The radical impact that the formulators envisioned the program would have on society as a whole has been deemphasized. In a sense the program is now used to *regulate* intergovernmental and intragovernmental relations rather than either to *manipulate* city conditions so as to *redistribute* resources in favor of the ghetto poor (the program formulator's original intent) or to *subsidize* a lot of cities on a growing scale (what the program did in 1967 and 1968 and might have done even more had Hubert Humphrey been elected President in 1968.)

Policy Outcomes

Because program funding began only in May 1969,[4] to expect measurable societal impact on core urban problems at the time of this writing (mid-1971) would be unrealistic. Data summarized at the beginning of this chapter suggest where the program money is going, although not very much money is going to go to any one city ($65 million for New York City will hardly make a dent in its problems). So far the main societal impact of the Model Cities program has been to stimulate local participation and interest. Sundquist's study of selected model cities indicates that neighborhood residents soon de-

[3] As already mentioned, in 1971 the Nixon administration was willing to take additional actions to shrink the program further. These actions included no request for new obligational authority for model cities for fiscal 1972, despite a request from HUD to the Office of Management and Budget that $575 million be included in the budget (the same figure as fiscal 1971 appropriation).

[4] At that time the first cities to receive funds were announced: Seattle, Atlanta, and Waco, Texas. As of 1 January 1970, 58 cities were receiving "action" funds. Romney and Hyde have, at least by implication, committed HUD to funding all cities submitting acceptable proposals.

mand greater influence and power in planning the allocation of funds. This reaction confirms the early experience of the community action part of the poverty program.[5]

The program has had some impact on city governments, mainly by encouraging them to engage in comprehensive planning and by strengthening the hand of the mayor by giving him and city officials the greatest share of control over program funds.

At the federal level the program has strengthened HUD's foothold in the executive establishment by building an important constituency supportive of HUD (the mayors and their principal organizations, the National League of Cities and the United States Conference of Mayors). It has only slightly improved interagency communication and the coordination of urban-oriented programs and has aggravated some interdepartmental rivalries. Some red tape and detailed federal controls over local implementations have been reduced in recent years. . . .

21

Congress, the Atom, and Civil Rights: A Case Study in Civil Wrongs

Theodore J. Lowi and Margaret Stapleton

Congress has lost most of its powers of initiatives, but Congress has not lost its powers. The power of the legislature in the twentieth century is changing, but it can still be formidable as long as the legislators maintain the will to confront the executive and to take seri-

[5] James L. Sundquist, *Making Federalism Work* (Washington, D.C.: Brookings Institution, 1969), p. 90.

Although the two authors take full responsibility for this case study, it is nevertheless the product of research done by them and several members of the senior author's Workshop in Public Policy Analysis at the University of Chicago. The other members were Elliot J. Feldman, Benjamin Ginsberg, Edward C. Hayes, Gregory Nigosian, Jonathan Pool, Allan Rosenbaum, Carlyn Rottsolk, Judy Van Herik, and Thomas and Julia Vittulo-Martin. All are co-authors of *Poliscide: Science and Federalism versus the Metropolis* (forthcoming).

ously the opportunities and options provided by the separation of powers.

The power that still resides in Congress may turn out to be the very thing all large industrial states need most: the institutionalization of second thoughts. A strong individual is nothing without superego. A strong nation needs the functional equivalent of superego. Rationality was the word of industrial governments and their planners in the first half of the twentieth century. Everything, even the most sincere democratic socialist, depended upon using government to maximize the use of resources, to improve relations between means and ends. But looking toward 2000, social conscience not socialism, ecology not economy, quality not quantity, and rights not comforts are the new criteria. And these require *self*-government more than government. Superego is a psychological phenomenon that does not inhere in institutions. The form it has to take would be some regular exercise of a larger view, a balanced or generalist view that deliberately cuts across the specialized views of the bureaucracies. Modern governments organize their executive branches into bureaucracies primarily to reap the profits of specialization, continuity, expertise, and the rest of the capitalist virtues — that is, rationality. But they pay a mighty price — myopia. Perhaps it is too much to expect agencies to take into account the full consequences of their own actions. But somebody should, and Congress can.

In our case study, Congress didn't. But its opportunities are clear. The building of the Western accelerator is an ideal study in congressional potential. It works all the better as a case study because it involves scientists — indeed, the elite among scientists, the high-energy physicists. Their failure to be any better than engineers or politicians at taking a cosmic view proves mainly that the arts and the demands of good government are larger than mere personnel. The failures of past governments and the potentialities of future governments lie ultimately with institutions, not personnel. Whether our institutions will be better will depend heavily upon what laymen do in Congress. And Congress could be better, at least in a small way, if it read our case and took its moral seriously.

THE SETTING

In December 1966, the Atomic Energy Commission announced the results of its long search for a site for the largest atom smasher in the world. In an unprecedented competition that involved sifting through two hundred site candidates from forty-six states, the AEC taxed its own staff and the staffs of the National Academy of Science

(NAS) and Congress's Joint Committee on Atomic Energy (JCAE), plus the patience and credibility of forty-six state industrial commissions and many major corporations, before settling upon Weston, Illinois.

The Weston area was an ideal location for any "clean industry." About twenty-five miles east of Chicago, close enough for commuters and yet far enough away to be in the open country, Weston was part of several thousand acres of metropolitan fringe which still held substantial options on future development. It could become commercial, industrial, or residential, and everybody seemed to realize that a few early commitments would probably determine the entire future development of the region. The village of Weston was directly surrounded by more than fifty farms; it had been a farm until the late 1950's when it was bought for speculative purposes by a local millionairess in anticipation of a national population boom that would ultimately spill over into any area of open country near major transportation routes.

Weston had been a controversial development from the beginning to the end of its six-year history. The county government had fought it at every stage. Residents in the area were hostile, and they regularly approved the hostile acts of their county board. Most major corporations were actively hostile. Neighboring villages were acutely hostile. Weston simply did not fit in with the plans of many major interests in the area for the orderly development of Du Page County, the fourth richest county in the United States.

A few concrete examples of their hostility help to provide the proper setting for the AEC's decision. County sanitation codes were applied with such rigidity to the plans for the construction of Weston that the developers were forced to provide both central water and sewerage facilities although the state law seems clearly to allow individual provision for only one (i.e., if central water is provided, septic tanks are legal; if central sewerage is provided, wells, or cisterns are permissible). This sort of pressure failed to halt construction, so that the county had to resort to the unprecedented strategy of seeking and appealing a *quo warranto* suit, seeking to block the incorporation of the village once it was constructed and had enough residents. Once any village qualifies with a minimum population and the passage of a referendum, incorporation is usually simple and uncontested. Yet it took Weston months and thousands of dollars in legal fees to gain its incorporation. State officials joined in by entering the *quo warranto* suit as *amicus curiae*. Chicago corporations joined in, among other ways, by preventing the developers from advertising houses for rent and sale in the metropolitan newspapers. On and on the parade of preventives went. They did not succeed because the potential for profit was so great. What these barriers did eventually do, however, was to turn the developers increasingly toward illegal means of getting money, including help from the "syndicate." Two area savings and loan banks went bankrupt in the process, and several officials involved in the bank and the development either ended up in jail, in protective custody, or in the Caribbean as fugitives.

Why the intense opposition to one more village development in the suburb? In that vast area it was a tiny village of 100 houses. Only 85 were occupied at the time of acquisition.

Weston represented an urban and proletarian direction for DuPage County in an area that was supposed to remain suburban and exurban. Although Weston was itself a small fish in an immense county pond, the Weston developers had the misfortune of picking an area in which one development could have tipped the development scale for the entire region. Or so the local influentials feared. The threat of urbanization was clear to its citizens, and a brief review of the situation will reveal why. The developers were going to offer the houses at first as rental property, planning to sell them during a second phase of development. The rentals, and eventually the sale prices, were set far below the value of the land and structures. This way the houses could be filled very quickly, and the village could move almost immediately to incorporation. This is important, because under Illinois zoning law, zoning power passes from the county to any village immediately on that village's incorporation. Thanks to the free exercise of its own zoning powers, DuPage County had so set minimum residential lot sizes that any house built on a lot for less than $30,000 would amount to an irrational use of resources. Yet, the Weston developers were talking values in the $13,000 to $18,500 range. Their scheme was clear to the local interests: The developers would build decent homes on these oversized lots and rent them cheaply to get their incorporation. Once zoning power passed to them, they could redraw the lots *to create a third lot between each pair of existing houses*. The major profit to the developers would come from the sale of the middle house.

This is the background of the AEC's decision. This background helps to explain why the state of Illinois would so eagerly agree to pay $30 million for 6,800 acres, 100 completed village houses, and more than 50 farm houses in good condition, and then turn these over to the AEC without charge, when the AEC had first asked for only 3,000 acres of unoccupied land. This background also helps explain some of the behavior of Illinois senators and congressmen when the selection of Weston came before the AEC, the JCAE, and Congress. But beyond all that, it was a background the AEC was almost completely unaware of.

To the national decision makers, the moral issues surrounding the Weston site were simply not fully relevant. In this particular part of the story we concentrate almost exclusively on the civil rights issues; but for civil rights as well as for all the socioeconomic issues, the scientists neither sought nor got information on the history of the area or on the motives and plans of the interested parties other than the vested interests. Their ignorance of the history and culture of the 6,800 acres they acquired is only a slight measure of the social and moral vacuum within which national decision makers appear to be operating. Many aspects of that story we tell elsewhere with several of our colleagues.[1] In this case study, we examine whether a larger social context can ever be provided through comprehensive congressional review.

We cannot overemphasize our sympathy with the fact that bureaucracies cannot operate without severe specialization and that bureaucratic agencies cannot be expected to take into account the full consequences of their own actions. But it is precisely that awareness that turns us to Congress as the place where a substantial counterbalance to the bureaucracy is supposed to occur. Congress has the power, and Congress occasionally exercises it. Budgetary review and substantive review, especially by the distinguished *Joint* Committee on Atomic Energy, provide Congress with frequent and substantial opportunities for the exercise of second thoughts about the general moral context of government action. Does Congress seize its opportunities? Not very frequently, we answer. And its exercise seems to be still less frequent where scientists are involved. Confidence about the capacity of scientists to make good decisions seems to lull Congress into a sense that the job need not be done at all. But the job of general review is almost never done for probably a stronger reason. We are in the field of public works, historically called the "pork barrel." It does not seem to make any difference whether the decision involves a $500 million project designed and executed by the cream of American culture or a $5 million project designed and executed by local hacks and jaded Army engineers.

[1] *Poliscide: Science and Federalism versus the Metropolis* (forthcoming).

THE AEC, THE SITE,
AND THE CIVIL RIGHTS ISSUE

DuPage County is not the place one thinks of as a land of opportunity for urban people. Median income is fourth in the nation, and, thanks more to biased zoning than explicit bigotry, the black population during the 1960's was a fraction of 1 per cent. At about the time of the Weston acquisition, the NAACP estimated that only 589 Negroes resided in a county of nearly four hundred thousand population.[2] A contemporaneous study estimated that a county whose population increase was from 313,000 to 394,000 between 1960 and 1967 included only 133 blacks.[3]

At no point did the AEC express any particular awareness of the restricted conditions in DuPage County, nor does the record show any serious effort on their part to consider the socioeconomic context or impact of its choice of site for the accelerator. When these issues came before the commission at all, they were delayed, deferred, or set aside as somebody's else's responsibility. During the site selection process the AEC revised its original criteria on several occasions, but neither the original [4] nor the refined [5] criteria ever stated that the level of development of a region be a factor favoring its selection. The only site criteria that might even remotely suggest that the AEC could use its new project to foster the economic improvement of a region were two points in the refined criteria covering utilization of facilities already owned by the federal government. In the first instance, the site evaluation committee was charged with the responsibility of taking into account federal installations and to weigh heavily the costs of any nonfederal land. The site evaluation committee was also supposed to take into account opportunities for more effective utilization of present AEC facilities.[6] However, these criteria ceased to be relevant when

[2] Press release from Syd Finley, NAACP National Office, Quad-State Field Director, to Mr. Lewis Morgan, Chairman of the Illinois Atomic Energy Commission, January 19, 1967.

[3] Pierre de Vise, *Chicago's Widening Color Gap,* Inter-University Social Research Committee, Report 2 (December 1967).

[4] Annex D(2) — Considerations Involved in Siting a Major New Accelerator. The document is included in *AEC Authorizing Legislation Fiscal Year 1968.* Hearings before the Joint Committee on Atomic Energy, Congress of the United States, 90th Congress, First Session, on General and Physical Research Program, Including Proposed 200 BEV Accelerator, Part 1, pp. 430–31.

[5] Annex D(1) — 200 BEV Accelerator Laboratory Siting Factors. The document is also included in *AEC Authorizing Legislation Fiscal Year 1968,* pp. 427–30.

[6] Ibid., pp. 428, 430.

states began to offer packages of free land. With the passing of acquisition costs went all incentive for consideration of land in economically depressed areas.

When interviewed in Spring 1969, AEC Commissioner James T. Ramey claimed that the AEC did consider economic improvement possibilities, but the only evidence he could offer was that the AEC tried to review all the sites that had been rejected by the blue-ribbon site selection panel set up by the National Academy (NAS). However, that is fairly flimsy because the NAS Panel had been following AEC criteria all along and because at no time did the AEC depart from any recommendation made by NAS.

The record is much clearer in the other direction, suggesting that the scientists made positive efforts to eliminate depressed areas from the competition. All their criteria stressed the very features that depressed areas lacked and would need most to become developed areas. Some samples of the NAS Panel's own interpretation of the AEC requirements dramatically reveal the effort to keep depressed areas out of contention:

> The first category of criteria includes the physical features, such as geology, science, configuration, climate and availability of power, water, and industrial support. The second category consists of those less readily measurable factors of environment likely to affect the recruitment of resident staff and the participation of visiting scientists.
>
> The site must be so located that management can mobilize and maintain the necessary specialized staff, both resident and non-resident, to accomplish the goals of the research program.[7]

Nearly a year later, after many site visits, and after fairly many sites had been eliminated from the competition, the AEC and the NAS Panel seemed even more firmly set on selecting a well-developed, upper-middle class region:

> This panel was primarily assembled to consider the physical criteria. However, we believe that a prime consideration is the attractiveness of the site and its environment for the permanent staff, and that this consideration should not be subordinated to the physical ones. . . . [A] poor choice of location could result in the assembly of a mediocre staff and consequently a mediocre facility.[8]

[7] "The Report of the National Academy of Sciences' Site Evaluation Committee" (March 1966), p. 430.

[8] "Report of the Panel of Accelerator Scientists, January 25, 1966." The document is also included in ibid., pp. 424–427, esp. 424.

The AEC claimed that the "civil rights atmosphere" around the potential sites was a constant consideration, although no mention was ever made of civil rights when the invitations went out for the site competition. Moreover, the civil rights question was never given as a reason for eliminating a particular site from the competition. The closest the AEC criteria ever came to expressing such concern was a vague and nebulous reference to "the availability of housing" for laboratory staff and the community's "ability of adapting to change." [9]

When under fire in February 1967, nearly two months after the announcement of the selection of the Weston site, AEC Chairman Glenn Seaborg responded in the same vague manner:

> . . . I want to begin by saying that the members of the Atomic Energy Commission do care about human rights, about non-discrimination, about open occupancy in housing. We are very concerned about this, and have been from the beginning and continue to be, and we are doing something about it. We believe that we have a positive program.[10]

Nevertheless, almost nothing in the record suggests any basis to this vague claim to conscience. According to Dr. Edward Goldwasser, a NAS Panel member, civil rights was a consideration to the panel only under the larger consideration of the site's potential for attracting adequate staff. The only active consequence of that consideration was the elimination of all sites located in the deep South.[11]

The AEC claimed that, aside from the presence or absence of such considerations in the NAS Panel deliberations, the civil rights question was brought up regarding the six finalists, once these were turned over by the panel to the AEC. Indeed, by Spring 1966, the general housing situation in Illinois was brought to national attention by Dr. Martin Luther King and his movement. This awareness was brought directly to bear upon the AEC and the Weston site by Clarence Mitchell, Director of the NAACP's Washington Bureau, who wrote Dr. Seaborg about housing discrimination in Illinois, comparing the Illinois site unfavorably, for example, with another finalist site near Denver, Colorado. Mitchell's letter cited Illinois Senator Dirksen's opposition to a national open housing statute as well as the Illinois Legislature's rejection of state open housing legislation as his evidence for doubt that Illinois could "give assurance that there would be adequate safe-

---

[9] "Accelerator Siting Factors," November 16, 1965. Also ibid., p. 430.
[10] Ibid., p. 157.
[11] Interview with Dr. Goldwasser, in Chicago, April 20, 1969, after his appointment as deputy director of the National Accelerator (Weston) Laboratory.

guards against persons being deprived of housing solely because of race. . . ." [12]

In responding to the NAACP pressure, Dr. Seaborg revealed that the AEC sought information from six important agencies of the federal government regarding the discriminatory practices of the six finalists.[13] Dr. Seaborg reported that "none of the agencies advised the AEC to eliminate any of the six sites." In fact, as he reported it, the civil rights records of all six sites were *rated about the same.*

However, this testimony underscores the absence of serious consideration for the contribution the accelerator might make to national civil rights. At no point did Dr. Seaborg indicate any effort on his part, or on the part of the consulted agencies, to add sites with a better civil rights record. It was clear almost from the beginning that future actions rather than present commitments or past records would determine civil rights considerations. This attitude completely freed the AEC to guide itself entirely by the "soft criteria" it had set for itself at the beginning of the site selection process. And quite clearly these added up to a single set of instructions to the panel: Get us a convenient, attractive, upper middle class white community that will give us no social problems at the outset. Consider our social contribution only as trimming on an already delicious cake.[14]

This amounted in practice to a request for "assurances of non-discrimination and equal opportunity . . . as well as assurances that there would be individual and common effort to prevent or offset discrimination and to deal with it promptly should it occur." [15] As promises are cheap, many assurances of support for these civil rights efforts were sent to the commission. The AEC in fact admitted that the situation in the Weston area was not satisfactory, but evasion seemed to be easy: according to the commission, their information created the impression of a "progressive attitude in the Weston site area toward equal employment opportunity, efforts to provide equality in suburban public school systems, and a number of community relations councils devoted to eliminating discrimination. . . . [While there are differing views in the area with respect to non-discrimination, the

[12] Ibid., p. 400.

[13] These were: Equal Employment Opportunity Commission, Community Relations Service, President's Committee on Equal Opportunity on Housing, Commission on Civil Rights, Civil Service Commission, and Office of Federal Contracts Compliance, Department of Labor.

[14] For further evidence on the eagerness of the Commission to consider only the future and not the present or past, see *AEC Authorizing Legislation 1968,* pp. 159, 160–65, 170–75, and passim.

[15] Ibid., p. 179.

Commission will expect] that with the leadership of the state and local governments and with the cooperation support of citizens and community organizations in the Chicago area, a broad satisfactory record of non-discrimination and equal opportunity will be achieved." [16] It is impossible to note this kind of optimism without recognizing the recent record of the state of Illinois and these same state and local leaders on state and local open housing ordinances.

The commission several times also sincerely noted its own intention to use its presence in the area to improve human relations. During the period of most intense civil rights pressure, the AEC's only black member, Samuel M. Nabrit, announced to Congress that the commission "will endeavor to exert our full leverage of power in promoting betterment in all areas of human relations in the metropolitan area and at state levels as well." [17] But even here, when it came to definite AEC policies, the commissioners returned to their vague expressions. Primarily, it steadfastly refused to be guided in its choice of site and its behavior on the site by civil rights considerations. At one time during the hearings, when asked by Rhode Island Senator Pastore, "What if you asked the town of Weston to give you an assurance of an ordinance with respect to open housing and they rebuffed you, would you still put it in Weston?" Chairman Seaborg replied lamely, "I would say that I wouldn't want the future of the accelerator to be determined on the basis of one ordinance of that type, where there are other ways of accomplishing the same thing. . . ." [18] This is the context within which Congress entered the scene in January 1967.

CONGRESS, THE SCIENTISTS, AND CIVIL RIGHTS: A STUDY IN LOST OPPORTUNITY

The accelerator issue became the official property of the United States Congress between January and July in 1967, when review of the project itself and of the choice of the Weston site came up as AEC Authorization Bills for Fiscal Year 1968. The AEC bills, introduced on January 24, 1967, requested a total authorization of $2.5 billion. The request included a mere $10 million dollars for the partial design and construction of the 200 BEV accelerator at Weston. The authorization request passed immediately to the Joint Committee on Atomic Energy, which opened its hearings on January 25. Although the ac-

[16] Ibid., p. 179.
[17] Ibid., p. 175.
[18] Ibid., p. 164.

celerator accounted for a tiny portion of the total request, it figured significantly in the JCAE's investigations, partly because the accelerator was considered such an important research tool, and partly because three members of the Joint Committee represented states whose site candidates had been among the six finalists. And, because those three members were joined with three others who were from the Northeastern states rallying to the cause of the Brookhaven, Long Island, site, it was almost inevitable that the JCAE would decide to concentrate "on selected matters that deserve particular attention" rather than to conduct its usual "comprehensive review of the Commission's entire program."

JCAE Chairman, Senator John O. Pastore (D. R.I.), was one dissident member of the committee who simply opposed Illinois. But he sought to make an issue of the Weston choice by raising the question of opportunities for minorities and how they could share in the benefits of the new accelerator. Ironically, the problem he and the other anti-Illinois dissidents faced early in the hearings was their uncertainty as to how to bring up the civil rights question and to make it an issue. Representative Melvin Price of Illinois, JCAE member and chairman of its Subcommittee on Research Development and Radiation, observed that " . . . as a committee we have not run into this problem before. Although we have located many atomic facilities in the past twenty years this question has not previously been raised." [19] This was a particularly damning piece of information, but the anti-Illinois faction managed for a brief moment to overcome the lack of precedent for raising moral issues in relation to atomic public works.

The first thing the dissidents did was to engage in their own friendly exchange to set the stage for a general inquiry into the civil rights aspects of this project:

> CHAIRMAN PASTORE: The point I mean to make, Senator Javits, is that we have a right either to authorize it or not to authorize it. I was going to ask you how far do you think the Congress can go in saying which one of the sites would it be.
>
> SENATOR JAVITS: As to picking a site, in my judgment the Congress has no right to pick a site and I don't think the committee has. I think it has an absolute duty to strike down a selection which it considers to be the wrong one because it has an independent authority to authorize or not to authorize. But it has not authority. It would not be wise in my judgment or good policy for the committee to put itself in the place of the AEC and say you pick Weston or you pick Brookhaven.

[19] Ibid., p. 139.

CHAIRMAN PASTORE: What guidelines do you think we should follow in this duty to strike it down? How should we superimpose ourselves over the unanimous judgment of the Commission?

SENATOR JAVITS: To start with, the most primitive of the guidelines, naturally if the committee found venality, fraud, misrepresentation, anything that would be against ethics, the committee would strike it down unhesitatingly. So we pass that. No one charges that here and the men of the Commission are very distinguished, and I am the first to say that. The other criteria would be these. One, were the selection criteria which the Commission itself chose adequate for the purpose in the judgment of the Congress or should there be any other criteria? For example, would it be proper to have a criterion that it is desirable to establish another national laboratory center in the Middle West? This would be a legitimate question. Congress would then be incurring a new responsibility, developing a new place, as it were, with its eyes open, realizing what it was.

The second criterion would be whether, in applying its own criteria, it omitted any criteria, and if so, whether it would be so material as to require a change in judgment. The third criterion would be whether or not they applied their own criteria in such a way as to require a reversal of judgment because it has so materially affected the decision as to be adverse.

The last criterion would be, does the Congress believe that there are overriding considerations in the national interest which require another selection.[20]

Having established that, JCAE went about its task with its usual seriousness and efficiency. Only occasionally did the parochial interests of committee members interfere with questioning witnesses. Many witnesses invited to testify were representatives from civil rights organizations, who testified almost exclusively on the civil rights question. And from all this, one extremely well-documented assertion was that DuPage County ranked among the worst possible places for the accelerator if minority group opportunities were to be increased.

As reported earlier, the AEC commissioners and staff reported on the consideration they gave to civil rights and attempted to defend their decision. However, the most effective witnesses before the committee were the Illinois senators and congressmen themselves. Senator Dirksen reminded the JCAE members of his own record of support for civil rights legislation, claimed that Illinois was making progress toward equal opportunity, and attributed the recent revelations of "untoward things" in Illinois to outside agitators.[21]

[20] Ibid., p. 71. Senator Javits was senior senator from New York, whose Brookhaven site was the most likely choice after Weston.
[21] Ibid., p. 80.

Charles Percy, the new junior senator who had only three months before defeated the famous Paul Douglas, naively attempted to use federal financing of the Weston houses as evidence that no discrimination existed: These homes "are held in title by the Federal Savings and Loan Insurance Corporation. I can't imagine this Government agency being charged with discriminating in the sale or rental of those homes." [22] Senator Percy also cited Argonne National Laboratory as an example of the fine civil rights record of another AEC facility in Illinois. Without giving any specific information, he attempted to claim special knowledge of Argonne on the basis of his membership on the Board of Trustees of the University of Chicago, the parent institution of the Argonne Laboratory. As Senator Percy said, "I have never heard a single case where a scientist, regardless of race, color, or creed — and there are thousands of technical personnel out there — has not found adequate housing. . . . As a Trustee of the University of Chicago I have had a degree of responsibility for that." [23] In his testimony, Senator Percy failed to point out a significant fact. As of January, 1967, 225 Negroes were employed at Argonne Laboratory, of which 223 had to commute over 70 miles round trip from their homes in Chicago or Gary.

Ultimately, John N. Erlenborn, congressman from the Weston district, probably got to the crux of the matter. He simply argued that although DuPage County did not have a very good civil rights record, *neither did any other place*. However, he was somewhat more devious about another damning fact about DuPage — the DuPage County realtors' attempt to prevent with an injunction the enforcement of Governor Kerner's executive order on open housing. In a remarkable display of eloquent sophistry, Congressman Erlenborn argued that the realtors' effort was simply an example of their professionalism:

> They have challenged the Governor's order because they believe it to be an illegal extention of the State's licensing power. As legislators, you gentlemen are cognizant of the necessity for watchfulness in this field of executive encroachment. These real estate brokers went to court, not because they are intent on keeping colored people out of DuPage County, but rather because of the principle involved in the Governor's licensing authority.[24]

Undaunted, Pastore pressed on. As chairman, he pressed witness after witness about the civil rights question in the Weston area. And Pas-

[22] Ibid., p. 83.
[23] Ibid., pp. 84–95.
[24] Ibid., p. 133.

tore's questions were typically leading: Would you say it would be tragic if Congress authorized the accelerator and then found discrimination in the area? Or, what should we do to avoid discrimination? Or, was a state housing ordinance an absolute prerequisite for authorizing the site? Or, should Congress delete the authorization altogether, or forcibly switch sites? He got his answers, especially from the civil rights witnesses, who obviously had a field day.

All this is accepted practice. Pastore was using the prerogatives of his chairmanship to head off a decision, or, failing this, to produce an unfavorable hearings record that might be useful during floor debate. And even if the decision on Weston were not prevented on the floor, this unfavorable record would nevertheless influence the implementing provisions of the responsible administrative agency, in this case the AEC. Hearings of this serious a nature are an intimate part of what is loosely called the "legislative history" and the "legislative intent."

As expected, Pastore failed to kill the Weston decision in committee. The committee majority voted to authorize the 200 BEV accelerator at Weston, and only two other members of the committee joined with Pastore to sponsor a minority report objecting to the Weston authorization altogether.[25] The pressure from this small minority seemed acceptable to a certain extent, inasmuch as the requested $10 million authorization was knocked down to $7.5 million. However, this was an empty victory. With the authorization coming late in the first year, the accelerator designers considered $7.5 million adequate. Moreover, the majority succeeded in removing from the authorization language a very significant clause: "AEC architect-engineer work only." [26] With that clause, funds would have been limited essentially to the drawing board. Its removal meant that some actual work on the site could begin, and that meant the AEC could irrevocably commit itself to the Weston site.

Pastore, through the minority report and other public channels, continued to press his objections to the authorization at Weston "at this time." He implored his colleagues to consider equal opportunity a "fundamental question of public policy." He persisted in reminding Congress of its independent responsibility to introduce such issues.

---

[25] *Report by the Joint Committee on Atomic Energy, together with Separate Views, Authorizing Appropriations for the Atomic Energy Commission for Fiscal Year 1968*, 90th Congress, 1st Session, House Report no. 369, June 19, 1967. This report with its Separate Views is printed in *House Miscellaneous Reports of Public Bills III,* Vol. 12753–3, House Reports 338–530, with exceptions, 90th Congress, 1st Session, pp. 57–59. Pastore was joined by Senator Jackson (D. Wash.) and Senator Aiken (R. Vt.).

[26] *JCAE Majority Report,* p. 36.

But suddenly, as the bill came up for debate on the Senate floor, Senator Pastore and his objections dropped almost out of sight. The senator had tripped over the pork barrel.

O'ER THE PORK BARREL WE WATCH: SELECTIVE VS. MYOPIC LEGISLATIVE OVERSIGHT

The House members of the JCAE brought the committee report to the House floor with their unanimous approval. The debate centered mainly on an amendment by a nonmember of the JCAE, John Conyers (D. Mich.), a black congressman, to delete the Weston item from the authorization bill. During the debate, two JCAE members urged avoiding the civil rights issue altogether. Chet Holifield, a California Democrat and vice chairman of the JCAE — confirming our own independent impressions — told his colleagues that civil rights had become an issue only late in the selection process of the AEC and had had nothing to do with the actual site selection criteria: "The (original) criteria that were set out had nothing in it in regard to open housing. It was subsequently brought into controversy through speeches by some of the Atomic Energy Commissioners." Another Californian, Craig Hosmer, was still more explicit. He denounced the AEC's handling of the site selection as "lurid, or dismal, or inept, or bungling," and he added that "also, during the process, the AEC allowed the extraneous matter of civil rights to loom large in the site selection criteria."

However, the most effective argument was not the weaknesses of the site selection process or the tardiness with which the AEC included the civil rights question, but rather the threat that application of the civil rights or equal opportunities criterion in this case would create a precedent that could easily apply to all public works projects. In a letter to committee member Holifield, Representative Erlenborn had pointed out that the position advocated by the civil rights supporters threatened further AEC spending in all the thirty or thirty-one states that did not have open occupancy laws. "If I am to take Chairman Seaborg at his word, then I am to assume that the Atomic Energy Commission will spend no more money in any of the thirty-one states without open occupancy satutes." Representative Holifield took that notion and applied it across the board, or across the barrel, to all federal projects, telling his colleagues in immortal prose, "No occupancy law, no federal funds."

We will probably never know whether the House members were swayed by the wisdom of accepting all unanimous recommendations made by committee members, or whether they were swayed by the precedent that would be set by applying the civil rights question to the selection. But on June 29, 1967, the House rejected the Conyers amendment by vote of 104 to 7 and sent the bill on to the Senate.

In the Senate the debate on the AEC authorization legislation took place almost entirely on one day, July 12, 1967, and, as in the House, the only controversial item in the debate was the authorization for the accelerator. Senator Pastore introduced an amendment to that authorization, in which he was joined by Senators Javits (R. N.Y.), Hart (D. Mich.), and Brooke (R. Mass.), the Senate's only black member, as cosponsors.

Although much of the Senate debate was occupied with civil rights questions in Illinois, it was less intense than the committee squabble or the House debate, despite the fact that the most recent events in Illinois should have made the debate more rather than less intense. First, although the neighboring communities of Wheaton and Joliet had passed open housing ordinances, the Illinois General Assembly had failed to pass any open housing legislation despite current pressures. Second, the AEC had yet been successful in securing commitment letters on open housing from a majority of communities in that area. Although the AEC was continuing to claim that its affirmative action program would "advance the cause and benefit of Negroes and other minority groups," the most recent evidence made that claim sound more and more vacuous.

Nevertheless, the Senate debate on civil rights in the site area got thinner and thinner. The best sign of this development was that Senator Pastore tried to keep the issue as narrowly defined as possible. During the debate he emphasized that he was not advocating rejecting Illinois or favoring some other state strictly on the criterion of the presence of open housing laws. He increasingly insisted that Congress should wait to see what happened in Illinois. Instead of insisting on the direct application of the civil rights criterion, as he had in his capacity as chairman of the JCAE, he more modestly urged that "time has a healing, helping way . . . we should give this good feeling a chance and postpone this project for another year." Moreover, he was increasingly vague about what he thought would be a sufficient guarantee of equal opportunity in Illinois or in the Weston area, even after the healing passage of time had come to an end. In addition to changing his tune about a year's postponement rather than absolute deletion, Senator Pastore also tried to provide his colleagues with several alternative reasons, rather than just one, for postponement or deletion or both. These reasons included (1) the proposition that the AEC was unsure of the type of machine it really wanted; (2) the proposition that an approaching budget deficit should militate against the projects that are merely "educational gadgets" having "nothing to do with national defense or national security"; (3) the technical question of whether Lake Michigan could legitimately be used as a source of water for the accelerator (although this was never contemplated); and (4) the original proposition that open housing and equal opportunity for minorities did not exist in the communities near the Illinois site.

Senator Hart, a cosponsor of the amendment and a notable civil rights leader, also tried to soften the issue by narrowing the class of cases to which a precedent set here would apply:

> When we are confronted with proposals to correct inequalities which have been the result of geography and history, we are told that so many things have been built up around them that we cannot unscramble them, that it is too bad, time will adjust it, but we cannot do anything very forthright. . . .
>
> . . . [H]ere is a situation where there is nothing but broad acreage and a proposal to put in a massive installation which will soon create a large population. Now is the time to make up our minds whether we are going to build a ghetto or not. We do have the opportunity this time, without upsetting or unscrambling anything, to practice what we preach around here.

Following that passage in the debate, Senator Pastore came up with still another effort to soften or narrow the meaning of the precedent:

> Perhaps we are setting a precedent and the precedent will be that any time a governmental agency brings up the question of . . . fair opportunity . . . they make that a predicate. We have a perfect right to defend that predicate.

It is doubtful Senator Pastore fully examined the alternative precedent he was setting here, which would be that social questions could be put on the agenda only by the bureaucracies!

However, these appeals were at least effective on some Illinois civil rights leaders, and they too attempted to soften the application of the civil rights formula. In a letter to Senator Hart, which was entered into the *Congressional Record,* black spokesmen Al Raby and Martin Luther King suggested the following test:

> We do not say as Representative Holifield of California has charged that *all* states without fair housing legislation are ineligible for federal projects because of Title VI (of the Civil Rights Act). We do say

that in this case and in similar cases, where a job opportunity is so totally dependent upon housing opportunity, Title VI stands against the project being located in Illinois as long as Illinois refuses reasonable cooperation in the creation of those conditions which are absolutely necessary for compliance with the federal law. [Emphasis in original.]

However, these strategies of getting votes by narrowing the application of the implied precedent were lost upon the masterful senior senator from Illinois, Everett Dirksen. As a seasoned member of the House and Senate Dirksen saw right through the Pastore-Hart effort to broaden their appeal for votes against the Weston site. He made quite clear and explicit to his Senate colleagues what he would do in the future if the amendment to delete the Weston authorization were passed in the Senate:

There are twenty states that have open occupancy laws. There are thirty states that have no such laws.

If Congress in its wisdom undertakes at any time to draw that line, then I want to say . . . that line is going to be firmly drawn, and it is going to be equally firmly held.

With respect to any authorization or appropriation bill, an effort will be made to strike every authorization and every appropriation for projects in any State in which this difference between open and non-open occupancy exists. We are going to see if that is going to be the case, that whatever is sauce of the goose is going to be sauce of the gander.

. . . I am going to keep a list handy. Just wait until some of the authorization and appropriation bills come around, and we will spend a lot more time in acting on them if they relate to States that do not have open occupancy laws. If that is to be the requirement, if that is to be the standard, then let us know it now.

To dramatize his intentions, Senator Dirksen arranged for a mock debate that is typical among the senior and more experienced senators. Senator Holland of Florida, acting as Senator Dirksen's straight man, would raise the names of specific federal installations which had been economic windfalls for the areas in which they were located — such installations as the space center at Cape Kennedy, the space center at Houston, Redstone at Huntsville, TVA, and Oak Ridge; Senator Dirksen answered each question with such comments as "We will come down and try to get it away from you"; and "It would not have been put there in the first place if this had been the rule." Few senators believed that Dirksen would actually carry out this threat. But all probably agreed that deletion of the Weston authorization would be an unpleasant precedent, at least as long as Senator Dirksen was around.

The Pastore amendment was defeated by a vote of 47 to 37. Senator Pastore himself attributed the defeat to the efforts of the two Illinois senators, Dirksen and Percy, who were able to get Republicans and Southern Democrats to unite against the amendment by framing it as a civil rights issue. And no doubt this was a consideration for many of the 47 negative votes. But for many others, including most of the 37 who voted for the amendment but did not strongly support it during the debate, it was the more general issue of writing social policy into public works decisions. Many on both sides even doubted whether Congress could legitimately penalize a state for failing to pass open housing laws, which would bend the principle of federalism. Others on both sides of the vote questioned whether the AEC was acting beyond its jurisdiction by raising the civil rights question. But one element overshadowed all the rest: maintaining the flow of public works projects into and out of the pork barrel. Social policy is all right, as long as it knows its place. Its place was definitely not inside, or anywhere near, the pork barrel. Even Senator Pastore began to waffle on this question. He did not reverse his position entirely. He only softened it almost out of existence. Yet, if he had not done that, he would not even have gotten 7 votes, certainly not 37.

ADMINISTRATIVE IMPLEMENTATION: HOW NOT TO REFORM A DRUNKARD

Because the clause that would have held the initial authorization to design work was eliminated, the $7.3 million for fiscal 1968 proved to be enough to commit the AEC irrevocably to the Weston site. Engineering problems could possibly force a removal, which was unlikely because of the excellent technological review of each site made by the NAS Panel. Therefore, when Congress approved the authorization, all opportunity to use the Weston site as a leverage for expanding opportunities in DuPage County disappeared, and the only prospect even for marginal influence passed to the local administrators of the newly named National Accelerator Laboratory.

On paper, the administrators revealed sincerity and an awareness of opportunities. In March 1968, the director and deputy-director of the National Accelerator Laboratory issued a "Policy Statement of Human Rights." Excerpts reveal a serious intention, without a practical plan:

> It *will be* the policy of the National Accelerator Laboratory to seek the achievement of its scientific goals within a framework of equal

employment opportunity and of a deep dedication to the fundamental tenets of human rights and dignity.

. . . [W]e have observed the destiny of our Laboratory to be linked to the long history of neglect of the problems of the minority groups. We *intend* that the formation of the Laboratory shall be a positive force in the progress toward open housing in the vicinity . . . we expect to create conditions for special opportunity by adopting aggressive employment practices and by instituting special educational and apprentice training programs.

Prejudice has no place in the pursuit of knowledge . . . in any conflict between technical expediency and human rights we shall stand firmly on the side of human rights. However, such a conflict should never arise. Our support of the rights of members of minority groups in our Laboratory and its environs is inextricably intertwined with our goal of creating a new center of technical and scientific excellence. . . .[27]

At least three things stand out in this statement: its utter sincerity; its total ignorance of the social surroundings within which the NAL was to conduct its hiring practices and locate its employees; and its complete naivete about the limitations of the project's influence on community life in the county once the location of the project was settled. Surely this is a case of the kindly lady who married the drunkard to reform him. And the record of the first four years of construction and operation seems to have developed accordingly.

As expected, the directors and planners of the Laboratory have conducted their own activities and policies in an exemplary manner. Eventually, the NAL will employ a permanent staff of 2,265, with 111 Ph.D.'s in high-energy physics, 486 B.S. and M.S. technical personnel and engineers, and around 1,660 other technical and clerical personnel. Experts estimate that about 1.5 other jobs in service areas will be created for each "basic" accelerator employee, and during the construction period alone 4,729 construction workers will have been employed. The AEC is of course obliged, under Executive Order 11246, to include a nondiscrimination clause in all of its construction and employment contracts. But the NAL has actually taken initiatives in expanding employment beyond the spirit or the letter of the law. After two years of construction and operation, Dr. Goldwasser reported that at least 20 per cent of the NAL's nonprofessional employees were black. The architectural engineering firm hired by NAL to do the design and construction work employed 270 people at the

[27] "Policy Statement of Human Rights," Robert R. Wilson and Edwin L. Goldwasser, March 15, 1968. (Emphasis in original.)

end of the period, and attempts were regularly made to maintain between a 10 and 20 per cent minority group composition among its employees.

To ensure maintenance and extension of the NAL's own employment practices, several AEC officials were assigned special responsibility for civil rights. Very early in the construction period, a former president of the DuPage County NAACP was hired by the NAL as equal opportunity and community relations officer. He has informed community minority group members of employment opportunities with NAL and NAL contractors and even met with two Chicago street gangs to inform them about opportunities and to recruit among them for specific programs.

The NAL also arranged for preapprenticeship training, run by Local 150 of the Operating Engineers Union, which until then had no black members. Of the 54 blacks enrolled in the program, 52 graduated and secured positions with NAL contractors. NAL staff also recruited over 20 black males from Chicago's ghetto to enroll in a 30 week technician training course at Oak Ridge, with guaranteed jobs, housing, and transportation when they finished. Clerical training programs were set up for minority groups at a neighboring city YWCA; welding training programs were set up at another city nearby; and the NAL also cooperated with the Council for Bio-Medical Careers in assisting minority high school students to develop special training with guaranteed jobs at the end. Minority group contractors were sought out and invited to solicit bids. During the six months of late 1968 and early 1969, 40 per cent of the purchase contracts for amounts of $10,000 or less went to minority group contractors.

Although all this creates the impression of NAL sincerity and dedication, it is less than a drop in the DuPage County bucket. All the NAL's efforts merely proved that a substantial influence could have been exercised only while the possibility remained of losing the site altogether. Indeed, in the years since the NAL became established, almost every part of Illinois has changed *except* DuPage County. Minority groups have come of age and are exerting pressure. Liberal support has improved in several ways. Before December 1966, only seven Illinois communities had adopted fair housing ordinances, and one was the now-defunct Weston. By Spring 1969, seventy-nine communities had passed such ordinances; but only seven of these were in DuPage County, one of the most populous Illinois counties outside Chicago's Cook County. According to the Illinois NAACP, nearly 67 per cent of Illinois' population lived in communities with some kind of open housing law, whereas before 1967 only 40 per cent did.

However, only a few of these people lived in DuPage County, which is one of the reasons why nonwhites continued into the 1970's to comprise less than 1 per cent of the DuPage County population.

In an interview after about eighteen months of operation, NAL's deputy-director reported that NAL's efforts to locate housing for their own minority group employees "had been successful in that, in every instance, suitable housing has been located, with a minimum of unfavorable incidents and in no derogatory publicity. Housing has been located in five adjacent communities." He was saying in effect that NAL was operating according to a policy of not causing anybody too much trouble. The NAL simply does not seem to understand, even now, the full consequences and meaning of their own actions. No explanation or apology was ever offered, for example, for the way NAL took over the village and the farm houses and wiped out all previous trace of community existence in the site area. All Weston street names have been changed; the post office relationship was switched from West Chicago to the more prestigious Batavia, so that now the official designation is "National Accelerator Laboratory, Batavia, Illinois." The elimination of all reference to Weston was carried out without any legal authority. In fact, it was more than two years later before the state of Illinois recognized this fait accompli and officially withdraw the Weston incorporation.

None of this is to deny that the scientists are concerned about the social uses of their site. They simply did not begin to exercise this consideration until the site was fully confirmed; even then these questions tend to complement the established upper-middle class values of the area insofar as the scientists' behaviors provide an example at all for the community at large. Perhaps the best example of their sincere but paltry intentions is this: soon after the construction of the accelerator ring was fully under way, the NAL office announced that they were going to set aside several acres of land on the site for a model farm to be run by a professional 4-H teacher by the name of Farmer Bob. They even decided to stock the farm with a small herd of buffalo. The children of the suburbs would, as a consequence, not forget the eternal verities of their agricultural heritage.

CONGRESS: GUARDIAN OR SILENT PARTNER?

The failure of this science project to fulfill any larger social goals is not a failure of the scientific mentality. It only proves that scientists are human beings and do not have any superhuman insights in the arts of government. The shortcomings of this decision are a reflection of the failure of Congress, not of scientists in particular or bureaucracy in general. It is the failure of the process or arrangement whereby public works decisions are made.

The pork barrel approach is tantamount to a conspiracy to keep the federal government out of social legislation. And the conspiracy works because of the committee system and through the committee system. The congressional process of authorization, appropriation, oversight, and control through specialized standing committees is ingeniously designed to deal with small questions and particularistic interests. Big questions get lost; they literally fall between the stools.

Apologists in Congress and among its students rely heavily on legislative oversight in committees to flesh out their theory of the separation of powers in the twentieth century. These apologists are not entirely unfounded in their optimism, but to hold strictly to their optimism requires almost deliberate negligence of certain unmistakable facts about committee oversight. Committees are organized along lines almost exactly parallel to administrative agencies and rarely, if ever, can exercise a view larger than the agencies. Thus, committee oversight becomes a substantial review of marginal items rather than a marginal review of substantial issues.

Committees should be called "little legislatures," not because they are smaller than the whole legislature but because each committee deals best in little things. Committees are designed to produce narrowmindedness. To be as generous as possible, each congressional committee tends to reinforce the lines of thought already developed in the bureaucracies and among the best organized constituent interest groups. The service the standing committees perform for Congress can be great only insofar as the limitations of committees are fully recognized and only inasmuch as Congress, in its parliamentary role, frequently seizes the initiative back from the committee.[28]

Granted, even where the will is present, the parliamentary aspect of Congress — that is, floor debate — appears most often unable to escape the confining influences of the committees. But the parliamentary Congress ought to be capable of taking the larger view at least where the pork barrel process is concerned. The Weston decision was important enough to reach the floor and to receive some debate, but nothing sustained the discussion at the level commensurate to the importance of the social problems associated with it. The potent influence of the pork barrel approach can best be appreciated by the fact that the technicians and congressmen (in the AEC and on the JCAE)

[28] For one approach to the problem of committees, see the proposals in Selection 26.

who had the greatest capacity for big thinking produced the least amount of it. They seemed incapable of escaping their own narrow definition of the terms of discourse.

Such cases as Weston, precisely because of the involvement of such highly qualified people, are ideal for questioning once again whether the present legislative system is capable of meeting the problems of our time. Although observers in the past have frequently raised this question, they generally consider its incapacity to understand technicallly complicated problems well enough to debate and legislate about them. We think this is patent nonsense. Congress, among its standing committees, its highly experienced senior members, its staff, and its ability to call outside experts through hearings and other consultations, can have as much expertise as exists on any subject. If Congress cannot deal with complexity, that is the same as saying government cannot.

If Congress is failing it is because Congress is no longer a place where laymen make fundamental decisions to guide and direct experts. Fundamental choices always have to be made by laymen, because on fundamental problems all men *are* laymen. Laymen need a forum. At present they do not have one. And they will not have one as long as Congress is so busy doing jobs it should not do — allocating projects — that there is neither time nor procedure for doing the job it should do. As a result, nobody is doing it.

22
The Day We Didn't Go to War
Chalmers M. Roberts

Saturday, April 3, 1954, was a raw, windy day in Washington, but the weather didn't prevent a hundred Americans from milling around the Jefferson Memorial to see the cherry blossoms — twenty thousand of them from watching the crowning of the 1954 Cherry Blossom Queen.

From Chalmers M. Roberts, "The Day We Didn't Go to War," *The Reporter* (September 14, 1954). Copyright Chalmers M. Roberts.

President Eisenhower drove off to his Maryland mountain retreat called Camp David. There he worked on his coming Monday speech, designed, so the White House said, to quiet America's fears of Russia, the H-bomb, domestic Communists, a depression. But that Saturday morning eight members of Congress, five Senators and three Representatives, got the scare of their lives. They had been called to a secret conference with John Foster Dulles. They entered one of the State Department's fifth-floor conference rooms to find not only Dulles but Admiral Arthur W. Radford, chairman of the Joint Chiefs of Staff, Under Secretary of Defense Roger Kyes, Navy Secretary Robert B. Anderson, and Thurston B. Morton, Dulles's assistant for Congressional Relations. A large map of the world hung behind Dulles's seat, and Radford stood by with several others. "The President has asked me to call this meeting," Dulles began.

URGENCY AND A PLAN

The atmosphere became serious at once. What was wanted, Dulles said, was a joint resolution by Congress to permit the President to use air and naval power in Indo-China. Dulles hinted that perhaps the mere passage of such a resolution would in itself make its use unnecessary. But the President had asked for its consideration, and, Dulles added, Mr. Eisenhower felt that it was indispensable at this juncture that the leaders of Congress feel as the Administration did on the Indo-China crisis.

Then Radford took over. He said the Administration was deeply concerned over the rapidly deteriorating situation. He used a map of the Pacific to point out the importance of Indo-China. He spoke about the French Union forces then already under siege for three weeks in the fortress of Dienbienphu.

The admiral explained the urgency of American action by declaring that he was not even sure, because of poor communications, whether, in fact, Dienbienphu was still holding out. (The fortress held out for five weeks more.)

Dulles backed up Radford. If Indo-China fell and if its fall led to the loss of all of Southeast Asia, he declared, then the United States might eventually be forced back to Hawaii, as it was before the Second World War. And Dulles was not complimentary about the French. He said he feared they might use some disguised means of getting out of Indo-China if they did not receive help soon.

The eight legislators were silent: Senator Majority Leader Knowland and his G.O.P. colleague Eugene Millikin, Senator Minority Leader Lyndon B. Johnson and his Democratic colleagues Richard B. Russell and Earle C. Clements, House G.O.P. Speaker Joseph Martin and two Democratic House leaders, John W. McCormack and J. Percy Priest.

What to do? Radford offered the plan he had in mind once Congress passed the joint resolution.

Some two hundred planes from the thirty-one-thousand-ton U.S. Navy carriers *Essex* and *Boxer,* then in the South China Sea ostensibly for "training," plus land-based U.S. Air Force planes from bases a thousand miles away in the Philippines, would be used for a single strike to save Dienbienphu.

The legislators stirred, and the questions began.

Radford was asked whether such action would be war. He replied that we would be in the war.

If the strike did not succeed in relieving the fortress, would we follow up? "Yes," said the chairman of the Joint Chiefs of Staff.

Would land forces then also have to be used? Radford did not give a definite answer.

In the early part of the questioning, Knowland showed enthusiasm for the venture, consistent with his public statements that something must be done or Southeast Asia would be lost.

But as the questions kept flowing, largely from Democrats, Knowland lapsed into silence.

Clements asked Radford the first of the two key questions:

"Does this plan have the approval of the other members of the Joint Chiefs of Staff?"

"No," replied Radford.

"How many of the three agree with you?"

"None."

"How do you account for that?"

"I have spent more time in the Far East than any of them and I understand the situation better."

Lyndon Johnson put the other key question in the form of a little speech. He said that Knowland had been saying publicly that in Korea up to ninety per cent of the men and the money came from the United States. The United States had become sold on the idea that that was bad. Hence in any operation in Indo-China we ought to know first who would put up the men. And so he asked Dulles whether he had consulted nations who might be our allies in intervention.

Dulles said he had not.

The Secretary was asked why he didn't go to the United Nations as in the Korean case. He replied that it would take too long, that this was an immediate problem.

There were other questions. Would Red China and the Soviet Union come into the war if the United States took military action? The China question appears to have been sidestepped, though Dulles said he felt the Soviets could handle the Chinese and the United States did not think that Moscow wanted a general war now. Further, he added, if the Communists feel that we mean business, they won't go "any further down there," pointing to the map of Southeast Asia.

John W. McCormack, the House Minority Leader, couldn't resist temptation. He was surprised, he said, that Dulles would look to the "party of treason," as the Democrats had been called by Joe McCarthy in his Lincoln's Birthday speech under G.O.P. auspices, to take the lead in a situation that might end up in a general shooting war. Dulles did not reply.

In the end, all eight members of Congress, Republicans and Democrats alike, were agreed that Dulles had better first go shopping for allies. Some people who should know say that Dulles was carrying, but did not produce, a draft of the joint resolution the President wanted Congress to consider.

The whole meeting had lasted two hours and ten minutes. As they left, the Hill delegation told waiting reporters they had been briefed on Indo-China. Nothing more.

This approach to Congress by Dulles and Radford on behalf of the President was the beginning of three weeks of intensive effort by the Administration to head off disaster in Indo-China. Some of those at the meeting came away with the feeling that if they had agreed that Saturday to the resolution, planes would have been winging toward Dienbienphu without waiting for a vote of Congress — or without a word in advance to the American people.

For some months now, I have tried to put together the bits and pieces of the American part in the Indo-China debacle. But before relating the sequel, it is necessary here to go back to two events that underlay the meeting just described — though neither of them was mentioned at that meeting.

On March 20, just two weeks earlier, General Paul Ely, then French Chief of Staff and later commander in Indo-China, had arrived in Washington from the Far East to tell the President, Dulles, Radford, and others that unless the United States intervened, Indo-China would be lost. This was a shock of earthquake proportions to leaders who had been taken in by their own talk of the Navarre Plan to win the war.

In his meetings at the Pentagon, Ely was flabbergasted to find that Radford proposed American intervention without being asked. Ely said he would have to consult his government. He carried back to Paris the word that when France gave the signal, the United States would respond.

The second event of importance is the most difficult to determine accurately. But it is clear that Ely's remarks started a mighty struggle within the National Security Council, that inner core of government where our most vital decisions are worked out for the President's final O.K. The argument advanced by Radford and supported by Vice-President Nixon and by Dulles was that Indo-china must not be allowed to fall into Communist hands lest such a fate set in motion a falling row of dominoes.

Eisenhower himself used the "row-of-dominoes" phrase at a press conference on April 7. On April 15, Radford said in a speech that Indo-China's loss "would be the prelude to the loss of all Southeast Asia and a threat to a far wider area." On April 16 Nixon, in his well-publicized "off-the-record" talk to the newspaper editors' convention, said that if the United States could not otherwise prevent the loss of Indo-China, then the Administration must face the situation and dispatch troops. And the President in his press conference of March 24 had declared that Southeast Asia was of the "most transcendent importance." All these remarks reflected a basic policy decision.

It is my understanding, although I cannot produce the top secret NSC [National Security Council] paper to prove it, that some time between Ely's arrival on March 20 and the Dulles-Radford approach to the Congressional leaders on April 3, the NSC had taken a firm position that the United States could not afford the loss of Indo-China to the Communists, and that if it were necessary to prevent that loss, the United States would intervene in the war — *provided* the intervention was an allied venture and *provided* the French would give Indo-China a real grant of independence so as to eliminate the colonialism issue. The decision may have been taken at the March 25 meeting. It is also my understanding that this NSC paper has on it the approving initials "D.D.E."

On March 29, Dulles, in a New York speech, had called for "united action" even though it might involve "serious risks," and declared that Red China was backing aggression in Indo-China with the goal of controlling all of Southeast Asia. He had added that the United States felt "that possibility should not be passively accepted but should be met by united action."

The newspapers were still full of reactions to this speech when the

Congressional leaders, at the April 3 secret meeting with Dulles and Radford, insisted that Dulles should line up allies for "united action" before trying to get a joint resolution of Congress that would commit the nation to war.

The Secretary lost no time. Within a week Dulles talked with diplomatic representatives in Washington of Britain, France, Australia, New Zealand, the Philippines, Thailand, and the three Associated States of Indo-China — Vietnam, Laos, and Cambodia.

There was no doubt in the minds of many of these diplomats that Dulles was discussing military action involving carriers and planes. Dulles was seeking a statement or declaration of intent designed to be issued by all the nations at the time of the U.S. military action, to explain to the world what we were doing and why, and to warn the Chinese Communists against entering the war as they had done in Korea.

In these talks Dulles ran into one rock of opposition — Britain. Messages flashing back and forth between Washington and London failed to crack the rock. Finally Dulles offered to come and talk the plan over personally with Prime Minister Churchill and Foreign Secretary Anthony Eden. On April 10, just a week after the Congressional meeting, Dulles flew off to London and later went on to Paris.

Whether Dulles told the British about either the NSC decision or about his talks with the Congressional leaders I do not know. But he didn't need to. The British had learned of the Congressional meeting within a couple of days after it happened. When Dulles reached London they were fully aware of the seriousness of his mission.

The London talks had two effects. Dulles had to shelve the idea of immediate intervention. He came up instead with a proposal for creating a Southeast Asia Treaty Organization (SEATO). Dulles felt this was the "united front" he wanted and that it would lead to "united action." He thought that some sort of *ad hoc* organization should be set up at once without waiting for formal treaty organization, and to this, he seems to have felt, Churchill and Eden agreed.

Just what the British did agree to is not clear, apparently not even to them. Dulles, it appears, had no formal SEATO proposal down on paper, while the British did have some ideas in writing. Eden feels that he made it plain that nothing could be done until after the Geneva Conference, which was due to begin in two weeks. But he apparently made some remark about "going on thinking about it" in the meantime.

At any rate, on his return to Washington Dulles immediately called a SEATO drafting meeting for April 20. The British Ambassador (who at this point had just read the Nixon off-the-record speech in the newspaper) cabled London for instructions and was told not to attend any such meeting. To cover up, the meeting was turned into one on Korea, the other topic for the Geneva Conference. Out of this confusion grew a thinly veiled hostility between Dulles and Eden that exists to this day. Dulles felt that Eden had switched his position and suspects that Eden did so after strong words reached London from Prime Minister Nehru in New Delhi.

EDEN AT THE BRIDGE

A few days later, Dulles flew back to Paris, ostensibly for the NATO meeting with Eden, France's Georges Bidault, and others during the week-end just before the Geneva Conference opened.

On Friday, April 23, Bidault showed Dulles a telegram from General Henri-Eugene Navarre, then the Indo-China commander, saying that only a massive air attack could save Dienbienphu, by now under siege for six weeks. Dulles said the United States could not intervene.

But on Saturday Admiral Radford arrived and met with Dulles. Then Dulles and Radford saw Eden. Dulles told Eden that the French were asking for military help at once. An allied air strike at the Vietminh positions around Dienbienphu was discussed. The discussion centered on using the same two U.S. Navy carriers and Philippine-based Air Force planes Radford had talked about to the Congressional leaders.

Radford, it appears, did most of the talking. But Dulles said that if the allies agreed, the President was prepared to go to Congress on the following Monday, April 26 (the day the Geneva Conference was to open) and ask for a joint resolution authorizing such action. Assuming quick passage by Congress, the strike could take place on April 28. Under Secretary of State Walter Bedell Smith, an advocate of intervention, gave the same proposal to French Ambassador Henri Bonnet in Washington the same day.

The State Department had prepared a declaration of intentions, an outgrowth of the earlier proposals in Washington, to be signed on Monday or Tuesday by the Washington ambassadors of the allied nations willing to back the venture in words. As it happened, there were no available British or Australian carriers and the French already were fully occupied. Hence the strike would be by American planes alone, presented to the world as a "united action" by means of the declaration of intentions.

Eden, on hearing all these details from Dulles and Radford, said that this was a most serious proposition, amounting to war, and that he wanted to hear it direct from the French. Eden and Dulles thereupon conferred with Bidault, who confirmed the fact that France was indeed calling desperately for help — though no formal French request was ever put forward in writing.

Eden began to feel like Horatius at the bridge. Here, on the eve of a conference that might lead to a negotiated end of the seven-year-old Indo-China war, the United States, at the highly informal request of a weak and panicky French Government, was proposing military action that might very well lead to a general war in Asia if not to a third world war.

DULLES' RETREAT

Eden said forcefully that he could not agree to any such scheme of intervention, that he personally opposed it. He added his conviction that within forty-eight hours after an air strike, ground troops would be called for, as had been the case at the beginning of the Korean War.

But, added Eden, he alone could not make any such formal decision on behalf of Her Majesty's Government. He would fly to London at once and put the matter before a Cabinet meeting. So far as I can determine, neither Dulles or Bidault tried to prevent this step.

Shortly after Eden flew off that Saturday afternoon, Dulles sat down in the American Embassy in Paris with his chief advisers, Messrs. MacArthur, Merchant, Bowie, and McCardle, and Ambassador Dillon. They composed a letter to Bidault.

In this letter, Dulles told Bidault the United States could not intervene without action by Congress because to do so was beyond the President's Constitutional powers and because we had made it plain that any action we might take could only be part of a "united action." Further, Dulles added, the American military leaders felt it was too late to save Dienbienphu.

American intervention collapsed on that Saturday, April 24. On Sunday Eden arrived in Geneva with word of the "No" from the specially convened British Cabinet meeting. And on Monday, the day the Geneva Conference began, Eisenhower said in a speech that what was being sought at Geneva was a *"modus vivendi"* with the Communists.

All these events were unknown to the general public at the time. However, on Sunday the New York *Times* printed a story (written in Paris under a Geneva dateline) that the U.S. had turned down a French request for intervention on the grounds Dulles had cited to

Bidault. And on Tuesday Churchill announced to a cheering House of Commons that the British government was "not prepared to give any undertakings about United Kingdom military action in Indo-China in advance of the results of Geneva" and that "we have not entered into any new political or military commitments."

Thus the Geneva Conference opened in a mood of deepest American gloom. Eden felt that he had warded off disaster and that now there was a chance to negotiate a peace. The Communists, whatever they may have learned of the behind-the-scenes details here recounted, knew that Britain had turned down some sort of American plan of intervention. And with the military tide in Indo-China flowing so rapidly in their favor, they proceeded to stall.

In the end, of course, a kind of peace was made. On June 23, nearly four weeks before the peace, Eden said in the House of Commons that the British Government had "been reproached in some unofficial quarters for their failure to support armed intervention to try to save Dienbienphu. It is quite true that we were at no time willing to support such action. . . ."

This mixture of improvisation and panic is the story of how close the United States came to entering the Indo-China war. Would Congress have approved intervention if the President had dared to ask it? This point is worth a final word.

On returning from Geneva in mid-May, I asked that question of numerous Senators and Representatives. Their replies made clear that Congress would, in the end, have done what Eisenhower asked, provided he had asked for it forcefully and explained the facts and their relation to the national interest of the United States.

Whether action or inaction better served the American interest at that late stage of Indo-China war is for the historian, not for the reporter, to say. But the fact emerges that President Eisenhower never did lay the intervention question on the line. In spite of the NSC decision, April 3, 1954, was the day we *didn't* go to war.

23

Legislative Effectiveness: Control and Investigation

John S. Saloma III

While public attention has been directed to the decline of Congress as a legislative body (i.e., to increased executive initiative in the legislative process), few observers have noted the significance of related developments in the control and investigative functions of Congress. Congressional participation in, and "oversight" or review of, the administrative process in government is one of the least understood functions that Congress performs. In this chapter we examine the control and investigative functions of Congress in the broader context of legislative performance.

THE RELATIONSHIP OF CONTROL AND INVESTIGATION TO LEGISLATIVE EFFECTIVENESS

Congressional control over administration has been an issue in American government since Congress attempted to specify the duties of the Secretary of the Treasury in the first Washington administration. The controversy over the investigative powers of Congress dates back to 1791 when Congress created a committee to investigate the disastrous expedition of Major General Arthur St. Clair to control Indians in the Ohio territory. The very exercise of these two related functions rests on certain assumptions about the role of Congress in the American political system. . . .

We have already suggested basic structural features of the American system that precluded the development of a parliamentary form of government and the tradition of a neutral civil service controlled by a cabinet ministry. The American solution of separated institutions sharing powers guaranteed the development of an open, politicized, executive bureaucracy subject to the competing directives of presidential and congressional executives. The rationalization of the executive bureaucracy has taken place within this framework of dual executives. While executive-centered government has meant great presidential *initiative* in the legislative process and enhanced control of the bureaucracy through the executive budget, it has implied a corresponding new emphasis on congressional *control* and *review* of both legislation and administration. It is understandable that the administrative mind should balk at this complex form of a rationalization with its inherent bar to unity of control. We merely note that dualism in administration is an inherited assumption of our contemporary political system. Once this assumption has been granted, Congress may adopt a number of legitimate aims in the exercise of its control and investigative functions. Broadly defined, they include:

Control of Unacceptable Forms of Bureaucratic Behavior. In sharing with the Presidency the objective of insuring a responsible bureaucracy, Congress must control bureaucratic growth and independent action, cases of administrative abuse or arbitrary actions affecting citizens, and malfeasance.

Effecting the Legislative Intent of Congress in the Administrative Process. Under the American system of representation, both the President and Congress (acting through separate majorities) have a responsibility to maintain popular control over the bureaucracy by ensuring that the bureacracy implements the policy objectives specified in the legislative process.

Efficiency and Economy in Governmental Operations. This goal assumes that policy objectives have been specified and enjoy congressional support. Congress controls and reviews the administrative process to ensure a balance between spending and revenues and the establishment of spending priorities. Occasionally, "economy drives" in Congress reverse policy decisions previously reached in the legislative process.

Achieving a Balance Between Control and Discretion or Flexibility in the Administrative System. In the exercise of control, Congress must also provide sufficient discretion or flexibility in the administrative system to permit the administrator room for initiative and efficient operation. Over-control may impede the very objectives Congress is attempting to realize.

Determining the Effectiveness of Legislative Policies. Ultimately, Congress exercises its control and investigative functions to determine the general effectiveness of legislation in meeting needs defined in the legislative process. If Congress is to share in guiding the direction of government, it must understand the impact of legislation on society. To be effective it must evaluate the consequences — actual and anticipated — of governmental action, utilizing the most advanced techniques of program analysis and evaluation that are available to top policy makers.

All these objectives are consistent with the assumption that Congress has a legitimate role in the administrative process. As we shall see, some critics of Congress are not willing to grant the assumption. Others would qualify the degree or forms of congressional participation. Before considering some of these arguments, we will clarify some of the terminology as it will be used in this analysis.

We shall define legislative "control" of administration to include *both* legislative *participation before* administrative action and legislative *review* or *oversight after* the fact. The terms "review" or "oversight" are sometimes used in the literature and within Congress itself in the broader sense of "control." Within this chapter, unless otherwise specified, "control" will be used in the broader sense and "review" or "oversight" in the more limited sense.[1]

Investigation is clearly a form or instrument of legislative control. In this chapter we shall define it as congressional study and research of specific problems that may require legislation. The focus of the control and investigative functions — the administrative bureaucracy on the one hand and the actual policy problems confronting government on the other — is distinct enough to justify separate consideration. In the first instance, Congress is concerned with the capacity of the executive bureaucracy to implement legislative policy; in the second, it seeks a clearer understanding of the problems for which it and the President legislate policy for the bureaucracy.

Finally, it should be noted that "legislative effectiveness," which we listed as one of several possible standards for evaluating congressional performance, is closely related to the functions of legislative control

[1] Joseph P. Harris, *Congressional Control of Administration* (Washington, D.C.: Brookings, 1964), p. 9.

and investigation. The efficiency-effectiveness criterion implies that Congress should be organized and should function so as to realize its will in the governmental process. If Congress is to be effective, then, it must exercise extensively its powers of administrative control and social inquiry.

THE CHANGING CONTROL
AND INVESTIGATIVE FUNCTIONS

The control of bureaucracy is a relatively new problem for American government. While Congress developed detailed legislative and appropriations specifications for the new executive departments early in the legislative history of the republic, the federal civil service numbered less than 50,000 at the start of the Civil War. The real period of growth began in the 1930's when the number of federal employees rose from 572,000 in 1933 to 1,014,000 in 1940. A dramatic indication of the growth of the executive bureaucracy is the fact that some three-quarters of the over 2½ million federal civil service positions today were established in the last thirty years.

This rapid growth, accompanied by the proliferation of new emergency agencies during the Depression and war years, provided a major impetus toward the development of the modern institutionalized Presidency and toward the rationalization of executive branch organization. Congress yielded its historic legislative power to organize the executive agencies in the Reorganization Act of 1939, giving the President the authority to draft reorganization plans subject only to a new "legislative veto." The first such plan submitted to the Congress in April, 1939 established the Executive Office of the President, including the White House Office, Bureau of the Budget, and the National Resources Planning Board.

The new equilibrium of roles under executive-centered government was confirmed by a rationalization of congressional organization in the Legislative Reorganization Act of 1946. This landmark legislation incorporated three basic provisions intended to strengthen congressional control of administration.

Rationalization of the Standing Committee System. Modernization of the standing committee system of Congress was, according to George B. Galloway, "the first aim of the act and the keystone in the arch of congressional 'reform.' " In the House, the number of standing committees was reduced from 48 to 19; in the Senate, from 33 to 15. Although a prohibition against special or select committees was struck from the bill, Congress was against this alternative to the recognized jurisdictions of the standing committees. The new standing committee structure was designed roughly to parallel the reorganized executive departments on a one-to-one basis.

This organizational formula has been closely adhered to by Congress since 1946. The only new standing committees have been the House Committee on Science and Astronautics and the Senate Committee on Aeronautical and Space Sciences, both established in 1958 with the initiation of the multi-billion dollar space program. Two new joint committees, the Joint Economic Committee and the Joint Committee on Atomic Energy, were established to meet special needs that arose almost coincidentally with the reorganization legislation. Some observers hold that the rapid growth of subcommittees has negated the reform. By 1955 the number of congressional committees and subcommittees of all types (exclusive of special subcommittees) had risen to 235 compared with 230 in 1945. However, the two situations are clearly not equivalent. The standing committees remain as coordinators and channels of legislative activity, and most of the parent committees retain considerable control over their subcommittees. While Congress may make marginal adjustments in the standing committee structure, to reflect new federal responsibilities in education and urban affairs and consequent realignments of executive departments, the 1946 Act appears to have given Congress a stable internal organization for the exercise of its control and investigative functions.

The Requirement of Legislative Oversight by Standing Committees. Section 136 of the 1946 Act stated that "each standing committee of the Senate and the House of Representatives shall exercise continuous watchfulness of the execution by the administrative agencies concerned of any laws, the subject matter of which is within the jurisdiction of such committee. . . ." While this authority was granted "to assist the Congress in appraising the administration of the laws and in developing such amendments or related legislation as it may deem necessary," the newly defined standing committees were to be the agents of the oversight function. The intention of the authors of the act was to achieve a three-stage performance of the oversight function: exercise of financial control before expenditure, by the Appropriations Committees; review of administrative structure and procedures, by the Expenditure (Government Operations) Committees; and review of the operation of substantive legislation by the legislative committees. Just how much "continuous watchfulness" has been achieved is a subject to which we shall return.

The Provision of Professional Staffs for Standing Committees. Before the reforms of the Legislative Reorganization Act of 1946, only the two appropriations committees and the Joint Committee on Internal Revenue Taxation, a staff arm of the two revenue committees, employed professional staff on a tenure basis. Section 202 of the act authorized each standing committee to appoint not more than four professional staff members and six clerks, although no ceiling was set for the appropriations committees and there was no great difficulty later in obtaining authorization for additional staff if the committee so requested.

While the development and utilization of professional staffs has been uneven, the 1946 legislation recognized the priority need to create congressional staff resources at the committee level if Congress were to perform its legislative and oversight functions. Additional staff and information resources were provided by establishing a Legislative Reference Service in the Library of Congress and by authorizing studies and expenditure analyses by the Comptroller General. Separate reforms in fiscal control, notably the attempt to establish a legislative budget, were never effectively implemented by Congress because, unlike the oversight requirement, they were not integrated with the standing committee structure.

These three basic provisions of the 1946 Act organized, directed, and staffed Congress for expansion of its control and investigative functions. A number of techniques of oversight were already available to Congress. Still others were rapidly developed. The basic *formal* means of control has remained the passage of legislation, through both the appropriations and the authorization processes. Through legislation, Congress has controlled the organization, programs, personnel systems, and funding of the executive departments. Although the President may now take the initiative in suggesting reorganization plans, the legislative committees have extended their control by replacing open-ended authorizations with annual or other forms of limited authorization. The two Post Office and Civil Service committees have closely watched over the federal personnel services and have consistently resisted (with congressional support) the centralization of personnel management under the President. The appropriations process is still generally considered the most important form of congressional control. Other formal controls include audit by the General Accounting Office (with review of audits by the Government Operations, Appropriations, and relevant subject-matter committees), senatorial confirmation of executive appointments, and authorized congressional investigations. One technique of control that has been rapidly extended is the "legislative veto" in several forms, including the committee veto.

Informal techniques of control do not enjoy the status of legislation or similar authoritative actions by the Congress. They are usually exercised by committees or individual members of Congress in their contacts with executive officials. They may be written into committee reports as "nonstatutory" directions or advice to the relevant agency, or they may enter the public record during committee hearings and floor debate. They may arise apart from the legislative process in a variety of contacts that a member of a congressional staff may have with an agency.

Both formal and informal techniques of control have expanded significantly since the Legislative Reorganization Act of 1946. Annual authorizations are now required in program areas such as space, foreign aid, atomic energy, and defense weapons systems, accounting for more than 35 per cent of the annual budget. The number of congressional investigations, which averaged slightly over thirty per Congress during the interwar years rose to over two hundred per Congress by the early 1950's, and funds authorized for congressional investigations almost doubled from $8.2 million in the 83rd Congress (1953–54) to $15.5 million in the 86th Congress (1959–60). The legislative veto has been utilized in more than twenty authorization acts since 1950. . . .

EVALUATIONS OF CONGRESSIONAL PERFORMANCE: INVESTIGATIVE STAFF FOR CONGRESS

Few would disagree that Congress should be informed in its decisions, should understand the nature of the problems on which it legislates, and should maintain an intelligent, continuing dialogue with the Executive on matters of public policy. These are canons of responsible legislative practice which even the executive-oriented critics of Congress admit. In advancing his case for establishing an Office of Legislative Evaluation, Daniel P. Moynihan chided some of the policy liberals inside and outside government who privately fear giving Congress full information on program operation:

> The usual whispered argument, of course, is that to be candid about public policies that don't produce much progress is to give a weapon to the enemies of progress. This is an unworthy argument; there are never grounds for concealing truth about public matters. . . . But it is also an absurd argument. The American public supports a fantastic array of social services, and does so in ever larger amounts. The issue, then, is not whether, but which.

It is equally clear that Congress can improve its understanding of ever more complicated matters of public policy only if it equips itself to do so. And this means enlarged, increasingly specialized, differentiated staff. Yet a strong argument against increasing congressional staff has been developed and is adhered to by a surprisingly large number of political scientists and executive officials as well as members of Congress.

The issue of congressional staff is pertinent to all congressional functions. Professional staff at the committee level is essential to congressional initiation in the legislative process and to exercising the control function. Staff attached to a congressman's office extends his performance in constituency service. While we have chosen to discuss congressional staff under the investigative function of Congress, the arguments we shall develop are generally applicable to congressional performance of all functions.

The cases for and against congressional staff, as in the debate we have just considered on the oversight function, rest on broader normative assumptions about the role of Congress in the federal system. Clearly, if one limits congressional control of administration to after-the-fact review or oversight, the staffing requirements will be quite different than if one takes an expanded view of the control function. Much of the criticism of congressional staff, then, is, more accurately, criticism of congressional activities with which the critic disagrees. In such a case, the criticism should be directed at the congressional function, not at the staff which was created by Congress to perform it.

The Trend Toward Executive Monopoly in Program Analysis and Evaluation

As the modern executive bureaucracy has grown, it has accumulated a "monopoly of skills" in critical areas of public policy such as space, defense weapons systems, foreign-policy intelligence, and urban redevelopment. Congress has been faced with the choice of how to develop its own understanding of new policy problems. It has, since the end of World War II, responded in a variety of ways. It has made adjustments in its committee structure. It has vested one committee and its staff, the Joint Committee on Atomic Energy, with extraordinary powers of access to executive information. It has developed new techniques of policy oversight like annual authorization. It has established a Science Policy Research Division in the Legislative Reference Service of the Library of Congress. In other areas the response of Congress has been limited or nonexistent. It has kept professional staffs on key committees, such as Armed Services and Space, small and generally nontechnical. It has virtually ignored the intelligence component of foreign policy. And it has just begun to reconsider committee jurisdictions and responsibilities in grasping the emerging domestic crisis of the urban ghetto.

In contrast the trend toward concentration of technical, specialized information in the Executive and the resulting dependence of Congress on the Executive for much of its policy information has been clearly discernible. Now that the Executive is moving into an important new phase of program analysis and evaluation research, symbolized by the Planning-Programming-Budgeting System (PPBS), the Executive's near-monopoly may be dramatically extended. The potential impact of the information revolution in government raises even more fundamental questions about congressional access to information and program evaluation. Daniel Moynihan concludes that "a new source of knowledge is coming into being" that is likely to raise the level of public discourse. However, the Executive branch has developed "a virtual monopoly on the product of evaluation research." Such an imbalance is dangerous because the findings of such research are not neutral. The situation should not be permitted to persist for a number of reasons:

> First, and most importantly, the Congress and other legislative bodies are put at a considerable disadvantage. A major weapon in the "arsenal of persuasion" is in effect denied them. Second, the executive is exposed to the constant temptation to release only those findings that suit its purposes; there is no one to keep them honest. Third, universities and other private groups which often undertake such research on contract are in some measure subject to constant if subtle pressure to produce "positive" findings.

The argument that Congress must equip itself to counter or check increasing executive expertise is a persuasive defense of its investigative function. It is supplemented by a more positive definition of Congress as a study and deliberative body. Former Congressman Thomas B. Curtis (R-Mo.) describes Congress, ideally and primarily, as "a mechanism for gathering together the knowledge and wisdom existing within the society to make judgments to solve the problems facing the society." According to Curtis, this investigative or study function of Congress is accomplished through three primary processes: (1) the distilled wisdom (publications and other forms of stored information) contained in the Library of Congress is further refined by the Legislative Reference Staff; (2) the current wisdom of the society is collected through the standing committees of Congress with the assistance of professional staff (committee hearings provide forums in which the knowledge of experts in the Executive branch and in the private sector is brought to bear on public problems); and (3) knowledge from individual citizens — how the laws as written and administered affect them — is gathered from the letters and conversations of constituents and interest groups. These three processes suggest three levels of staff assistance: institutional staff assistance attached to Congress, the professional staffs of congressional committees, and congressional office staff servicing constituent needs. We shall limit our analysis to the first two. . . .

The Debate over Enlarged Congressional Staff

Opposition to increased congressional staff, and especially to the establishment of a legislative bureaucracy, is based on a number of negative assessments of congressional staff. One major concern not discussed at length here is the potential for increased competition between executive and legislative staff bureaucracies with corollary interference in the executive process by legislative actors. With regard to the investigative function at least, competition in ideas and evaluation is probably a positive gain. Other concerns are discussed below.

The Problem of Congressional Control of Staff. Critics of large congressional staffs fear that they may develop into independent power centers in the legislative and administrative process. Staffs may usurp congressional roles and become "wheelers and dealers." They may develop cosy relationships with congressmen, agency personnel, and interest representatives and facilitate the growth of subgovernments that are difficult for both the President and Congress to control.

Advocates of enlarged staffs reply that staffs only exercise power that is derived from immediate political superiors. At every point, the extent of discretion staffs enjoy depends upon the working relations established with members of Congress. A staff serves as an extension of the personality of the congressman himself. It enables the member of Congress to play several roles simultaneously where he otherwise might be severely limited in his effectiveness. Staffs play a variety of political roles in the legislative process. They participate extensively in the hearings and committee phase and may even do the bulk of questioning of committee witnesses. Because of the political context of their employment, the temptation of a staff member to "play congressman" is great. In fact, this aspect of congressional staff work may be one of the basic rewards provided by the system. Yet Congress could hardly function today if congressional staffs did not mimic or anticipate the behavior of their congressional superiors. Ultimately it is the responsibility of the congressman to define the acceptable range of behavior for his congressional staff. The advocates of an enlarged staff assume that congressmen individually and collectively can keep order in their own house.

Abusive or Partisan Behavior of Congressional Staff. A related concern voiced by critics of congressional staff is that an investigative staff in particular, sometimes aided by unscrupulous members of Congress, will abuse the civil rights of witnesses and pursue investigations designed to advance the personal political fortunes or limited partisan aims of their superiors. The Senator Joseph McCarthy period generated some particularly searching criticisms of the investigative powers of Congress.

Advocates of investigatory staff reply that Congress has moved to adopt rules and standards of conduct that protect witnesses. Moreover, the Supreme Court, notably in *Watkins* v. *U.S.,* has suggested procedural limits to the investigative powers of Congress. The criticism of *particular exercises* of congressional investigation does not negate the basic value of the *general* power of Congress to act in such a capacity. As Stephen K. Bailey notes, formal investigations are "virtually the only means available to Congress for examining social and economic questions outside the framework of the federal bureaucracy." A partial list of congressional investigations of national consequence includes: studies of Negro migration after the Civil War (1880), immigration of foreign contract labor (1888), strike breaking by railroads (1892), western land reclamation (1909), structural reform of banking and finance (1912), communist activities (1930), the operation of the securities market and stock exchange (1931), the munition industry (1934), migratory labor (1937), and monopoly (1939). More recent investigations into war production and the drug industry by former Senators Harry Truman (D-Mo.) and Estes Kefauver (D-Tenn.) have become classic examples of congressional initiative and responsible performance. In sum, any instrument may be used for limited ends or abused. The proper course is to limit such abuse as far as may be practicable, not to deny the use of the instrument.

Preserving the Lay Element in Legislative Thinking. Another concern is that the growth of legislative bureaucracy will insulate the congressman from, or dilute his relationships with, either his constituents or executive officials. Arthur Macmahon believes that it is the duty of the congressman, immediately in touch with his constituents, to bring "practical public sense" to bear in the oversight of administration. The congressman interjects the criticism of a "robust, imaginative, lay mind" into highly technical operations. Macmahon fears that these values might be lost if the politician-legislator dealt with administrative officials vicariously through an intermediate legislative bureaucracy.

The advocates of a technically trained staff for Congress reply that the presence of a staff does not preclude direct legislator-administrator dealings. More likely a staff may actually increase the amount and level of interchange by giving the legislator the capacity to understand what the specialist is talking about. The romanticized ideal of the lay legislator confuses the ability to deal with specialized subjects with the commitment of the specialist. As the complexity of public policy issues has increased, the job of a congressman has of necessity become a more professional occupation. Congressmen will require more staff assistance simply to maintain intelligent or informed dialogue with the Executive. A case in point is the growth of a new "analyst" profession in government. With the extension of PPBS, Congress must acquire new professional staff skills in appropriations if it is to keep up with the dialogue that is already changing in the Executive branch. Congressmen, if they are to serve in an effective mediating role between governmental policy and their constitutions, must constantly upgrade their understanding of government. So long as the legislator is subject to re-election and the administrator is responsible for implementing his program, there is little likelihood that the separate value perspectives of nonspecialized and specialized minds will be lost.

The Limits of Staff Effectiveness. Perhaps the most cogent criticism of the opponents to increased staffing is that staffing in itself cannot solve many problems. Whether a member of Congress or committee will initiate an investigation, follow through on hearings and committee action, and actually vote for legislation may depend on a range of factors completely apart from the availability of staff. Simply adding staff not only may fail to accomplish its desired objective; it may also yield undesirable side effects such as those already noted. Many problems are essentially intractable. Staff offers an illusory hope that congressmen can escape the burdens of uncertainty, difficult choice, and continuing frustration.

The advocates of increased staff reply that their definition of staff requirements is selective and in demonstrated areas of need. They admit that a basic problem is one of educating members of Congress to use staff effectively. (Congress has virtually unlimited power to increase its own staff if it so desires.) While they may disagree exactly how increased staff should be allocated within the congressional system, they share an optimistic assessment that Congress could improve its functional performance significantly — in investigation and elsewhere — if it were only adequately staffed.

Staffing for the Investigative Function of Congress

If one grants that the advocates of increased congressional staff have the better argument, as the author is inclined to do, a number of problems remain. A significant increase in congressional staff can only be accommodated outside the existing committee system. Moynihan, for example, suggests that the staff of a new Office of Legislative Evaluation be located either in a separate agency responsible to Congress, in the Library of Congress, or in the General Accounting Office. Decisions on this and other proposals, such as a RAND-type of Congressional Institute and the use of congressional commissions, will require careful attention to design, supervision, and effective utilization.

The fundamental problem of allocating staff resources remains. An overall increase in the quality and quantity of congressional staff should alleviate the expressed staffing inadequacies of the minority as well as of junior members of committees. It is important to realize, however, that staff resources are an important element in the basis of congressional power and that an increase in such resources will inevitably affect the distribution of power in Congress. The allocation of staff will also have consequences for congressional performance in specific functional areas such as oversight and constituency service.

Finally, it should be noted that the debate over a professional staff for Congress since 1946 will soon be transformed by innovations in other areas. The information processing and screening functions of a staff will be radically transformed by the development and application of computer-based information systems in government. A whole new area of social investigation will be opened by the steady improvement of budgetary analysis, coupled with a new base of social indicators and simulation techniques. As Bertram Gross depicts the passing order, executive officials and members of Congress alike have been "misled by *inadequate interpretation* of *bad information* based on *obsolete concepts* and *inadequate rearch* and collected by *underfed and over-lobbied statistical agencies.*"

Congress has great potential for contributing to basic social and economic investigation in the coming decades. Such a function is consistent with the historical use of congressional powers. Its further development, however, will require congressional adaptation to a new era of governmental decision making. And not the least of these requirements for adaptation will be the intelligent and effective use of congressional staff.

24

Congressional Staff and Public Policy-Making: The Joint Committee on Internal Revenue Taxation

John F. Manley

Many students of Congress have observed that, due to the increased scope and complexity of governmental activity, congressmen need expert staff assistance if they are to legislate in an informed way and retain some independence of the executive branch and its expertise. Confronted with multifarious demands on their time, the argument goes, legislators have a difficult time mastering the intricacies of substantive policy proposals; partly as a result, many policy-making functions theoretically reserved for the legislative branch have been transferred, in fact if not always in form, to the executive. Carried out to its logical conclusion this development would appear to culminate in the suggestion made by Samuel P. Huntington that Congress give up whatever lawmaking power it still has: "Explicit acceptance of the idea that legislation was not its primary function would, in large part, simply be recognition of the direction which change has already been taking. It would legitimize and expand the functions of constituent

From John F. Manley, "Congressional Staff and Public Policy-Making: The Joint Committee on Internal Revenue Taxation," *Journal of Politics*, 30 (November 1968), pp. 1046–67.

service and administrative oversight which, in practice, already constitute the principal work of most congressmen." [1]

Should Congress arm itself with a professional staff which may equip it to compete with the sources of information available to the executive and help it stem the tendency toward de facto executive lawmaking? Or should Congress recognize its inability to legislate and maximize the functions for which it is best suited: constituent service and administrative oversight? . . .

Like other questions of congressional reform the question of staff has been raised before political scientists have produced descriptive and analytical accounts of the activities of the staff which Congress already employs. Shooting from the hip does not necessarily mean that one will miss the target but Ralph Huitt makes a persuasive argument that the low level of knowledge about how Congress works impedes the effectiveness of suggestions for change. . . .

The purpose of the present study is to analyze the role of one staff in the policy-making process. . . .

The Joint Committee on Internal Revenue Taxation (JCIRT), established forty-two years ago, is the oldest joint committee of Congress. As originally planned by the House in the Revenue Act of 1926 the "Joint Commission on Taxation," as it was called, was to be composed of five Senators, five House members, and five members appointed by the President to represent the general public. The job of the Commission was to investigate the operation, effects, and administration of the internal revenue laws with the purpose of simplifying the statute and improving its administration. Better phraseology and administration of tax law, not policy innovation, were the objectives of the Commission as envisaged by the House. The Commission, expected to last less than two years, received an authorization to spend $25,000 on clerical and traveling expenses; quarters were to be provided by the Secretary of the Treasury.

The Senate drastically altered the House plan. Making liberal use of its authority to amend revenue bills passed by the House, the Senate called for a Joint Committee on Internal Revenue Taxation made up solely of congressmen: five Senators and five Representatives. The primary stimulus for this action was the sensational revelations of tax evasion aided by misconduct on the part of Internal Revenue Bureau

[1] Samuel P. Huntington, "Congressional Responses to the Twentieth Century," *The Congress and America's Future,* in David B. Truman (ed.) (Englewood Cliffs, N.J.: Prentice-Hall, 1965), p. 30.

employees, revelations which stemmed from the work of a select committee headed by Michigan Senator James Couzens. The new Joint Committee, *through its staff,* was designed to: (1) obtain information from taxpayers to assist in the framing of future revenue legislation; (2) gain a "closer insight" into the problem of the administration of the tax laws (a euphemism for preventing corruption in the Internal Revenue Bureau); and (3) gather data bearing upon revenue legislation. The House receded on the Senate amendments and the Joint Committee, a combination watchdog and law-simplifying organization, was set up — with a staff.

Shortly after its inception the Joint Committee was given the job of reviewing large tax refunds planned by the Bureau of Internal Revenue. Today, the Joint Committee relies upon its staff (three of whom actually work in the Internal Revenue Service) to review the refunds. The Joint Committee, which has only an informal veto over refunds, acts mainly as an appellate court for IRS when the congressional staff and IRS cannot resolve a case. Under the current Chief of Staff, Dr. Laurence N. Woodworth, the Joint Committee has not yet reversed its staff; it did rule in favor of the Bureau under Woodworth's predecessor, Colin F. Stam, in rare instances.

In addition to checking on refunds the Joint Committee has met in recent years to discuss tax regulations and to be briefed on the computerization of tax returns, but it has not evolved into a policy-making body for revenue legislation. With no role in the general policy process the importance of the Joint Committee is that it serves as the institutional excuse for maintaining the joint staff, a body of experts which early in its history was praised for its work on the technical aspects of tax law.

From modest beginnings, and with an uncertain future, the joint staff grew until for the period July 1, 1966 to July 1, 1967 it employed three dozen people at a cost of almost $440,000. Twenty of the 36 were professional staff, including three economists. Most of these people spend their time helping the Ways and Means Committee and the Senate Finance Committee write tax laws; the staff needs of the Joint Committee as such are minimal.

It may be true that in some fields Congress needs more staff assistance but in the area of revenue legislation the Joint Committee staff provides the legislature with a professional, independent, highly reliable source of information. The few studies which mention the staff invariably cite its competence, expertise, and influence with congressmen. Two articles, one in *Business Week* and the other in the *Wall*

Street Journal, stress the quality of the staff,[2] and in a well-known book Roy M. Blough observes that the members of the tax committees place "heavy reliance" on the Chief of Staff and that the staff plays a "highly important" role in tax legislation.[3] A member of the Ways and Means Committee goes so far as to contend that, "Between the Joint Committee staff and the House Legislative Counsel, Congress has developed a more competent staff for drafting tax legislation than has the Treasury." [4]

Congressional experience with the Joint Committee staff is so favorable that this device has been taken as the model for changes in the legislative process. In the recent hearings before the Joint Committee on the Organization of Congress, for example, Senator John L. McClellan (D.-Ark.) used the JCIRT to support his proposal to establish a Joint Committee on the Budget. This arrangement, he felt, would give Congress the same type of technical assistance in the appropriations field as it enjoys in the revenue field, and as the Budget Bureau provides the executive branch.[5] The National Taxpayers Conference and the Tax Foundation stated that the JCIRT could be a precedent for a similar organization to deal with expenditures, and Senator Boggs used it as the prototype for a fully-staffed Joint Committee on National Strategy. These proposals may never materialize but the fact that the JCIRT is taken as the model for further institutional innovations is evidence that in many quarters the view of the joint tax staff is a positive one.

What does the Joint Committee staff do for the tax committees which leads people to think that a similar device would be useful in different contexts? Are members of House Ways and Means and Senate Finance happy with the work of their staff; if not, why? What is the staff supposed to do for these committees and does it live up to congressional expectations?

The most obvious, and in some ways the most important, function of the Joint Committee staff is one of linkage: what continuity the tax legislative process has, apart from informal contacts between leading members of the committees, arises from the central role of the staff in

[2] "Where Tax Bills Run the Gauntlet," *Business Week,* June 11, 1966, p. 106. Arlen J. Large, "Help on the Hill," *Wall Street Journal,* June 25, 1965.

[3] Roy M. Blough, *The Federal Taxing Process* (New York: Prentice-Hall, 1952), p. 64.

[4] Thomas B. Curtis, "The House Committee on Ways and Means: Congress Seen Through a Key Committee," *Wisconsin Law Review* (Winter, 1966), p. 8.

[5] *Op. cit.,* p. 477. McClellan's proposal has passed the Senate many times but to date leaders of the House Appropriations Committee have responded negatively.

both the House and Senate deliberations on tax bills. In the executive sessions of the Ways and Means Committee the staff is not merely on tap for the members but it is actively engaged in the examination of policy proposals made by the members, the Administration, interest groups, and lobbyists. After explicating for Ways and Means how individuals and groups will be affected by changes in the Internal Revenue Code the staff, and most prominently the Chief of Staff, crosses the rotunda and explains the bill to the Finance Committee, going through the same basic routine except that now there exists a detailed bill instead of the tax message with which Ways and Means normally begins. For many years, and until Russell Long (D.-La.) became chairman of Finance in 1965, about the only professional staff available to the Finance Committee was the joint staff.[6]

In performing its tasks for the Ways and Means Committee and the Senate Finance Committee the staff is expected to follow certain norms. Three such norms are: objectivity, bipartisanship, and neutrality. As a body of professional tax experts the Joint Committee staff is supposed to be objective in its handling of data, bipartisan in its handling of member requests, and neutral on public policy questions. "Our job," says the present Chief of Staff Laurence N. Woodworth, "is to see that members of Congress get the facts on both sides so they can make their own decisions." "If I can come away from those meetings," he has said, "knowing that the committee has made its own decisions in the light of this knowledge, then I'm satisfied." The staff's job, according to Ways and Means Chairman Wilbur Mills (D.-Ark.), is "to bring facts together for our use, to do the spadework for us." A former Republican staff assistant noted the bipartisan nature of the staff: "When I tell Woodworth or those guys something I expect confidence and I get it." Recruited without regard to party affiliation ("I'm very proud of the fact that Mr. Stam [former Chief of Staff] never asked me my party politics and as far as I know never asked any other member of the staff.") the staff, as one aide put it, acts "as a coordinator for the Ways and Means Committee. We serve Curtis and Byrnes [Republicans], Boggs and Mills [Democrats], in addition to Senator Byrd." Woodworth has on occasion, helped write the ma-

[6] In justifying his successful request for more staff Long contended: "Under our Government the legislative branch is not supposed to be a lackey or the tool of the executive and is not to take the word of the executive on matters but should be able to acquire information itself." *Congressional Record*, April 20, 1966 (daily edition), p. 8239. He admitted that the Joint Committee staff does a good job but when they are working for Ways and Means the Finance Committee has only a secondary claim on their services. Long also argued that Finance has much nontax work to do and needs help which the joint staff cannot provide.

jority report on a bill and then turned around and helped the minority write its dissenting views.

Given the controversial nature of tax policy, given the well-known complexity of the Internal Revenue Code which puts a high premium on technical advice, given the difficulty of facing choices without forming opinions, and given the strategic role of the quartermaster corps in the conduct of any war it is not surprising that the staff, which obviously affects the decisions made by the policy-makers, has been criticized for failing to live up to the above norms. One norm in particular, that of neutrality on public policy, has, some policymakers feel, been broken by the staff, especially while Colin F. Stam was Chief of Staff.

"It has been estimated," Stephen Bailey and Howard Samuel note, "that Stam exercised more influence on the preparation of tax legislation than any other single person in the federal government." [7] Little known outside of Washington, Stam accumulated so much influence with the Ways and Means Committee and the Senate Finance Committee that only one (Harry Byrd) of 20 people interviewed by E. W. Kenworthy for his perceptive study of Stam was willing to have his views of the corpulent technician attributed to him. Stam did not control tax policy, in Byrd's opinion, but he "has made very many vital decisions. He has made recommendations that have carried great weight with both committees. . . ." [8] And, to cite but one more piece of evidence, a Republican Senator commented on Stam,

> He'd been here so long that he wasn't like other staff men. He was the only staff man I knew who could tell a senator to go to hell without getting his face slapped. Not that he did it, understand, but there wasn't any of this subjugation or kowtowing which you sometimes see in the staff, no "sir" business. He was here when I first came in . . . and he cut quite a figure then.[9]

Inevitably associated with influence in Washington is controversy, and Stam had influence in the tax field despite his stated view of himself as a technician who merely supplied analyses and counsel to the decision-makers. Not everyone would agree with the citation on his Rockefeller Public Service Award given "in recognition of distin-

[7] Stephen K. Bailey and Howard D. Samuel, *Congress at Work* (New York: Henry Holt & Co., 1953), p. 342.

[8] E. W. Kenworthy, "Colin F. Stam," in *Adventures in Public Service,* Delia and Ferdinand Kuhn (eds.) (New York: Vanguard Press, 1963), p. 115.

[9] After an apprenticeship with the Internal Revenue Bureau Stam joined the Joint Committee staff in 1927, became Chief of Staff in 1938, and ran it for a quarter of a century until his retirement in 1964. He suffered a stroke and died in January, 1966.

guished service to the government of the United States and to the American people." Specifically, Stam's activity as Chief of Staff has been severely criticized by liberal Senators concerned with making changes or, as they see it, "reforms" in the internal revenue laws.

For these Senators not only was Stam of little help but his expertise was sullied because it buttressed, in the main, the views of their antagonists, men who were in effective control of both committees. Though Stam was certainly not the linch-pin in the conservative coalition which Senate liberals feel has controlled tax policy for many years, he was a conservative, he identified with the conservative leaders of Finance and Ways and Means, and his key position and acknowledged mastery of the Code were used to frustrate liberal attempts to "purify" the tax laws — so, at any rate, say the liberals. . . .

It appears, then, that the impact of the staff's work leaned toward the conservative side under Stam's leadership — norms of neutrality and objectivity to the contrary notwithstanding. What the staff does to some extent affects what the committees decide, and even the conservative members of Finance admit that in Stam they had an important friend. "Colin Stam's personal philosophy," said a Senator in praise of the staff chief, "was that the tax law should be used for raising revenue and not for social reform. If that makes him a conservative then I suppose he's a conservative. I think this is Larry Woodworth's philosophy too, and it's certainly mine." Commenting on the demands for more minority staff, a Republican Senator confirmed the liberals' charges when he observed that on Finance the minority, plus the Byrd Democrats, had all of the staff they needed because Stam was a conservative. "Gore and Douglas and a few others were the ones who didn't have any staff," he chortled: "our coalition had the staff." . . .

Given the difficulty of remaining neutral in the policy-making process it would be tempting to look upon the above policy consequences of the staff attitudes as all but inevitable. Men in Washington form preferences, the political system is designed for the airing and resolution of preferences, and it may be unrealistic to ask any man to be a policy eunuch, especially one who must operate amid the competing demands which surround the tax legislative process. But the history of the joint tax staff since Stam's retirement and the ascendancy of Woodworth to the top position necessitates caution in accepting this conclusion. Perfect conformity to the norms of neutrality and objectivity is probably impossible but the degree of attainment and deviation varies with different individuals. And, experience shows, there is no reason to conclude that the staff *cannot* both serve and please diverse masters.

When Woodworth took over as Chief of Staff in 1964 he was aware of the liberal criticism of Stam and he took steps to restore the staff to its position as a useful aide to *all* members of the Senate Finance and Ways and Means committees. He assured Senate Liberals that he and his assistants stood ready to assist all members, regardless of policy considerations, and that, in effect, the staff would not play politics on revenue bills. Woodworth's campaign worked: the critics of Stam laud his successor. "I'd say the staff is 500 per cent improved over what it used to be," said one liberal Senator. Hired by Stam in 1944, Woodworth is more skillful than his mentor in retaining the confidence of the factions that make tax policy. Whether or not he can always avoid all commitments to individual policy positions, or operate in such a way that although the staff research does in fact enhance one position at the expense of others he does not alienate any members, remains to be seen, but at present he is doing precisely that. "I honestly have no idea whether he's a Democrat or a Republican," says one long-time associate of Woodworth's. "He's about as straight down-the-middle as you can get." If Woodworth can function in accordance with this inclination he may be able to play his role as he — and the congressmen — think it should be played.

It should be noted, in passing, that criticism of the joint staff has been found on only one side of the Capitol: the Senate. The Ways and Means Committee is populated with Democrats whose voting behavior is as liberal as the Finance Committee reformers, but there are crucial differences in style between the two groups. There are really no reform-minded liberals like Paul Douglas (D.-Ill.) (before his defeat) or Albert Gore (D.-Tenn.) [before his defeat] on the House Committee, although some House members would no doubt vote for the same reforms — if pressed. The one Ways and Means member who in personal philosophy and public statements most closely resembles the Senate tax reformers is Chairman Mills, but in practice if not preachment he has been a disappointment: "Wilbur Mills has always been for reform right up to the opening day of Congress. . . . He pulled this three or four times until he found out he couldn't fool anyone anymore." This statement, whether an accurate assessment of Mills or not, indicates that to date not much steam for tax reform has come from the House. Consequently, not much criticism of the staff for blocking reforms has come from the House either. The general attitude was probably well illustrated by a liberal Ways and Means Democrat who, in reply to a question about the criticism of Stam, dismissed it with the observation: "I think that's just a characteristic of some liberal Senators. They have to have something to complain about and if it's not the staff it's something else. I think complaining is their common denominator."

As a link between the two tax committees of Congress, in summary, the Joint Committee staff, as seen by the policy-makers, has had mixed results. Possessed of so much expertise that one House member was led to observe that "they are the legislators, we are the politicans," the staff has played its role appropriately under one head and inappropriately, in light of the norms which the members and staff espouse, under another. Having gone through the process on the House side the staff is equipped to inform the Senate Finance Committee on the technical — and political — problems involved in various sections of the bill. But it is a job which affects the kind of decisions made in the legislative process; as such, it is endowed with influence and, potentially, controversy. The existence of the former and avoidance of the latter is delicate business. Under Stam the expertise of the staff resulted in some disaffection; under Woodworth the expertise of the staff, in no way diminished, has been used in a more neutral — or less offensive — way. Time will determine whether or not this is a permanent revolution.

In addition to linking the Ways and Means and Senate Finance committees directly in the legislative process, the Joint Committee staff acts as an important point of contact between the committee and two key participants in the tax-making process: the Treasury Department and interest groups. In this section we will analyze the staff's relation with these actors, putting special emphasis on the initial stage of the process which revolves around the Ways and Means Committee.

WAYS AND MEANS —
TREASURY DEPARTMENT RELATIONS

It is a maxim, by now, that although the Constitution separates authority among the three branches of government there is a good deal of overlap among the institutions and that, in fact, they share power and responsibility for legislation. To date, however, there are relatively few empirical studies of how the branches have bridged the formal separation and organized their interaction; there are even fewer studies of arrangements between individual congressional committees and related executive department agencies.[10] Congressional oversight of administration has received a fair amount of attention but much work remains to be done on the interaction between the branches in formulating policy, marking up bills, and striking a balance between the competing demands which are involved in the policy-making process.

One bridge between the branches is through the professional staff of Congress and its counterpart in the executive departments. For many years Joint Committee staff experts, under Stam and continuing under Woodworth, have worked with Treasury Department experts on technical tax problems in what are called staff "subcommittees." A member of the Joint Committee staff summed up the purpose of these subcommittees:

> We work very closely with Treasury people. Before a message is sent by the President we have these staff subcommittees composed of Joint Committee on Internal Revenue Taxation staff, Treasury people, and IRS [Internal Revenue Service] people. We discuss proposals drawn up by the Treasury's economists. These economists compose big ideas and general notions as to what Treasury ought to do on taxes — this is where it all starts. Then we get together in our subcommittee and discuss these ideas as to feasibility and technical possibility. Many times they aren't practical. We represent the Ways and Means Committee and let them know what the Committee may or may not accept. What we do in these meetings is kick ideas around, we brainstorm ideas.

The primary task of the subcommittee is to discuss, in a professional way, various tax proposals, the technical problems involved in drafting the language necessary to put them into effect, and the likelihood of congressional policy-makers responding positively or negatively to them.

Through the staff mechanism, then, the Ways and Means Committee members may learn what the Treasury Department is contemplating or not contemplating and Treasury receives technical assistance and valuable information about what the Committee is likely to accept or reject. Neither staff contingent has the authority to bind the policy-makers, of course, and the Joint Committee staff is careful

---

[10] Notable exceptions include: J. Lieper Freeman, *The Political Process: Executive Bureau-Legislative Committee Relations,* rev. ed. (New York: Random House, 1965); Richard F. Fenno, Jr., *The Power of the Purse* (Boston: Little, Brown, 1966), chs. 6, 7; James A. Robinson, *Congress and Foreign Policy-Making* (Homewood, Ill.: Dorsey Press, 1962), chs. 5, 6.

about appearing to speak for its superiors. But policy questions are discussed, technical barriers to changing the Internal Revenue Code are resolved, and the subcommittees do serve as a way of combining the expertise of both staffs in the initial stage of the policy-making process. The prognostications of the congressional staff may or may not be heeded by Treasury. For example, in 1963 the joint staff warned the Department that Ways and Means would not approve the controversial proposal to limit itemized deductions to five percent of the taxpayer's adjusted gross income, but Treasury, committed to the five percent floor, proposed it anyway. The issue was not even put to a vote in Ways and Means. In other cases, however, the views of the congressional staff are taken into account when Treasury is deciding what to include in a tax message, and in this way the probable response of the Ways and Means Committee has a bearing on the initiation of tax legislation.

After the preliminaries are over and the Ways and Means Committee is in executive session, the Joint Committee staff, having spent hours in consultation with Treasury Department experts, is prepared to explain arcane tax proposals to the members. Since Ways and Means allows Treasury officials to attend and participate in its executive deliberations both staffs are involved in explaining the Treasury Department's proposals to the Committee. If the Secretary of the Treasury is especially well-versed in tax matters, as was Douglas Dillon on the proposal which became the Revenue Act of 1964, he will carry a large part of the burden of presenting the Department's case, and the Treasury staff will serve as a backstop to him. (One Committee member said Dillon spent so much time with the Committee in 1963 he began to wonder if the Secretary was using Ways and Means as a "hideout.") But the Joint Committee staff, playing the role of *Congress's* staff, ensures that the Committee hears all sides of the issues and, by so doing, the staff affects the decisions that are made. . . .

When there is disagreement among the experts the Committee members are inclined to rely on their staff, not Treasury's. The general feeling is that the Joint Committee staff, which generates its own studies and data independent of the Treasury Department, has demonstrated that in a dispute with Treasury its studies are more reliable than the executive's. Two examples, one pertaining to the reduction of excise taxes, the other to raising the national debt limit, illustrate the Committee's faith in its staff and the ways in which the work of the staff affects policy outcomes.

In 1965, as part of a long-awaited excise tax reduction bill, the

Administration proposed that the excise tax on automobiles be reduced in steps from ten percent to seven percent, and then to five percent by 1967 at which time the five percent levy would be permanent. Detroit's spokesman on the Ways and Means Committee, Martha Griffiths (D-Mich.), proposed that the tax be removed altogether and at once, a proposal that would have cost the federal government over $1 billion in revenue. The Treasury Department, not wanting to increase the budget deficit by this much, opposed the Griffiths motion, and so did Chairman Mills. In the course of building his argument against the motion Mills argued that the Committee could not lift the automobile excise and stagger the tax on telephone service, so he asked Treasury how much reducing the telephone tax all at once would add to the deficit. Assistant Secretary Stanley Surrey replied that it would cost a half billion dollars. At this point Eugene Keogh (D-N.Y.) asked how much a compromise proposal on the auto excise would cost and Mills then recognized Woodworth, the Chief of Staff. Woodworth informed the Committee that the joint staff figures showed that the federal budget deficit would be higher than that estimated by the Treasury, an observation which further argued against the Griffiths proposal. Representative Keogh asked a rhetorical question about whose estimates have usually been nearer the mark, Treasury's or the Joint Committee's staff, and Mills answered for Woodworth: the congressional staff. With the case made against the car makers' amendment Ways and Means voted. Griffiths, beaten on a voice vote, did not bother to press for a roll call. Mills, the Joint Committee staff, and Treasury, in concert, defeated the Griffiths amendment.

In the case of excise taxes the expertise of the Joint Committee staff buttressed the Treasury Department, but the congressional staff's work also helps the Committee take and support positions contrary to that of the Executive Branch. One such incident was the Committee's handling of the 1966 debt bill. On the basis of calculations about federal finances made by its staff, Ways and Means rejected the Administration's request for a $332 billion temporary limit on the national debt and recommended instead a $330 billion ceiling. The $2 billion cut was predicated on the joint staff's studies which showed that federal receipts would probably exceed the amount estimated by Treasury, the deficit would consequently be less than expected, and, therefore, a lower ceiling could be justified. The Committee's faith in its staff was not misplaced: a week after the House passed the bill Treasury Secretary Fowler acknowledged before the Senate Finance

Committee that the Department, though squeezed, could live with the House figure.[11]

Thus Congress, through the staff of the Joint Committee on Internal Revenue Taxation, has a body of professionals which links its principal revenue-raising organs bicamerally, which serves as a communications link between the Ways and Means Committee and the Treasury Department, and which is so expert that the legislature has an in-house check on the expertise of the Executive Branch — so much so that the congressmen feel they can rely on their staff even in the face of conflicting information from the executive. Important as these functions are they do not exhaust the functions of the staff. One more aspect of the staff, its relations with interest groups, needs to be explored before one can appreciate the extent of the staff's services for the Ways and Means Committee.

WAYS AND MEANS — INTEREST DEMANDS

Access to the Committee on Ways and Means is obtained in many ways. Members of the Committee act as the spokesmen for particular interests (e.g., the oil industry), the practice of holding public hearings on major bills is firmly rooted, and group spokesmen have on occasion been invited into the Committee's executive session to assist it in writing legislation (e.g., representatives of Blue Cross–Blue Shield were summoned to a closed meeting on medicare in 1965). Another line of access is through the Joint Committee staff. The staff is a common target for informed Washington lobbyists and the first stop for many constituent demands.

There is abundant evidence in the anecdotes which travel the Washington grapevine, the public record, and the perceptions of those involved in the policy-making process to support the observation that contacts between the staff and interested parties are frequent, legitimate, and important.

On the anecdotal level the story is told of Colin Stam that he carried so much weight with the formal policy-makers that a lobbyist who had difficulty getting to see him bought a dog and walked the canine around Chevy Chase Circle in hopes of encountering the tax

---

[11] Hobart Rowen, "Fowler Accepts House Debt Action," *Washington Post,* June 14, 1966. Before the Rules Committee, with Woodworth sitting behind him, Mills backed the Committee's action in these words: "I'm prone to believe that the staff itself may be more accurate than the Treasury."

expert on his nightly dog-walking strolls. Apocryphal, perhaps, but the circulation of the story testifies to the importance of the staff to interest groups. "Nobody's been up to my neighborhood to see me yet," Woodworth has been quoted as saying, but this may be because no one has yet had difficulty seeing him at the office.

Normally, access to the staff is not difficult. Stam, for example, used to hold quasi-hearings at which lobbyists would present their views on tax matters (a measure of his influence in the process), and Woodworth does the same. Many lobbyists have heard a member of Ways and Means or Senate Finance say, "See Stam" (and now, "See Larry"). . . . "Stam's staff," as one Ways and Means member put it succinctly, "is very influential and that's why they are lobbied so much."

By receiving and analyzing tax proposals the staff increases the Committee's contacts with interested parties, which is an important part of the Ways and Means Committee's job, and at the same time it helps the members cope with the tremendous number of demands for changes in the Code. Many times, in fact, these demands are stimulated by the Committee itself as part of its legislative procedure. Prior to the passage of the 1954 Revenue Act, for example, the staff mailed a tax questionnaire to thousands of individuals and groups. Over 15,000 replies were received and over two dozen national associations did studies of various tax proposals before passage of the Act, the first major revision of the Code since 1939. So much of the work was done by the staff that one member, Jere Cooper (D-Tenn.), argued that the Committee, with six weeks labor, still did not understand the bill reported to the House:

> The staffs of the Joint Committee on Internal Revenue Taxation and the Treasury Department together have spent over two years preparing recommendations for the bill. Extensive hearings were held, and some 15,000 replies to questionnaires were reviewed preparatory to making recommendations to be included. In contrast to this, the committee deliberated on the bill for only six weeks. In my opinion, such a complete overhauling as this bill proposes to make involving the most complicated laws which Congress has ever written, would require at least one year to fully understand. . . .

Another revealing example of the contacts between interest groups and the staff occurred in 1956 when the House considered a bill dealing with the renegotiation of government contracts. In this case the Committee did not make policy as much as it legitimatized the recommendations of the staff and business organizations. Thomas Jenkins (R-Ohio) said of the bill:

> Mr. Speaker, this bill is the result of an exhaustive study by the staff of the Joint Committee on Internal Revenue Taxation. This study was conducted pursuant to statutory directive and lasted for many months. *Industry had a complete opportunity to present its problems to the staff.*[12]

Jenkins acknowledged that it may have been unfortunate that Ways and Means did not hold hearings but: "On the other hand, I believe that Mr. Stam and the joint committee staff did a magnificent job in developing these needed improvements in the act." Small wonder that interest groups and individuals pay attention to the staff.

The testimony to the important role of the staff which is found in the public record is, of course, the reflection of the staff's activities in countless private meetings with lobbyists and in the executive sessions of the Ways and Means Committee. When the members of Ways and Means descend from their dais and begin marking up a tax bill the staff becomes an integral part of the process. According to Thomas B. Curtis (R-Mo.), when the doors are closed the staff represents the views of the people with whom it has been in contact:

> The role of the Joint Committee staff is even more important during executive sessions when administration officials are the only outsiders present. Then the staff must represent the views of all other "interests" whose positions are often discounted by the sometimes parochial outlook of Treasury and Internal Revenue Service officials and experts.

The staff, in other words, brings to the discussion the results of its meetings and communications with people on the outside, thereby keeping the Committee informed on the views and arguments of those who will be affected by the Committee's decisions.

One example of this part of the staff's role will be cited. In 1965, when the Committee was considering President Johnson's proposed cut in excise taxes, the question arose as to whether or not the announcement of excise tax reductions would induce consumers to postpone buying certain items until the tax was removed, thus, in effect, creating a buyer's strike. Woodworth reported to the meeting that the Joint Committee staff had contacted different industries to see if they thought a refund of any tax paid on such goods was

---

[12] *Congressional Record*, 84th Cong., 2nd Sess, 1956, 102, Part 9, p. 12726. Emphasis added.

needed to ward off a drop in sales. It first appeared, he stated, that the electrical appliance industry favored the refund idea, but consultation with the national organization of electrical manufacturers revealed that the only appliance to which the refund should definitely apply, due to the closeness of the summer selling season, was air conditioners. He also informed the meeting that many manufacturers were not too anxious to pass the tax cut on to consumers by way of lowered prices, and providing for a tax refund would increase the pressure on them to do so. This, together with the administrative burdens of handling the refund, argued against applying refunds to articles other than air conditioners. Ways and Means, guided by the information gathered by the staff from interested parties, decided to make the refund applicable to air conditioners.

Interest group representatives in Washington go where power is, or where they think power is, and the Joint Committee staff is not shortchanged when it comes to contacts with lobbyists. A favorable response from the staff does not *assure* the same reaction from the tax committees, but with the complexity of tax legislation and the concomitant need of congressmen for expert guidance the likelihood of the decision-makers following the advice of the fact-finders is high. This does not mean that congressmen are captives of their staffs. By and large the staff probably reflects the views of the members more than it determines those views. But the above evidence shows that the staff can and does play an active role in the process. The input of the staff, one more variable for students of policy-making to consider, has received scant attention to date but it may warrant greater attention in the future.

CONCLUSION

From a case study of one staff it is impossible, of course, to answer the question of whether or not Congress needs more staff in order to compete effectively with the executive branch. All we can say is that in one significant area of public policy, revenue legislation, Congress is equipped to do much more than service constituents and oversee the bureaucracy. The House Ways and Means Committee is so well-equipped in this area that the Treasury Department usually presents its requests in the form of a tax message as opposed to a draft bill. The bill is the *product* of the Committee's work, not the start of it.

Having shown how the Joint Committee staff may affect the decisions of policy-makers, and discussed the linkage functions of the staff, we may speculate on some of the variables which are pertinent to the role of the staff. First in probable importance is, obviously, the nature of the subject matter handled by the committee. As the complexity of the decisions facing legislators increases so too does the likelihood that the staff will exert influence on the outcomes. Tax policy, infinitely complex, maximizes the importance of expertise. The importance of the staff is likely to vary on other committees with different tasks (e.g., the House Rules Committee, Government Operations).

Another factor that affects the influence of the staff is the scope of the decision. It is no accident that much of the criticism of Stam centered around his role in drafting and defending narrow tax provisions which helped particular industries, companies, or, in the case of Louis B. Mayer, one individual.[13] The more salient the issue is to a large number of participants the less likely the judgment of the staff will direct the decision. On purely economic grounds, for example, the Chief of Staff believed in the fall of 1967 that a tax increase was advisable but Chairman Mills led 19 other Ways and Means members in tabling the President's request until Congress and the President resolved the question of limiting federal expenditures. Staff studies, though not without some importance, bowed to the political barriers to passing a tax increase in the House.

Highly personal factors such as the relationship between the staff and leading members of the committees also deserve attention. There is in Congress a cadre of professional staff assistants who, like Stam, develop firm ties with influential congressmen, thus partaking of their sponsors' influence while they simultaneously contribute to it. . . .

Other interesting questions about the role of the staff in the legislative process are not hard to imagine. On a committee such as House Post Office and Civil Service, for example, what are the consequences of having an unstable committee membership but a long-term professional staff director? How does the staff of a highly centralized committee (e.g., Ways and Means which does not work through subcommittees) differ from the Appropriations Committee which does almost all its work in subcommittees? Why is it that not one member of the current Democratic party leadership in the House has a staff confidant other than House Parliamentarian Lewis Deschler? How do congressmen rely on the staff without becoming captives

---

[13] For a study of special tax provisions see Stanley S. Surrey, "How Special Tax Provisions Get Enacted," pp. 203–213, in this volume. — Eds.

of the staff? Why are some highly capable men willing to refuse lucrative jobs outside of Congress in order to toil anonymously and at relatively low pay for congressmen? These questions, and others, will not be easy to answer but they appear to be sufficiently important to require some investigation.

It should be noted, in conclusion, that it is very difficult if not impossible to determine how much "power" the staff has in the policy-making process. On certain kinds of issues under certain conditions a staff man such as Colin Stam did indeed have power. But it was a curious kind of power. It depended upon the congruence between his judgment on policy and the judgment of the majority whom he served. In their frustration over the failure to change the internal revenue code one would expect the liberal critics of Stam to exaggerate his importance as a pillar of the status quo. Future research will demonstrate, I think, that Stam and other leading staff experts perform important functions in the legislative process but, in the final analysis, they take more cues from the formal policy-makers than they give.

25

HISC Investigates: The Strategy of Exposure, with and without a Legislative Purpose

[In May 1965, Dr. Jeremiah Stamler was subpoenaed by the House Un-American Activities Committee (later renamed House Internal Security Committee) to testify about his political past and that of his friends and associates. This was part of a general HUAC investigation of the so-called resurgence of Communist activities in the Chicago area. Dr. Stamler chose neither to cooperate nor to plead the Fifth Amendment. Instead he brought suit against the committee to enjoin it from carrying out its investigation, on the grounds that it was in violation of its own rules as well as the spirit of the First Amendment.

From Albert Jenner et al., Appendix 4 to Jurisdictional Statement (October Term of the Supreme Court of the United States, 1968), pp. 2–76.

The case has been up and down the courts for nearly eight years, and about a year after the suit was entered with Stamler as plaintiff, he was made defendant in a criminal trial for contempt of Congress. During this time over $300,000 has been raised and spent; much of the money went for research to prepare briefs for the two cases. One supporting document was a careful study of the strategies, tactics, and products of the committee during its history of investigations in Washington and in the field. The following are all excerpts from that document, Appendix No. 4 to "Jurisdictional Statement," accompanying lawyers' appeal to the Supreme Court from the U.S. District Court for the Northern District of Illinois, October Term, 1968.[1]

As is true of any brief, the presentation gives only one side: whether the committee has exceeded its own or Congress' powers. Nevertheless, the review is the best available study of the investigatory process, for very similar strategies have been used by committees whose work is supported by those people who damn HUAC-HISC. The strategies are worth reviewing for themselves. The question of whether they constitute a violation of the First Amendment cannot be dealt with here, although the student can use these materials to make his own evaluation of the investigatory process in general, as well as of its use to uncover political activities. — Eds.]

COMMITTEE INTERACTION WITH WITNESSES

The Committee has its own "friendly" witnesses, makes repeated use of them on the same subjects, and is aware of the testimony to be given:

Elizabeth Bentley testified in public session three times.

Matthew Cvetic testified in public session four times.

John Lautner testified in public session on ten separate occasions between the 84th and 86th Congresses.

Barbara Hartle testified in public session four times between 1954 and 1960.

In four days of testimony, *Mrs. Mildred Blauvelt,* a "red squad" agent of the New York City Police Force, supplied the Committee with the names and, in most cases, the addresses of 450 people. She gave further testimony along the same lines in public session in the 1955 Los Angeles hearings.

---

[1] The case began as *Stamler et al. v. Willis* (HUAC Chairman at that time). Four years later, when the courts held that HUAC might not be susceptible to suit under provisions of Article I giving members of Congress immunity when on business, the case became *Stamler v. Mitchell* (the Attorney General at that time). — Eds.

Charles Regan testified in public session at least twice.

Armando Penha testified in public session five times in the same year.

Berenice Baldwin testified in public session in three hearings.

The Committee's most frequent witness has been *Irving Fishman,* a customs agent who over a five-year period testified in public session twelve times in ten cities. Each time his testimony was substantially the same.

Committee witnesses list names without providing details.

Reading the transcripts of the Committee's hearings reveals that a major portion of the public testimony of friendly witnesses places in the public record the names of those persons whom the Committee has determined are "subversive" or "un-American." Names are listed with the sketchiest of descriptions. The Committee rarely inquires into the witness's knowledge of activities on the part of the persons named.

> MR. NITTLE: Now, you have before you a list, prepared by you, which identifies some of those who were in attendance; is that correct?
>
> MISS HOLMES: Yes I have.
>
> MR. NITTLE: Now, will you tell the Committee, please, whether you know those persons who were in attendance at the State convention?
>
> MISS HOLMES: I know all of them very well: Ben Friedlander, Mollie Gold, David Englestein —
>
> THE CHAIRMAN: Start reading the list and go slow so that the reporter can get it.
>
> MISS HOLMES: Mollie Gold, David Englestein, Fritzi Englestein, Dorothy Davies, James West, Mollie West, Samuel Kushner —
>
> . . . Milton Cohen, L. Kimmel —
>
> . . . Otto Wangerin as observer; Marcia Starr —
>
> . . . Charles Sotis, Romolo Passarelli —
>
> . . . Flora Hall, Lou Diskin, Geraldine Lightfoot, Claude Lightfoot, Lester Wickstrom, Esther Eisenscher Wickstrom.
>
> . . . Gertrude McBain, Fran Vivian, Joseph Mazeika —
>
> . . . Daniel Queen, Arpad Balla . . . Lucius Armstrong —
>
> . . . Charles Wilson and Joseph Zawadowski.
>
> There were others. I don't have their names at the moment. (Counsel's questions about spelling names omitted.)

Payments are made to committee witnesses.

. . . Rep. Hays inserted into the Congressional Record the following list of persons who had been under contract with the Committee during the previous five years and the amounts of their contracts (Daily Record, October 20, 1966, p. 85454) (this material does not appear in the permanent edition of the Congressional Record):

Committee on Un-American activities contracts approved

	Name	Date Approved	Amount
87th Cong.	Lillian E. Howard	May 3, 1961	$ 1,800.00
	Maurice Malkin	June 8, 1961	400.00
	Ruth Taylor Hunter	Feb. 1, 1962	1,800.00
	Total		4,000.00
88th Cong.	*1st Sess.*		
	John Santo	Mar. 14, 1963	$ 2,500.00
	George H. Lynch	July 17, 1963	1,000.00
	Margaret Ann Kerr	Do	1,800.00
	John Lautner	Dec. 11, 1963	1,000.00
	Herbert Romerstein	Do	1,000.00
	Total		7,300.00
	2d Sess.		
	Margaret Ann Kerr	Aug. 24, 1964	$ 800.00
	Andrew J. Berecz	Oct. 2, 1964	200.00
	Charles S. Weatherholt	Do	378.59
	George H. Lynch	Jan. 2, 1965	4,500.00
	Total		5,878.59
89th Cong.	*1st Sess.*		
	John Sullivan	June 25, 1965	$ 3,600.00
	William Hendrix	July 2, 1965	250.00
	George H. Lynch	Aug. 20, 1965	3,000.00
	John D. Sullivan	Sept. 2, 1965	3,600.00
	Do	Dec. 28, 1965	3,600.00
	Total		14,050.00
	2d Sess.		
	Phillip Abbott Luce	Aug. 22, 1966	$ 1,000.00
	George H. Lynch	Oct. 11, 1966	3,000.00
	Total		4,000.00

The Committee often accuses unfriendly witnesses, rather than attempting to elicit information from them.

The Committee routinely asks witnesses whether they were members of the Communist Party. The form and substance of these and similar questions, often highly argumentative, make it clear that the function of these questions is not to obtain information, but rather to expose and accuse: . . .

Baltimore, 1957

Mr. ARENS: Then stand up like a red-blooded American and deny that you are a member of the Communist Party. [Applause.]

Mr. WILLIS: We will not have any such outburst in the courtroom either favorable or adverse to any witness. This must be enforced.

Mr. ARENS: Will you kindly answer the question?

Mr. NICHOL: I think that my service in the Army speaks for itself as regards my Americanism and conduct as a citizen.

I respectfully decline, however, under the circumstances surrounding this whole hearing, and so forth, under the first and fifth amendments to answer that question. . . .

Newark, 1958

Mr. ARENS: Why don't you stand up like a red-blooded American, and deny that you are a Communist?

Mr. LEAVY: Because, as a red-blooded American I am going to uphold the Constitution of the United States including the first and the fifth amendments.

Chicago, 1965

. . . Mr. NITTLE: Now, Mrs. Jennings, in the light of our information that you had had an initial break with the Communist Party in 1961 because of a dispute with another party member, we should like to inquire whether you have, in fact, had further contact with the Communist Party or cooperated with it in any way since that time?

COUNSEL: May I object to the form of the question, it presupposes she was a Communist Party member. That is one of the issues in this hearing, I believe.

Mr. NITTLE: If there is any factual content in that question which the witness finds to be untrue, she now has the opportunity under oath to state the fact. . . .

The Committee already has the answers to defamatory questions it puts to unfriendly witnesses.

Charlotte, 1956

... MR. ARENS: Were you present when Mr. Charles Childs was initiated in the Communist Party? . . .

MR. FELDMAN: Same answer.

MR. ARENS: You helped induct him in the Communist Party; did you not?

MR. FELDMAN: I offer the same answer.

MR. ARENS: You did not know when you inducted him into the Communist Party that you were inducting in the Communist Party an FBI agent, did you?

MR. FELDMAN: I offer the same answer.

MR. ARENS: To that extent the committee is in your debt for inducting into the Communist Party an FBI agent. . . .

Minneapolis, 1964

MR. NITTLE: Now I want to pose another question, which I don't think you can claim to be an innuendo.

In testimony before the Subversive Activities Control Board on January 13, 1954, Barbara Louise Roehrich, who was identified by Mrs. Gordienko as a member of her cell at the University of Minnesota, stated, testified that she executed an application for membership in the Communist Party during February of 1949. She further testified that Rachel Tilsen was the chairman of the University Village Club of the Minneapolis Communist Party and Minnesota State treasurer of the Labor Youth League and that she, Rachel Tilsen, took her application for membership in the Communist Party during February of 1949. Mrs. Roehrich also testified that Kenneth Tilsen and several others asked her to join the Communist Party. Now, did you during February of 1949, or at any time during the year 1949, ask Barbara Roehrich to join the Communist Party?

MR. TILSEN: I respectfully decline to answer that question on all of the grounds already urged. . . .

The Committee's questions often relate to events alleged to have occurred many years before the hearing.

Chicago, 1965

... MR. NITTLE: Prior to taking up your residence in Chicago in 1949, were you a member of a Communist cell or group in San Francisco? (More than 16 years earlier.)

MR. NITTLE: Were you in attendance at that meeting of the Communist Party held in the home of Willie Mae Smith on December 16, 1949 at 333 East 60th Street in Chicago? (15 years earlier.)

MR. NITTLE: Did you not, in fact, attend and be employed at

Commonwealth College, in Mena, Arkansas, during the period 1930 to 1933? . . . (32 to 35 years earlier.)

Washington, D.C., 1961

Mr. TAVENNER: When was this picnic?

Mr. SCOTT: I'd forgotten all about it until now. I couldn't say definitely when it was.

Mr. TAVENNER: That was between 1945 and 1949, was it not?

Mr. SCOTT: I think so, some place in there. I don't even remember the year it was.

Mr. TAVENNER: Who were some of the more prominent Communists that you recall attended? . . . (12–16 years earlier.) . . .

Cleveland, 1962

Mr. NITTLE: Our investigation discloses that at a meeting in the Music Hall, Cleveland, Ohio, on April 30, 1949, it was announced that you were among the largest contributors to the Progressive Party. Was that announcement correct? . . . (13 years earlier.)

Mr. NITTLE: You were also in attendance at a concert sponsored by the Progressive Party at Music Hall on March 20, 1950, which featured Paul Robeson, were you not? . . . (12 years earlier.)

The Committee often demeans unfriendly witnesses.

San Francisco, 1960

. . . Mr. IZARD: I avail myself of the first amendment, which you have already trampled upon, and I avail myself also of that citizen's shield of the Republic, the privilege of not being forced to testify against myself, under the fifth amendment.

Mr. SCHERER: A very fine speech, coming from a Communist. . . .

Washington, D.C., 1962

Mr. NITTLE: I suggest, Mr. Chancey, that you are a hard-core Communist and that the tears in your voice are quite unbecoming, would you comment on that? . . .

Lansing, 1954

Mr. CLARDY: That means you shall not be compelled to incriminate yourself. Let us not fence with the English language. You know what it means and that it is only invoked by people who are, in my humble opinion, apprehensive that they will do so. You leave that impression every time you raise it, and I don't care how many people argue to the contrary. . . .

Washington, D.C. 1959

THE CHAIRMAN: You are not under any compulsion. You say, "I must decline." You are not under any compulsion whatsoever. If you want to help the Congress and the country, you will not decline to answer.

Minnesota, 1964

MR. NITTLE: Have you been instructed by Communist Party functionaries to invoke the fifth amendment in response to questions of this committee? . . .

Michigan, 1951

REP. POTTER: I think it's significant to point out that anyone who hides behind the Fifth Amendment, who in answer to the question as to whether he was or had been a member of the Communist Party refuses to answer because his reply might tend to incriminate him, leaves the committee with only one choice, to believe that he is a member of the Communist Party. If he were not a member, had not been a member, certainly a truthful answer would not incriminate him and there would be no purpose in seeking the protection of the Fifth Amendment. . . .

The Committee persists in interrogating unfriendly witnesses despite their refusals to testify.

. . . It is commonplace that the Committee puts a line of defamatory questions despite the witness' continued declinations to testify. The Committee moreover does so despite express statements by the witness that no further such questions will be answered.

For example:

Washington, D.C., 1961

MR. NIXON: . . . and I will for the same reason refuse to answer other questions that I deem to be of the same character.

I should like to say in conclusion that when and if you ask further questions of this nature, and I say I decline for the reasons already stated, I have reference to all of the reasons that I have just described to you.

MR. SCHERER: Now, Witness, are you still a member of the Communist Party?

MR. NIXON: Did you hear my statement just now, Mr. Scherer?

THE CHAIRMAN: Answer the question.

MR. NIXON: Well, the reason I ask whether you heard my statement is because it is a categorical refusal to answer all such questions, and there should be no question in your mind that I am going to answer that question, I refuse to answer for all of the reasons that I have just described.

MR. TAVENNER: Were you a member of the Communist Party in 1958, the year of the publication of the Statement of the Awards Committee?

Mr. Nixon: You are wasting your time. I am not going to answer your question.

Mr. Tavenner: It is noted that the address given of the office for The Fund for Social Analysis is Room 2800, 165 Broadway. Have you met with the officers of this association at that address?

Mr. Nixon: As I said before, I am not going to answer any questions regarding the Fund.

Mr. Tavenner: Then you refuse to answer. And I am going to continue to ask the questions that you ought to be asked.

Mr. Nixon: You understand what I said?

Mr. Tavenner: I understand what you said, but I always live in hopes that a person may change his mind, even you, Mr. Nixon.

The Committee, frequently, invites or expressly permits the witness to express his grounds for refusal to testify in a shortened form.

Washington, D.C., 1961

Mr. Aptheker: My answer is the same, and is it necessary for me to repeat the entire phraseology?

Mr. Tavenner: No, it is not; if you say "on the same grounds," I think that the Chairman will accept that.

Counsel for witnesses have been verbally and physically mistreated.

Los Angeles, 1956

Mr. Arens (Committee counsel), addressing Mr. John Porter, counsel for several witnesses:

Comrade Porter, let's not have any further outbursts from you.

Mr. Arens: I suggest that Comrade Porter be admonished that if we have further outbursts of this kind he will be removed from the room.

Mr. Arens: Comrade Porter, you just read the rules on the ethics before this committee, and content yourself with that. We will take care of the proceedings here.

Mrs. Doran [witness]: You said everyone would be courteous. My counsel's name is Mr. Porter, P-o-r-t-e-r.

Mr. Arens: He has been identified as a comrade. One man was identified as a doctor of philosophy. So we called him a doctor. This man has been identified as a comrade.

Mrs. Doran: For the record and in order to protect myself, I refuse to answer the question, if I can still remember it, by citing the first and fifth amendments. And I want everyone here to remember that my counsel's name is Mr. Porter. And I believe that is the way we address each other in this country.

MR. ARENS: Do you address him in any other capacity any place else besides in public session?

MR. PORTER: Just a minute.

MR. DOYLE: Just a minute.

MR. PORTER: I rise to a point of personal privilege, and charge that counsel is violating —

MR. ARENS: I suggest that counsel submit himself to an oath if he wants to engage in these proceedings with reference to whether or not he is a comrade or, else, that he restrain himself and read the canon of ethics of the American Bar Association here, which among other things, set high moral standards for practitioners of the law who are sworn to uphold the Constitution of the United States. . . .

Washington, D.C., 1966

An attorney was forcibly removed from the hearing room when he attempted to register an objection to a question put by the Committee counsel concerning his client. When the Committee Chairman requested that the attorney be returned to the hearing room, it was learned that he was already in jail.[2] . . . Subsequently, seven attorneys for other subpoenaed witnesses withdrew, and in a prepared statement read by one of them they said . . .

". . . although we have been able to bail Mr. Kinoy out of jail, and he stood beside me an hour ago, the brutal treatment offered him has all but destroyed any chance we may ever have to represent our clients adequately. Attorneys cannot function in an atmosphere of terror and intimidation. The fundamental constitutional right to be represented by counsel means counsel free from brutalization and terrorization. . . ."

The Committee engages in exposure for exposure's sake.

Rep. Harold Velde — 1952

The principal objectives of the committee, during this Congress, have been to expose subversive elements in the motion-picture industry and in essential defense areas in the United States, to expose the complicity of American Communists and their part in the destruction of freedom in the Far East, and to expose the manner in which Communists and espionage agents have gained employment in the Federal Government.

Rep. Francis E. Walter [former Chairman] — 1955, 1961

Unlike most congressional committees, in addition to the legislative function we are required to make the American people aware if possible the extent of the infiltration of Communism in all phases of our society. . . .

[2] The attorney's conviction for disorderly conduct was reversed in *Kinoy v. District of Columbia* (D.C. Cir. July 29, 1968, Docket No. 21262).

It is most important that we remember . . . that most of the extensive information the Federal Bureau of Investigation collects on the operations of the Communist conspiracy in this country, for a number of good reasons, is kept absolutely secret. For the most part, it is never revealed to the public except in the case of a court trial.

Because the FBI is purely an investigating agency and has neither the legislative nor the informing function of a congressional committee, it, alone, cannot do a thorough job of protecting this country from communism. . . . (1961.) . . .

Rep. Edwin E. Willis [former Chairman] — . . . 1967

The subversive activities of the Communists should be a primary concern of the American people, and we on the committee consider it our main duty and responsibility to keep the public informed by focusing attention on Communist activities endangering the welfare of our Nation. . . .

Rep. Gordon Scherer — 1957

In October, 1957, a witness objected to being asked to identify an application for employment because he felt the sole purpose of the question was to lead to an exposure of his beliefs and associations. Representative Scherer responded:

"Witness, it will lead to an exposure of you being a colonizer for the Communist Party in this area. It has nothing to do with your beliefs. . . ."

Rep. Bob Casey (non-member) — 1961

The Un-American Activities Committee has effectively unmasked those among us who have succumbed to this ideology, and who are the enemies of our people, our economic system and our Nation. . . . (1961.)

Rep. Thomas J. Lane (non-member) — 1961

The House Committee on Un-American Activities is ever alert to this peril. Through its patient, searching, and well-documented investigations, it has exposed both these organizations in their devious methods. The information gained as a result of these investigations has helped the American people to understand how the Communist conspiracy works.

. . . We must defend ourselves against the insidious practices and one of the most potent means is to unmask those individual organizations that serve as a front for treason. . . . (1961.)

Rep. Thomas Abernethy (non-member) — 1961, 1965

I do not know of any tribunal, court, branch or segment of our Government which has contributed more to ferreting out the anti-Americans than the Committee on Un-American Activities. In instance after instance it has turned the light of day on the un-American activities of many un-American people. . . . (1961.)

The prime objective of the Un-American Activities Committee is to expose communism wherever and whenever it can be found in the United States. . . . (1965.)

Rep. Harlan Hagen (non-member) — 1961

It has exposed to public knowledge the identity of persons who have been members of subversive apparatus in this country. This exposure cannot be accomplished at the national level by any agency outside of the Congress. . . . (1961.)

Rep. Richard Ichord [Chairman] — 1964

It is the committee's hope that the information produced here will have a further use and that it will help to, that is, it will help to keep the American people generally, and the people of this area, alert to the fact that communism is a very real problem and danger, both here at home as well as abroad; that it must be fought here as well as abroad. Here it must be fought fairly, intelligently, and effectively, if our freedoms as Americans are to be preserved. . . .

Rep. Joe Pool — 1968

The tremendous work the Committee has done in the past few years in exposing militant pro-Peking Chinese Leftist Communists, who are on the campuses of many of our universities here in America.

I think that the House Committee on Un-American Activities is actually the "court of last resort" to the people of America to come and find out what's going on in the way of infiltration by enemies, the Communists and by other groups who would destroy America as we know it. . . .

LEGISLATIVE PRODUCT OF THE COMMITTEE

. . . In response to . . . criticisms, at the Committee's request the Leislative Reference Service of the Library of Congress in 1958 published a study of the legislative recommendations of the Committee as well as the success of the Committee in having them enacted into law. Legislative Reference Service, *Legislative Recommendations by the House Committee on Un-American Activities,* 86th Cong., 2d Sess. (rev'd ed 1960). . . .

A careful analysis of this report along with the subsequent annual reports of the Committee through 1966 indicates that the Committee's actual legislative product is very much smaller than found by the Legislative Reference Service. In fact, the Committee's publications claim only 32 different enactments. Of these, seven are contained in the McCarran-Walter Immigration and Nationality Act of 1952, and nine are contained in the Internal Security Act of 1950. (Four of the

McCarran-Walter Act sections superseded sections of the Internal Security Act of 1950.)

A summary of the Committee's legislative product follows:

McCarran-Walter Immigration and Nationality Act of 1952, 8 U.S.C. §§1101 et seq. The Committee takes credit for seven provisions of the Act relating to subversive and un-American activities. The enactment of this major revision of the immigration law would seem more properly attributable to Representative Walter's position as Chairman of the House Committee on Immigration and Nationality.

Internal Security Act of 1950, 50 U.S.C. §781 et seq. This legislation was to be a comprehensive act requiring disclosure and regulation of the Communist Party of the United States of America. But the act has been ineffective because the courts have held that to require compliance with the registration requirements would violate the registrant's rights under the Fifth Amendment. . . .

18 U.S.C. §3291. This statute established a ten-year statute of limitations for certain crimes relating to citizenship and naturalization and passports and visas. The usual statute of limitations under the federal Criminal Code for these crimes would be five years.

38 U.S.C. §1789. This section of the War Orphans Educational Assistance Act prohibits using educational benefits for war orphans at institutions on the Attorney General's list of subversive organizations. . . .

Communist Control Act of 1954, 50 U.S.C. §§841–44. This statute contains a Congressional finding regarding the Communist Party of the United States and deprives it of all "rights, privileges, and immunities" under law. Members of the Party are declared to be members of a Communist action organization for purposes of the Internal Security Act. This statute has had only one application. . . .

Espionage and Sabotage Act of 1954, Section 201, amending 18 U.S.C. §794. This statute increases the penalty for peace-time espionage and alters the sentencing authority for espionage by increasing the penalty to death or life imprisonment or any term of years.

Act of August 20, 1954, amending 18 U.S.C. §3486. This statute permits the granting of immunity from prosecution after the Fifth Amendment privilege has been claimed.

Act of June 30, 1954, 18 U.S.C. §798. Extends the expiration date of a specific espionage statute, 18 U.S.C. §794, until six months after the termination of the national emergency period proclaimed on December 16, 1950.

Communist Control Act of 1954, §13 A(e) as amended by the Act

of July 26, 1955, 50 U.S.C. §792a(e). The report of the Legislative
Reference Service refers particularly to section 792a(e)(1) providing
that the Subversive Activities Control Board shall give consideration
to Communist Party membership of an organization's officers within
the past three years in determining whether an organization is Communist infiltrated.

Act of August 1, 1956, 50 U.S.C. §851 et seq. This statute requires
the registration of persons engaged in or trained in espionage, sabotage or similar fields by a foreign government. The constitutionality of
the aspects of this statute requiring disclosure of criminal activity is
brought into question by the recent Court decisions.

Act of July 24, 1956, amending 18 U.S.C. §§2384–85. This statute
increases penalties for seditious conspiracy and advocating the over-
throw of the government.

*Labor Management Reporting and Disclosure Act of 1959, §504,
29 U.S.C. §504.* The statute prohibits persons who have been members of the Communist Party within the previous five years from serv-
ing as union officers. The provision was declared unconstitutional in
United States v. Brown, 381 U.S. 437 (1965).

Public Law 87–301 adding 8 U.S.C. §§349(c), 1105a. These sections place the burden of proof on the question of loss of nationality
on the government and also relate to the exclusiveness of judicial review on deportation orders. The committee report on the bill was
issued by the House Committee on the Judiciary rather than the
Committee on Un-American Activities.

Public Law 87–369 repealing 18 U.S.C. §791. This statute ended
the limitation of the espionage and censorship provisions of the criminal code to the Admiralty and Maritime jurisdiction of the United
States. This bill was reported by the Committee on the Judiciary.

Public Law 87–486 amending 18 U.S.C. §2385. This statute de-
fines the term "organize" in the Smith Act so as to avoid this Court's
construction that the term referred only to acts entering into the creation of a new organization.

Public Law 87–793, §305, adding 39 U.S.C. §4008. This statute
permitted the Postmaster General to detain Communist propaganda
sent through the mails and to determine whether the recipient wanted
to receive the materials. The statute was declared unconstitutional in
Lamont v. Postmaster General of the United States, 381 U.S. 301
(1965).

Public Law 88–290, adding 58 U.S.C. §831 et seq. The statute
relates to security clearances for employees of the National Security
Agency.

Public Law 87–474, §1(b) amending 50 U.S.C. §784. This statute relieves the Secretary of Defense of the obligation to publish a list of those defense facilities at which members of Communist-action organizations are prohibited from employment. This statute removed a deficiency from the Communist Control Act of 1954. The provision had been rendered moot since 50 U.S.C. §784(a)(1)(D) was declared unconstitutional in *United States v. Robel,* 389 U.S. 258 (1967).

P.L. 90–237, amending the Internal Security Act of 1950. The act, inter alia, amends the Internal Security Act of 1950 to establish a system of public disclosure of Communist and Communist-front organizations and their members, requires the disclosure of Communist organizations using the mail to solicit money, provides a grant of immunity for compulsory testimony and production of evidence over self-incrimination claims, and prescribes penalties for misbehavior in the presence of the Subversive Activities Control Board. . . .

[Is there sufficient "legislative purpose" in the history of HUAC–HISC to satisfy the requirements of the constitutional provisions, as interpreted by the Supreme Court? The opinions of the committee's own members about the goal of exposure leaves one wondering whether legislative purpose is very important to them. And the very thin record of legislative accomplishments after nearly thirty years as a standing committee tends to add to the question. On the other side, would the committee be in even greater jeopardy if it did legislate more frequently? The First Amendment is unmistakably clear when it provides that "Congress shall make no law. . . ."

The Stamler case is the most important instance, to our knowledge, where the whole record of the committee is put before the court. It is ideal for study because it is a veritable textbook of investigatory techniques, yet it suggests that this aspect of congressional power is problematic and, we hope, not settled for all times.

Studying these issues should also cast further light, and shadows, across the noble sentiments expressed in the Cooper-Church debate in Part I. All Americans, especially those most favorably disposed toward representative government, are ambivalent about democratic power. We particularly want a powerful legislature, but somehow we cannot decide how it should use its power. The editors have their own values which are reflected in the choice of materials in this volume. But we feel that careful study of these materials is absolutely necessary before any reasonable position on legislative power can be sustained. — Eds.]

VI

REFORMING REPRESENTATIVE GOVERNMENT

Legislative politics is a fact. Representative government is an ideal. We are constantly trying to put the two together and usually end up chasing our tails. Everyone who ever sought to understand Congress or any other American legislature eventually has tried to bring facts and ideal closer together through "reform." Some facts are closer to the ideal, if only we could make them facts.

A large number of reform proposals have been made in the 200-year history of modern legislative politics in the United States. The number and variety of proposals suggest that Congress and its sister institutions have not stood still, and perhaps even that some changes have occurred because an occasional reform proposal was adopted. But the variety also suggests that students of legislative politics do not understand the facts or the ideal in the same way.

Two very different approaches to reform are presented here by the editors, expressly for this book. Yet the editors have experienced many of the same studies in the vast literature on legislative politics and have agreed on the selections to be presented in this volume. The divergence should work as no discouragement to the student. He should see it is evidence that the subject is tremendously complex and as an opportunity to become a watcher and a reformer of legislatures himself. Any number can play. And, at least up to now, all have been welcome. That will always be the beauty of conducting politics in legislatures.

26

Congressional Reform:
A New Time, Place, and Manner

Theodore J. Lowi

Congressional reform movements usually happen every two or four years in January when a new Congress is about to be convened. This is an unfortunate time because the reform proposals are too narrow and formed mainly by recent frustrations; they are usually just a little more than rhetorical honorings of eloquent campaign promises.

In 1971 reformers threw themselves with unusual zeal upon the hard rock of cloture in the Senate and seniority in the House. Yet they succeeded only in getting a concession that might as well have been written in disappearing ink. This concession was a decision to lodge the power to select committee chairmen in the party caucuses rather than leaving it to the automatic workings of seniority. But power always did reside in the party caucus, whenever a majority of the caucus determined to use the power. In previous years the nonagenarian Theodore Francis Green was replaced by William Fulbright as chairman of the Senate Foreign Relations Committee. Adam Clayton Powell was relieved of his chairmanship of the House Committee on Labor and Education following the battle over his conduct. But the sorry point is that no party majority determines to do anything of the sort except in ridiculously extreme cases.

The 1971 reform was worse than an empty gesture. Formalizing the power of the parties over selection of committee chairmen may have strengthened seniority by legitimizing it. From now on a party caucus will be taking the nearly automatic process of seniority and making the results appear to be the positive choices of the party. As Senator Mathias (R. Md.) said, the reform adopted by the House was merely a change "from an era of divine right into an era of constitutional monarchy."

A majority of Congress probably favors seriously reforming the seniority system and other structural impediments to rationality, but it is no paradox that the majority vanishes every time the issue is faced squarely. Congress may be constantly thwarted by seniority, but most members are experienced enough to know that seniority is a fact of all organized life. Most also realize that without some automatic criterion of selection no substantive business would be done during the first several weeks of each new Congress. And even after that the senior men would probably win more often.

If serious reform is intended, first of all, it should be staged at a new time in the electoral cycle — toward the end of an old Congress rather than the beginning of a new one. A new Congress is fresh from victories, especially the reelection and reinforcement of the senior and most powerful members. All that is fresh in the minds of members of an old Congress is the awareness of defeat: defeat of good proposals during the past two frustrating years in office, and the defeat that threatens at the polls a few months later. If there is wisdom in pain, the attack must be staged before Congressmen pass through the apotheosis of election, into weak and uninstructive memory.

A new place and manner of attack should also be determined by recognizing that cloture and seniority are not the real problems. Cloture is so irrelevant because it is never hard to get when a majority is intense and determined. The cloture rule appears to foil the majority only because hypocrites hide behind it. Cloture is not a problem of congressional reform but of general character reform, for which even the mightiest of governments has insufficient powers.

Seniority comes closer to a problem within Congress's power and obligation to change. But even seniority is not as important as the rigid and maladaptive committee structure. Seniority is a problem only because it is tied to committees, reinforcing them, rigidifying them.

Few casual observers realize that the so-called seniority system is tied to the committee system, that it means continuous service on a single committee, not total years of Senate or House membership. Committee supremacy and committee seniority make an almost unbeatable team against rational treatment of junior members and against rational treatment of a great deal of innovative legislation.

The ill effects of this unbeatable team go even further. The system locks talent into congressional careers. The time a congressman or senator invests in his rise to committee power becomes too valuable, after a certain point, to allow him to consider other ambitions. This isolates Congress and robs it of valuable influence it might have on the executive branch. In the nineteenth century, before the triumph of seniority, indeed on into 1910, this kind of interchange did occur. The contemporary exceptions — a few senators who strike out for the presidency — tend to prove the rule. The presidency is one office in the executive branch a senator can seek with the assurance that his failure only lands him back in the Senate, except during the year when he must seek reelection (as Goldwater did in 1964; McGovern did not have to face reelection until 1976).

The committee-seniority system also rigidifies the whole governmental process. Most standing committees in both chambers are organized along jurisdictional lines precisely parallel to major executive departments and agencies. The ties between a committee and an agency become intimate over the years, and they are usually supported by the dominant interests in that particular subject. This triangular trading is the basis for the "military-industrial complex" and the many other complexes that comprise the stable political alliances that make public policy at the federal level. The most stable element of this complex is the committee. The top bureaucrats are birds of passage in comparison.

These are the ills and diagnoses that cry out for reform. Congress wants to do more than ensure the rise of an occasionally qualified young member. Congress wants to be and remain part of the center of governmental power. A mature committee system makes legislative government possible by enabling it to carry out complex tasks. But the same arrangement seems now to be imposing serious limits on the very same legislative power. How can this structure be reformed without being seriously weakened as a tool of effective legislative government? This is the major problem, not how to help junior members or how to improve the regional distribution. How can the structure of Congress be loosened so that it can effectively govern in times of complexity and crisis? I have three proposals for reform.

First, the number of standing committees in the Senate and in the House should be *expanded* rather than reduced. Twenty-five years under the 1946 LaFollette-Monroney reforms have proven that reducing the number of committees makes for little improvement. Students of Congress tend to feel that the result is the reverse, because the power of the chairmanship actually increased and the seniority formula was not weakened. The power of the chairman increased because the jurisdiction of each remaining committee was correspondingly larger, as well as because the chairman retained the power to appoint the chairmen of each of his subcommittees. The Democrats in the House have restricted the committee chairman to one chairmanship for himself, but neither party in neither chamber has seriously diminished the power of chairmen over their subcommittees.

Adding committees would immediately increase the available chairmanships. This could take some frustration away from members of middling seniority, which would also include a larger number of

Senators and congressmen from competitive districts. This sudden increase in chairmanships would produce excellent opportunities for party leadership, because new openings increase startling low patronage possibilities.

Expanding the number of standing committees would very probably also loosen and expose the rigid and intimate relations between the present standing committees and executive agencies. Jurisdictions would inevitably overlap, and overlapping jurisdictions produce healthy political competition.

Second, an alternative to seniority (naming sponsors of legislation) should be used for selecting the chairman of *new* standing committees. But it should be emphasized that this rule has almost as much status in Congress as the seniority rule. It is well-established in both chambers that when new legislation leads to the creation of a new committee, the chairmanship goes to the sponsor of the bill, regardless of his seniority. For example, the very junior Senator Brien MacMahon became the first chairman of the important Joint Committee on Atomic Energy, because of his role in drafting and sponsoring the Atomic Energy Act of 1946. More precedents are found in the appointments of subcommittee chairmen.

This method of expanding committees and granting chairmanships to sponsors of the legislation is ideally designed to provide incentives for legislative initiative. Yet in no way does it seriously threaten the seniority system.

Third, prompt enactment of a tenure-of-statutes Act is the most fundamental reform, and would give special significance to the first two proposals. For reasons far beyond mere reform of congressional structures, Congress should on principle limit every statute and program to a life of no more than ten years. Nothing is more unjust and oppressive than obsolete laws. The most irrational and oppressive bureaucracies are those that operate under obsolescent statutory authority. Military-industrial and other complexes spawn in stagnant statutory waters.

Automatic ten-year life sentences for statutes would not overly burden the modern congressman. Although they might force him to displace routine business and private bills with substantial legislative concerns, everyone would gain. As recent squabbles over executive privilege show, congressional control through the power of legislative oversight is almost completely illusory. The only effective power Congress ever held over the executive was statutory. Also, most statutes need very little attention after ten years. Review and reenactment in those cases would take little time. The ten-year death sentence would simply provide an automatic opportunity for substantive review rather than incremental review by appropriation.

Moreover, limiting statutes combined with increasing committees (the second proposal) would give ample incentive to congressmen to review all statutes after ten years. If their creativity is rewarded with chairmanships, there is every assurance that some creativity will flourish. This way, congressional structure would be kept more relevant to existing social problems rather than to the problems of a generation before. Rewards would be meted out for accomplishment, and jobs would be lost because of complacency or incompetency rather than increasing age.

These three proposals, if adopted, would meet the demands of congressional reform. Obviously, some surface confusion would be produced by overlapping committee jurisdictions and competition for legislative roles. But this kind of confusion is not a problem. It is the political process, reintroduced to Congress, where in recent years it may have become a stranger. Overlapping jurisdiction would arise out of conflict among statutes, and this problem is met with statutory reform, perhaps a more encompassing single statute, ending in a fusion of two preexisting committees.

All this would have the salutory effect of pushing present committee chairmen to greater vigor to maintain their chairmanships. And more often than not, chairmanships would continue to go to the senior members, because in Congress they tend to be more effective people and enjoy more respect. But this way, senility would be replaced, while other senior members could prove that knowledge and skill increase with age. Meanwhile junior members would not be discriminated against. Their opportunities would arise with every new social problem and every time an old statute came up for its ten-year review.

But far beyond those advantages, these proposals would almost guarantee for Congress a place at the center of government, a place it has yearned for since it was moved to the periphery a half century ago. Congress has known for years that review through substantive committees or through appropriation yields little but frustration. As one observer once said, Congress strains at gnats, then swallows large budgets. In contrast, substantial preparation would be necessary for a review that was required after ten years, especially because administrators would be keenly aware that failure in the review would mean the termination of the program. Such a review would shake up established relationships, expose unholy alliances, reveal unhappy precedents. The process might even lead to the elimination of a few useless programs.

Such reforms would contribute another value to the system — the introduction of a greater role for rule-of-law. Most major statutes are passed under pressure of time and ignorance, necessitating far broader delegations of power to administrators than any congressman would willingly grant. But somehow, these broad delegations never seem to get narrowed; and Congress has been the least likely place where any such narrowing is provided. Congress authorizes the job, then promises itself it will catch up during annual appropriations sessions. But with every such general and unguided authorization, we move closer to a purely bureaucratic state. A tenure-of-statutes act, coupled with ambitious, chairman-seeking legislators, would provide Congress with the means for reentering the center. At least every tenth year Congress could decide whether experience took away the pressure and the ignorance surrounding the original enactment. During the first ten years of any program, many agencies actually work out important rules of law to guide themselves through a class of cases or problems. These actions have the force and effect of law already. Congressional review could not possibly hurt. Adopting these rules into the statute would increase their stature. Codifying these rules into tidy chapters and titles could not fail to simplify the law for the agency and for the citizen. Europeans discovered many years ago that codification is nine points of the law.

These three proposals should appear to be desirable even if seniority were not at issue. If they meet present legislative problems and help to solve even more fundamental issues as well, then the case for their adoption ought to be compelling. And, unless reformers revere time-honored failures for their own sentimental value, they should welcome a new case, a new time and a new and broader method of attack. If they are doomed to failure anyway, why not fail on a grander scale?

27

The Impact of Congress
on Public Policy:
Goal-Oriented Performance

Randall B. Ripley

THE SOCIAL FUNCTIONS OF CONGRESS

In a sense, Congress performs one major function: it helps, or at
least tries to help, to resolve societal conflict. If it is mostly successful
and if other institutions of society are also mostly successful, then
society is likely to be relatively stable. If Congress and the other
institutions of government are unsuccessful in resolving conflict, then
societal instability may develop. Failure is, of course, possible; the
American Civil War is a classic example of what happens when
societal conflict cannot be resolved through normal institutional
channels.

Despite the ultimate importance of this overarching function, it
does not have much analytical utility. Rather I have chosen four
categories for ordering the discussion of the functions of Congress: (1)
lawmaking, (2) oversight of administration, (3) education of the
public, and (4) representation. These categories do not include everything Congress does that can affect society, but they do include the
major ways Congress influences public policy (thus, for example, the
limited judicial function of Congress is omitted) and those functions
that can be consciously and directly manipulated by members of the
two houses (Congress's leadership selection function — most dramatically for presidential candidates — is, for example, omitted because,
although important, its performance is determined mostly by events
and circumstances outside the control of the specific preferences and
actions of senators and representatives).

Congress has great latitude in performing these four functions. Congress is principally the collection of individuals who happen to serve
in it at any given time. The wishes and preferences of those members
and the behavior based on those wishes and preferences can make a
real difference in how the functions are performed. Some outer limits

of congressional behavior may be immutably fixed but they are far from confining; the range of congressional choice in the performance of these functions is great.

Congress and Lawmaking

Before the Civil War, congressional lawmaking activity in the domestic sphere was basically limited to promoting the development of the nation. This sort of interest has, of course, persisted to the present and Congress is still heavily involved in subsidizing a wide range of private development activities.

By the end of the nineteenth century Congress became involved in regulating railroads and trusts. Since then congressional regulation has greatly expanded to include such diverse matters as unfair business practices, all modes of transportation, power, radio and television, food and drugs, labor relations, and the securities market.

From 1929 until the beginning of World War II, Congress also began to get heavily involved in redistributing the economic and social benefits of society, and made some attempts to redraw more equitably the social and economic lines the mythical "free market" had produced. Changes in the tax code and laws dealing with wages and hours, social security, medical care for the aged, aid to depressed geographic areas, public housing, aid to inner city public education, and job training all involve debates over equality or inequality and degrees of redistribution, and all became part of the congressional agenda. Following World War II, congressional interest expanded to encompass questions of racial discrimination.

Congress is unlikely to surrender willingly any of the lawmaking activities in the domestic realm in which it is already involved. It certainly could, however, show some aggressiveness in seeking out new areas of endeavor or it could deliberately seek simply to maintain the status quo in terms of the range of citizen activities in which it is involved.

In foreign affairs Congress has, especially in recent years, usually been peripheral and reluctant to assert itself. Whether this "normal" posture of Congress toward this part of its lawmaking authority will continue or not seems open to some question. Will Congress again pass a Tonkin Gulf type of resolution, for example? (Several such resolutions have been passed since World War II that give broad and amorphous mandates to the president to act in appropriate ways, including militarily, in large areas of the world. They have involved not just Southeast Asia but also Western Europe, the Mid-east, and the Far East.) Or will a president even feel confident enough to ask for such a resolution? Congress cannot absolutely control foreign affairs and probably should not do so. But it can show varying degrees of assertiveness or unassertiveness in dealing with such problems.

Another important element of variance in congressional performance of the lawmaking function is the degree of specificity in the standards for administering various laws that are included in the organic statutes themselves. Congress can decide about the level of specificity in many different ways. At one extreme, for example, the Social Security Act of 1935 contains remarkably clear standards to guide subsequent administration of the law. At the other extreme, the phrase "maximum feasible participation" (of the poor) in the Economic Opportunity Act of 1964 meant many different things to federal administrators, city officials, and actual or potential beneficiaries.

Congress and Oversight of Administration

Congress can oversee administrative activities in a variety of moods. It can pursue very narrow questions such as "What did you do with the $10,000 for new downspouts at Fort Sill?" It can also pursue very broad questions, such as "What should the role of the federal government be in relation to the development of the nation's urban areas?" Much congressional oversight approaches the Fort Sill end of the spectrum. Some members of Congress seem intent on becoming day-to-day managers of specific programs (some would, for example, charge that Congresswoman Edith Green (D. Ore.) was more interested in "running" programs in juvenile delinquency or education rather than "overseeing" them). But a good deal of the other kind of oversight also takes place. In recent years in the Senate, the hearings on the federal government and the cities chaired by Abraham Ribicoff (D. Conn.), the hearings on manpower chaired by Joseph Clark (D. Pa.), the hearings on national security organization chaired by Henry Jackson (D. Wash.), and the hearings on hunger chaired by George McGovern (D. S.D.) all qualify as policy oversight of administration of the broadest kind — considering not just administrative details but the scope and direction of policy in large and important areas as well.

Congress and Education of the Public

Perhaps inevitably, Congress as an institution has never devised an appropriate mode of communicating with the public. As a multiheaded institution of equals with differing party affiliations and policy views it is hard to imagine "the Congress" ever appearing as a single-minded entity to the public. There is no single spokesman for Congress, even on relatively noncontroversial issues, and especially not on controversial ones. When some members of Congress and the president have locked horns over some issue, the natural advantage lies with the president. He can state his position clearly in public with immediate and thorough coverage by the mass media. The majority leaders can try to counteract it, but the congressional posture is almost always muddied because a vocal minority in Congress will always publicly support the presidential position.

But individual members of Congress certainly can and do engage in public education. Again any senator or representative can take various stances. At one extreme stand those members who only try to gauge what is popular at any given time and assure themselves (they hope) of continued electoral success by following "the voice of the people." At the other are those who try to lead their constituents, sometimes in directions they know to be unpopular.

Congress and Representation

Congress is representative in many senses and it has many interests it can represent — including interests as expressed by interest groups, but also including interests of constituencies, of such territorial units as cities, districts, states, or regions, and of the nation. Individual representatives and senators can and do undertake several kinds of representative activities:

1. Members of the House and Senate support the interests of individuals in "casework" activities. These cases typically involve deportation and immigration, selective service, social security, and tax matters.

2. Members of the House and Senate also pursue cases involving corporate entities. Typically these cases involve enforcement and interpretation of the tax code or exemptions from certain kinds of enforcement of regulatory provisions. For example, when strict enforcement of federal safety standards threatened the last steamship on the Ohio River with extinction, interested members of Congress from the region had different standards applied to this particular vessel. Defense contractors involved in cost overrun disputes with the government can regularly count on some congressional intervention on their behalf.

RANDALL B. RIPLEY   377

3. Members of the House and Senate also intervene in the division of federal largesse, for example, creating new post offices, providing dams for specific localities, and assigning contracts to specific companies.

4. Senators and representatives can also seek to represent broad classes or races. Some black members consider themselves as representatives of the interests of all black; some conservative white southerners consider themselves as representatives of the interests of all southern whites and perhaps all whites. Some members consider themselves as spokesmen for all the poor or for some segment of the poor — perhaps urban, perhaps Appalachian, perhaps Indian.

5. Senators and representatives can choose to try to represent "the national good." Presumably most take this stance at least occasionally, and some members are even led to take stands that are unpopular and may cost them their seats. The early opposition of Senators Morse and Gruening to the war in Vietnam is a case in point.

Most members of Congress, in fact, pursue a mixture of these representative activities, although different members certainly weight the activities differently. It is not unusual to see a senator like Morse vigorous in his anti-war stance one day and vigorous in support of high tariffs to protect Oregon cherries the next. Neither is it unusual to see Senator Fulbright simultaneously pursuing "national interests" and the welfare of Arkansas chicken and rice growers.

ALTERNATIVE GOALS FOR CONGRESS

Congress is, of course, a large and very diverse group of individuals. Therefore, different individuals and clusters of individuals often hold diverse goals for it. It is possible, however, for most members to articulate and pursue (with varying levels of consciousness) some broad institutional goals designed to put Congress in a position to have specific effects on public policy.

Three alternative institutional goals seem particularly relevant to Congress unless its members are simply content to pursue reelection for all incumbents without much coherent attention to policy. The first is to maximize support for the substantive program of the president. This might be called the "presidential model."

The second possible goal is to maximize the independent influence of Congress on positive policy actions by the government — a "separation of powers model."

The third possible goal is to maximize Congress' ability to limit governmental innovation and to restrain the increase in governmental activity — a "status quo model."

In fact, contemporary spokesmen have taken each goal as the single proper goal for Congress to pursue and they urge their respective positions with considerable vigor. James MacGregor Burns is one of the most visible spokesmen for the position that Congress should concentrate its efforts on maximizing support for the president's program. Theodore Lowi holds that Congress should strive to maximize its independent influence on positive policy actions. James Burnham has made the case that Congress should primarily maximize its ability to limit governmental innovation and restrain the increase of governmental activity.

Most public debate on the proper role of Congress considers the conflict between the Burns position (presidential model) and the Burnham position (status quo model) and the seeming radical antithesis between them. Until recently, little public attention has been given the Lowi position (separation of powers model).

The Burns and Burnham positions do, to be sure, conflict. As stated by their proponents, they are wedded to differing ideologies — the Burns position to a liberal position and the Burnham position to a conservative position, at least on domestic matters. (Vietnam has muddied the ideological pool somewhat.) In an important sense, however, these two positions are quite similar in that they make Congress dependent rather than independent. In the Burns positions Congress is dependent on the president. In the Burnham position Congress is dependent on and at the mercy of the existing order of programs and bureaus.

CONGRESSIONAL PERFORMANCE OF FUNCTIONS TO REACH DIFFERING GOALS

The way in which Congress performs its functions of lawmaking, oversight of administration, education of the public, and representation will help determine which goal or goals are in fact being sought. To be prescriptive, Congress should choose certain modes of performance if it seeks the presidential model, it should choose different modes if it seeks the separation of powers model, and it should choose still different modes if it seeks the status quo model. If, as is often the case, Congress consciously chooses no single goal and no single mode of performing its functions, then probably bits and pieces of all three goals will be sought simultaneously. Such a situation probably also means that Congress appears confused and incoherent in its policy role even to interested parts of the public.

The following discussion suggests briefly the general outline of how each function should be performed to maximize the attainment of each goal.

Achieving Maximum Support for the Program of the President — The Presidential Model

If Congress pursues the presidential model, it should perform its *lawmaking* function by enacting whatever legislative proposals the president supports and submits.

Congress should perform its *oversight* function very generally, if at all, in the case of agencies and programs that seem to meet with presidential approval. If, for example, the president seems pleased with the activities of the Department of Defense, then the uncritical stance of Mendel Rivers or of F. Edward Hebert is quite appropriate. The president may, however, be worried about or annoyed with the activities of some agencies and programs theoretically under his control and might well welcome careful congressional scrutiny to help him influence matters that otherwise might be independent of any real checks. In these cases the president could make clear to various congressional committees those programs and agencies that he viewed as fair game for careful oversight and Congress could then dutifully help.

Congress should perform its *public education* function by propagandizing in favor of presidential proposals before enactment and on behalf of presidential performance after enactment.

Congress should perform its *representation* function by concentrating on narrow activities (casework for individuals and dividing federal largesse for corporations) to avoid conflict with the executive branch on broader questions — except in those few cases in which the president might view such conflict as beneficial to his program.

Achieving Maximum Independent Influence on Positive Policy Actions — The Separation of Powers Model

If Congress pursues separation of powers it should perform its *lawmaking* function by including explicit standards for administering new programs enacted into law. Congress can either demand that the executive branch include such standards in draft legislation or it can add them by amending bills coming from the executive branch or it can include them in bills initiated in Congress. Both houses should take floor debate and floor amendments very seriously if they seek to work toward separation of powers. The natural tendency of committees when writing legislation is to become very cozy with the relevant executive branch agencies and interest groups. Floor action can rectify any particularistic excesses that get reported out in bill form.

Giving limited tenure to all legislation as Lowi suggests in the previous article would also help propel Congress toward the goal of maximum independent influence.

Congress should perform its *oversight* function by looking at broad areas of national interest and examining the role of specific federal agencies and programs in meeting or not meeting those needs. This form of oversight should uncover new areas and problems in which legislation is needed. Lowi's suggestion to expand and reshuffle the standing committees might prove useful here. Oversight to meet the goal of maximizing independent congressional impact should also be designed to insist on rigorous adherence by executive agencies to the standards of performance included in the statutes authorizing the programs these agencies administer. And this form of oversight should also insist that agencies develop rigorous standards for evaluating performance and relative degrees of success or failure. Ideally, congressional committee members and staff members could themselves help to develop such standards.

Congress should perform its *public education* function by selecting specific substantive areas in which efforts to stimulate public attention and support should be concentrated. Congress has little impact when it tries to educate the public on every side of every issue simultaneously. But if there is some genuine consensus (either bipartisan or at least in the majority party in Congress) on which few issues need special and constant attention, then Congress — through its most visible members — can appear institutionally to be educating at least the attentive part of the public.

Congress should perform its *representation* function by concentrating considerable attention on "national good" kinds of questions, although such activity should probably be limited to a few subject areas for maximum impact. If almost every issue is claimed to involve profound principles and the national good, then the claim becomes diluted. Representation of class in support of specific substantive goals is also appropriate. In a Congress striving for the separation of powers model much of the representative function and the public education function become fused.

Naturally, Congress will also continue the narrower kinds of representation (cases for individuals and corporations and division of federal largesse), which are perfectly proper activities as long as they do not conflict with the limited number of broader results being sought by the other kinds of representative activities.

Achieving Maximum Ability to Limit Governmental Innovation and to Restrain the Increase in Governmental Activity — The Status Quo Model

If Congress pursues the status quo goal it should perform its *law-making* function by enacting only a few new laws at most. Those that are enacted should contain "legislative veto" provisions guaranteeing continued tight congressional control. Similar provisions should be added to existing legislation.

Congress should perform its *oversight* function by constantly involving itself in the details of the administration of all programs. Representative Edith Green's proprietary attitude toward some juvenile delinquency and education programs would become the model for congressional behavior. Relationships with key bureaucrats and interest group representatives to maintain the status quo in a wide range of programs should be cultivated.

Congress should perform its *public education* function by propagandizing about the dangers of big government (for example, invasion of privacy, economic problems) and too much spending (for example, inflation). If parts of the executive branch seem disposed to be unacceptably innovative, then constant hearings on their programs and proposals which require endless justifications should be held. Little energy or desire is left for innovative activity if every movement provokes new hearings. Simultaneously, small public education efforts should be undertaken to support existing specific programs (for example, cotton price supports; Defense Department relations with the aerospace industry or with specific companies within it; and the Appalachian development program).

Congress should perform its *representation* function by concentrating exclusively on casework and federal largesse division.

CONCLUSION

Congress has a single set of functions to perform and techniques with which to perform them. Individuals of both houses must select specific techniques and modes and times of using them that promote both